17th-Century Men's Dress Patterns

1600–1630

17th-Century Men's Dress Patterns

1600–1630

WRITTEN AND ILLUSTRATED BY
Melanie Braun, Luca Costigliolo,
Susan North, Claire Thornton
and Jenny Tiramani

PHOTOGRAPHY BY
Henrietta Clare, Pip Barnard
and Paul Robins

WITH OVER 1,300 ILLUSTRATIONS

This book is dedicated to Norah Waugh, Linda Crouch and Mark Rylance for their pioneering work in publishing, comprehending and wearing patterns of 17th-century men's dress.

On the cover: pattern (front) and x-ray (back) of crimson silk grosgrain doublet (pattern by Jenny Tiramani)
Page 2: detail of embroidered silk damask cloak

First published in the United Kingdom in 2016 by Thames & Hudson Ltd, 181A High Holborn, London WC1V 7QX, in association with the Victoria and Albert Museum, London

Reprinted 2022

17th-Century Men's Dress Patterns 1600–1630
© 2016 Victoria and Albert Museum, London/ Thames & Hudson Ltd, London

Text and original line illustrations © 2016 Melanie Braun, Luca Costigliolo, Susan North, Claire Thornton and Jenny Tiramani
Photographs © 2016 Victoria and Albert Museum, London, unless otherwise specified
Design and layout © 2016 Thames & Hudson Ltd, London

All Rights Reserved. No part of this publication may be reproduced or transmitted in any form or by any means, electronic or mechanical, including photocopy, recording or any other information storage and retrieval system, without prior permission in writing from the publisher.

British Library Cataloguing-in-Publication Data
A catalogue record for this book is available from the British Library

ISBN 978-0-500-51905-9

Printed and bound in China by Artron

Be the first to know about our new releases, exclusive content and author events by visiting
thamesandhudson.com
thamesandhudsonusa.com
thamesandhudson.com.au

V&A Publishing
Supporting the world's leading museum of art and design, the Victoria and Albert Museum, London

Contents

Foreword 6
Men's wardrobes, 1600–30 6
Clothing terms 9
Dressing men, *c*. 1600–30 10
Tailoring the doublet 14
Sewing stitches 20
Embroidery stitches 22
How to use this book 24

The patterns 25

1 | Green silk velvet doublet 26
1600–10
Claire Thornton
Details 28
Pattern 32
Construction 38

Sir Rowland Cotton's Suit

2A | Doublet of   **2B | Slashed silk**
slashed silk satin 48   **satin trunk hose**
c. 1618   **with canions** 70
Melanie Braun   *c*. 1618
Details 50   *Melanie Braun*
Pattern 54   Details 71
Construction 62   Pattern 74
                                       Construction 77

3 | Sword girdle and hangers 80
c. 1618
Jenny Tiramani
Details 82
Pattern 84
Construction 86

4 | Crimson silk grosgrain doublet 88
c. 1620
Jenny Tiramani
Details 90
Pattern 96
Construction 102

5 | Slashed doublet of stamped ivory silk satin 112
1625–30
Luca Costigliolo
Details 114
Pattern 118
Construction 124

6 | Embroidered silk damask cloak 134
c. 1560–1600
Claire Thornton
Details 136
Pattern 138
Construction 140

7 | Felt hat 142
1590–1620
Luca Costigliolo
Details 143
Pattern 144

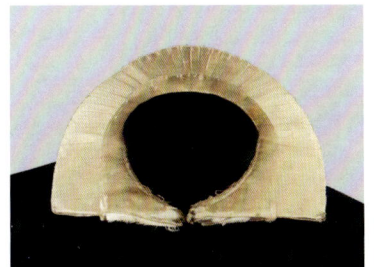

8 | Silk satin picadil 145
1600–20
Luca Costigliolo
Details 146
Pattern 149
Construction 150

9 | Embroidered linen nightcap 152
1600–25
Claire Thornton
Details 154
Pattern 156
Construction 157

10 | Linen nightcap liner 158
1600–80
Susan North
Details 159
Pattern 160
Construction 161

11 | Crimson silk velvet mittens with embroidered tops 162
c. 1600
Jenny Tiramani
Details 164
Pattern 166
Construction 168

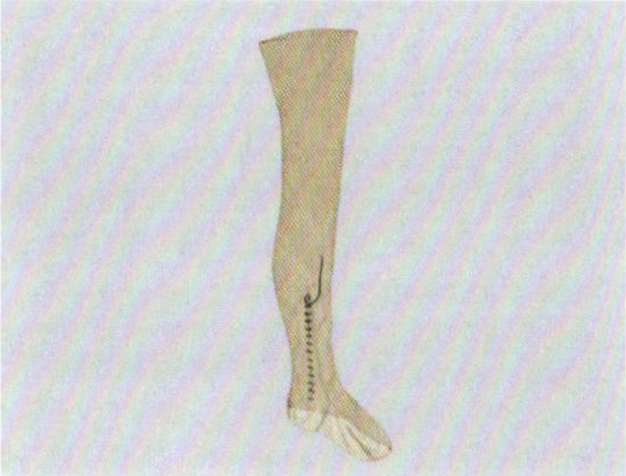

12 | Embroidered linen stocking 170
1590–1630
Susan North
Details 171
Pattern 172
Construction 173

Select bibliography 176
Acknowledgments 176

Foreword

This volume continues the series of pattern books launched with *Seventeenth-Century Women's Dress Patterns*, Books One and Two. It incorporates the experience we gained from these, plus a few advances. A major one is the addition of colour to the construction diagrams, enhancing the clarity of all the illustrations, particularly those showing the many layers of the doublets.

For beginners, the linen stocking offers an introduction to the tailor's art and the damask cloak bridges the technical leap between the latter and the doublets. For embroiderers, this volume provides a range of techniques and levels of difficulty. The simple embroidery on the linen stocking can easily be mastered, while the night cap, mittens, sword girdle and hangers provide more complicated designs and stitches, in both silk and metal threads. Silver-gilt embroidery appears in its full glory on the damask cloak.

Accessories are often overlooked in histories of fashion. Unlike modern clothing where hats, belts and gloves are optional, in the early 17th century everyone required these accessories, however plain and humble. The mittens, picadil, sword girdle and hangers examined here demonstrate not only the complexity of their structure and decoration, but also the range of technical skills required to make them. Although very simple in technique, the felt hat is extreme in its shape, literally stretching the hatmaker's skills to their limit.

We do want you to try these patterns at home, but recommend that you read through the patterns and the introductory chapters carefully before taking scissors to cloth. Many of the sewing techniques these garments employ are very different from those used in modern tailoring – and indeed may seem counterintuitive. Mastering the construction of a doublet may require 'unlearning' standard conventions. Some of these garments lend themselves to a collective approach to making. Rounding up some fellow tailors for a 'picadil party' or collaborative doublet-making session will save time and maximize the level of expertise as well as reflecting early 17th-century practice.

Men's wardrobes, 1600–30

Many garments are missing from the V&A's collection of 17th-century men's dress; for example, there are no shoes, shirts, ruffs, jerkins, night gowns, cassocks or coats from the period between 1600 and 1630. Wills and probate inventories of this period (a number are easily accessible in published format) fill in these gaps and offer an overview of the clothing worn by people from various levels of society. In wills, depending on the wishes and possessions of the testator, clothing is sometimes specifically mentioned. Inventories often just give a total value for 'his apparel and his purse', but about a third itemize the clothing, occasionally with details of colour and fabric. There are enough with fairly detailed lists of the deceased's wardrobe, across the social scale and covering most of England, to fill in the blanks remaining in museum collections. The probate inventories of mercers, drapers, haberdashers, glovers and shoemakers provide information on a range of accessories and the materials from which they were made. Household accounts record the purchase of clothing during the wearer's lifetime and these too often list materials purchased, including linings, reinforcements and trimmings, as well as the sums paid for making particular garments. Examining these records across the social strata reveals the very basic items of clothing worn by most of English society, and the additions and variations that increasing wealth and different occupations made to a man's wardrobe.

A probate inventory was taken after death to assess the value of the deceased's estate, settle any debts and prove his will. Only those whose estates were worth more than £5 were required to make a will, so in general, probate inventories span English society from rural labourers to royalty. This survey of men's wardrobes from 1600 to 1630 begins with Samuel Browne of Marlborough in Wiltshire. He died in 1601, his occupation was not given and his estate was valued at only £1 19s 8d, but he owned the following:

1 dublet and 1 jurkyn [jerkin – usually a sleeveless garment echoing the shape of a doublet and worn over it], 6s 8d
1 pair of shoes, 1s 4d
1 cloke, 4s
1 pair of breeches, 1 pair of drawers, 1 wastecote, 2s 2d
1 other dublet, 2s 6d
1 hat, 8d
2 pair of old stockins, 6d
2 shirtes, 2s
3 bandes and a cap, 1s[1]

Browne had all the basics of a man's wardrobe with shirts as underwear, coverings for his legs, feet and head, and a cloak as his outer garment. Inventories survive for husbandmen (farmers whose restricted access to landholding limited their prosperity). John Sheppard was one of the wealthiest; his estate was valued at £55 17s 8d, but his wardrobe held only a few more garments than Browne's: an additional doublet, another pair of breeches, five more bands, two more caps, a purse and a girdle, a coat and a mandilion – a loose, thigh-length coat that was pulled on over the head.[2] The will of husbandman Edward French of Banbury in Oxfordshire included his fustian (fabric with a linen warp and cotton weft, brushed to simulate broadcloth) doublet and a russet cloak – the word russet describes either the cloak's fabric or its colour.[3]

The wardrobes of some of the more prosperous yeomen are similar in the number and type of garments, suggesting that their greater wealth did not always require more lavish clothing. The estate of Anthony Stevens, a Wiltshire yeoman, was valued at over £90, yet he had the same number of clothes as Samuel Browne.[4] Wills for yeoman often distinguish between 'Sunday best' and 'workaday' clothes. William Briggs of Durham left his son-in-law 'a paire of white britches, a white dubblett and a payre of white stockins and a sherte', and his 'work day' breeches, doublet and cap to a friend.[5] Thomas Bethome of Durham left to his cousin, 'my best suyte of apparel, wch I weare on the sabboth dayes, viz. a dowlett, a paire of breaches

The fashionable version of a cassock, 1626 | From the garments of Vaclav Vilem Lobkowicz | The Regional Museum in Mikulov, the Czech Republic

Pinked leather shoes, *c.* 1630 | Livrustkammaren (The Royal Armoury), Stockholm | Photograph: Göran Schmidt (CC BY-SA)

Cutwork satin jerkin, 1620s | Hessisches Landesmuseum Darmstadt | Photograph: Wolfgang Fuhrrnannek

Linen ruff, 1620s | Livrustkammaren (The Royal Armoury), Stockholm | Photograph: Göran Schmidt (CC BY-SA)

Linen cuff, *c.* 1600 | Skokloster Castle Collection | Photograph: Skokloster Castle | Photograph: Jens Mohr (CC BY-SA)

of fustin, and the stockings thereunto belonging'. Another cousin got his 'next best suyte of apparel, being of kersey and stockings and the black dowlett, and the workaday cloake wch I usually were together'.[6] Many of the yeomanry were upwardly mobile with aspirations to gentility as the will of Thomas Faulkner of Cheshire reveals. He gave his brother his best stuff (worsted) suit, riding coat, boots, sword and dagger with silver buckle and spurs. He was clearly wealthy enough to own a horse and a sword, the essential early 17th-century accessory of a 'gentleman'.[7]

Wills and inventories survive for a range of craftsmen including shoemakers, tanners, blacksmiths, butchers, tailors, joiners and masons, and the wardrobes of the most humble were equivalent to those of husbandmen. Gowns appear in several inventories, perhaps reflecting the difference between the indoor sedentary occupations of some craftsmen and the outdoor work of rural farmers. The estate of Ipswich joiner Richard Cornellis was worth over £59; the presence and the value of the gowns in his wardrobe suggests that he may have been supervising a large workshop of joiners, rather than doing such work himself:

1 murry gowne, £2 10s	2 doublytts, £1
1 stuffe gowne, 13s 4d	1 Jerkyn and 1 pare of bretchies
1 Cloake, £1 10s	and an old cloake, £1.[8]

It was probably in the professional interests of tailors to dress fashionably; George Piner from Banbury had two ruffs in his inventory, as well as silk garters and a 'gold gerdell', while tailor John Pearce from Gloucester had five 'ruffbands'.[9]

The 'Stroud-water red' waistcoat, a garment that men wore between their shirt and doublet, was probably a necessity for Richard Saunders' trade as a Bristol plumber, although the dozen old silk, silver and gold points, the silver bodkin and two old silk and silver hatbands in his inventory may represent payment to him in lieu of cash.[10] Tradesmen such as innkeepers and vintners were financially on a par with many of the craftsmen and yeomen, but more expensive fabrics and fashionable garments appear in their inventories. Banbury ironmonger Edward Hadley's estate was worth over £54 and his wardrobe included:

3 shirtes, 10s 6d	A purse and girdle, 1s
2 ruffe bandes, 5s	A hat and band, 4s
3 nighte capes, 1s 6d	2 payre of stockins, 3s 4d
A silk rash dublett, 13s 4d	A purse and girdle, 1s
A payre of black briches, 5s	A dublet and 2 payre of hose, 8s
A French green jerkin with 2 dossen of silver buttons, 11s	2 dossen of silver buttons, 6s
A dublet and paire of hose, 5s	An old hatt, 1s
A payre of stockings, 5s	2 payer of bootes, 2s
A cloke lined, 12s	3 payer of shooes, 1s 8d
	An old cloke, 3s 4d.[11]

Innkeeper Thomas Dixon's 'Spanish leather jerkin' was more fashionable than the plain leather or frieze jerkins of farmers. He also had a gown edged with fox fur, one lined with lamb and faced with marten, a nightcap and 13 ruff bands along with a sword, buckler and dagger.[12] Further up the mercantile social scale, the wardrobe of Bristol merchant George Lane, whose estate was valued at £850, was comparably modest: a furred gown, three cloaks, three doublets, three pairs of breeches, eight pairs of stockings, three pairs of shoes, six shirts, six handkerchiefs, one jerkin, two hats, four ruff bands, two girdles and two pairs of gloves.[13]

Forming yet another layer of Jacobean society were the professional classes such as doctors, lawyers, clerics and schoolmasters who were all distinguished by their education: they had usually studied at university. The value of the wardrobe of John Ratcliffe, a schoolmaster in Hertfordshire, whose estate totalled £5 7s, equalled that of the poorest husbandman, while a minister in Banbury, who was worth over £98, had three suits, two gowns, two cloaks, three hats, with an unspecified number of shirts, bands, caps, handkerchiefs, stockings, shoes and boots.[14] Thomas Wainwright, a curate and schoolmaster in Liverpool, included in his will his satin breeches, branched-taffeta (figured) breeches and a velvet jerkin, his best hat, lined with velvet, two gowns and an old cassock – the old-fashioned style of gown associated with his profession.[15]

Only three published inventories were identified as belonging to 'gentlemen' and only one was wealthy. The estate of John Bayley of Banbury was worth a mere £11 and most of it related to his clothing: a cloak, coat, jerkin, two doublets, two pairs of breeches and uncounted accessories: shirts, bands, stockings, shoes, boots and spurs.[16] Cuthbert Bates of Durham had an estate worth over £269. No clothing was listed in his inventory, just the weapons and armour essential to a gentleman:

A longe sword	2 jackes [plated jackets]
A shorte sword	2 preavye coates [armoured coats]
A gylted dagre	
11 staves	1 payre of plate britches
4 goones [guns]	2 payre of plate sleaves [sleeves]
2 pystalls	2 payre of plate stokens [stockings].[17]
2 steall capps	

The inventories of the craftspeople who provided the materials and made the clothes and accessories offer another perspective on the wardrobes of middle England outside London. Glovers in Bristol, Derbyshire, Oxfordshire and Surrey sold a range of leather gloves made from the skins of sheep, deer, calves, as well as knitted wool ones.[18] The stocks of clothiers and drapers indicate the wool fabrics commonly worn: kersey, russet, durance (glazed worsted), cotton (napped wool), frieze, serge and fustian. Black and grey predominated, but there were also fabrics in white, red, blue, green, tawny, orange, maiden hair (bright tan), primrose, sage, mouse colour, as well as medleys and stripes.[19] A Wigan mercer's shop sold a wide range of linens for shirts including the expensive imported holland and cambric, as well as a cheaper coarse canvas.[20] The furs that men in rural society wore included rabbit, sheepskin, polecat, fox, otter, squirrel and rat skin, to line and face loose gowns.[21]

'Cloth stockings' in a Chesterfield hosier's inventory and woollen knit hose in that of a Bristol hosier demonstrate that both styles were made and worn.[22] As well as the local mercer, travelling chapmen and chapwomen sold fabrics, trimmings and accessories to rural customers, including bandstrings, bone and

Men's wardrobes, 1600–30

Man's linen shirt, embroidered with silk, 1620s | The Warwickshire Museum

Purple silk damask gown, 1605–15 | Claydon House, Buckinghamshire | National Trust | Photograph: Judith Hodgkinson

bobbin laces, woven laces of silk and wool, points, gartering and buttons, as well as pins, thread and needles for sewing.[23]

Some garments were available ready-made. The 1619 inventory of an Ipswich merchant included 47 coarse falling bands described as 'sale ware' (i.e., ready-made) and that of a Wiltshire tailor in 1615 listed 20 'sale' doublets, 12 pairs of breeches and six jerkins.[24] A form of shoe sizing was in use during this period: a Bristol shoemaker's inventory listed a range of sizes from two through to 12.[25] The money needed to pay for all these items was carried in leather purses made by the whitawer (white-tawed leather worker).[26]

There was a clear sartorial distinction between commoners and aristocrats. A list of clothes delivered in 1615 to the steward of Henry Percy, 9th Earl of Northumberland illustrates that this difference manifested itself in the number of garments owned, the materials they were made of and how richly they were decorated. Percy's wardrobe included a laced velvet cloak lined with wrought velvet, two pairs of gold-embroidered hangers and girdles, an inlaid sword and a hatched rapier, a pair of black garters laced with silver and gold lace with matching shoe roses, a pair of carnation silk stockings, a black beaver hat and a white beaver hat with gold hatbands.[27] The probate inventory, dated 1614, of Henry Howard, Earl of Northampton listed three gowns, 15 cloaks, two suits, four doublets and ten pairs of hose, all of silk – mostly velvet – and decorated with slashing and applied laces. He also had two shirts with lace insertions, a dozen plain ones, 16 'ruff bands' and three girdles and pairs of hangers embroidered with seed pearls.[28]

Richard Sackville, 3rd Earl of Dorset was notorious for living beyond his means and spent vast sums on his wardrobe. An inventory of part of his wardrobe taken in 1617 lists six separate ensembles of cloak, doublet, hose, stockings, gloves, hatband, garters, shoe roses, sword belt and hangers, all of matching silks, elaborate embroidery and precious metal laces.[29]

At the pinnacle of English society was the young and stylish Henry, Prince of Wales, whose wardrobe accounts for 1608 record the clothing ordered and made for him. These included a doublet and hose of green satin and a green velvet cloak, all trimmed with silk lace, a doublet and hose of white satin striped with silver, slashed to reveal a carnation silk lining, a green camlet hunting coat, a jerkin of black frizade (a napped woollen fabric) lined with shag (silk or wool with a pile) and two embroidered linen waistcoats. Gloves of cordevant (Spanish leather) and stag's leather, all trimmed with metal lace and fringe, silk hose and garters, points (ribbons with metal aiglets at each end for lacing together doublet and hose), hatbands, feathers for hats, holland for shirts and beaver hats of 'diverse colours' are also listed. In addition, 157 pairs of shoes and 34 pairs of boots, a sword and dagger damascened with gold were purchased for the prince who until his untimely death in 1612 was England's male fashion icon.[30]

The garments described in the following pages are clearly clothing for the gentry; neither the elaborate court dress seen in portraits nor the everyday garments of the working classes survive. As bills, inventories and portraits illustrate it was the quality of the fabrics and trimmings that distinguished the clothing worn by each level of society. During this period, most Englishmen relied on the second-hand clothing market for their cloaks, doublets and hose, resulting in a degree of time lag between the latest fashions of the rich and aristocratic and those who wore their cast-offs. At the same time, the many rural tailors listed in the inventories were making men's clothes for a local clientele of all classes. Allowing for these differentiations of style, fabrics and decoration, the patterns provided here may be adapted to make clothing for many ranks of Englishmen between 1600 and 1650.

Susan North

1. Iris Lorelei Williams and Sally Thomson, eds, *Marlborough Probate Inventories, 1591–1775*, Wiltshire Record Society, vol. 59, 2007, p. 15
2. John S. Moore, ed., *Clifton and Westbury Probate Inventories, 1609–1761*, Bristol: Avon Local History Association, 1981, p. 1
3. J. S. W. Gibson, ed., *Banbury Wills and Inventories: Part One 1591–1620*, Banbury Historical Society, vol. 13, 1985, p. 277
4. Williams, *Marlborough*, p. 22
5. Herbert Maxwell Wood, ed., *Wills and Inventories from the Registry at Durham, Part IV*, Surtees Society, vol. 142, 1929, p. 93
6. Ibid, p. 139
7. Paul B. Pixton, ed., *Wrenbury Wills and Inventories, 1542–1661*, Record Society of Lancashire and Cheshire, vol. 144, 2009, p. 135; Angus Patterson, *Fashion and Armour in Renaissance Europe*, V&A, 2009, p. 18
8. Michael Reed, ed., *The Ipswich Probate Inventories, 1583–1631*, Suffolk Record Society, vol. 22, 1981, p. 76
9. E. R. C. Brinkworth and J. S. W. Gibson, eds, *Banbury Wills and Inventories: Part Two, 1621–1650*, The Banbury Historical Society, 14, 1976, p. 48; John S. Moore, ed., *The Goods and Chattels of our Forefathers: Frampton Cotterell and District Probate Inventories, 1539–1804*, London and Chichester: Phillimore, 1976, p. 51
10. Edwin and Stella George, eds, *Bristol Probate Inventories, Part 1: 1542–1650*, Bristol Record Society, vol. 49, 2002, p. 70
11. Gibson, *Banbury, Part One*, p. 164
12. Jeanne Jones, ed., *Stratford-upon-Avon Inventories 1538–1699: I: 1538–1625*, The Dugdale Society, vol. 39, 2002, p. 207
13. Patrick McGrath, ed., *Merchants and Merchandise in Seventeenth-Century Bristol*, Bristol Record Society, vol. 19, 1955, p. 71
14. Meryl Parker, ed., *All my Worldly Goods II Wills and Probate Inventories of St Stephen's Parish, St Albans, 1418–1700*, St Albans: Bricket Wood Society, 2004, pp. 167–68; Gibson, *Banbury, Part One*, p. 263
15. J. P. Earwalker, ed., *Lancashire and Cheshire Wills and Inventories 1571 to 1696*, Chetham Society, vol. 28, new series, 1898, pp. 33–34
16. Gibson, *Banbury, Part One*, p. 265
17. J. C. Hodgson, ed., *Wills and Inventories from the Registry at Durham, Part III*, Surtees Society, vol. 112, 1906, p. 183
18. George, *Bristol*, pp. 68–69; D. Marion Herridge, ed., *Surrey Probate Inventories, 1558–1603*, Surrey Record Society, vol. 39, 2005, pp. 380–81; Brinkworth, *Banbury, Part Two*, pp. 173–74, 209
19. Earwalker, *Lancashire*, p. 19; C. B. Phillips and J. H. Smith, eds, *Stockport Probate Records, 1578–1619*, Record Society for Lancashire and Cheshire, vol. 124, 1985, pp. 56–57; J. M. Bestall and D. V. Fowkes, eds, *Chesterfield Wills and Inventories, 1604–1650*, Derbyshire Record Society, vol. 28, 2001, p. 134; J. A. Atkinson et al, eds, *Darlington Wills and Inventories, 1600–1625*, Surtees Society, vol. 201, 1993, pp. 111–14
20. J. J. Bagley, 'Matthew Markland, A Wigan Mercer: The Manufacture and Sale of Lancashire Textiles in the Reigns of Elizabeth I and James I', *Transactions of the Lancashire and Cheshire Antiquarian Society*, vol. 68, 1958, pp. 45–68
21. George, *Bristol*, p. 57
22. Bestall, *Chesterfield*, p. 202; George, *Bristol*, p. 37
23. Atkinson, *Darlington*, p. 113; Jones, *Stratford-upon-Avon*, p. 329
24. Reed, *Ipswich*, p. 77; Williams, *Marlborough*, p. 47
25. George, *Bristol*, p. 40
26. Gibson, *Banbury, Part One*, p. 177
27. G. R. Batho, *Household Papers of Henry Percy*, Camden, 3rd series, vol. 93, 1962, p. 108
28. E. P. Shirley, 'An Inventory of the Effects of Henry Howard', *Archaeologia*, vol. XLII, part 2, 1869, pp. 3, 47–78
29. Peter and Ann MacTaggart, 'The Rich Wearing Apparel of Richard, 3rd Earl of Dorset', *Costume*, vol. 14, 1980, pp. 41–55
30. William Bray, 'Extract from the Wardrobe Account of Prince Henry, Eldest Son of King James I', *Archaeologia*, vol. 11, 1794, pp. 88–96

Clothing terms

The names of various parts of doublets and hose are given here. Many terms are from Randle Holme's, *The Academy of Armory*, 1688, which was compiled over many years and includes descriptions from the earliest years of the century, as well as those closer to the date of its publication. In a section of the volume called 'Canting Terms used by Beggars, Vagabonds, Cheaters, Cripples and Bedlams' (Book III, Chapter III, page 167) Holme defines the word for 'Cloaths' as 'Dudes'.

The terms **lacing tab** and **girdle loop** are contemporary terms chosen by the authors for parts that are not defined in 17th-century literature. The image shows a half-scale reconstruction of the crimson silk grosgrain doublet on page 88, with trunk breeches based on extant examples.

Jenny Tiramani

'**Sleeve hands**, the lowest part of the sleeve next the Wrist.'
The Academy of Armory, Book III, Chapter III, p. 96

'**The Belly Peeces**, the inward stiffning of the Breast of the Doublet.'
The Academy of Armory, Book III, Chapter III, p. 95

Lacing tab

'**The Peake**, is the bottom or point of the Stomacher, whether before or behind.'
The Academy of Armory, Book III, Chapter III, p. 94
This definition is given in the section for women's dress but is appropriate for the same position at the base of the pointed front on a man's doublet.

'**The Waist-band**, is a ‑‑‑‑‑‑‑‑ [sic] under the skirts to which the straps are fastened. Straps, are peeces of Leather fastnd to the Waistband instead of Eyes, or holders.' *The Academy of Armory*, Book III, Chapter III, p. 95

'**The Eyes**, or **Holders**; are small Wiers made round through which the Breeches hooks are put, to keep them from falling.'
The Academy of Armory, Book III, Chapter III, p. 95

'**The Pockets**, are little bags set in the sides of the Breeches to put or carry any small thing in.'
The Academy of Armory, Book III, Chapter III, p. 96

'The **Cod=peece** [sic], or open of the Breeches before.'
The Academy of Armory, Book III, Chapter III, p. 96

'In a **Mans Suite** of cloaths there are these several parts: as The **Doublet**, it is the whole covering for the upper part of the man: in which there is these pieces and terms.'
  a. The two Fore Bodies
  b. The two Back Parts
The Academy of Armory, Book III, Chapter III, p. 95

'**Trunk**, or **Sailers Breeches** ... This was the fashion of the Gentry in the beginning of King James his Reigh ... the Breeches full in the wast, that they fell into Pleats and Folds, and being gathered at the Knees, they swelled round out: as in many Munuments to be seen, where they are tied above the Knees, and the hose also gathered under the Knees.'
The Academy of Armory, Book III, Chapter II, p. 19

'The **Linning**, is fine Flaxed or Linnen: called the out lining.'
The Academy of Armory, Book III, Chapter III, p. 95
All four doublets with patterns in this book have silk linings but the word 'lining' reveals the strong connection with linen, the textile commonly used for linings.

'The **Cottonings**, is that with which the cloth or outward stuff of the Breeches are Lined.'
The Academy of Armory, Book III, Chapter III, p. 96
The trunk hose on page 70 have a fustian lining (a linen warp and cotton weft).

'The **Collar**, is that part that compsseth [sic] the Neck.'
The Academy of Armory, Book III, Chapter III, p. 95

'**Eiglet** or **Aiglet** – used now for the tip of the point but also for the whole point.'
[*aiguillette*: a point; *aiguilletter*: to trusse, or tye points]
Randle Cotgrave, *A Dictionarie of the French and English Tongues*, 1611, f. 30

'The **Wings**, are **Welts** or **peeces** set over the place on top of the Shoulders, where the Body and Sleeves are set together: now Wings are of diverse fashions, some narrow, others broad; some cut in slits, cordy Robe like; other Scalloped.' *The Academy of Armory*, Book III, Chapter III, p. 94

Girdle loop

'The **Waist**, is the length from the shoulder to the middle, now in a Doublet it may be the fashion to be Short Waisted Side Waisted.'
The Academy of Armory, Book III, Chapter III, p. 95

'**Eylet holes**, or **Eiglet holes**, little round holes whipt-stitched about, through which laces are drawn to hold one side close to the other.'
The Academy of Armory, Book III, Chapter III, p. 94

A Point: A length of ribbon, lace, braid or leather, usually with metal Eiglets or Aiglets on either end, to tie items of clothing together.

'**Turn ups**, or **Cuffs**; are the turning up of the end of the Doublet next the hand.'
The Academy of Armory, Book III, Chapter III, p. 96

'The **Skirts** or **Laps**, because one lieth a little over another, they are distinguished by the fore skirts, side skirts and hinder skirts; sometimes the custom is to have them more or less, big and little: narrow or short, and large or deep.'
The Academy of Armory, Book III, Chapter III, p. 95

'The **Seat**, the hinder part on which we sit: also the inner part which is at the Breech.'
The Academy of Armory, Book III, Chapter III, p. 96

'The **Inner Lining**, is Canvice, Buckram, or such like, next to the cloth or stuff, between it and the Foresaid Lining.'
The Academy of Armory, Book III, Chapter III, p. 95

The inner lining, or interlining, is not visible here because it is sandwiched between the outside layer and the lining.

Dressing men, *c.* 1600–30
Cloaks
Doublet and hose

1. Detail of *Portrait of a gentleman, traditionally identified as Henry, Prince of Wales*, *c.* 1620 (see page 89). The majority of portraits in this book show their sitters wearing cloaks draped over the left shoulder, leaving the right arm unencumbered in case of the need to draw a sword.

3. Detail of *An Elegant Company*, 1632, by Pieter Codde. Mr and Mrs Martin, Ryerson Collection © The Art Institute of Chicago.

2. Detail of a portrait of Philip IV of Spain (see page 135). Painted in 1622, it shows Philip IV of Spain wearing his cloak draped around both shoulders in a somewhat formal manner.

4. Detail from Girard Thibault's *Academie de l'Espée*, 1628, plate XX, Skokloster Castle / CC BY-SA. This man has the rear points hanging loose from his hose.

A linen shirt was the garment worn next to a man's skin. Over the shirt a doublet and hose were put on, followed by various outer garments such as jerkins, cassocks, coats, gowns and cloaks. By 1600 doublets were quite snug-fitting with armholes cut high in the armpit and with the top of the undersleeve cut very high to enable maximum movement of the arms. Even for those men who did not favour the tightest fit, it was essential that the doublet was tight around the waistline to support the sword girdle and weapons. In his autobiography, Thomas Raymond records that James Hay, 2nd Earl of Carlisle (1612–60) was chastised by his father when he complained that the doublet of his masking suit was too straight: 'Fye, boye', said the Earl, 'are you not ashamed to complayne of that? Whie, when I was a masker and the mode was to appear very small in the wast, I remember I was drawne up from the grounde by both hands, whilst the taylor with all his strength buttoned on my doublet.'[1]

This tightness may explain the appearance of lacing tabs on the inside of doublet fronts in the early 17th century. A lace was tied through them first, to take the strain off the buttons while doing them up. From at least the 14th century a man's hose were tied to his doublet with points, somewhere between his waist and his hips, depending on the fashionable doublet length at the time. Early in the 16th century it settled around the natural waist (between the bottom ribs and the top of the pelvis). A high waist was introduced in the early 1600s as is shown in images 5 to 8. Seventeenth-century portraits do not always show clearly whether the points are actually tied to the hose because they were increasingly being used for decorative purposes alone by then. The youth kneeling in image 3 has loose ribbon points hanging from eyelet holes in his laps that may be either. However, image 4 clearly shows a man fencing with his back points hanging from the hose alone, unconnected to his doublet. This arrangement gave him greater physical freedom for the activity and his linen shirt can be seen in the resulting gap between doublet and hose. The illustrations opposite show the four V&A doublets with patterns in this book, worn with matching hose, although they could all have equally been worn with hose of contrasting fabrics. In image 5 the system of attaching the green doublet to a pair of hose did not necessitate an internal waistband. Points would have been threaded through pairs of holes in the waistband of the hose first, then threaded through the eyelet holes in the doublet laps and tied in bows on the outside, whereas on the doublet and hose in image 6, the points remained hidden under the laps. About 1610 metal hooks and eyes appear in mercers' inventories and on extant doublets and hose, as they do on the crimson doublet in image 7. In addition to the hooks and eyelets respectively used for practical purposes, both this and the doublet in image 8 also have eyelets for purely decorative points. By the 1630s decorative ribbons tied in bows were often stitched directly onto the top of the doublet, or bottom of the hose, without being threaded through any eyelet holes at all.

1. G. Davies, ed., *Autobiography of Thomas Raymond and Memoirs of the Family of Guise of Elmore, Gloucestershire*, Camden Society, 3rd series, vol. 28, 1917, p. 28; J. L. Nevinson, 'A New Suit', Connoisseur, vol. CXXIII, 1949, p. 100

5. The green silk velvet doublet, *c.* 1600–10, on page 26, has one set of worked eyelet holes that are worked through the top of the laps. This method of connecting the doublet and hose without an internal waistband of eyelets was used for several hundred years before 1600.

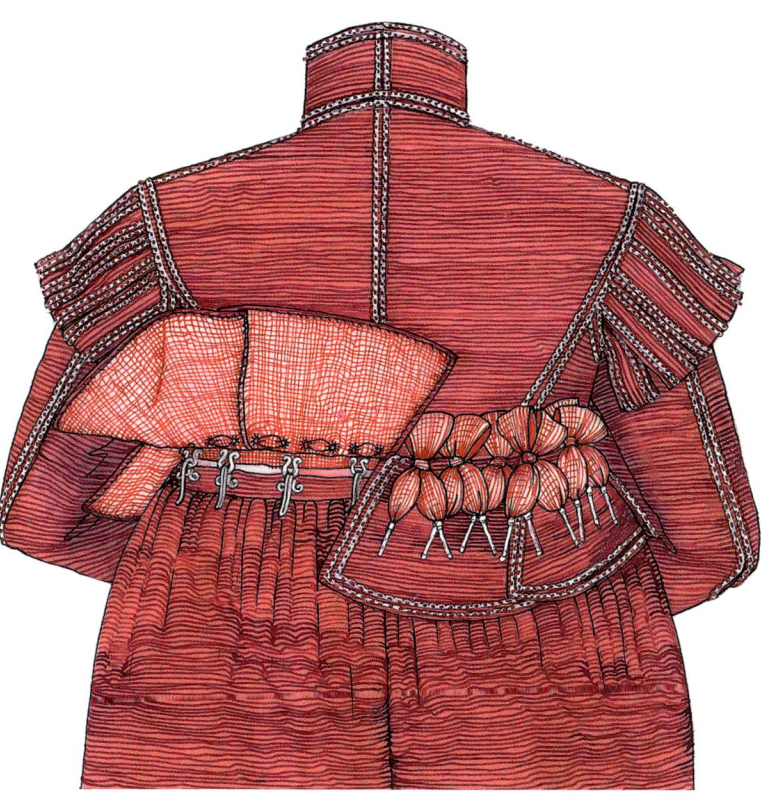

7. The crimson silk grosgrain doublet, *c.* 1620, on page 88, has metal eyes on the waistband, from which metal hooks in the waistband of the hose would hang. There are also worked eyelet holes in the tops of the laps for visible ribbon points to be threaded through. These may have been for decorative points only, or for the doublet to be worn with hose with pierced holes at the waist.

6. The doublet of slashed silk satin, *c.* 1618, on page 48, has a waistband of worked eyelet holes and unworked pierced holes in the waistband of the trunk hose. The points were hidden under the laps when worn.

8. The slashed doublet of stamped ivory silk satin, *c.* 1625–30, on page 112, has worked eyelet holes in the waistband for tying points from the hose and another set in the laps for visible decorative points.

Dressing men, *c.* 1600–30

Sword harnesses

In the 17th century men with the social rank of gentleman or above still had the right to carry arms and many did so, especially in public. Even when they unhooked and removed the hangers, it was commonplace to wear the sword girdle as seen in image 10. In the 16th century the protruding shape of the peascod doublet helped to keep the sword girdle in place. However, once this style of doublet gave way to one with a smooth front in around 1605, keeping the girdle on the curved waistline became more problematic. All four doublets surveyed in this book have the means to support a girdle at the front in the form of a pair of loops. In addition, the girdle was tied with a point through eyelet holes at the front peak of the doublet. It was essential to wear the girdle fastened tightly around the waist so that it could support the sword hanging on the left-hand side and prevent it from sagging in an ungainly manner. Image 11 shows the front girdle strap worn swooping over both the girdle at centre front and the small laps at the side, but as the fashion for longer laps became popular this strap is often seen worn underneath them in portraiture, as it is in image 12.

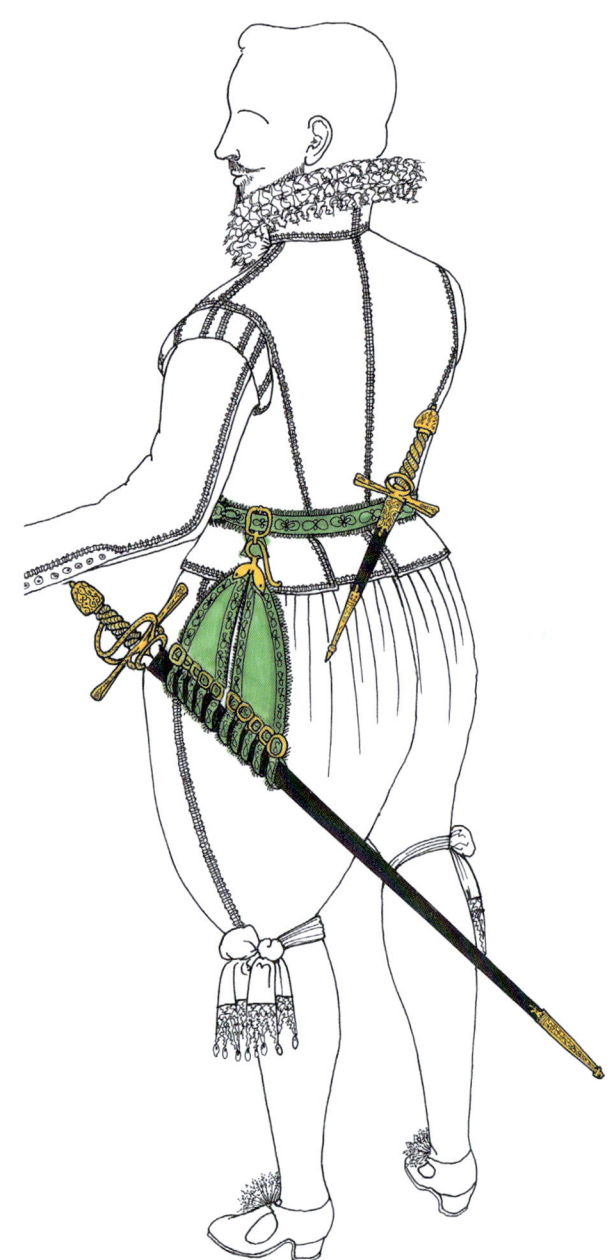

9. A dagger and scabbard were often fastened to the back of the girdle in such a way that both sword and dagger could be drawn at once, should the need arise.

10. Detail of the 1610 portrait on page 70.

11. Detail of the 1615 portrait on page 80.

12. Detail of the *c.* 1629 portrait on page 112.

13. Detail of Robert Radcliffe, Earl of Sussex, known as 'The White Knight', *c.* 1593, English School, Royal Armouries (I.36), © Royal Armouries. He wears a girdle over armour with the sword, scabbard and hangers in his left hand.

Stockings and hose

Garters

Trunk hose with canions such as those in images 13 and 14 and on page 70 are often shown with stockings worn over them above the knee. The stocking tops are folded over several times, possibly concealing a narrow garter tied above the knee. Silk garters served both as practical and decorative devices for men and women. A pair of silk taffeta garters was found on the exhumed body of Margaretha Franziska de Lobkowitz (d. 1617) in the church of St Wenceslas in Mikulov in the Czech Republic. The garters, 6 feet long and 14 inches wide, were wound around her legs four times and then tied in double bows.

Lacing Bands

Rather than relying on garters alone, an alternative, and much more secure way of holding up stockings, was to stitch or lace them directly to the round trunk breeches or hose. Extant hose such as those in the Galleria Parmeggiani, Reggio Emilia in Italy, which date from around 1615 to 1620, have leg bands with eyelet holes around them for this purpose. In the Livrustkammaren in Stockholm there is a pair of knitted silk stockings (inv.gr.3378) with two rows of eyelet holes worked around their tops, one row ½" below the other. Perhaps the stockings stretched and the lower row was added to prevent wrinkles.

Points

By the end of the 1620s the fashion for points tied around the bottom of hose was well established. In image 18 the points are threaded through pairs of eyelet holes in the breeches and through those in the stocking tops. There is a set of ribbon points that date from around 1632 in the Verney Collection at Claydon House, Buckinghamshire. It is possible that their purpose was similar to those here. The points survive with a doublet and some other elements from a single outfit, but the doublet has no eyelet holes at the waist, so the points were most probably from a pair of breeches.

Jenny Tiramani

14. Detail of 1603 portrait on page 162.

16. Detail of 1622 portrait on page 135.

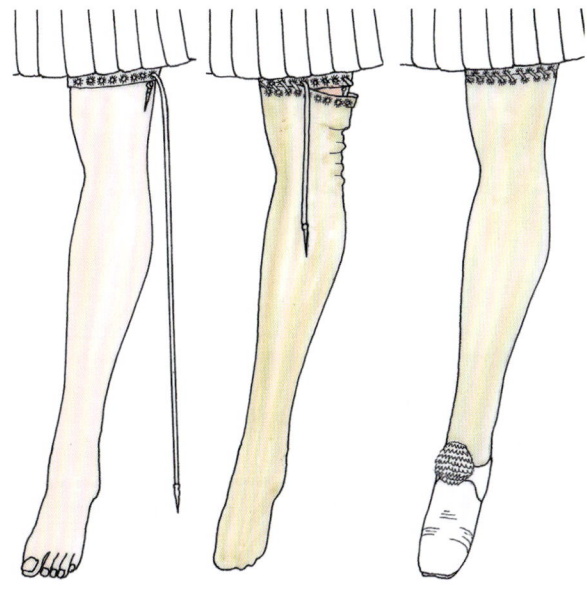

18. Detail of *c.* 1629 portrait on page 113.

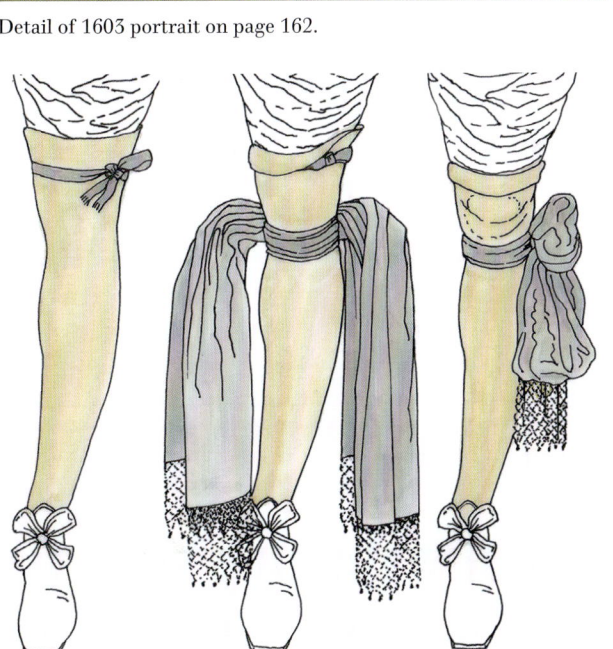

15.

17.

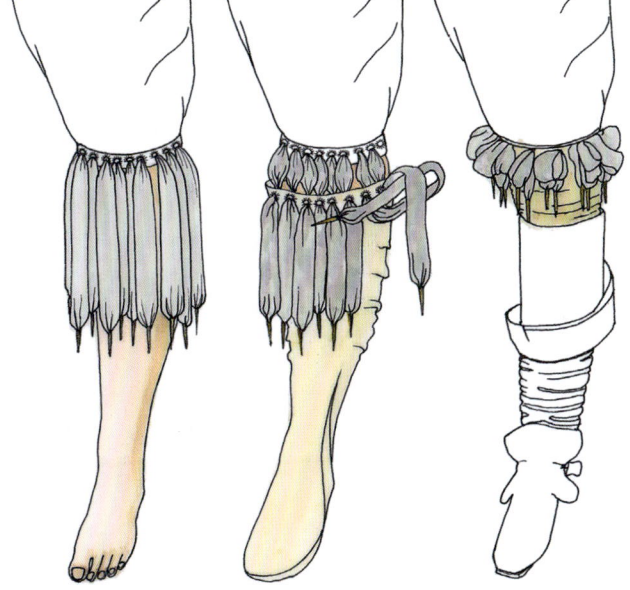

19.

Dressing men, *c.* 1600–30

Tailoring the doublet

1. Hans Heinla, tailor, 1610, from *Die Hausbücher der Nürnberger Zwölfbrüderstiftungen*, Amb. 317b.2°, f. 79v. (Mendel II)
© Stadtbibliothek Nürnberg

2. Bartl Harder, tailor, 1613–30, from *Die Hausbücher der Nürnberger Zwölfbrüderstiftungen*, Amb. 279.2°, f. 83r. (Landauer I)
© Stadtbibliothek Nürnberg

Surviving clothing must be studied carefully and techniques should be observed rather than assumed. A knowledge of modern tailoring techniques is invaluable but the craft has evolved over the past 400 years and the methods employed often vary from those used today. Hand-sewn clothing needs a different approach from machined garments and not every technique is easily adapted. The 17th-century tailor had to be a master of many skills and techniques and had to know how to adapt them for use on a variety of fabrics and garment styles. He also had to be proficient at using expensive fabrics economically; at a time when the making of the garment often accounted for the smallest amount on the bill the tailor had to work in the most efficient way possible. Evidence of the tailor's skill is seen in the four doublets presented in this book. Worn throughout Europe for almost 300 years, the doublet underwent many stylistic changes. Dating from around 1605 to 1630, these four represent a tiny fragment in the history of the doublet. It was a period in which the waist rose dramatically from its natural line and the belly piece evolved fully.

The doublets surveyed include one of green silk velvet (1600–10), one of slashed silk satin (c. 1618), worn by Sir Rowland Cotton, one of crimson silk grosgrain (c. 1620) and a slashed doublet of stamped ivory silk satin (1625–30). These all have a silk outer layer and are made from a range of other materials: linen, fustian, woven and unwoven wool, and paper, baleen, cork and bents.[1] Wood, silk, linen and metal threads are used for their buttons, laces and stitches.

Tailors' workshops

The tailors' workshops in images 1, 2 and 4 appear to be small businesses, comprised of the tailor himself and one or two apprentices or journeymen. At this time, a tailor needed only a few tools to set up a shop: a pair of shears, a measuring stick and a large table on which to cut the fabric. In image 1, the tailor is cutting fabric for the apprentice to stitch; it is possibly part of a suit, of which the finished hose or possibly a length of fabric hang on the rail suspended from the ceiling. A further piece of equipment essential to the tailor was the pressing iron, seen here at the tailor's feet. The warrants for Elizabeth I record her tailor, Walter Fyshe, taking delivery of 'one pressing Iron being very well steled', in 1595.[2] Pressing irons could gently press a seam before it was stitched down permanently. By the beginning of the 17th century, the fashion for heavily quilted doublets had begun to be replaced with a sleeker style, achieved by the subtle shaping of fabric layers, worked by the tailor with stitching and pressing, to mould the form.

Image 1 depicts the apprentice, seated on a stool by the window so he could take advantage of the daylight, stitching part of a garment in his lap. He has a small table with raised edges for his equipment – a pair of shears, a piece of wax and possibly a ball of thread. The scene in image 2 is viewed through a window, with a mirror on the opposite wall reflecting the daylight, and increasing the light in the workshop. On the table are other tools vital to the tailor – a bodkin for making eyelet holes and a pair of compasses or dividers alongside the measuring stick and the shears. The tailor sits on a wooden stool with a little compartment at its base, as does the apprentice in image 1. This may be for collecting fabric scraps (known as cabbage), or it could have housed a small metal pot with hot coals to warm the stitcher. The tailor's workshop in image 4 shows the two apprentices sitting cross-legged on a board; their knees were ideal shapers over which to stitch and add form to a garment. The figure to the left is sewing, while the figure on the right appears to be threading a needle. Hanging on the wall behind them are skeins of stitching thread.

Measurements, patterns and materials

The Spanish tailor, Juan de Alcega, was one of the first to write about the use of geometry and scale measurement in his pattern book published in 1589. Contemporary images show dividers as part of the tailor's equipment. These were used in the art of casting or drawing patterns using geometry. When casting a pattern with dividers, the proportions of the body were used along with units of measurement that varied across, and within countries: in England, the ell or yard was used, in France, the *aune*, and in Italy, the *braccio*. These were divided and subdivided evenly within themselves. Alcega states that the Castilian ell or *bara* (equal to 33") is 'divided into a twelfth, an eighth, a sixth, a quarter, a third and a half ell: and all of these divisions of the ell are perfect fractions relative to the ell itself'.[3] The tailor recorded his client's measurements by knotting a length of string or cutting notches in a parchment strip. To today's number-dependant eye, this seems confusing, but it gave the tailor a much better understanding of his customer's bodily proportions than a modern measuring tape.

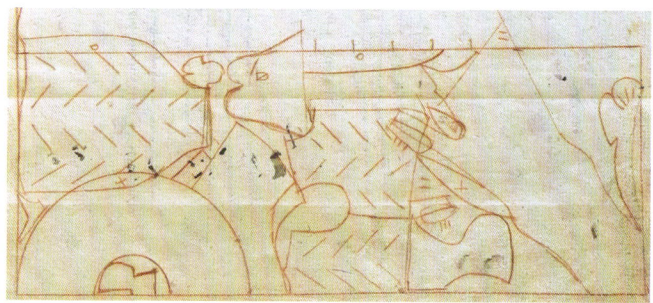

3. Pattern of garments for a knight in combat with a hood, gloves, cloak and hose. 'Item einen Ritter ins Feldt, einem Mutzen, Hentzschken, Kappen undt Hossen', 1604, #61, from *The Book of Patterns by the Guild of Tailors from Chomutov* published in Šimša, Martin, Tailor's Pattern Books in the Czech Lands in the 16th–18th centuries (NULK, 2013). Photograph © Martin Šimša, 2013 (English translation by Melanie Braun)

Surviving tailors' pattern books from the 16th century onwards offer fabric layouts and explanations of how to allow for the direction of pattern and nap.[4] Information on drafting garments was not offered, neither was the choice of interlinings, or stitching information. The tailor was expected to be knowledgeable about such things.

The pattern layout in image 3 offers a whole outfit, including the doublet with a slashing pattern, hose with codpiece, a hood, cloak and mittens. The one-piece sleeve and hose were slightly old-fashioned in style by 1604. It also shows where to cut large piecings. Smaller piecings were generally not shown in pattern layouts and were cut from the cabbage. Laps and wings were often pieced together from these small scraps, as in the case of the green velvet doublet (pages 28, 29 and 30).

Fabrics

A variety of silks were used as a top layer for all of the doublets in this book, as well as some of the less heavily tailored garments such as the damask cloak. The silk velvet was probably the most costly of all the fabrics due to the complexity of the weaving process and the amount of silk thread it required. In 'A proclamation against the excesse of Apparel, 6. July 1597' made by Elizabeth I silks were restricted to certain members of her court.[5] Silk velvet was limited to even fewer wearers than satin, damask, taffeta and grosgrain, all of which feature on the garments in the book.

The customer himself purchased the fabric and decoration he wanted for his doublet and chose its style, but left the method of construction to the expertise of the tailor. The wide range of fabrics available varied in texture, weave and flexibility, all of which the tailor had to take into account when deciding which linings and interlinings to use. The interlinings were as important as the top fabrics, as they provided the foundation on which the tailor shaped and formed the doublet using a variety of methods and materials.

Each doublet in this book is based on a single layer of medium to heavy weight, densely woven linen, and all are further supported at the centre fronts by belly pieces. The stiff, tightly woven velvet of the green doublet (page 26) needed no additional interlinings other than scraps of linen, loosely stitched around the shoulders, as its structure came from the layer of wool quilted into the taffeta lining. The crimson doublet (page 88) and stamped satin doublet (page 112) had extra pieces of linen applied to their foundation layer to shape the front and back shoulder. This was enough to support the tightly woven, crisp crimson grosgrain. Much of the surface of the stamped doublet is covered with applied couched decoration, which was stitched through to its linen foundation, stabilizing the layers. The interlinings of Sir Rowland's doublet (page 48) had an additional layer of coarsely woven wool applied to its shoulders. The satin outer layer was backed by a thin blue silk: they were slashed and pinked as one. Another thin silk, this one white, sat between the slashed layers and the linen interlinings.

Threads

All the threads used in the construction of these garments are 2 'S' ply of various thicknesses in either linen, hemp or silk. Linen and silk were employed in the construction seams and stitches that held the garment together. The 2 'S' hand-plied thread used here is elliptical in cross-section and 'flattens in the stitch' in contrast to modern threads made for the sewing machine, which are 3 'Z' plied and circular in cross-section.[6]

4. Jan Georg van Vliet, *Kleermaker*, 1635, Rijksmuseum, Amsterdam

On silk garments, linen seemed to be the tailor's most popular choice for seams that needed to take strain or that were concealed by lining, decoration or layers of fabric. Seams at the shoulders, sides, sleeves, armholes and waist were stitched with sturdy linen thread, sometimes used doubled and/or waxed. These threads were either bleached or unbleached. Dyed linen can also be found, for example, the brown thread used in the construction of the green doublet. The use of a strong thread enabled the tailor to achieve a durable seam, which could withstand considerable strain with the minimum number of stitches, a great benefit in an age before the invention of the sewing machine. In some cases, such as the crimson doublet, the side, shoulder and sleeve seams have been stitched with red silk thread. The lace covering the seams is very narrow and natural linen thread might have shown on the red silk once this was put under strain. However, linen thread was used to stitch the sleeve to the armhole and the waistband of eyes, where most strength was needed. Silk threads, dyed to match the doublet, appear to be used for strong seams only when the seam is likely to be on view, whether outside or inside the garment, such as attaching the lacing tabs to the belly pieces.

Silk thread is also used for any finishing stitch in silk-lined garments, such as the felling of the lining on body and laps, as well as for eyelets, buttonholes, worked bars and attaching decoration.

Shaping, pad stitching, quilting and stiffening

There are several ways to achieve shape in a garment: through the cut, the use of curves and the joining of a curved edge to a straight edge. Also important is pad stitching – moulding and shaping the garment with sewing. Evident in 16th-century garments, pad stitching has undergone changes, but has always been used to give form to multiple layers of fabric. It is still in use today to give collars and lapels their shape.

Pad stitching is created by columns of slanted stitches, applied through all the layers of fabric. These run up, then down to create broken 'v' shapes ' \/\/\/ ' on one side of the fabric, and a series of horizontal lines '------' on the other (see also figs 12a and 12b on page 21). In the first half of the 17th century, pad stitching was worked so that the stitch facing the tailor would be the horizontal line. This was achieved by working the stitches in a down and then upwards movement (see also figs 12a and 12b on page 21). The typical \ / is created on the underside, invisible to the person working the stitch, as seen in image 5 above. The stitches are easy to control and often regular. The stitch direction can change up to 90 degrees, with the work being turned in the hand so that the next line of stitches appears at right angles. A good example is the pad stitching on Sir Rowland's doublet (step 2, page 62), which was worked from the neck out to the shoulder and then turned and worked from the shoulder to the waist. In modern tailoring pad stitching is worked in a staggered \ / pattern, stitched so that the \ / is visible to the tailor.

Pad stitching can be found on almost every garment in this book. It gives a gentle curve around the wrist to the mitten tops and shapes the larger laps of the doublets. Around the shoulders and shoulder blades, the three short-waisted doublets are given their shape with pad stitching. The tailor created a curve to mould around the contour of the shoulder blades in the back, which also allowed for the roundness of the shoulder joint in the front and the hollow space just below the collar bone. In these three doublets, the pad stitches appear to be of similar size and spacing; these would have given a

5. Detail of the collar of a silk doublet, c. 1625–30, V&A: 170–1869 © Victoria and Albert Museum

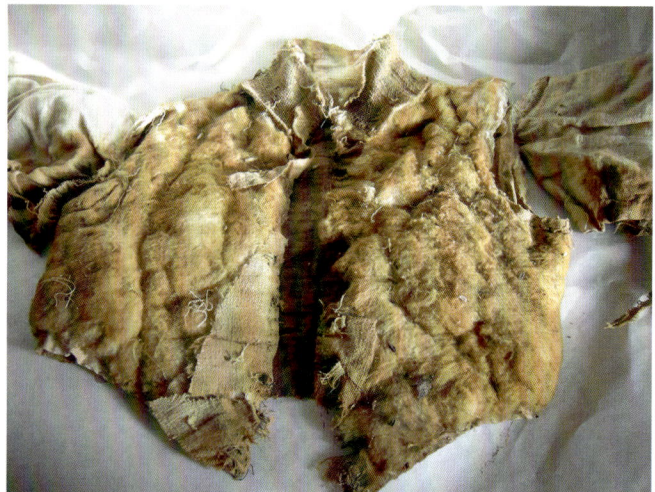

6. Remains of a child's *giubbone*, mid-16th century, Church of San Domenico Maggiore, Naples. Courtesy of Ufficio Diocesano Beni Culturali Ecclesiastici e Arte Sacra, Napoli. Photograph: Roberta Orsi Landini

three-dimensional shape over the shoulders and around the armholes when new.

Collars were also firmly pad stitched in order to shape them to the curve of the neck, as well as to stiffen them and hold all the layers of interlining together. Of these doublets, only three survive with collars. Both Sir Rowland's doublet and the stamped one have three layers of linen, formed over the hand and closely pad stitched, while the crimson has two linen layers, with a pasteboard piece inbetween, and a further layer of soft wool, closest to the neck. These layers made the collar extremely stiff, but the shaping over the hand while pad stitching ensured that it encompassed the neck comfortably. Another V&A doublet (image 5), similar in shape and cut to the stamped doublet, was pad stitched from the outside of the collar. Bents were sewn between the layers of linen to achieve the rigid shape.

On both the green doublet and Sir Rowland's doublet the laps are smaller than in the two later examples, where they become longer and wider. Pad stitching was a means of controlling the form of these larger laps. In the stamped doublet, the four laps at the front have a double layer of canvas, pad stitched with large stitches. All of the laps on the crimson doublet are interlined with a double layer of canvas and pad stitched. The front laps have only nine horizontal rows of big stitches to make them lie flat and smooth; these also prevent the edges from curling up, as they are wont to do without them. The side-back laps have 14 rows of small stitches where the intention was to make them sit over some full hose in a rounded fashion, rather than standing out as stiff flat plates. This was another style current during the same period.

Shoulder wings too sometimes feature pad stitching. For example, the green doublet had a layer of linen and wool pad stitched together over the hand, giving a gentle curve to the wing. The shape of the wing *always* echoed and enhanced the line of the sleeve head; the arched edge of the wing was always stitched into the armhole. The straighter lower edge sits in close to the bicep of the wearer.

Quilting

Quilting can be related to pad stitching in that it can also be used to attach two or more layers of fabric together. It is almost always practical, whether for warmth or protection, and it also gives form, smoothing out any irregularities in the body, or providing a fashionable shape. Only the green doublet in this book is quilted; it dates from the very end of the style for the heavily stuffed or bombasted, peascod-bellied doublet.

Linen-armourers were associated with tailors from at least the beginning of the 14th century. They made, as the name suggests, fabric armour that was worn under, over, or instead of, the metal version. Quilting two or more layers of fabric together, usually with an unwoven material such as wool, cotton, silk or horsehair inbetween, protected the wearer. Quilted garments were worn by both civilians and the military, and various quilting techniques were used. Possibly the simplest method was found in the green doublet, in which a layer of unwoven carded wool was placed between the linen interlining and silk lining, and running stitched. The stitched columns give the garment form, and make the layers sufficiently pliable to shape around the body. Other quilting techniques included stitching and then stuffing, or stitching and stuffing simultaneously.

Most of the outer fabric of the mid-16th century child's *giubbone* in image 6 has rotted away, leaving tiny fragments of a cloth-of-gold camlet. This reveals the layer of quilting, with pieced triangles of soft linen at the waist on each centre front. The green doublet has similar triangles in unstiffened blue wool, visible in the x-ray (image 7). On both doublets, these appear to be early forms of the belly piece.

Belly pieces

All the doublets in this book were stiffened with belly pieces. In the earliest in style of the four – the green silk doublet (image 7) – these consisted of a triangular linen panel, elongated at the top to reach the neckline and cut on the fold at centre front. Two strips of baleen were inserted into each front to keep them smooth, and the panel was stitched to the canvas foundation of the doublet. A triangular piece of blue wool was stitched onto each boned linen panel at waist level. When the doublet was worn, the front was very straight and smooth from the neck to the peak. In this less evolved type of belly piece, the paired baleen strips were mostly responsible for the straight profile, although the mere act of stitching the soft blue wool to the baleen panel created form.

The belly pieces used to stiffen the fronts of the three high-waisted doublets are much stiffer and use a variety of materials. Although at first glance their shape might look very similar, each one has a different construction from the other, giving a slightly different silhouette when the garment was worn. Compared to the other doublets, the belly pieces on Sir Rowland's (image 8) are relatively soft. Layers of canvas were pad stitched together to create two flat rigid panels and two strips of baleen, as long as these panels, were inserted at centre front on each side to prevent them from wrinkling. The belly pieces were attached to the canvas interlining and a lacing tab on each side, stitched at waist level, helps draw the edges together. When the doublet was worn, the centre front was smooth, gently curving over the chest.

The belly pieces of the crimson doublet (image 9) were made of cork carved into triangular panels, the thickness tapering from the diagonal side, which were wrapped in a layer of linen and pad stitched. A second layer of linen extending to the neckline at the top was cut double the width of the belly pieces and then folded on itself to create a pocket at the centre front for a strip of baleen reaching from the neck to the peak. This piece covers the outer surface of the belly pieces and was cut so that when it was folded at the centre front one layer is slightly smaller than the other along the inner edge, graduating the thickness of the layers of canvas to avoid any ridges showing through the top fabric. The two lacing tabs drew the two fronts together and pushed their centre front edges outwards to create a pointed, rather than flat, effect.

The belly pieces of the slashed doublet (image 10) were made of bents, skilfully arranged and stitched together, to create two rigid panels. A layer of wool, cut in a similar way to the boned linen layer of the crimson doublet, was glued around the bents and pad stitched. The top edge reached the neck to create a smooth line and the belly pieces were stitched to the lining, waist seam and centre front edge as in the crimson doublet. The thickness of the panels and similarities in the position of the lacing tabs suggest that this belly piece was also intended to fasten into a pointed front. The absence of a baleen strip results in a gentle curve over the chest. This shape was unavoidable with the long vertical slashes that break the tension of the fabric in the upper part of the body. The use of materials such as canvas stiffened with glue, bents and baleen in the construction of these belly pieces was closely related to staymaking, an art that was still carried out by tailors at the beginning of the 17th century. Layers of canvas and pasteboard, pad stitched together and glued, resembling belly pieces, can be found on many extant 18th-century stays, suggesting that this knowledge was retained once staymaking became a separate trade in the second half of the 17th century.

Seam allowances, seams, stitches and alterations

In terms of the four doublets, all heavily tailored garments, the seam allowances observed both by eye and x-ray image differ in size. Where wide seam allowances were not required for future alterations there was often a minimum amount left, to avoid creating bulky seams and wasting precious fabrics.

X-ray images of the belly pieces on
the left-hand side of the doublet fronts
Left to right from top left:
7. Green silk velvet doublet, *c.* 1600–10
8. Sir Rowland's doublet of slashed silk satin, *c.* 1618
9. Crimson silk grosgrain doublet, *c.* 1620
10. Stamped ivory silk satin doublet, *c.* 1625–30

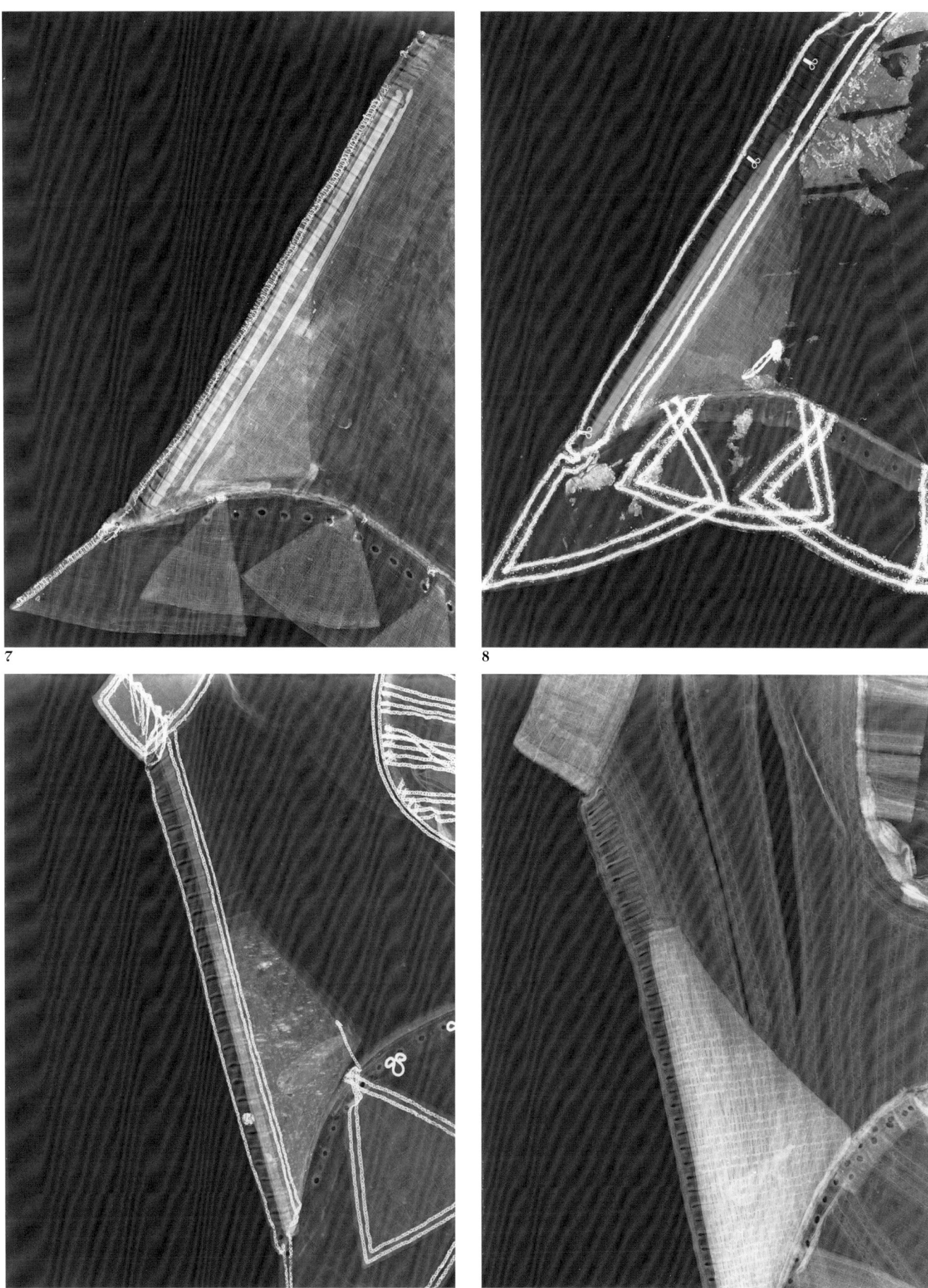

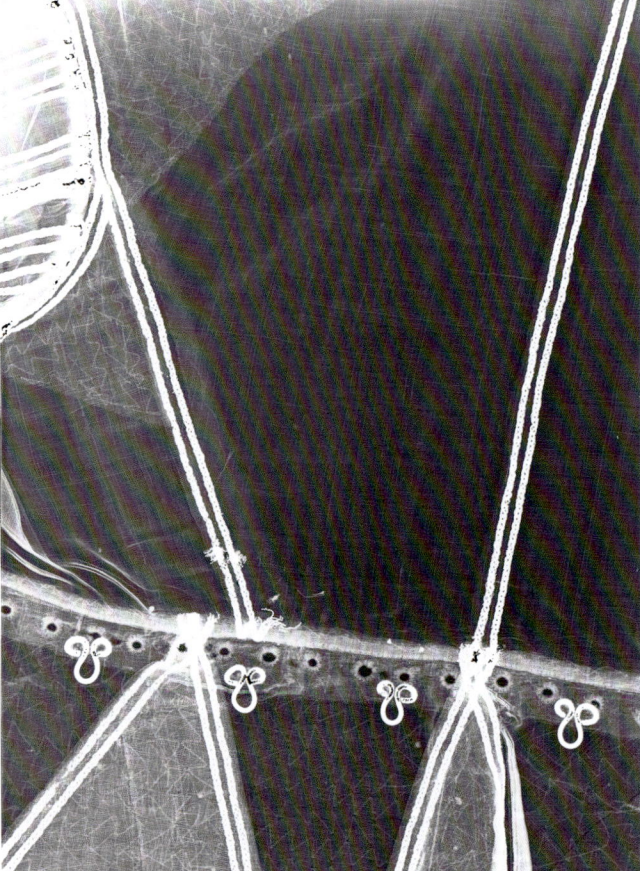

All four doublet fronts and wrist openings were cut net, without an over- or under-wrap for the buttons and buttonholes, which were positioned almost on the edge. A flap was created at the centre front through which the buttonholes were worked. This allowed the top layers and the quilting and belly pieces all to sit edge-to-edge when the doublet was closed without compromising the shape. However, in each of these doublets, the tailor cut a larger seam allowance on the side seams of the silk outer fabrics. This appears to have been done at the same time as the interlinings were cut, as alterations were made at the front side seam, probably after a first fitting, to the green doublet, Sir Rowland's and the stamped one. The crimson doublet had large seam allowances on the shoulders and side seams, but was never altered. The reason for this extra seam allowance at the shoulders was only to maintain the balance of the neckline at a fitting, as it is not possible to drop the shoulder without changing the whole neck, which would make it too big. The tailor then kept the seam allowance to further support the strong sculptural shape of the shoulders.

A comparison of seam treatments can be made between different parts of a doublet. The sleeve seam has the least strain placed on it, compared to the waist seam, which supports the hose and has to allow for the movement of the lower body, yet the same stitch can be used for both. The strength of the seam was essential, relying on the strength of the thread, of the fabric, or of both.

In *The Academy of Armory*, Randle Holme gives 'Several Terms used in Sowing of Cloath', among them, 'Basting… Backstitch. Fore stitch. Whip-stitch. Privy-stitch. Fine Drawing'.[7] Most of these were used on the doublets. Back stitch was the most commonly used, and gives a strong seam between several layers of fabrics, for example, to attach the laps to the waist of Sir Rowland's doublet. It was also worked through just two thicknesses as in the green silk doublet's sleeves and centre-back seam.

Running stitch (or fore stitch, as described by Randle Holme) is mainly used today for basting or gathering. Its use as a seaming stitch has been completely superseded by the sewing machine. In the 17th century, however, it was used as a primary stitch, perfect for joining seams that were under little tension, such as petticoat or trunk-hose seams. It also uses less thread than a back stitch. The crimson doublet has its sleeves running stitched in red silk thread, an example of seams under little strain. In the green silk doublet the side seams are joined and the wings and sleeves are attached with running stitches. As these seams were all running stitched through at least four layers, the use of this stitch may have been an attempt by the tailor to keep the seam pliable. The strength of the seam relied completely on the strength of the brown linen thread.

Whipping was used to work the raw-edged, net-cut seams of the stamped doublet's sleeves, and waist-to-lap seam on the green one. In each case, doubled linen thread was used. The edges of the sleeve seams were sealed with glue before whipping.

Side seams with seam allowances of the four doublets, left to right from top left:
11. Green silk velvet doublet, *c.* 1600–10
12. Sir Rowland's doublet of slashed silk satin, *c.* 1618
13. Crimson silk grosgrain doublet, *c.* 1620
14. Stamped ivory silk satin doublet, *c.* 1625–30

11, 12 and 14 show seam alterations.
13 is an x-ray image, which is the only way to see the seam allowance as the lining is fully intact.

The doubled thread used for the green silk doublet's waist seam (image 11) was heavily waxed before stitching, strengthening it further. The tailor would also have relied upon the six layers of fabric (velvet, lining and interlining on the body and the laps) being tightly caught together and bound by the whip stitch.

Both the stamped and the crimson doublets have their sleeveheads whip stitched into the armholes. On the stamped doublet, the edges at the top of the sleeve were left raw, with a ⅛" seam allowance. They were coated in a glue to prevent them fraying and stitched with sturdy doubled linen thread. The edges of the crimson doublet were strengthened by other means. Here, the seam allowance of the sleeves was folded and whip stitched into the armholes through the edge of the fold, so the threads passed through four layers of silk. This technique, used for the same purpose, can be observed on 18th-century silk garments. Except for Sir Rowland's, each of the doublets had its sleeves attached by working from the body into the sleeve, regardless of stitch, rather than from the sleeve into the body – a practice necessitated by the sewing machine.

When working the half-scale toiles to check the construction sequence for each doublet, we found that some stitches were worked more easily in a certain direction, or with the garment placed in a particular way, for example, in the lap, or placed flat on a surface. Stitches such as felling or whipping are directional, showing which way the seam was worked, whereas the direction of a running or back stitch is less obvious. There is even evidence of left-handed stitching. On Sir Rowland's doublet, the felling of the lining to the waist seam (step 44, page 67) feels awkward with the right hand, but flows easily with the left.

Alterations

Alterations can be found on three of the four doublets. The changes were made at different stages during the garments' lifetime, either early in the construction process after a fitting, or at a later date, perhaps when the wearer gained weight. The doublet might have been handed on to a person of different stature, and altered accordingly. Both Sir Rowland's and the green doublet appear to have been let out at the side seam by the addition of a piecing of linen in the interlining layer only. The silk outer fabrics have not been pieced, indicating that they were cut slightly larger to allow for such an alteration. The lack of seaming stitch holes in the silk confirms that these alterations to the interlinings were made during construction.

The stamped doublet has a similar alteration with an extra linen piecing in the interlining. The satin here was also cut with extra seam allowance, but it has stitch holes, so could have been altered at a later stage. The threads used throughout the construction appear to be the same as the alteration threads, suggesting that it was altered by the same tailor. The crimson doublet has no alteration, but the x-ray images show that at the side seam a larger seam allowance was cut on the front than on the back.

How were the doublets worked?

It is uncertain how much of these garments was worked when they were still in flat pattern pieces. Many of the details, such as buttonholes and applied laces, could have been done before a doublet was joined at the shoulders and its three-dimensional shape was created. Some details – such as the slashing and pinking on Sir Rowland's doublet and hose – had to be carried out flat, especially as there are two layers of silk slashed as one. However, it is evident from their construction sequence that the canions were slashed after the seam was joined.

Except for the crimson doublet they all had their linings applied while flat. In the case of the green silk doublet, the quilted linings had to be joined to the velvet early in the construction sequence. In the crimson doublet, the body and the lining each had their shoulders stitched and then the lining was prick stitched to the body. This method was quick and efficient, and could have been worked over the tailor's knee.

In the illustrations of the tailors' workshops on pages 14 and 15 there is little space for the stitchers to spread out their work. The majority of the table space was given over to the cutting, which was always a separate task and the preserve of the master tailor. With space at a premium, a doublet was the ideal garment to be constructed by more than one person. Several hands would be able to work on the different components of the garment at the same time, but the final assembling would have been left to the most skilled tailor in the workroom.

These final processes could be completed independently of each other, and the sequence may have varied. We have debated these issues and can only pose the question: did the tailors of these doublets put in the collar first or the sleeves? For the final fitting on the customer, it would certainly have been advantageous to baste on the collar and pin or baste the sleeves temporarily, to check the balance. However, the final stitching could then be completed in either order.

This brief analysis of just four doublets demonstrates that for the 17th-century tailor there was no standard means of construction. He worked with a diverse range of materials and an understanding of how to modify his skills and techniques subtly so as best to suit the garments that he produced.

Melanie Braun, Luca Costigliolo,
Claire Thornton and Jenny Tiramani

---

1. Bents are grass-like reeds, rushes, sedges, and other plants with stiff or rigid stems. (OED online)
2. Janet Arnold, *Queen Elizabeth's Wardrobe Unlock'd*, Leeds: Maney, 1988, p. 182
3. Juan de Alcega, *Tailor's Pattern Book*, 1589, facsimile, Carlton: Ruth Bean, 1979, f.vii
4. Nap is the surface given to cloth by raising and then cutting and smoothing the short fibres. (OED online)
5. A Booke containing all such Proclamations, as were published during the Raigne of the late Queene Elizabeth, 1618, http://www.bl.uk/collection-items/proclamation-against-excess-of-apparel-by-queen-elizabeth-i
6. Philip A. Sykas, 'Re-threading Notes towards a History of Sewing Thread in Britain', in Mary M. Brooks, ed., *Textiles Revealed: Object Lessons in Historic Textile and Costume Research*, London: Archetype Publications, 2000, p. 124
7. Randle Holme, *The Academy of Armory*, 1688, Book III, Chapter III, p. 96

15. Mark Rylance as Vincentio, Duke of Vienna in *Measure for Measure*, Hampton Court Palace Horn Room, 2004 © Shakespeare's Globe. Photograph: John Tramper
His doublet, hose and cloak are of patterned silk/metal fabrics, trimmed with metal laces and his sword hangers, girdle and glove tops are of embroidered black silk velvet. Silver-gilt bobbin lace edges the hatband and glove tops.

16. Colin Hurley as William Shakespeare in his dressing room for *The BIG Secret live 'I am Shakespeare' webcam daytime chatroom show Minerva Theatre, Chichester, 2007*. Image: Jenny Tiramani
He wears a doublet and hose of wool camlet decorated with silver-gilt bobbin lace, and a closed-front picadil with a linen band and cuffs.

These reconstructed *c.* 1610–15 garments were researched, designed, cut and hand stitched using patterns of extant garments and primary written and visual references. All materials used are comparable to those found in 17th-century garments.

Clothing by Jenny Tiramani, Melanie Braun, Luca Costigliolo and Armelle Lucas

Sewing stitches

1

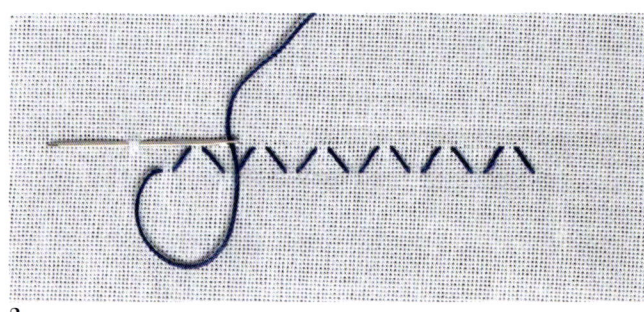
2

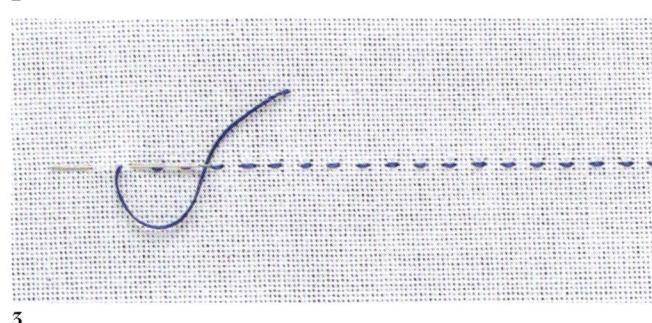
3

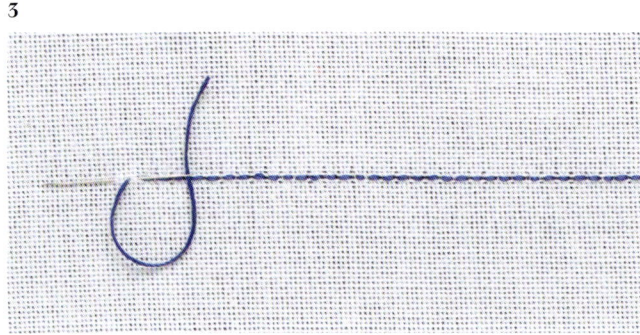
4

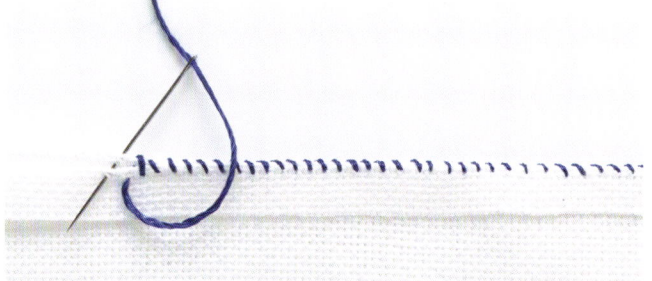
5a

5b

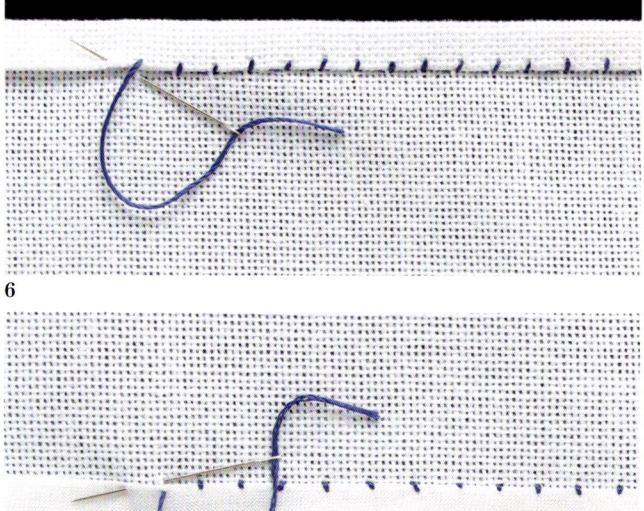
6

7

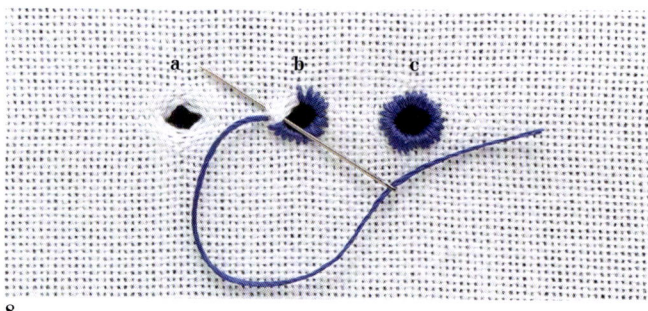
8

a

b

9

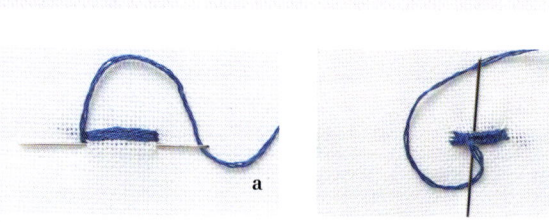
10a

The names used for stitches found on the garments in this book have changed radically since the 17th century. The identifiable stitch names shown here in bold were recorded in Randle Holme, *The Academy of Armory (1688)*. Where similar stitches were used for different purposes they have sometimes been given different names for clarity.

VARIANTS OF RUNNING STITCH:
1. **RUNNING STITCH** or **FORE STITCH**; when used as a temporary stitch it's called **BASTING**.
2. **RUNNING STITCH** worked in a zig-zag path.

VARIANTS OF BACK STITCH:
3. **HALF-BACK STITCH**: the stitches have space between them; called **PRICK STITCH** when worked through several layers to keep them together.
4. **BACK STITCH**: the stitches meet edge to edge.

VARIANTS OF WHIP STITCH:
5a. **WHIP STITCH** or **OVERSEWN** from right to left.
5b. **WHIP STITCH** or **OVERSEWN** from left to right.
6. **HEMMING** or **FELLING**; used mainly by seamstresses.
7. When sewing a lining or a binding: **FELLING** (possibly **PRIVY STITCH**). Used mainly by tailors who sometimes refer to it as **WHIP STITCH**.

8. **EYE-LID HOLE** or eyelet: (a) a hole pierced with a bodkin, (b) the hole being WHIP STITCHED or WHIPPED all around the edge, (c) the finished eyelet.
9. **INTERLOCKING RUNNING STITCH** worked with two needles simultaneously while the work is held between clamps to join, for example, bundles of material such as bents. Shown here through one layer of linen: (a) both needles are pushed through the same hole from opposite sides, (b) the needle is pulled out on each side to create an interlocking stitch.

STITCHES ON GARMENTS IN THIS BOOK USED BY THE TAILOR ONLY:
10. **UNWORKED** and **WORKED BAR**: (a) the threads are laid on the ground fabric and secured at either end, (b) for a WORKED BAR, a BLANKET STITCH is worked over the threads.

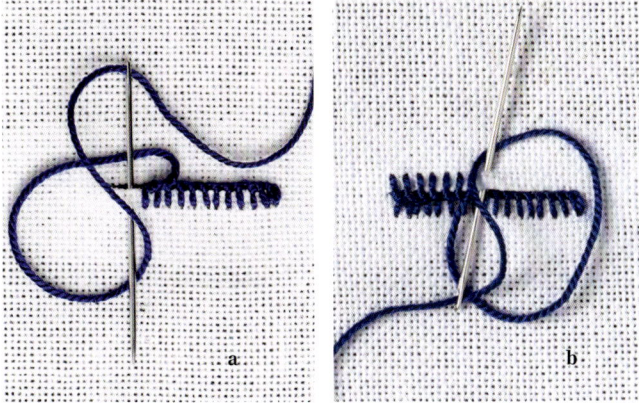
11a

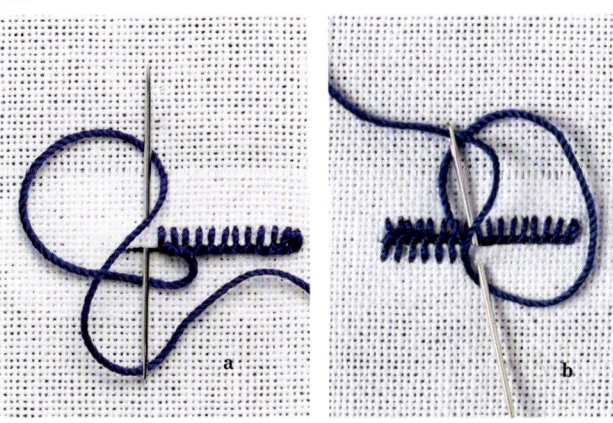
11b

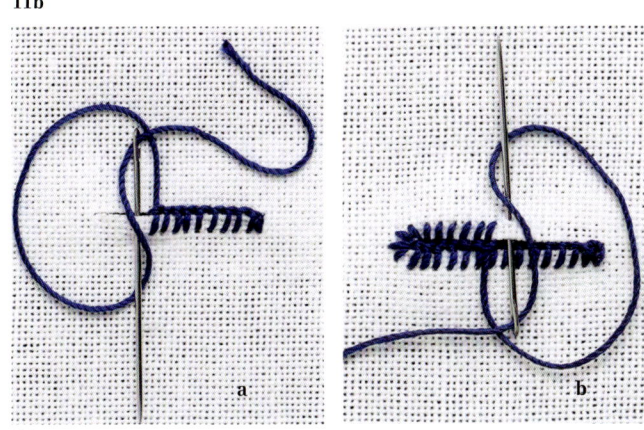
11c

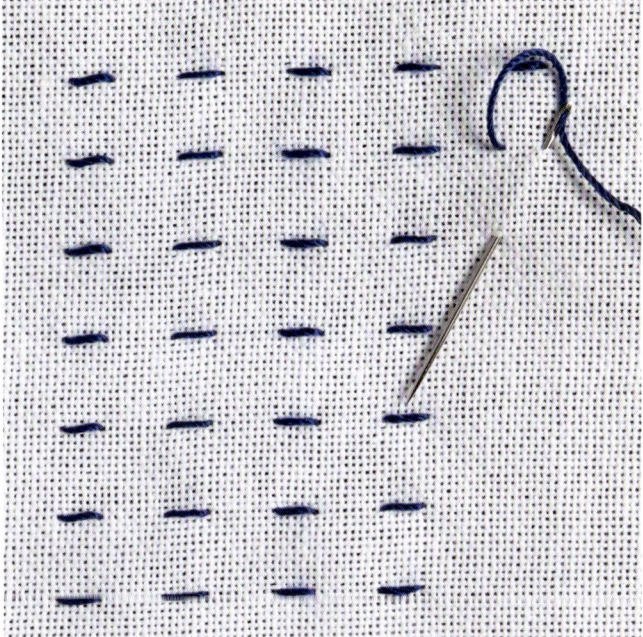
12a

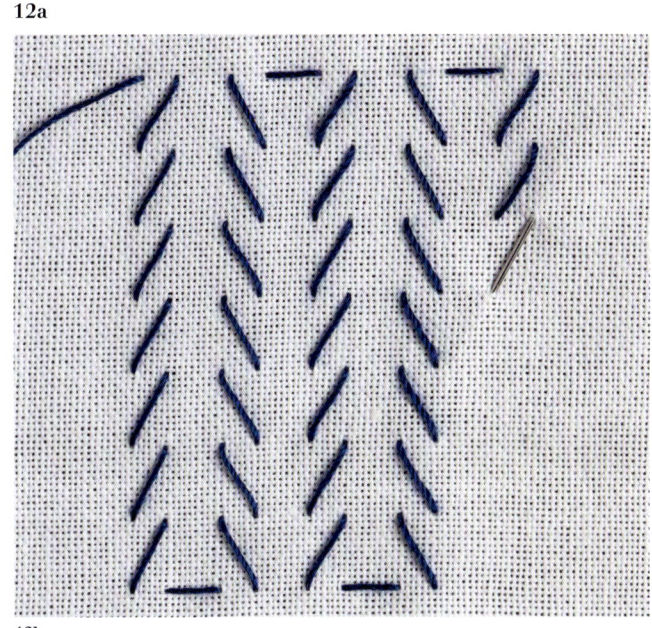
12b

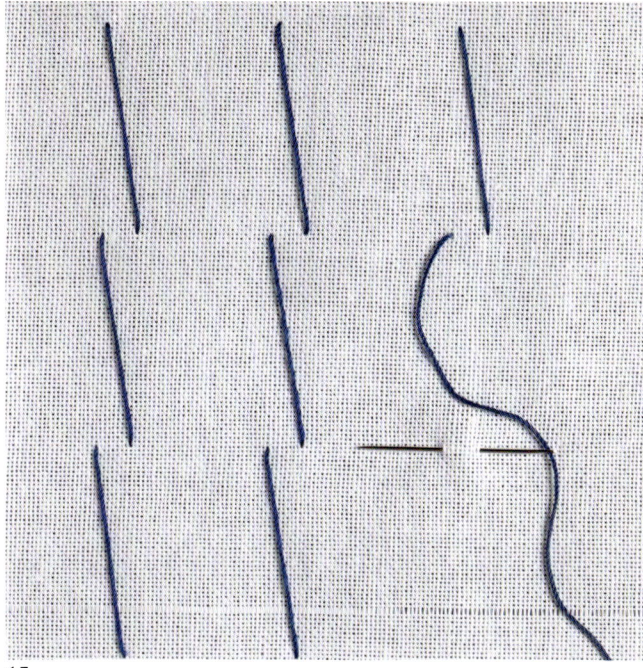
13

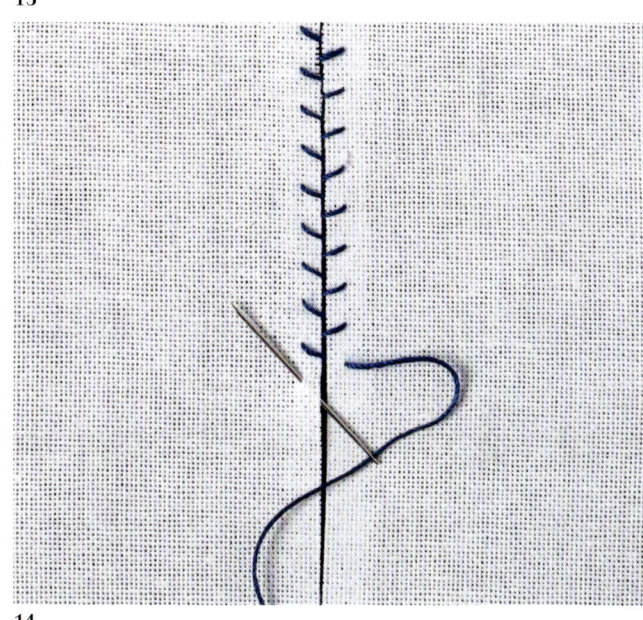
14

11a. BUTTONHOLE worked in two stages from right to left:
 (a–b) a BUTTONHOLE STITCH is worked over both sides of the cut edge.

11b. BUTTONHOLE worked in two stages from right to left:
 (a–b) a BUTTONHOLE STITCH is worked over both sides of the cut edge.

11c. BUTTONHOLE worked in two stages from right to left.
 (a–b) a BUTTONHOLE STITCH is worked over one side of the cut edge and stitched around the front corner and continued at the other side of the cut edge.

12. PAD STITCH is the only stitch used exclusively by the tailor, by which means he gives a three-dimensional shape to the garments: (a) right side, (b) wrong side.

13. PAD STITCH used for BASTING to hold layers together.
14. JOINING SEAM worked over the selvedges of the fabric to create an extremely flat seam.

The term STAB STITCH can be used for any linear stitch and for PAD STITCH (1, 2, 3, 4, 5, 12, 13, 14) worked in two stages to hold layers of fabric together. The initial stab of the needle down through the layers is followed by it being brought back up to the surface in a different position.

The term CATCH STITCH indicates a series of different stitches, such as WHIP STITCH, FELLING and HALF-BACK STITCH, worked along the same path. It is sometimes used to attach decorative laces over the seams of garments.

Sewing stitches

Embroidery stitches

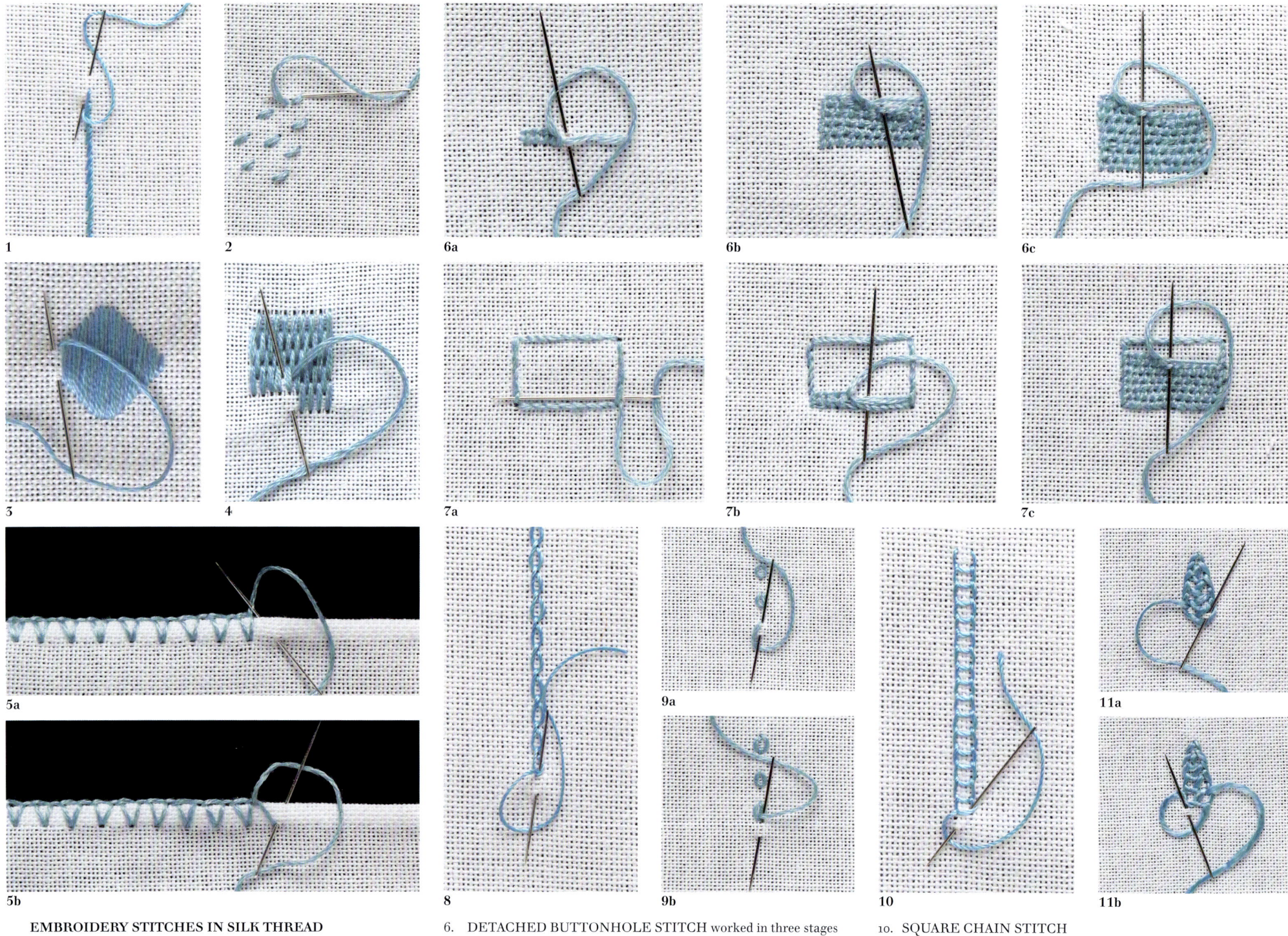

EMBROIDERY STITCHES IN SILK THREAD FOUND ON THE GARMENTS IN THIS BOOK
1. STEM STITCH
2. DOT STITCH
3. **SATIN STITCH**
4. OVERLAPPING SATIN STITCH
5. TWO-STAGE EDGING STITCH
6. DETACHED BUTTONHOLE STITCH worked in three stages over an extra thread bar, starting from a.
7. DETACHED BUTTONHOLE STITCH, with a STEM-STITCH outline; worked in three stages over an extra thread bar, starting from a.
8. **CHAIN STITCH**
9. SPACED CHAIN STITCH, worked in two stages.
10. SQUARE CHAIN STITCH
11. LINKED CHAIN STITCH, worked in two stages.

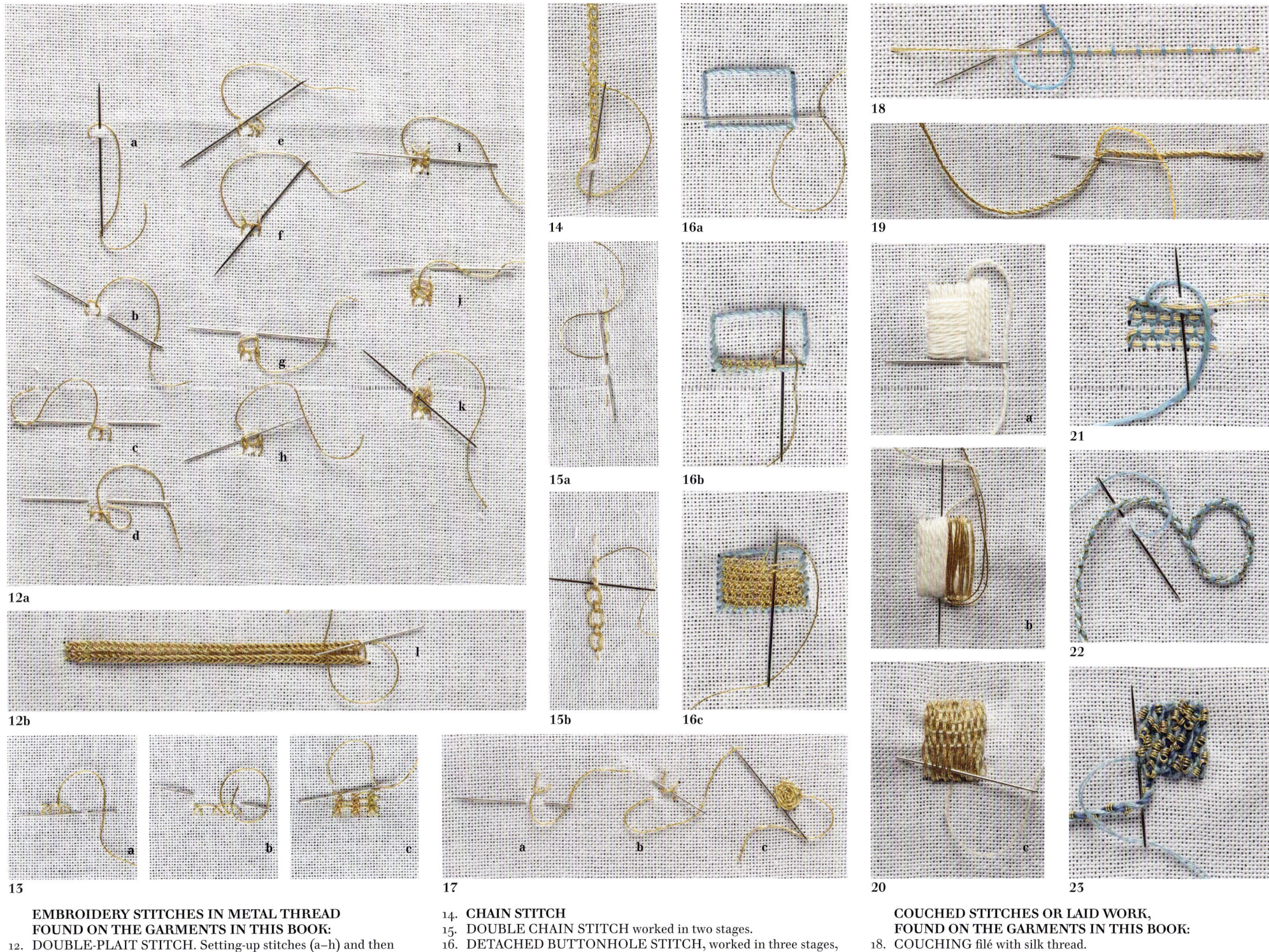

EMBROIDERY STITCHES IN METAL THREAD FOUND ON THE GARMENTS IN THIS BOOK:
12. DOUBLE-PLAIT STITCH. Setting-up stitches (a–h) and then a four-stage stitch (i–l).
13. PLAITED FILLING STITCH worked in three stages.
14. CHAIN STITCH
15. DOUBLE CHAIN STITCH worked in two stages.
16. DETACHED BUTTONHOLE STITCH, worked in three stages, starting from a.
17. WEAVING STITCH: setting up stitches (a, b).

COUCHED STITCHES OR LAID WORK, FOUND ON THE GARMENTS IN THIS BOOK:
18. COUCHING filé with silk thread.
19. INVISIBLE COUCHING a twist with a silk thread of the same colour.
20. COUCHING over a linen thread foundation to give a raised effect, starting with a.
21. COUCHING paired filé with BLANKET STITCH with silk thread.
22. COUCHING a twist of partially wrapped silk, with silk thread.
23. COUCHING a silk thread, partially wrapped with purl, with silk thread.

Stitch samples by Claire Thornton, Luca Costigliolo and Melanie Braun

Embroidery stitches

How to use this book

Terms and abbreviations

Selvedge: the woven edge of the fabric
Warp: the threads running parallel to the selvedges
Weft: the threads running from selvedge to selvedge
Straight grain: the direction of the warp/selvedges
Cross grain/bias: 45 degrees to the straight grain
Fold: where the fabric is folded once
Turn: where the fabric is folded twice to form a hem

Net pattern: the pattern shape without any seam allowance
Seam allowance: the margins added to the edges of the net pattern when cutting out the fabric

CF: centre front of the garment
CB: centre back of the garment
RS: the right side, i.e., the outer side of the garment
WS: the wrong side, i.e., the inside/wrong side of the garment
Verso: used on photographs to show the position of a detail, which is on the reverse of the side photographed
RHS: the right-hand side, i.e., the right-hand side of the garment as it relates to the right-hand side of the body
LHS: the left-hand side, i.e., the left-hand side of the garment as it relates to the right-hand side of the body

Thread: linen or silk fibres that have been spun and plied
Floss: strands of silk that are not plied
Filé: thread with a silk core wrapped in metal strip
Twist: two or three filés plied together
Purl: a coiled length of copper, silver or silver-gilt wire

Baleen: found in the mouths of some whales, in place of teeth, it is made of keratin and has a firm, yet flexible, structure which can be split into very thin, narrow strips. It was called 'whalebone' from the 16th to the early 20th centuries, and is still popularly known by that term. Both words for the material are used in this book.
Bents: grass-like reeds, rushes, sedges and other plants with stiff or rigid stems; these are gathered into narrow bunches and used to stiffen clothing.
Cork: the light, tough and elastic inner bark of the cork-oak tree; used in historical clothing either as a stiffener or to create volume.

Using the patterns
Unless otherwise shown, the pattern pieces are laid out with the warp of the fabric running vertically and the weft horizontally. No seam allowance is added to the patterns. A number of pieces in this book are cut 'net', i.e., without a seam allowance. Except where noted, however, the seam allowance should be added to the pattern shapes given in this book before cutting them out in fabric.

Using the construction drawings
These have been worked out from the junctions of seams and stitching on the right sides and wrong sides of the garments, from the x-ray images and by making the reconstructions. Where possible, the drawings are oriented so that the reader is in the same position as the person carrying out the process shown.

Interpreting the x-ray images
X-ray images (radiographs) provide invaluable information concerning the materials and construction beneath the surface of an object, hidden from sight. X-rays are a form of electromagnetic energy that can penetrate materials that look opaque to the human eye. The denser materials show up as the brighter, whiter parts of an image. For example, areas of seam allowance appear paler than the rest of the fabric because they are of double layers of fabric and metal threads are very white. Other hidden features revealed by x-rays include pad stitching, basting, the weave of interlinings and reinforcements in the form of cork, bents and baleen. Except where noted, all the x-ray images in this book were taken from the RS of the garment.
For more information on the subject, *X-Radiography of Textiles, Dress and Related Objects* (2007) by Sonia O'Connor and Mary M. Brooks provides an extensive explanation of techniques, applications and analysis.

Imperial and metric measurements
All the garments in this book were made before the advent of the metric system. They were cut and sewn using imperial measures, so the patterns presented here use that system.

Using imperial, rather than metric measurements, when reconstructing garments based on these patterns will result in clothing much closer to the proportions and dimensions of that made in the 17th century. For those unfamiliar with imperial measures, the metric equivalents are given on the scale rulers below.

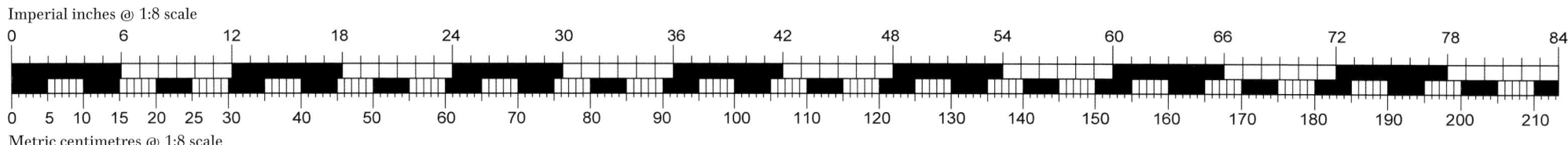

Imperial inches @ 1:8 scale
Metric centimetres @ 1:8 scale

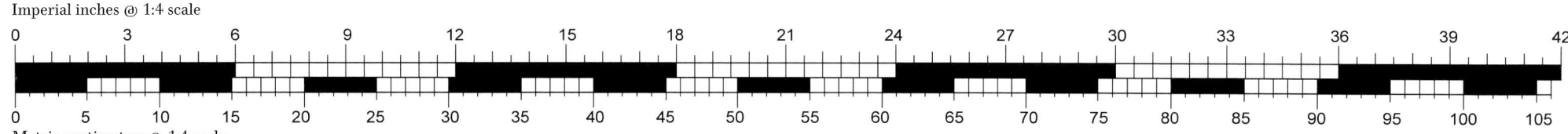

Imperial inches @ 1:4 scale
Metric centimetres @ 1:4 scale

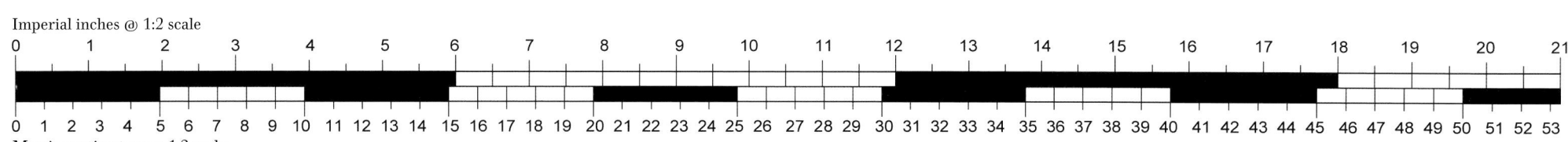

Imperial inches @ 1:2 scale
Metric centimetres @ 1:2 scale

The patterns

1 | Green silk velvet doublet

English, 1600–10, V&A: 183–1900

Pattern by Claire Thornton

This doublet is part of the Isham collection, purchased from Sir Charles Isham of Lamport Hall, Northampton, by the South Kensington Museum for £500 in 1899. Although no written evidence connects the Isham garments to known family members, the doublet may have belonged to Sir John Isham (1582–1651). Made of green silk velvet, the doublet is decorated with a narrow edging lace of green silk floss and silver-gilt filé, applied in pairs; the decoration is now very worn and only remains on the wings. The rest was removed, possibly to be recycled on a different garment. The velvet is uncut with a voided satin ground, although the tips of the loops have worn away over most of the surface, giving the appearance of a cut pile. The looped pile can still be seen under the wings. The finest patterned velvets were made in Italy in the early 17th century and this example is possibly Florentine.

Patterns of horizontal stripes worked as slashing, or applied bands of decoration, were popular from about 1550 to 1615. In this velvet, the stripes are woven into the pattern and they are similar to the design seen in the portrait opposite, which shows a doublet of cloth-of-silver with silver-gilt woven bands, filled with rows of individual foliate motifs.

The inside of the doublet is lightly padded with carded (and now slightly felted) wool, quilted in rows under a silk taffeta lining. The taffeta, which is in a relatively good condition, has a green warp and a yellow weft – this would have been described in the 17th century as 'changeable' and is now known as 'shot'. It lines the doublet throughout, as befitted the social status and wealth of the Isham family. Other surviving quilted doublets of the period have linen or fustian linings with silk only facing the garment and lining the laps.

This doublet is the earliest example in this book and it demonstrates the transition between two styles. Its external shape takes the form of the new flat-fronted style of doublet, but on the inside it retains the quilted layer that had shaped doublet fashions previously. After a heavily exaggerated 'peascod' shape that required several pounds of bombast (stuffing), a lighter, less extreme style became fashionable at the beginning of the 17th century. In this doublet, the quilting is thicker at the fronts, gradually decreasing in depth to leave the centre back unpadded. The waist is free of padding, possibly to make it appear sleek.

The colour green was associated with both hunting and the outdoors, and was considered appropriate for the young. The Royal Collection's portrait of Henry, Prince of Wales with Robert Devereux by Robert Peake the Elder, painted in 1605 (contemporary with this doublet) shows the prince and his companion both dressed in green. In this portrait Henry's suit is cloth-of-gold, but his wardrobe accounts of 1608 list other green ensembles for hunting: 'Making a side hunting cote of green chamblett, wrought all thicke with green silk galowne in 2, together with a whood of the same chamblett, and laid all thick with the same lace, the bodies, and sleeves, and whood, lined with greene velvet, the side skirts lined with green taffata, silke buttons, loope lace, silke, stichinge, and sewings, and buckeram'. The camlet, velvet and taffetas cost £14 4s in total and the tailor was paid £5 to make the ensemble.[1]

The collar of this doublet was later cut away, probably in the 19th century. Careful examination of the remaining raw edges and scraps of collar lining suggests that it originally had a 'grown-on' collar, i.e., with the back of the collar cut as part of the back of the doublet and two separate pieces sewn to the front neckline, forming the collar fronts.

There are 12 laps remaining; originally there were 13, but the fourth lap from the centre right front is missing. It was removed carefully – again possibly in the 19th century – as there is no pulling or tearing on the thread holes or fabric. Laps were usually placed in pairs, so it is likely that there was intended to be a fourteenth that was never attached, or was somehow lost. The shape and number of laps on doublets change as the century progresses. Here, they are numerous and short, but by the 1620s, they became fewer and deeper. The odd number here (including the thirteenth) would give 57 eyelet holes for pointing the doublet to the hose. As points were usually tied through pairs of eyelet holes, creases in the velvet of the centre-back lap suggest that a point was threaded through the eyelets on either side of the centre back hole, missing it completely.

1. William Bray, 'Extract from the Wardrobe Account of Prince Henry, eldest Son of King James I', *Archaeologia*, vol. 11, 1794, pp. 88–96

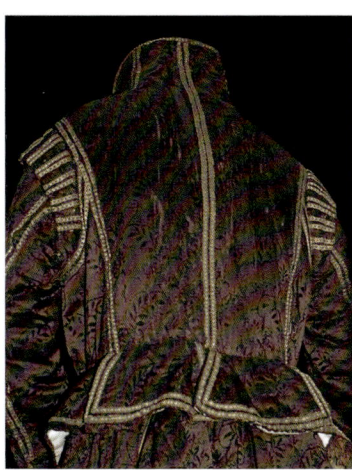

Above: Mulberry uncut silk velvet doublet, *c.* **1605**
Grimsthorpe and Drummond Castle Trust
This doublet has a 'grown-on' collar similar to the one that the Isham doublet may have once had. The conjectured collar given in the pattern and the construction sequence is partially based on this example.

Right: Portrait of a Gentleman, 1609
Anglo-Flemish School
Private Collection. Photograph © Philip Mould Ltd, London/Bridgeman Images
He wears a splendid cloth-of-silver doublet with stripes and foliate motifs, similar in design to the V&A doublet. He also wears a starched needle-lace band over a closed-front picadil similar to the one on page 145.

Pattern by Claire Thornton

DETAILS
Right side (RS) details

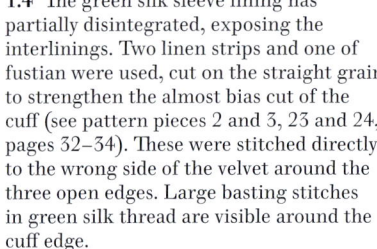

1.1 A front view of the doublet laid flat. Including the missing lap, there are 59 worked eyelet holes around the waist.

1.2 and **1.3** Partially hidden by the wing are two piecings in the top and undersleeve. The top sleeve itself was cut along the selvedge, the edge to which the piecings at the top and wrist were sewn. The striped selvedge is visible at the wrist where the velvet has disintegrated slightly. Neither the grain nor the pattern of the piecings matches the sleeve. A few small greyish stripes can be seen at the cuff. These are oxidization marks, left by the unpicked braid.

1.4 The green silk sleeve lining has partially disintegrated, exposing the interlinings. Two linen strips and one of fustian were used, cut on the straight grain to strengthen the almost bias cut of the cuff (see pattern pieces 2 and 3, 23 and 24, pages 32–34). These were stitched directly to the wrong side of the velvet around the three open edges. Large basting stitches in green silk thread are visible around the cuff edge.

1.5 The green silk stitches of the quilting can be seen on the flap of the lighter-weight linen interlining that holds two baleen strips. The green silk facing the buttonhole stand extends beyond the neckline and probably lined the original collar. A selvedge can be seen to the right of the buttonholes. The pale green stitches at the neckline were done after the removal of the collar.

1.6 A short length of stitching at the right centre front has come undone. Seen here is the folded edge of interlining holding two baleen strips whipped to the blue wool – the belly piece. The selvedge on the right is from a strip of lining used as a facing. The thread used to attach the buttons works from one to the next without cutting and finishing it in between each one.

1.7 On the LHS centre front, a silk facing folds into the 'ditch' separating the buttonhole stand from the quilted lining. The edge of the quilting finishes ¼" away from the front edge.

28   1 | Green silk velvet doublet

1.14 The small, almost square step at the top of the side seam. The seam is bulky because the stiff velvet and heavy linen interlinings were stitched as one, but this would have been disguised by the braid.

1.17 The quilting at the back shoulder gives it depth even when lying flat.

1.8 A back view of the doublet laid flat.

1.15 The third lap on the LHS was cut upside down, perhaps to use up a scrap. In fig. 1.1 it has a golden glow due to the difference in pile. Four parallel lines to the right of the lap show the position of the unpicked braid.

1.18 At the top of the image is the right shoulder wing where the velvet has worn away at the edge, exposing the two interlinings, one linen, possibly glued, and the other a heavy black, felted wool. At the end of the wing, to the right of the image, is a short length of the striped selvedge. The wing is lined with scraps of velvet. Under the wing, to the left, is a scrap of green silk. This is the armhole binding and is only visible because the seam is open, due to the rotting of the brown linen thread.

1.9 The fourth lap on the RHS is missing.

1.10 The neat edges of the remaining fabric layers indicate that the lap was deliberately unpicked, rather than torn away.

1.11 Edging lace in green silk floss and silver-gilt filé. It was applied in pairs.

1.12 Hidden under, and protected by the wing, the looped pile of the velvet is still intact.

1.13 The domed wooden core of the buttons.

1.16 The buttons were woven in a chevron pattern, with a six-point star at the top, in green silk floss and silver-gilt filé.

1.19 This lap spans the centre-back seam. Laps are usually paired, but this doublet originally had 13 (see the missing lap in fig. 1.9). There is no lacing band on the inside, so these eyelets fastened the doublet to the hose. Eyelets were usually laced in pairs, but this doublet has an odd number. The point at the back may have spanned three holes, resulting in the folding to the left of the central eyelet hole. The binding lace, applied in three pieces, hides and neatens the waist seam.

Pattern by Claire Thornton

Wrong side (WS) details

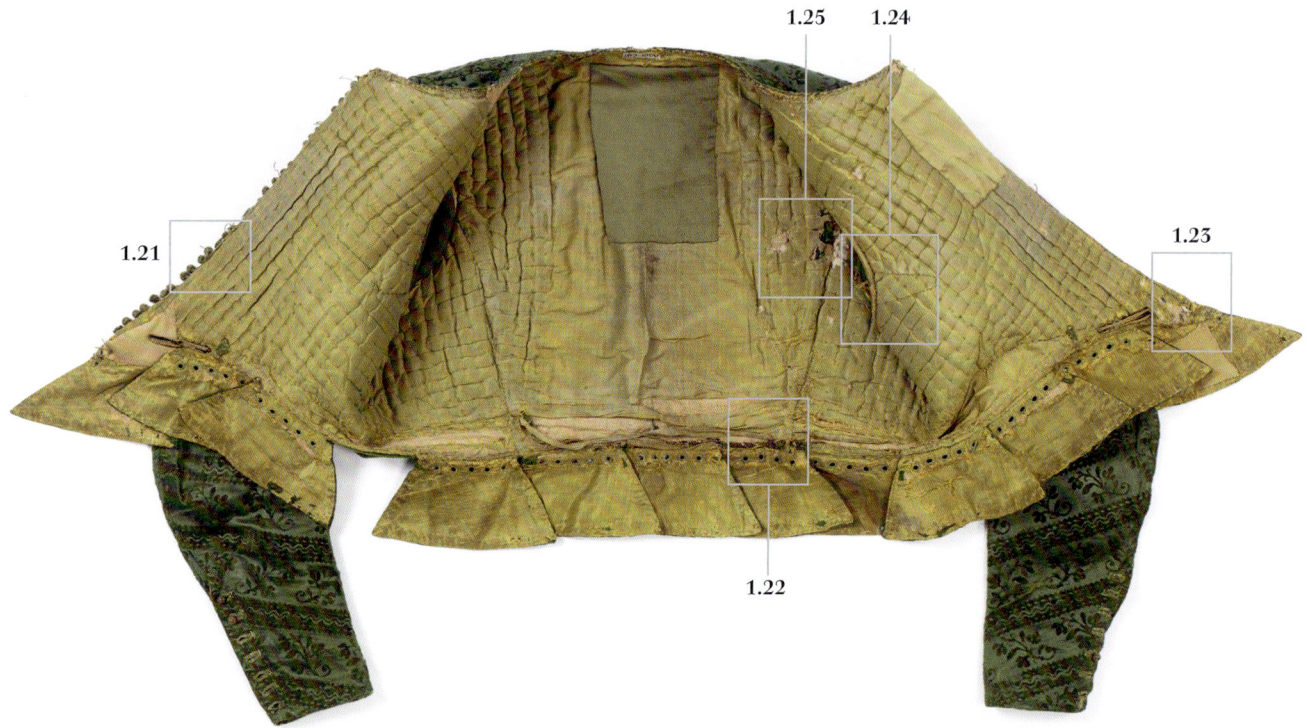

1.20 Left
The front of the doublet laid open. The quilting varies in thickness over the body: it is deepest at the centre fronts and graduates to nothing at the back. The curved line of stitches above the waist is the bottom edge of the quilting, tapering away to nothing and leaving no wool padding at the waist. The lining at the centre-back waist has worn away to show the strongly whipped waist seam.

1.21 Right
The button side has a facing of silk applied onto the quilting to close the front edge. This may be intentional, or it may have been attached when the lining finished short. The deep indents in the quilting where the stitching has pulled the silk into the wool padding indicate that it was about ⅜" thick.

1.22 Left
The back laps were whipped to the waist with a doubled, waxed, brown linen thread and then whipped back in the opposite direction, giving a very strong seam. Towards the bottom centre of the image is a large knot. The heavy, close woven linen gives a strong foundation.

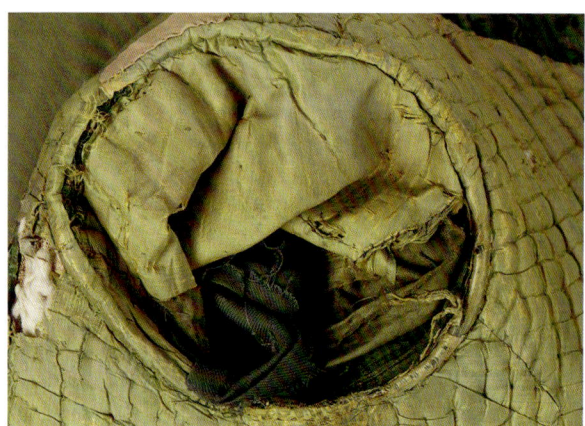

1.23 The lower corner of the quilted lining has been pulled back slightly from the front edge and stitched. Small fragments of the blue wool interlining are visible where the silk has rotted. The lacing loop of satin appears to have been re-attached; this is the only piece of satin on the doublet.

1.24 The quilting stitches holding the wool to the top-sleeve lining are visible within the sleeve head. A trapezoid piecing was stitched into the lining at the front armhole.

1.25 The velvet, linen and wool quilting at the left side seam are exposed. This small piece of wool is slightly felted. To the left is a single, large brown linen stitch: it is either for basting the wool layer, or is a pad stitch.

1 | Green silk velvet doublet

X-ray images

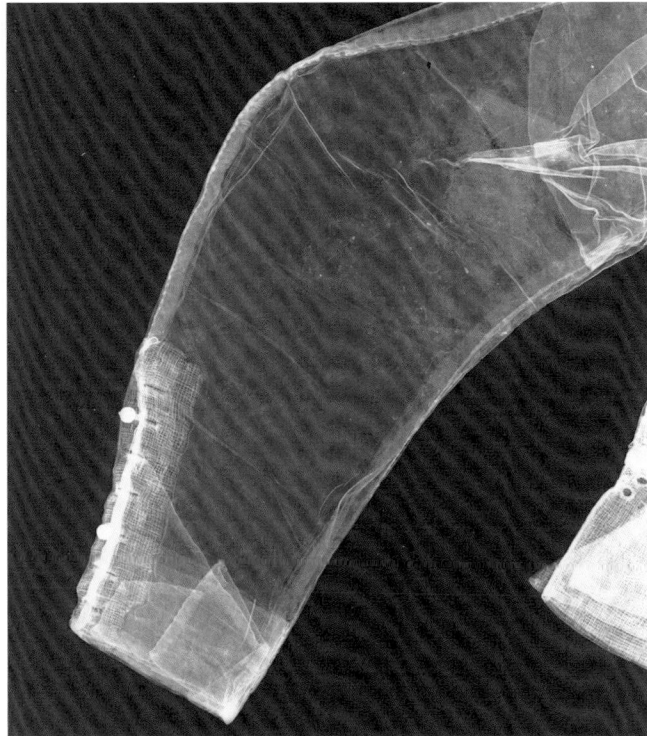

1.26 Left sleeve: the weaves of the linen and fustian strips interlining the cuff are noticeably different. The back-stitched back sleeve seam appears as a line of loops.

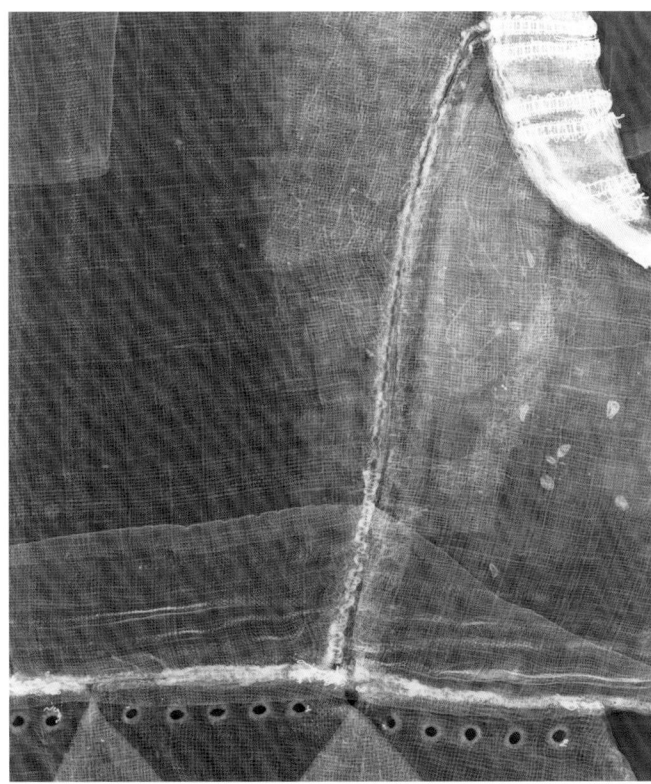

1.27 Side seam, RHS: it is just possible to make out the wool quilting, but no stitches can be seen. The pad stitching on the interlinings is visible as large irregular zig-zags. Tiny fragments of edging lace are caught in the waist seam.

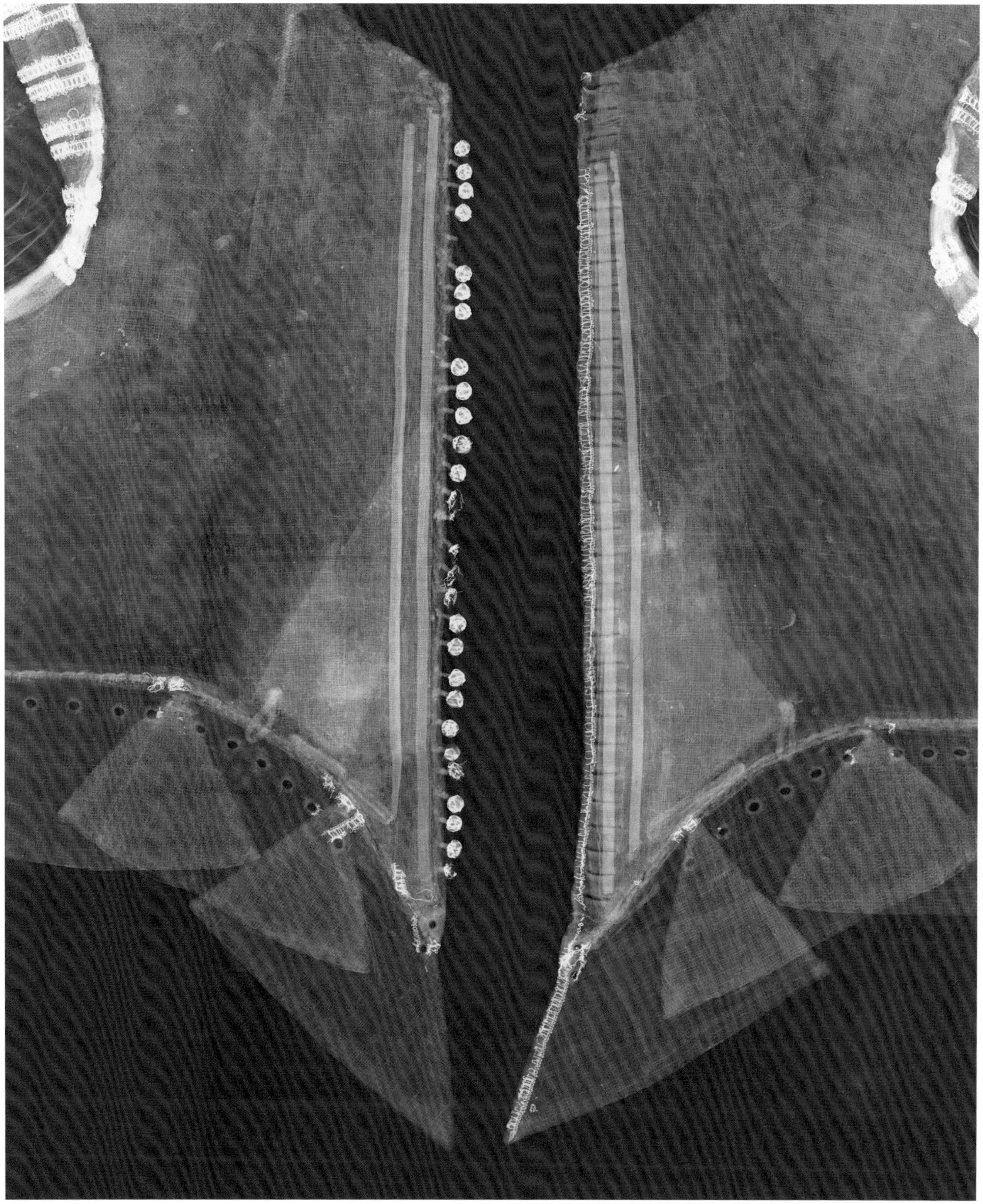

1.28 Centre fronts: the interlining holding the baleen has running stitches for the channels that are just visible between and beside the baleen strips. The blue wool layer (seen as white triangles) is pad stitched and whipped. At the bottom edge, the cloud-like clumps of quilting wool curve up and away from the centre fronts.

Pattern by Claire Thornton

PATTERN
Pattern of the velvet top layer

SCALE 1:4

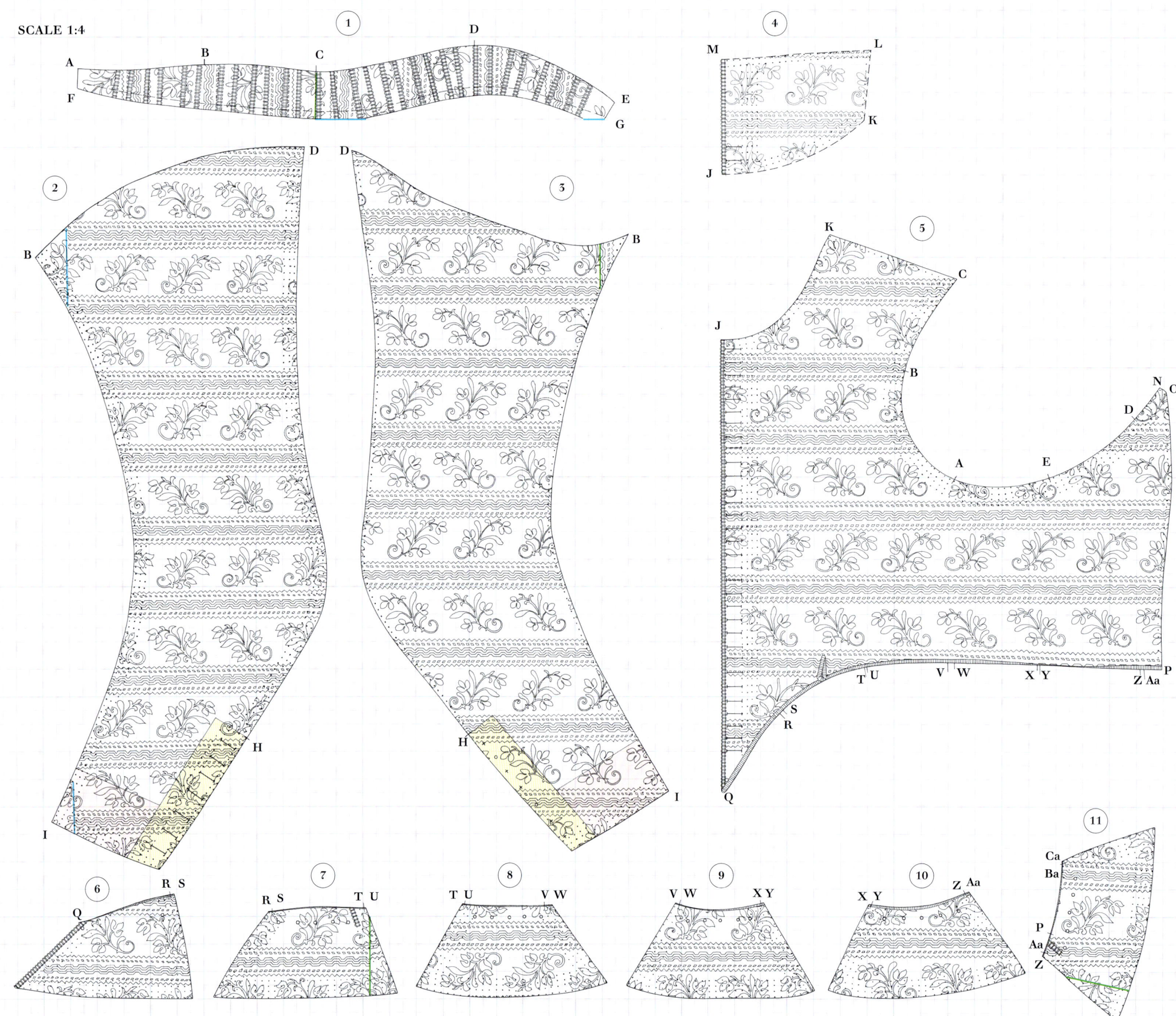

1 | Green silk velvet doublet

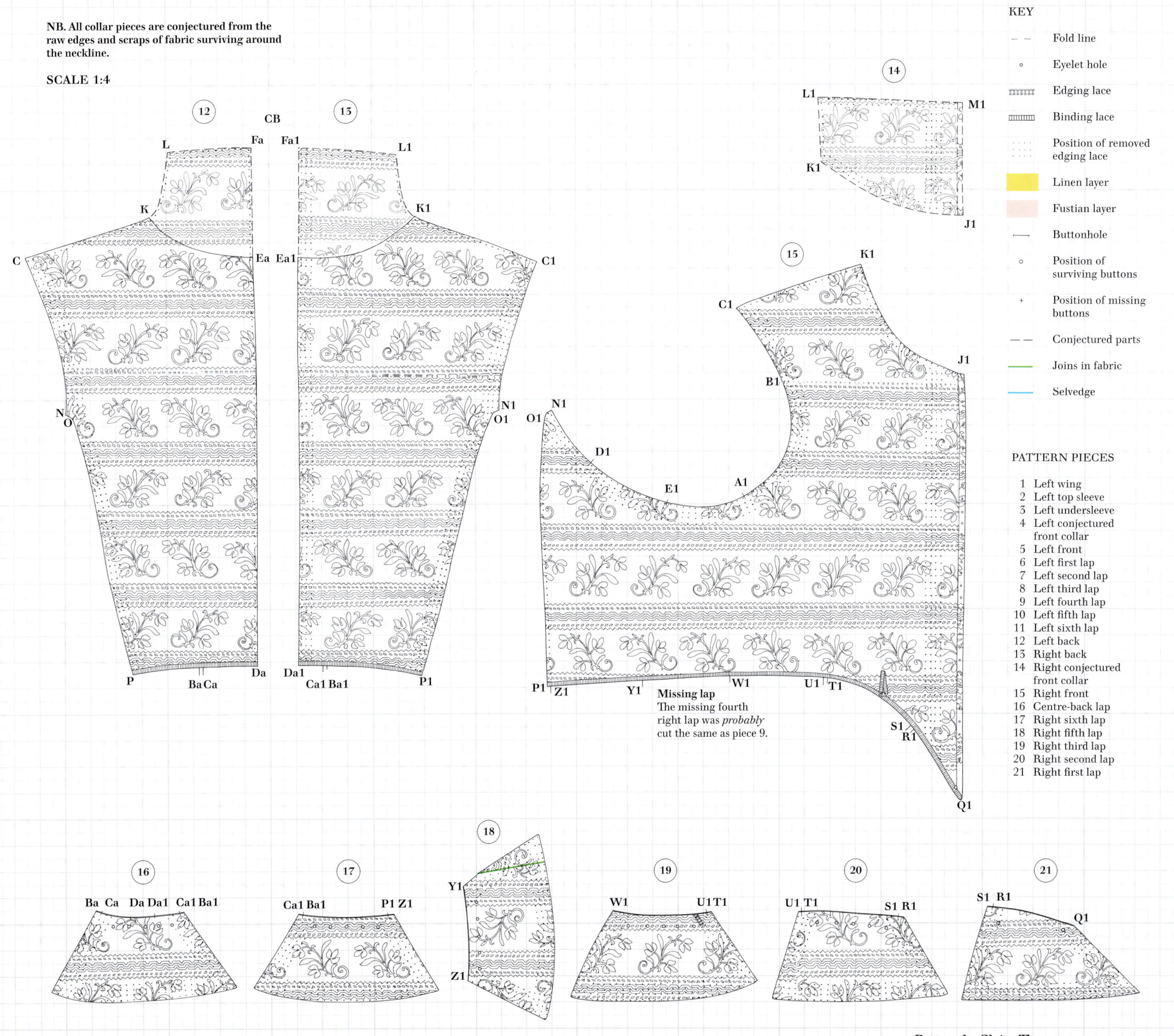

Pattern of the velvet top layer CONTINUED

SCALE 1:4

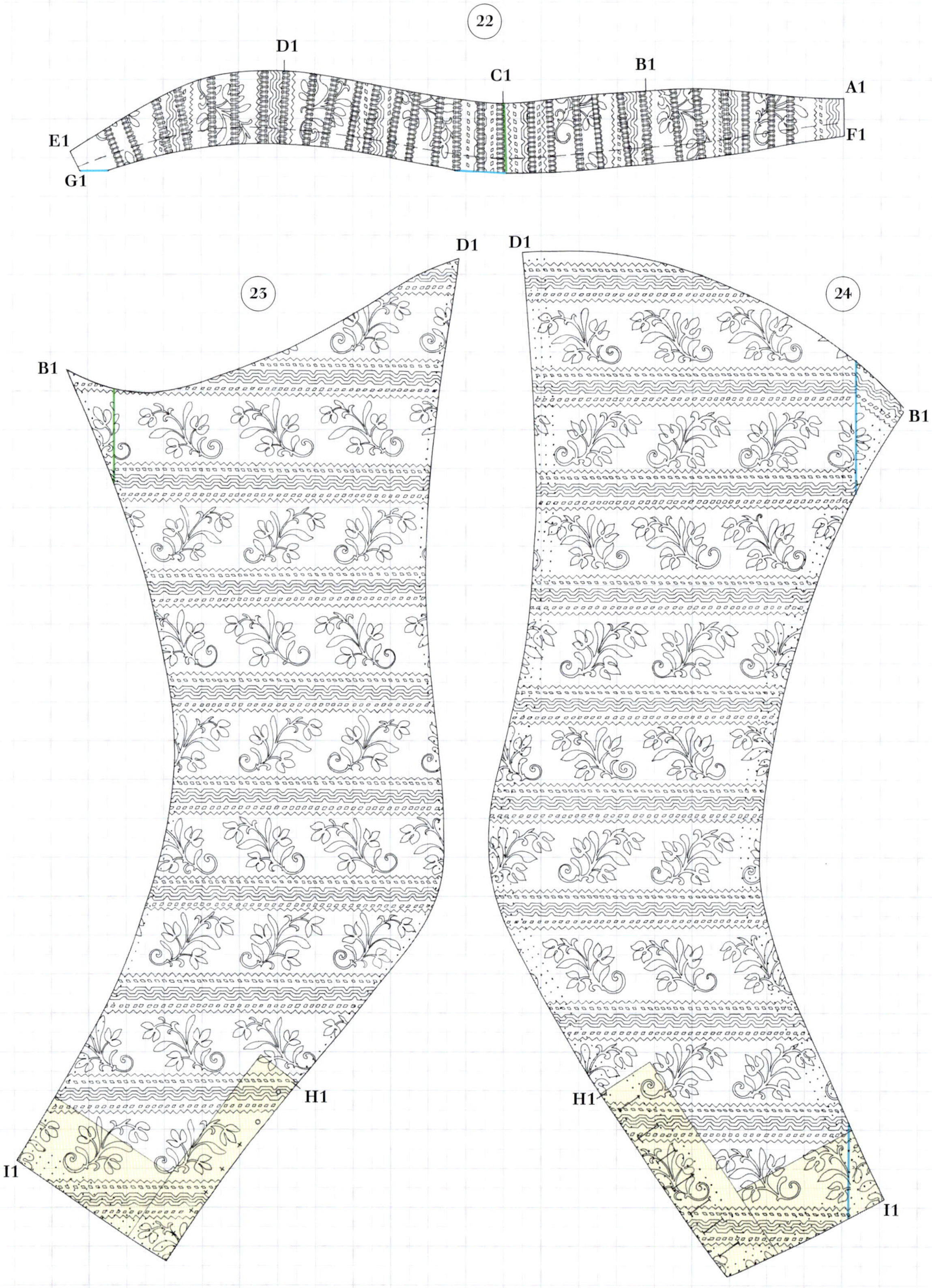

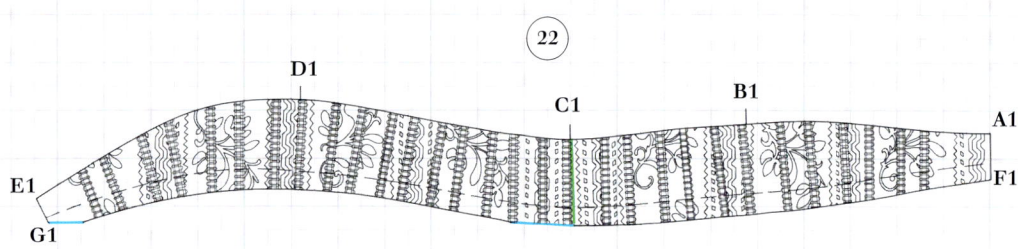

Pattern of the quilted layers

SCALE 1:4

NB The pattern of the quilted layer was taken from the WS, as opposed to the pattern of the velvet, which was taken from the RS, therefore the pattern of the quilting and its velvet counterpart appear mirror-imaged.

A layer of non-woven, lightly carded wool was stitched between the interlinings and the silk linings. (The pattern for the interlinings hidden by the wool are shown on page 37.) The slightly larger size of the silk linings (pattern pieces 27, 29 and 32) allowed for the volume of the wool, but would *probably* have been cut even larger still, and trimmed after stitching.

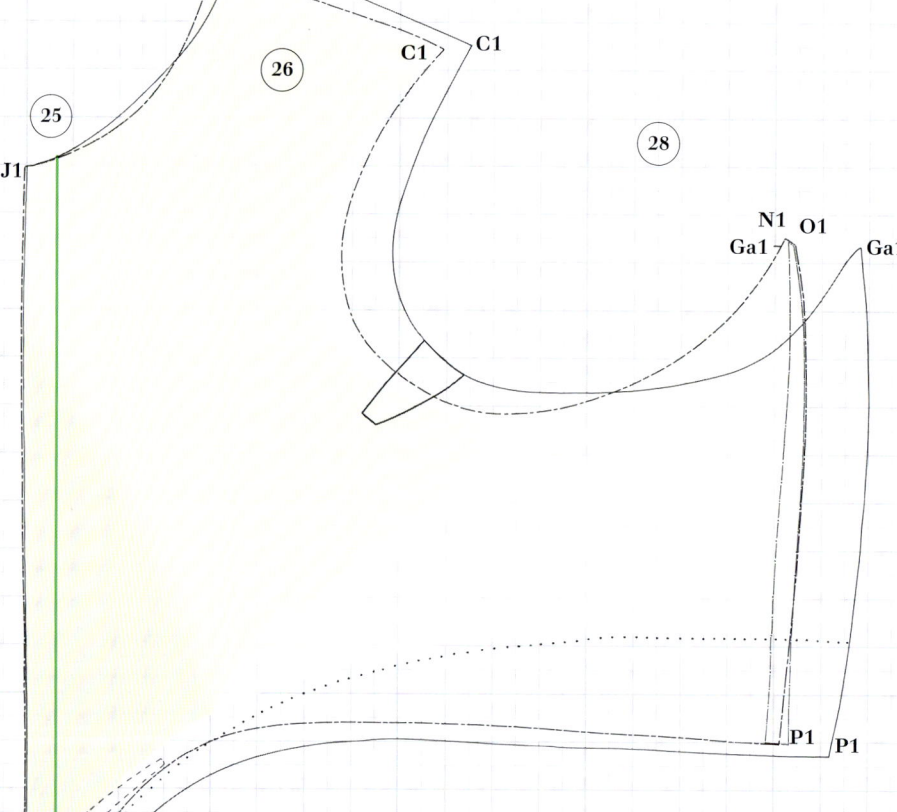

The quilted squares are ½", but do vary slightly in size and would have been worked by eye.

On the left front there are 28 squares from top to bottom, and 32 from front to back.

On the right front there are 28 squares from top to bottom, and 28 from front to back.

The back has two full columns of 29 squares from top to bottom. The depth of quilting grades from ⅜" at the centre front to nothing at the centre back, and from ⅜" at the shoulder to nothing at the waist. The distribution of the wool is shown in the cream areas on pattern pieces 26, 30 and 33.

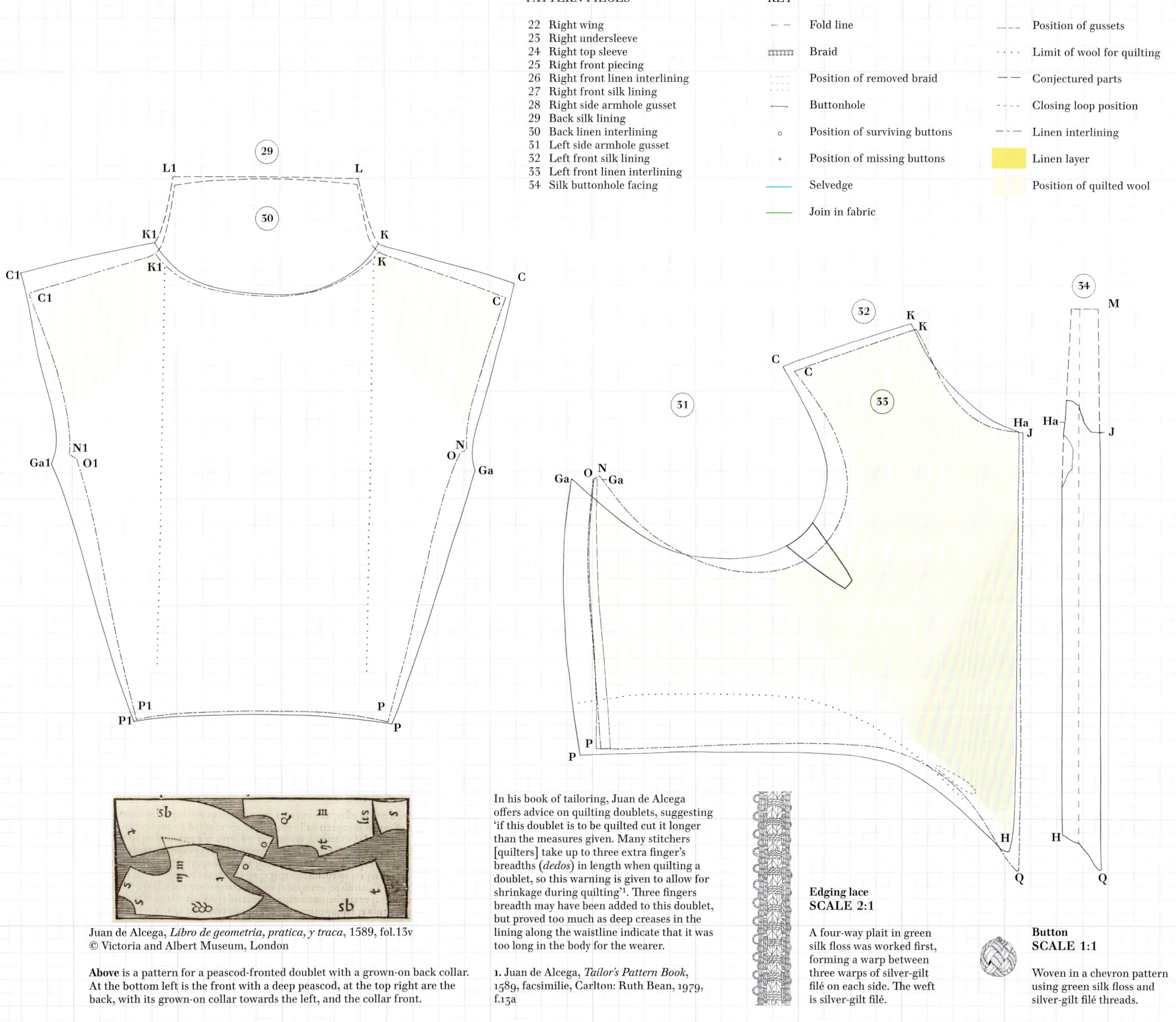

Pattern of the linings

SCALE 1:8

PATTERN PIECES

35 Velvet left wing lining
36 Velvet right wing lining
37 Silk left top-sleeve lining
38 Silk left undersleeve lining
39 Silk right undersleeve lining
40 Silk right top-sleeve lining
41 Silk right first lap lining
42 Silk right second lap lining
43 Silk right third lap lining
44 Silk right fifth lap lining
45 Silk right sixth lap lining
46 Silk centre-back lap lining
47 Silk left sixth lap lining
48 Silk left fifth lap lining
49 Silk left fourth lap lining
50 Silk left third lap lining
51 Silk left second lap lining
52 Silk left first lap lining
53 Left wing linen and wool
54 Right wing linen and wool
55 Conjectured right collar linen layers
56 Right linen shoulder piece
57 Back linen layers
58 Left linen shoulder piece
59 Conjectured left collar linen layers
60 Right belly piece
61 Right front linen and wool layers
62 Left front linen and wool layers
63 Left belly piece
64 Right first lap
65 Right second lap
66 Right third lap
67 Right fifth lap
68 Right sixth lap
69 Centre-back lap
70 Left sixth lap
71 Left fifth lap
72 Left fourth lap
73 Left third lap
74 Left second lap
75 Left first lap

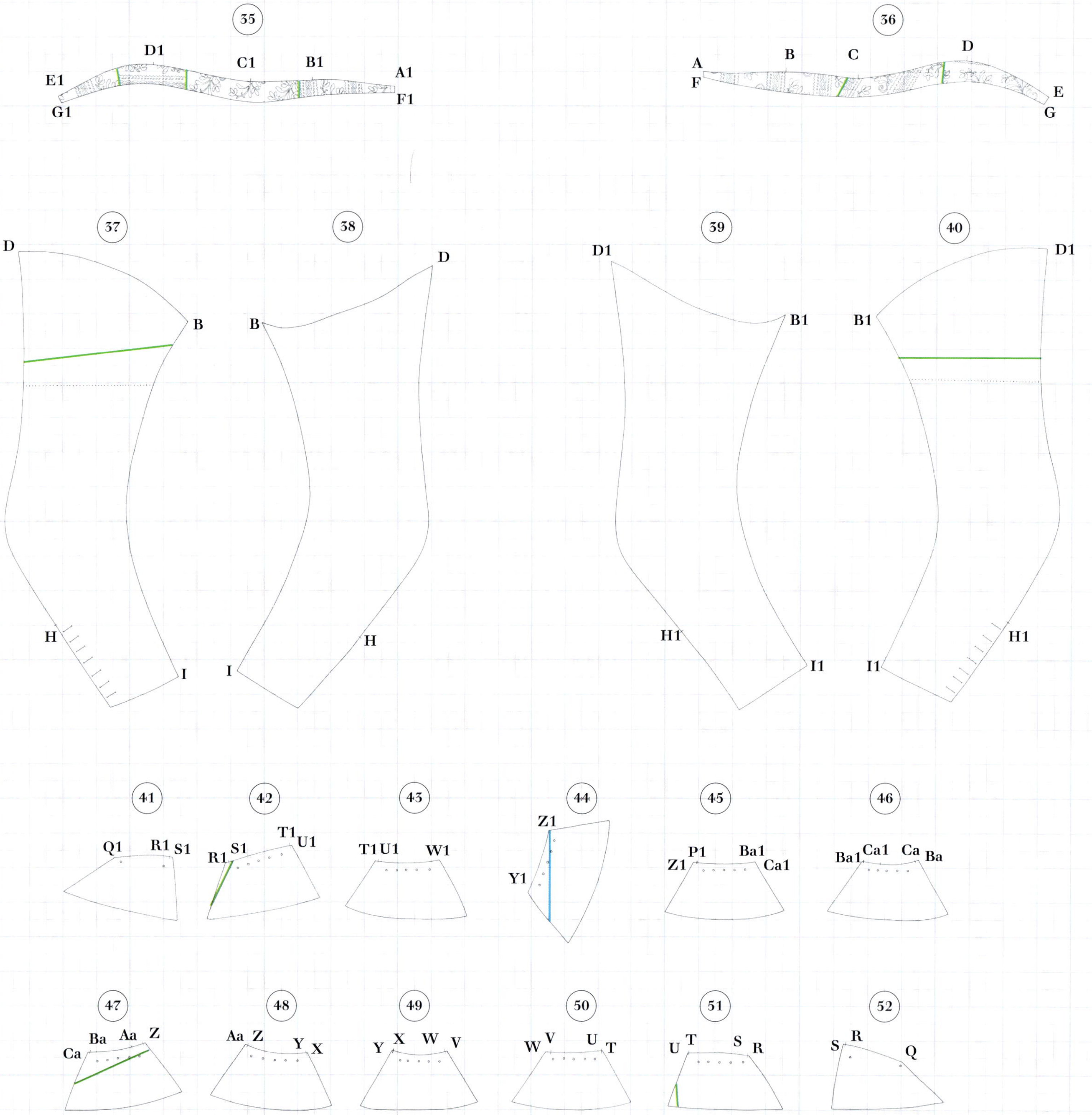

1 | Green silk velvet doublet

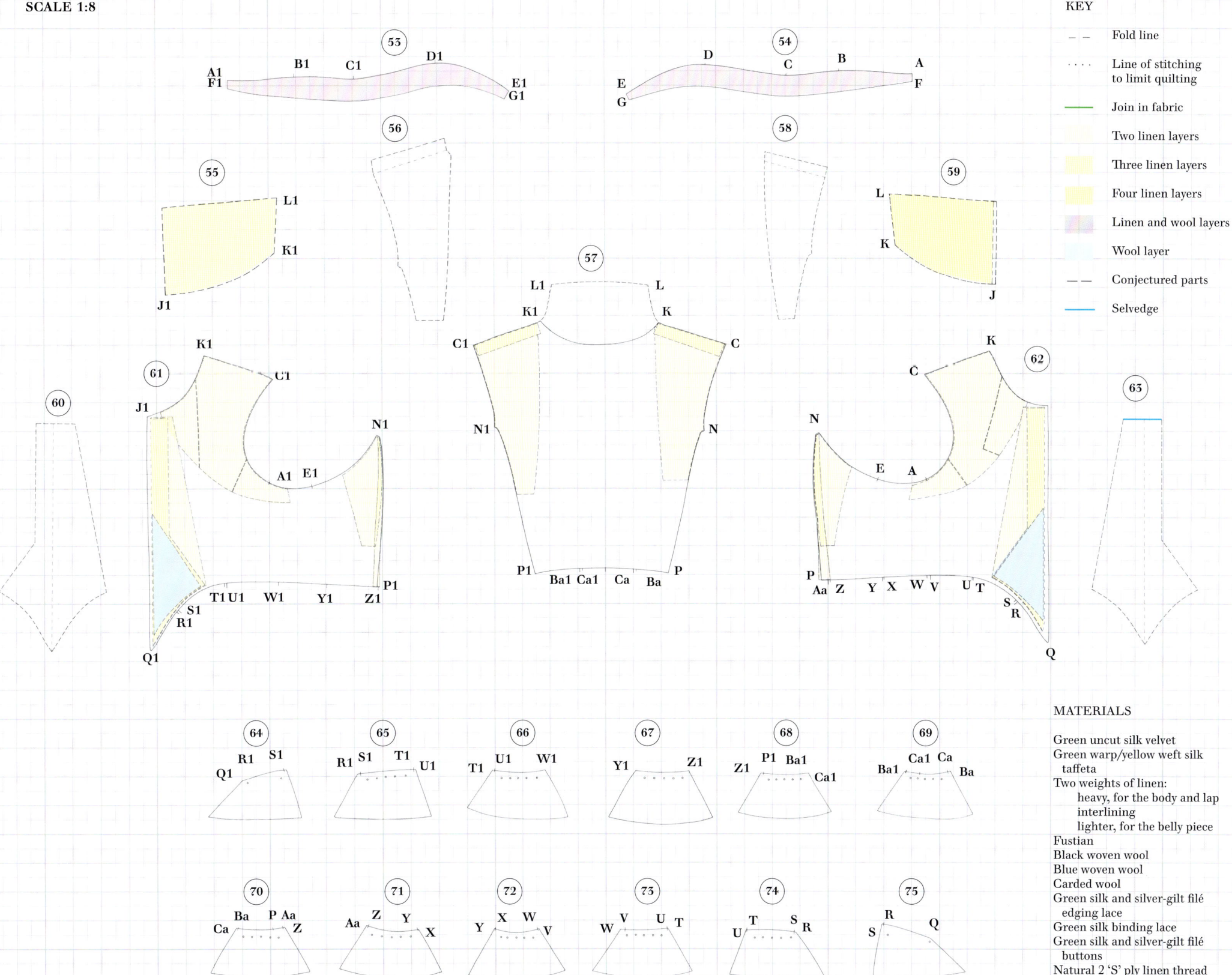

CONSTRUCTION
Construction of the body

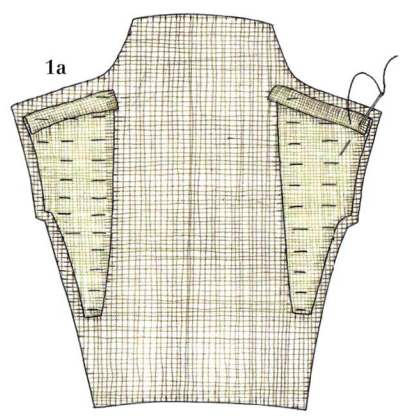
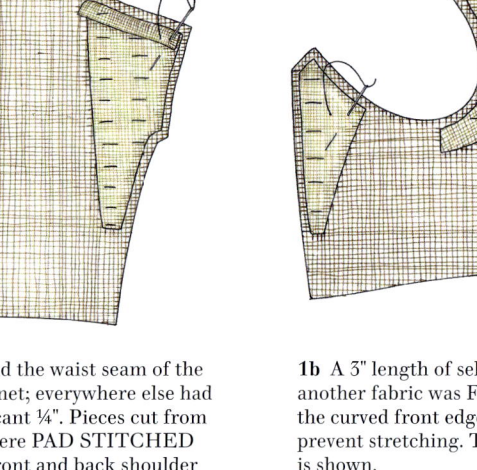
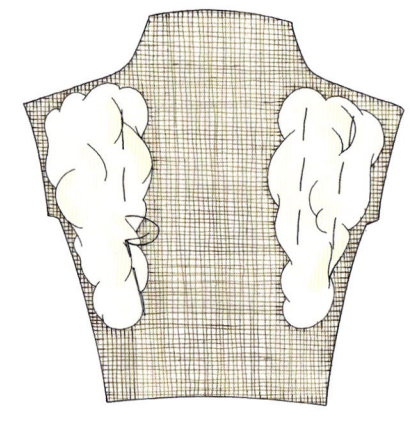
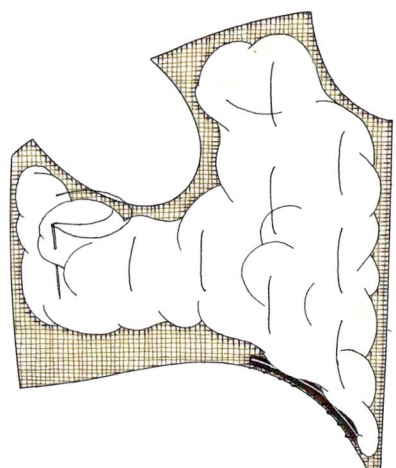

1a The centre fronts and the waist seam of the interlinings were CUT net; everywhere else had a seam allowance of a scant ¼". Pieces cut from scraps of a finer linen were PAD STITCHED to the WS around the front and back shoulder for support. On the back shoulder, the piecing is FOLDED over 1" and STITCHED through.

1b A 3" length of selvedge from another fabric was FELLED to the curved front edge, *probably* to prevent stretching. The left front is shown.

5 A layer of washed, carded and slightly felted wool was PLACED over the shoulder blades on the back interlining, and over the whole front, leaving the seam allowances, the waist and the centre-back area free. The wool layer is thicker at the centre front and over the shoulders. It was *probably* BASTED into place.

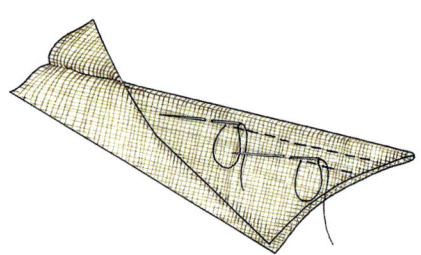
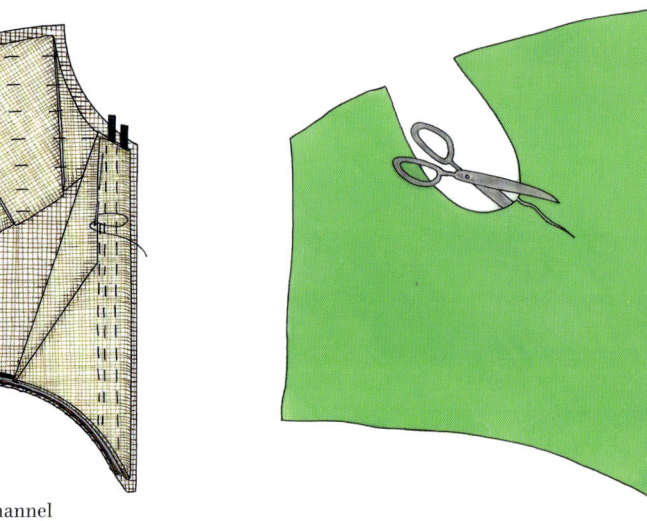
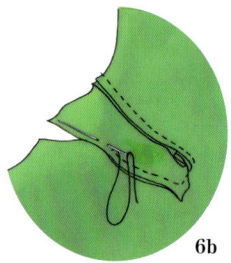

2 The belly piece was FOLDED and two rows of running stitches were worked ⁵⁄₁₆" apart, in brown linen thread.

3 A baleen strip was INSERTED into each channel and then the entire piece was PLACED onto the front interlining, ¼" away from the centre front edge. It was RUNNING STITCHED behind the baleen channels, 1⅝" from the centre front.

This layer carries the wool quilting and leaves a narrow flap of the linen to support the buttonholes. Although the RHS button front does not need the flap, it is still worked in the same way.

6a The green silk linings for the front and back were CUT larger than the linen pieces to allow for some shrinkage while quilting. A 2" slit was CUT in the front armhole, to allow for a piecing.

6b With RS together, a blunt-tipped triangular piecing was RUNNING STITCHED into the slit in green silk thread.

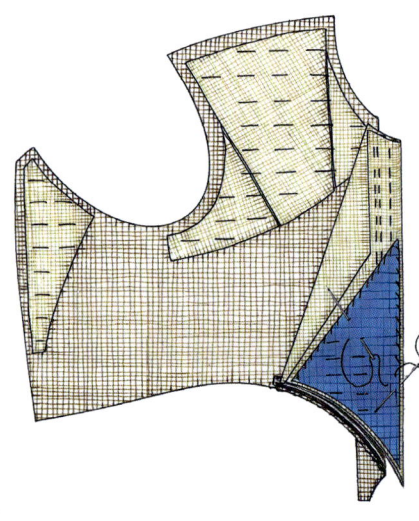
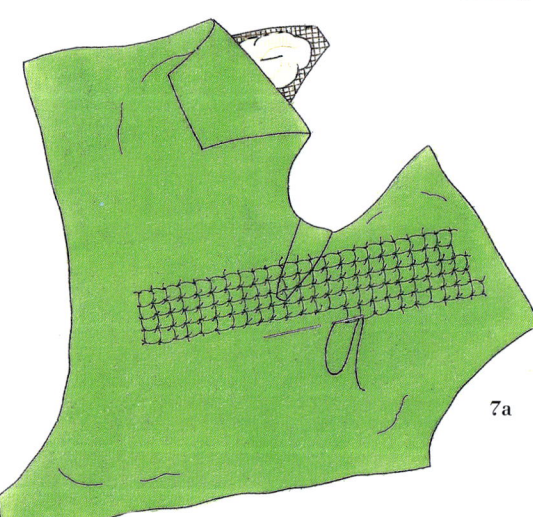
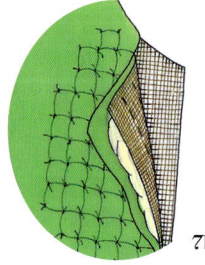

4 Holding the narrow flap of linen out of the way, a triangle of blue wool was PAD STITCHED onto the belly piece and then FELLED all around.

7a With WS together, the front lining was PLACED over the wool layer on the front interlining. Rows of RUNNING STITCHES forming ½" squares were worked up and down the length, *probably* starting from the armhole, in a dark green silk thread. The square sizes vary slightly, so were *probably* worked by eye.

7b At the centre front, the narrow flap of linen must be held out of the way.

1 | Green silk velvet doublet

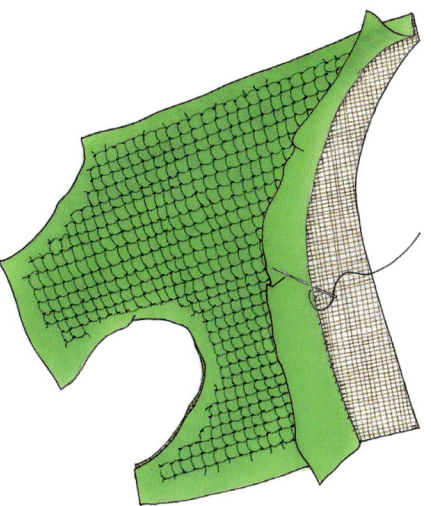

8 The lining was FOLDED up against the bottom edge of the quilting rows and FELLED onto the linen interlining, forming a row of prick-like stitches on the RS.

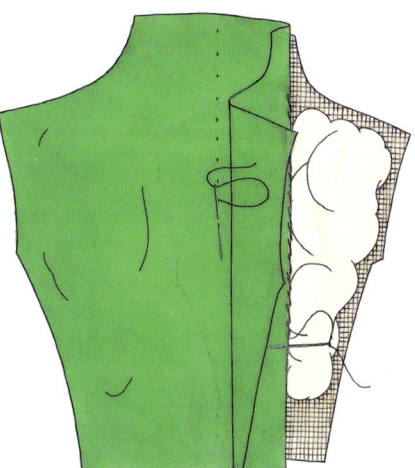

9 With WS together, the back lining was PLACED directly over the wool layer. A row of RUNNING STITCHES was worked centrally down the back to hold the fabric. The lining was FOLDED back and FELLED to the interlining next to the wool.

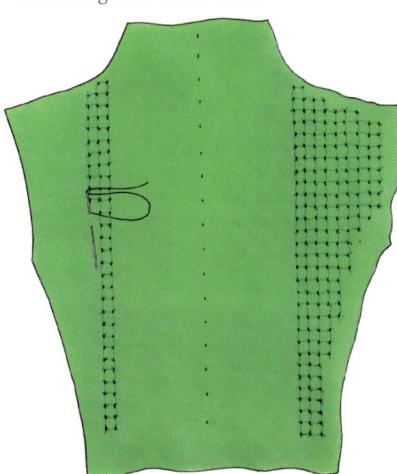

10 RUNNING STITCHED rows were worked as in step 7, away from the centre, towards the shoulder, leaving the central area free.

11 With RS together, the centre-back seam, with a ⅜" seam allowance, of the velvet was BACK STITCHED in brown linen thread.

12 Two rows of edging lace were FELLED, in green silk thread, working first down one side and then back up the other side, one covering the back seam and the other to the left of it, leaving a ³⁄₁₆" gap between.

13 The WS of the velvet was PLACED over the WS of the lining (linen side up), matching the edges of the velvet to the linen. Then it was BASTED.

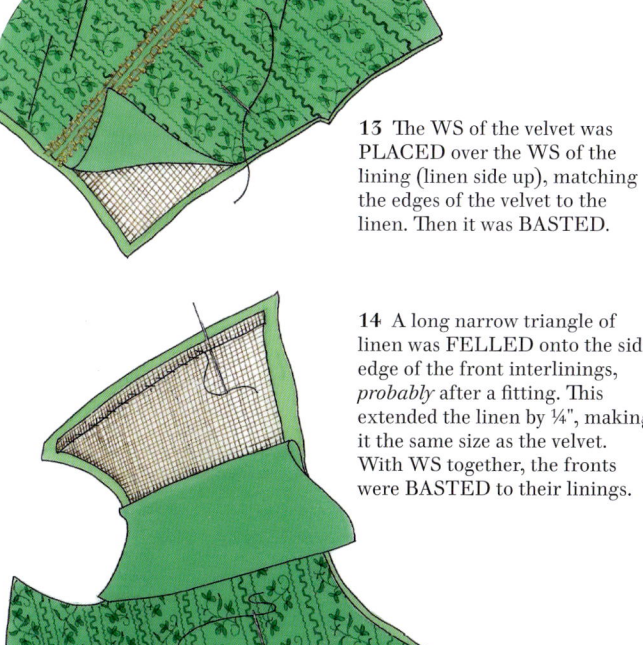

14 A long narrow triangle of linen was FELLED onto the side edge of the front interlinings, *probably* after a fitting. This extended the linen by ¼", making it the same size as the velvet. With WS together, the fronts were BASTED to their linings.

Conjectured construction of the collar

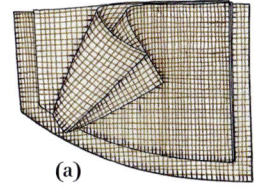 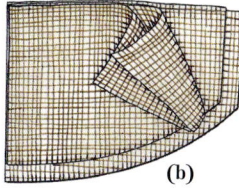

(a)   (b)

15 Three pieces of linen were CUT net for each front collar. The LHS collar pieces are ¼" narrower at the front edge to allow for the buttonholes (a). Two additional pieces were CUT to the same size as the RHS collar (b) with a ¼" seam allowance on the back and bottom edges.

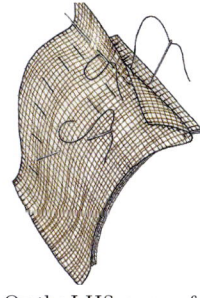 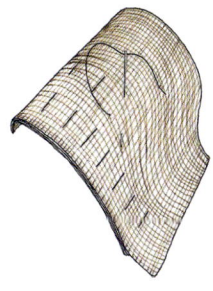

16 On the LHS, a row of small PAD STITCHES was worked down the centre front through the three net layers only. A row of RUNNING STITCHES was worked behind them through all the layers, then small PAD STITCHES were worked through all the layers, giving a curved shape to the collar.

17 On the RHS, small PAD STITCHES were worked through all the layers.

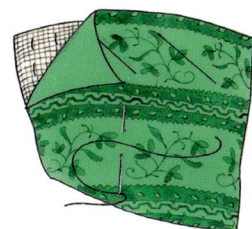 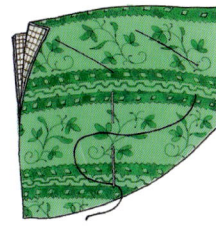

18 Both of the velvet collar pieces were CUT with a ¼" seam allowance all around except the CF. On the RHS, the RS of the velvet was PLACED on the interlinings and PAD STITCHED.

19 On the LHS, the WS of the velvet was PLACED on the RS of the interlinings, and PAD STITCHED, leaving a flap at the front of the one linen layer and the velvet.

 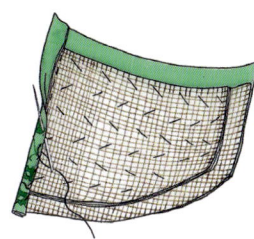

20 On the RHS, with RS together, a 1" wide strip of velvet was RUNNING STITCHED a scant ¼" from the CF through all the layers, to make a binding.

21 The binding was then FOLDED ¼" to the WS and FELLED to the inside of the collar.

Pattern by Claire Thornton

Construction of the front left-hand side (LHS) – buttonhole side

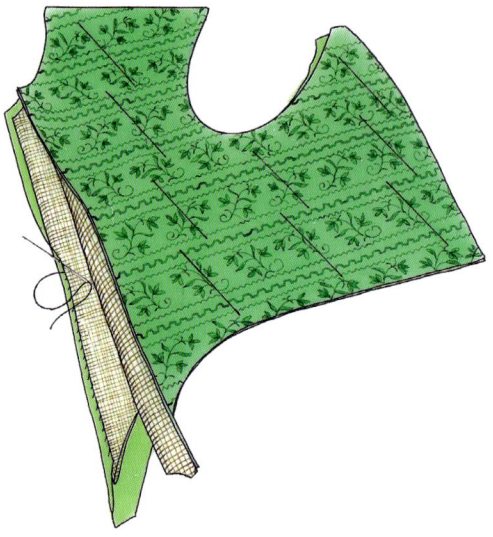

22 The ¼" seam allowance of the silk lining was FOLDED around to the reverse of the baleen panel and FELLED in green silk thread.

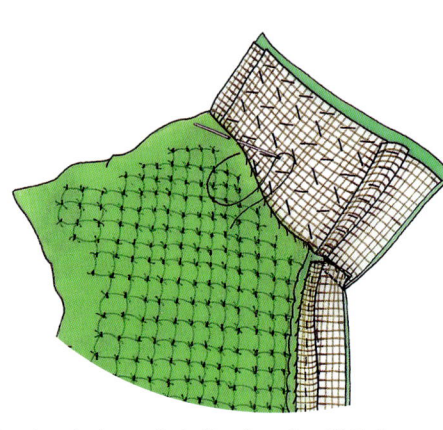

25 Keeping the buttonhole flap free, the silk lining was FELLED to the collar.

28 The long edge of the facing was FOLDED ³⁄₁₆" to the WS and HALF-BACK STITCHED to the RS of the very front edge of the velvet (a scant ⅛"), in green silk thread.

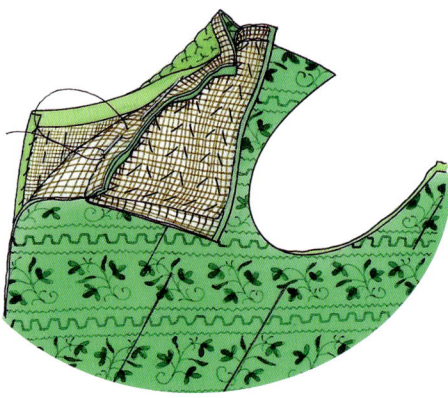

23 With RS together, the collar and the front were *probably* BACK STITCHED, with a ¼" seam allowance, keeping the lining out of the way. The seam allowances were *probably* TRIMMED to ⅛"–³⁄₁₆".

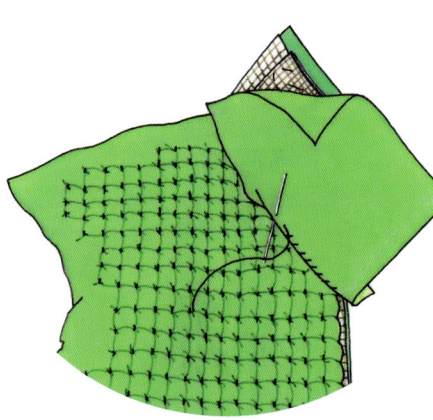

26 The seam allowance of the lower edge of the collar lining was FOLDED to the WS and FELLED to the silk lining of the body.

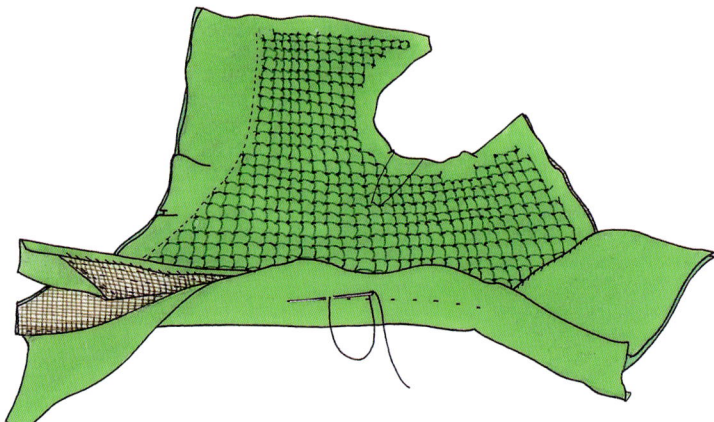

29 With the baleen panel held back against the quilted layer, the facing was FOLDED to the WS and HALF-BACK STITCHED into the 'ditch' (1" from the CF) between the quilting and the velvet/linen layer, using green silk thread.

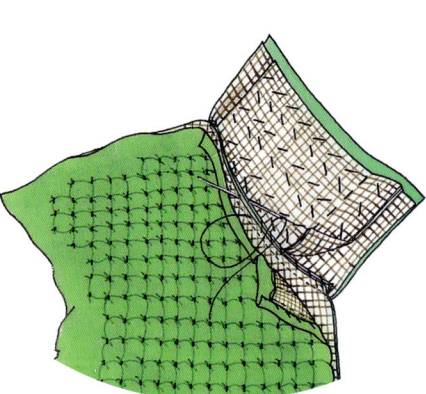

24 Again keeping the linen collar flap free, the seam allowance was FELLED to the collar.

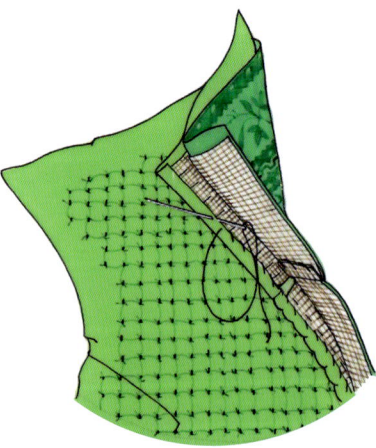

27 The seam allowance of the front edge of the collar lining was FOLDED around to the WS of the linen collar flap and FELLED.

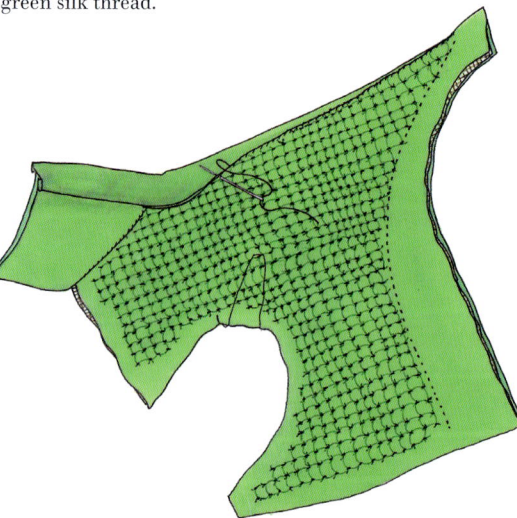

30 The ¼" seam allowance of the facing was FOLDED to the WS and FELLED to the quilted lining and baleen panel on the front edge, with green silk thread.

Construction of the right-hand side (RHS) – button side

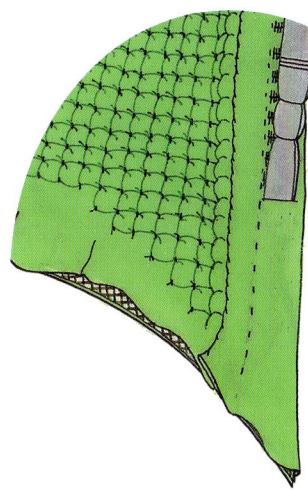

31 Working through the buttonhole stand only, each buttonhole was CUT with a chisel, ½" apart and just less than ¼" from the front edge. They were then worked in green silk twist from the collar down as follows.

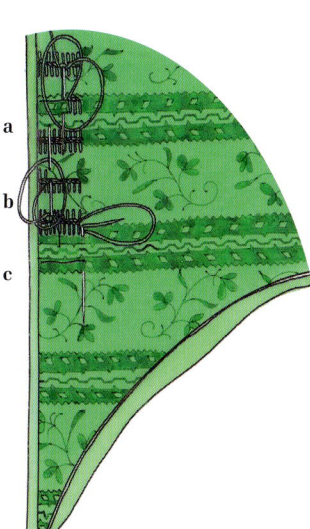

32 Thirty-four buttonholes (two on the collar) were BUTTONHOLE STITCHED, starting each along its bottom edge, from right to left (a), with the knot at the end of each stitch pointing left. No stitches were made at the front end of the slit. They were worked along the top edge only, from left to right (b). The final stitch in the previous buttonhole was worked invisibly through the layers to begin the next one (c).

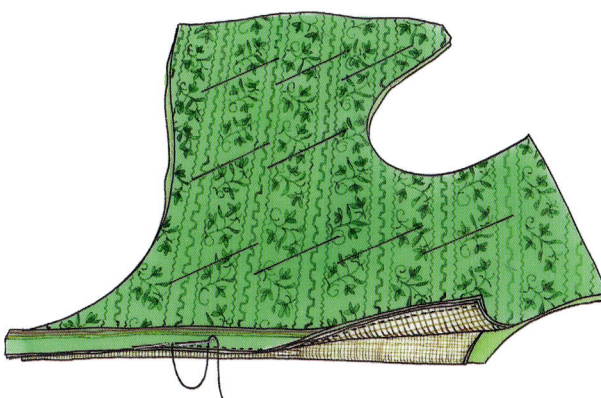

33 With RS together, and working through the velvet and linen only, a 1" strip of velvet was RUNNING STITCHED ¼" from the CF edge, in order to bind it.

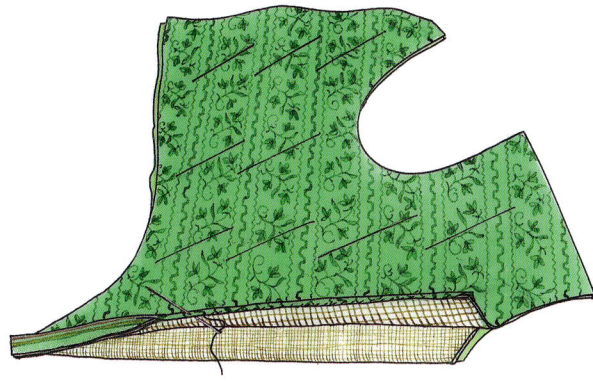

34 The velvet binding was TURNED ¼" to the WS and FELLED to the linen interlining.

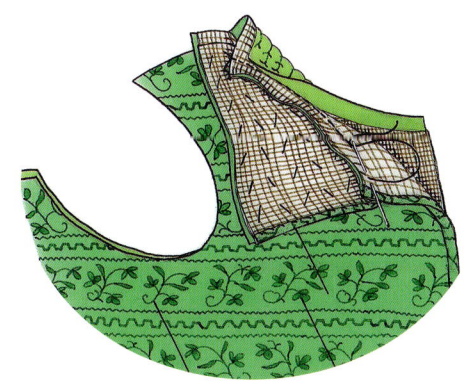

35 With RS together, the collar and the front were *probably* BACK STITCHED, with a ¼" seam allowance, keeping the lining out of the way. The seam allowances were *probably* TRIMMED to ⅛"–³⁄₁₆".

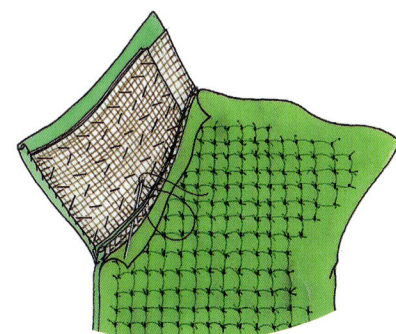

36 Keeping the silk lining out of the way, the trimmed-down seam allowance was FELLED to the collar.

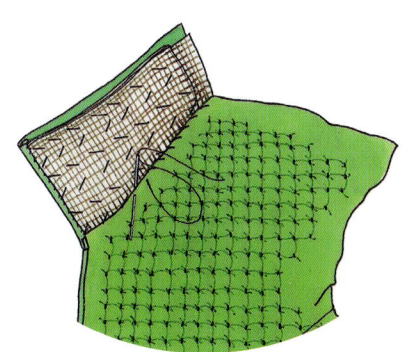

37 The silk body lining was FELLED to the collar.

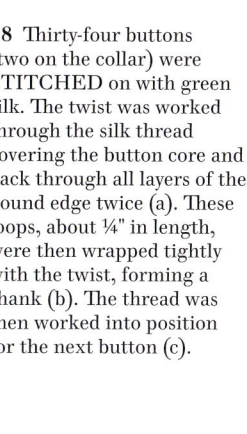

38 Thirty-four buttons (two on the collar) were STITCHED on with green silk. The twist was worked through the silk thread covering the button core and back through all layers of the bound edge twice (a). These loops, about ¼" in length, were then wrapped tightly with the twist, forming a shank (b). The thread was then worked into position for the next button (c).

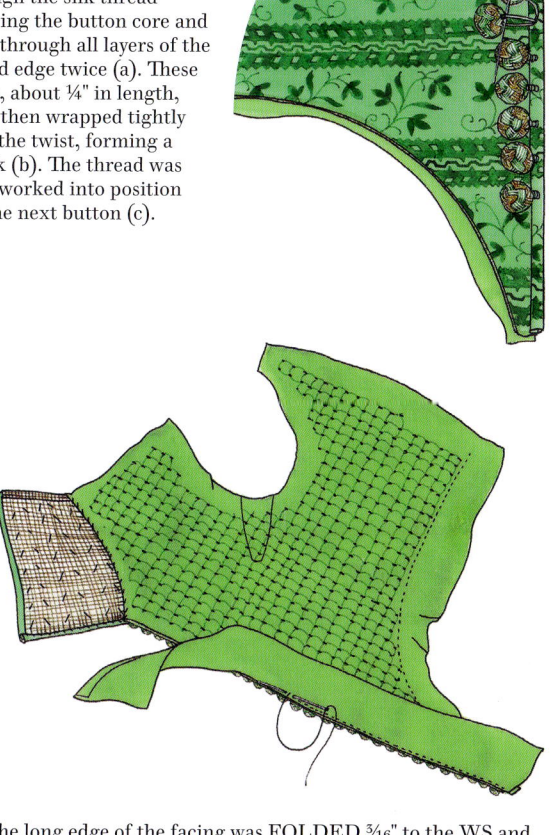

39 The long edge of the facing was FOLDED ³⁄₁₆" to the WS and HALF-BACK STITCHED to the velvet binding along the CF edge in the green silk thread.

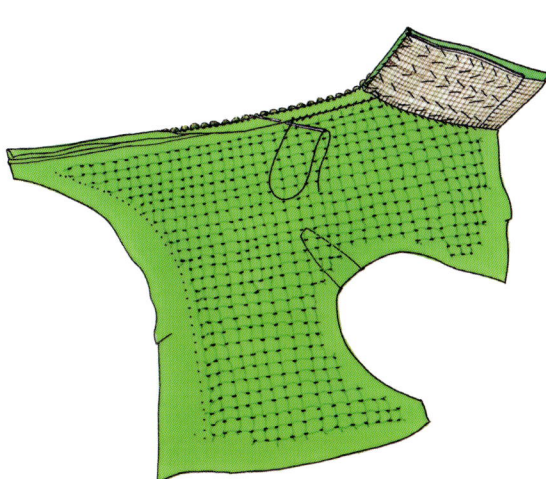

40 The other edge of the facing was FOLDED ³⁄₁₆" to its WS and FELLED to the quilting layer in green silk thread. The finished strip is almost ⅞" wide.

Pattern by Claire Thornton

Construction of the right-hand side (RHS) – button side   CONTINUED

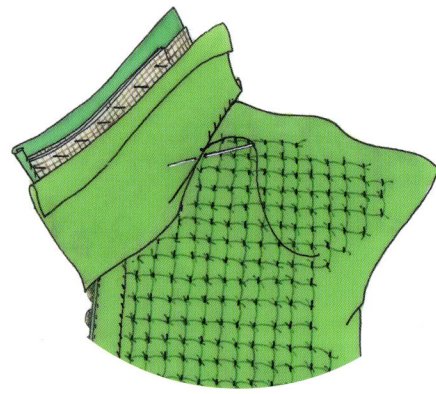

41 The seam allowances at the bottom and front edges of the collar lining were FOLDED to the WS and FELLED into place, finishing at the top edge of the collar.

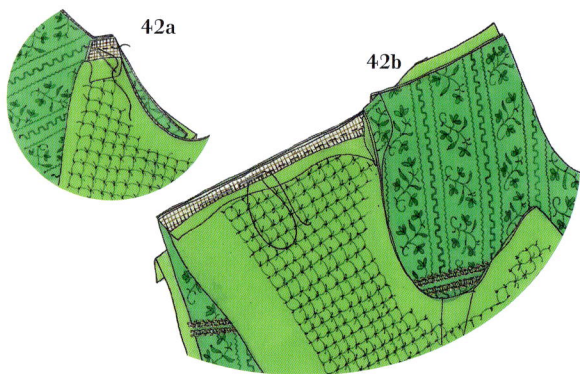

42a The side seam was *probably* STITCHED in two separate stages; the 'step' near the armhole first. With RS together, and the silk lining kept out of the way, two or three running stitches were worked.

42b With RS together, the front and back side seams were lined up. Keeping the linings out of the way, they were RUNNING STITCHED together through the velvet and linen layers in the brown linen thread, with a 5⁄16" seam allowance.

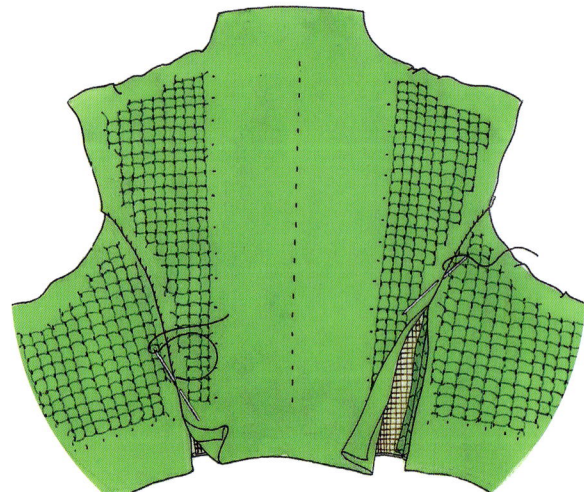

43 On both seams the ¼" seam allowance of the back lining was FOLDED to the WS and FELLED to the ¼" seam allowance of the front lining. Below the quilting lines the lining is only STITCHED to itself, leaving it free for finishing the waist later.

44 Two lengths of edging lace were FELLED to each front edge from the waist to the collar seam, in green silk thread. On the LHS the first row is inside the buttonholes and the second is 3⁄16" from the first. On the RHS, the first row is 7⁄8" from the CF and the second is 3⁄16" from the first. Two additional lengths were *probably* STITCHED 3⁄16" up from the collar seam to the top of the collar, the same distances from the CF's as before.

46 Starting at the front length of edging lace on the collar, another length was FELLED, 3⁄16" up from it, and echoing the line of the collar seam. Another length of edging lace was FELLED to the edge of the LHS, leaving enough to finish off the collar.

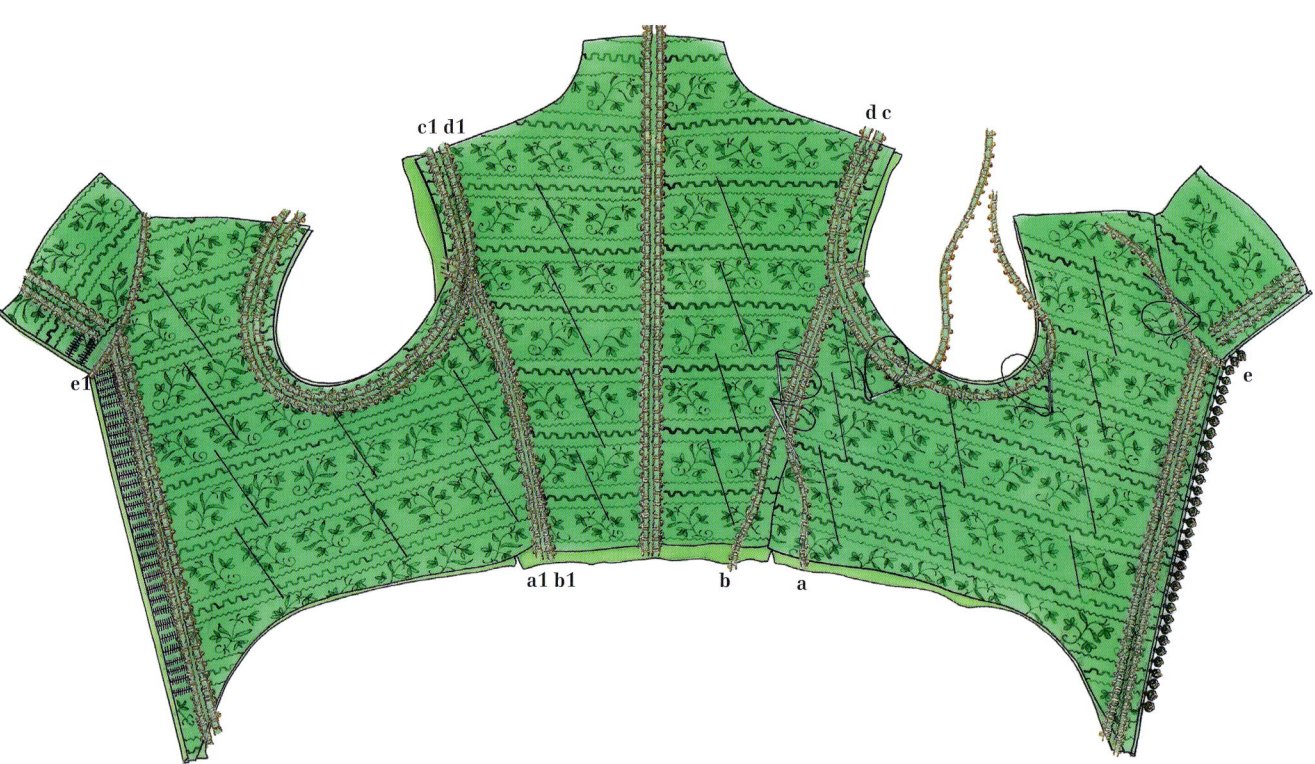

45 Three pairs of braid were FELLED to each side of the doublet in the green silk thread:

a, a1 covering the side seam and **b, b1** inside them towards the centre back

c, c1 next to the ¼" seam allowance of the armhole and **d, d1** 3⁄16" away from them

e, e1 on the fronts, under the seam of the collar (**e, e1** should be folded under and stitched down at the centre front edge)

Construction of the laps

> Some of the velvet and silk linings of the laps were pieced. These layers of the laps were CUT net at the top only.

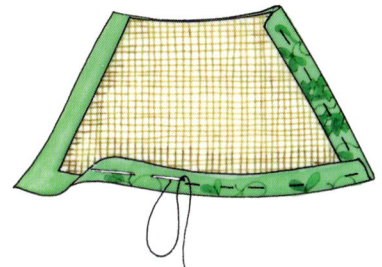

47 The interlining for each lap, CUT net, was PLACED on the WS of the velvet and then the ⅜" seam allowance around three sides was FOLDED to the WS and RUNNING STITCHED.

48 Two lengths of edging lace were FELLED to each lap, one on the outside edge, the other ³⁄₁₆" away from the first.

49 With WS together, the lining was PLACED over the linen interlining, the ⁵⁄₁₆" seam allowances were FOLDED to the WS and HALF-BACK STITCHED.

50a Five eyelet holes were PIERCED with a bodkin on 11 laps, ½" apart. Each hole was WHIPPED around with green silk thread.

50b Both the centre front laps had only one eyelet worked.

51 With RS together, the laps were positioned along the waist and *probably* BASTED. They were WHIPPED in doubled, waxed, brown linen thread and an extra line of WHIPPING was worked in the opposite direction, across the back between the two side seams.

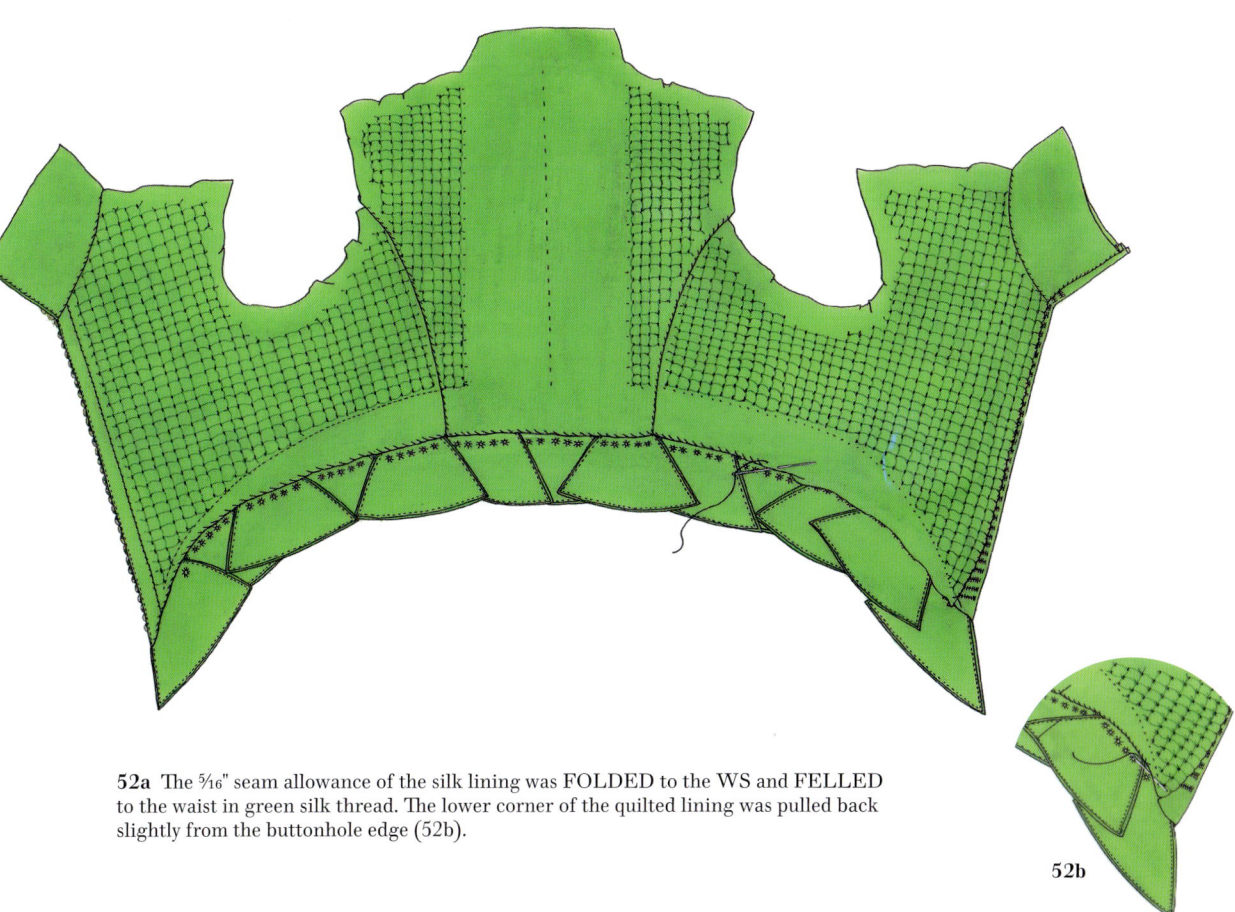

52a The ⁵⁄₁₆" seam allowance of the silk lining was FOLDED to the WS and FELLED to the waist in green silk thread. The lower corner of the quilted lining was pulled back slightly from the buttonhole edge (52b).

Pattern by Claire Thornton

Construction of the laps CONTINUED

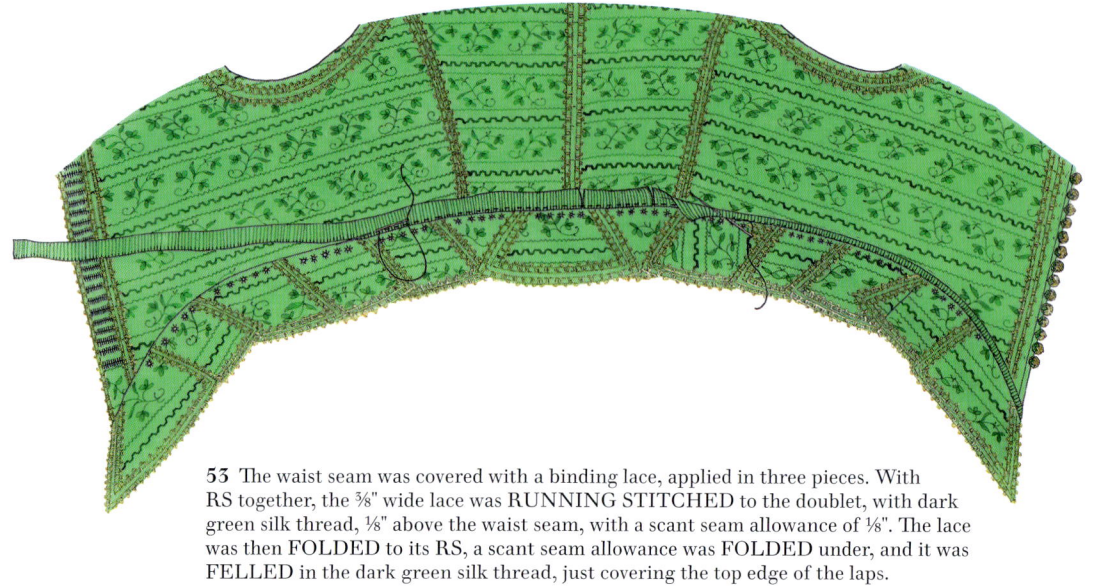

53 The waist seam was covered with a binding lace, applied in three pieces. With RS together, the ⅜" wide lace was RUNNING STITCHED to the doublet, with dark green silk thread, ⅛" above the waist seam, with a scant seam allowance of ⅛". The lace was then FOLDED to its RS, a scant seam allowance was FOLDED under, and it was FELLED in the dark green silk thread, just covering the top edge of the laps.

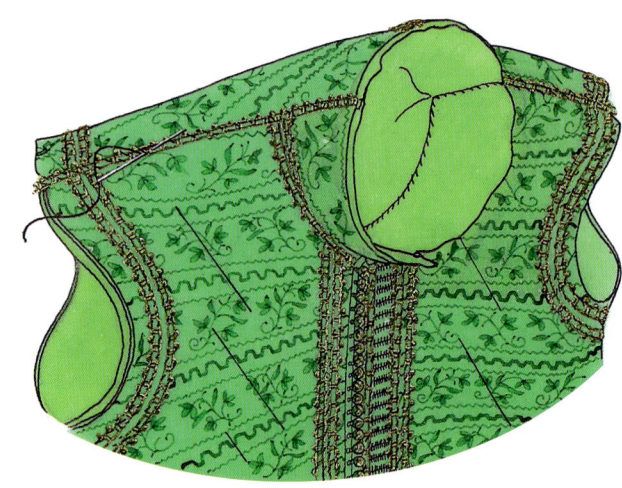

57 A single length of edging lace was FELLED along the shoulder and collar seam.

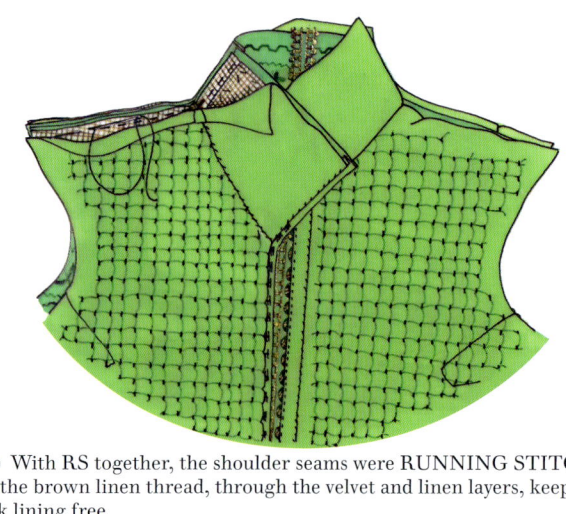

54 With RS together, the shoulder seams were RUNNING STITCHED in the brown linen thread, through the velvet and linen layers, keeping the silk lining free.

55a The velvet seam allowance at the top of the collar was FOLDED to the WS and FELLED to the interlining. At the buttonhole end the strip of silk for the buttonholes was tucked in and FOLDED over all of the interlining layers (55b).

56 The seam allowance of the back shoulder lining was FOLDED to the WS and then FELLED to the front shoulder lining in green silk thread. All of the armhole layers were then BASTED together.

55b

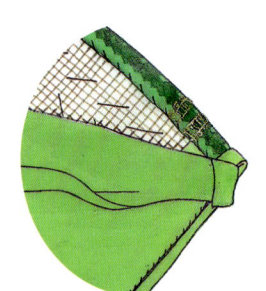

58a The seam allowance of the lining at the top of the collar, on the buttonhole side, was FOLDED to the WS, completely sealing the flap.

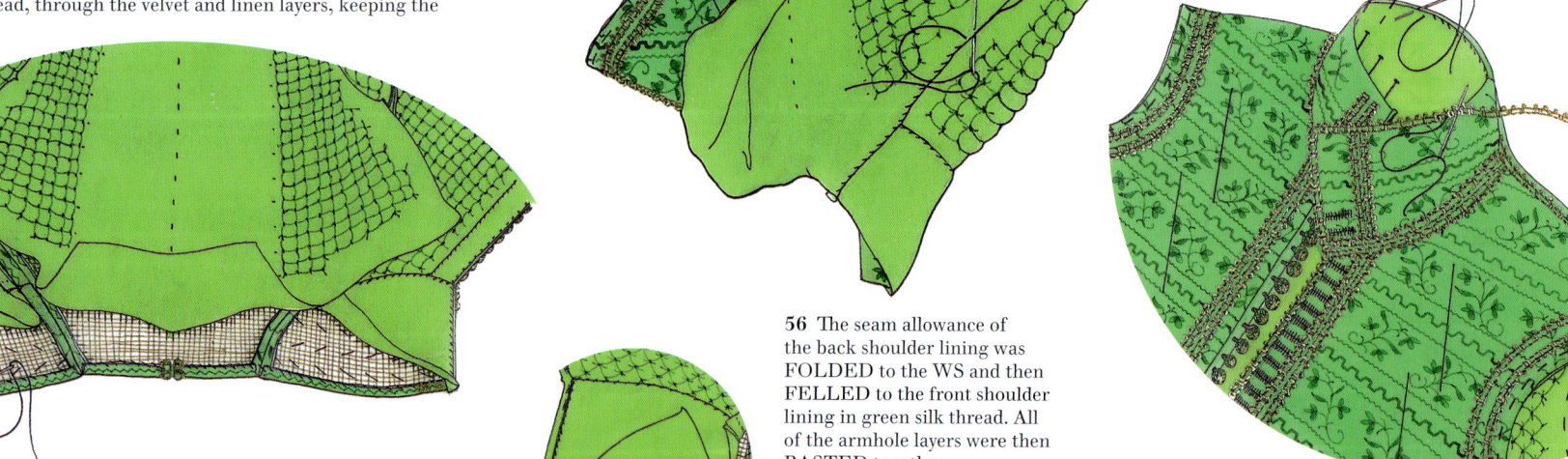

58b The seam allowance of the silk collar lining was FOLDED to the WS and FELLED. The extra length of braid was then FELLED around the top edge of the collar.

Construction of the sleeves

59 With RS together, three piecings were RUNNING STITCHED with brown linen thread.

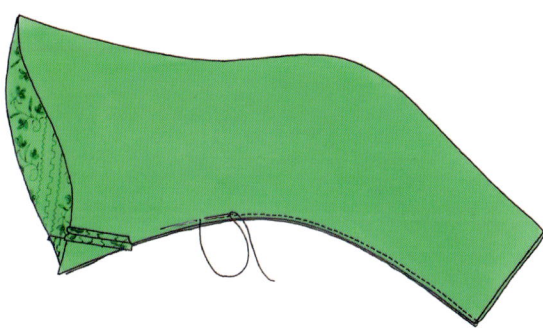

60 With RS together, the inside seam at the top and the undersleeves were BACK STITCHED in brown linen thread, ⅜" seam allowance.

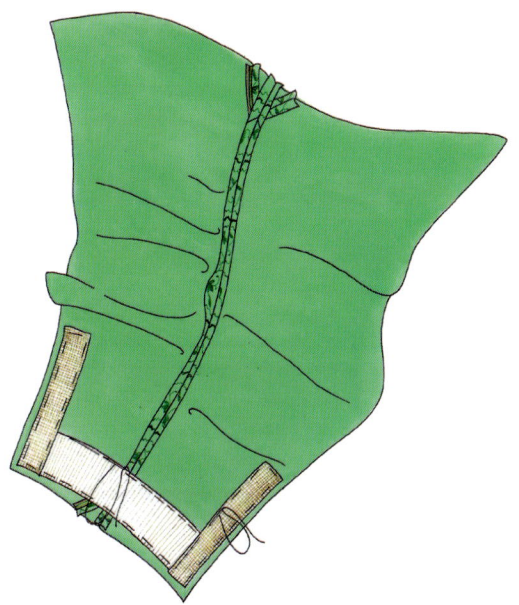

61 To support the wrist opening, two linen strips were *probably* BASTED on the WS, within the ⁵⁄₁₆" seam allowance of the outside edge of the sleeve. A strip of fustian was PLACED between them and *probably* BASTED.

62 A pair of edging laces was FELLED to the RS, the first covering the seam and the second ³⁄₁₆" away on the top sleeve.

63 With WS together, the sleeve piecings were RUNNING STITCHED in green silk thread.

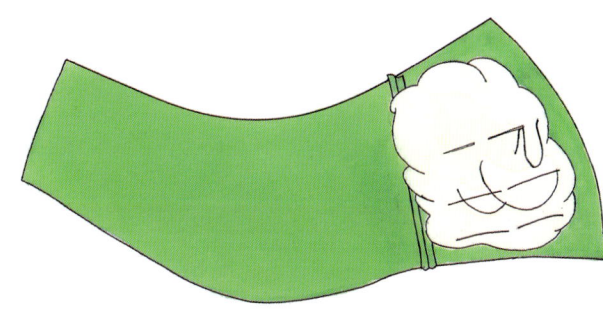

64 A light layer of the carded wool was positioned on the WS of the top-sleeve lining. It was RUNNING STITCHED with large, loose stitches in green silk thread.

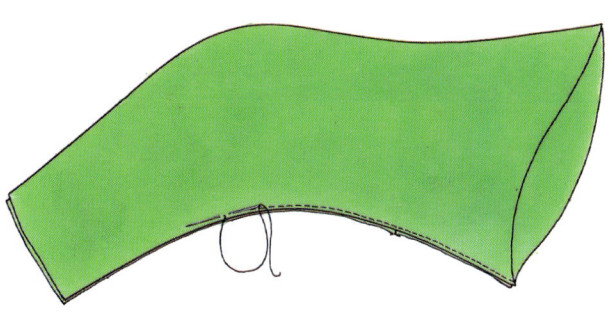

65 With RS together, the inside seam of the lining top and undersleeve was HALF-BACK STITCHED in dark green silk thread, with a seam allowance of ⁵⁄₁₆".

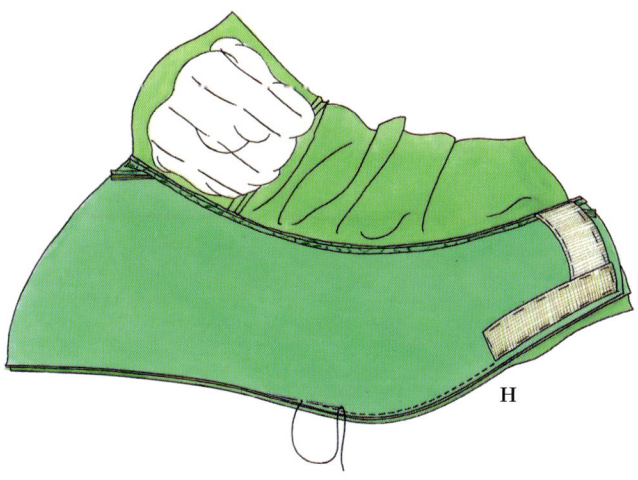

66 The sleeve lining was laid open, WS facing up. The velvet sleeve, still RS together, was PLACED over it, undersleeve to undersleeve, matching up the inside sleeve seams. The outside seam was then BACK STITCHED in brown linen thread from **H** to the top, working through both velvet layers and the undersleeve lining layer, with a ⅜" seam allowance.

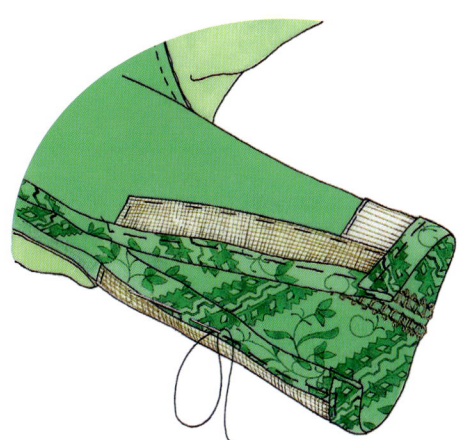

67 At the wrist opening the ⁵⁄₁₆" seam allowance of the velvet was FOLDED to the WS and RUNNING STITCHED to the interlinings with green silk thread.

Pattern by Claire Thornton

Construction of the sleeves CONTINUED

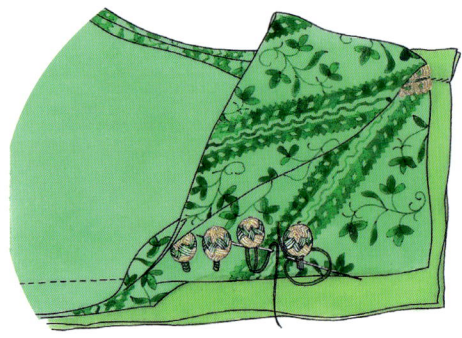

68 Seven buttons were sewn to the undersleeve, at the wrist, ¼" from the finished edge, and ⅝" apart, as in step 38.

71 Seven buttonholes were sewn on the top sleeve, ¼" away from the front edge, and ⅝" apart, lining up with the buttons, as in step 32.

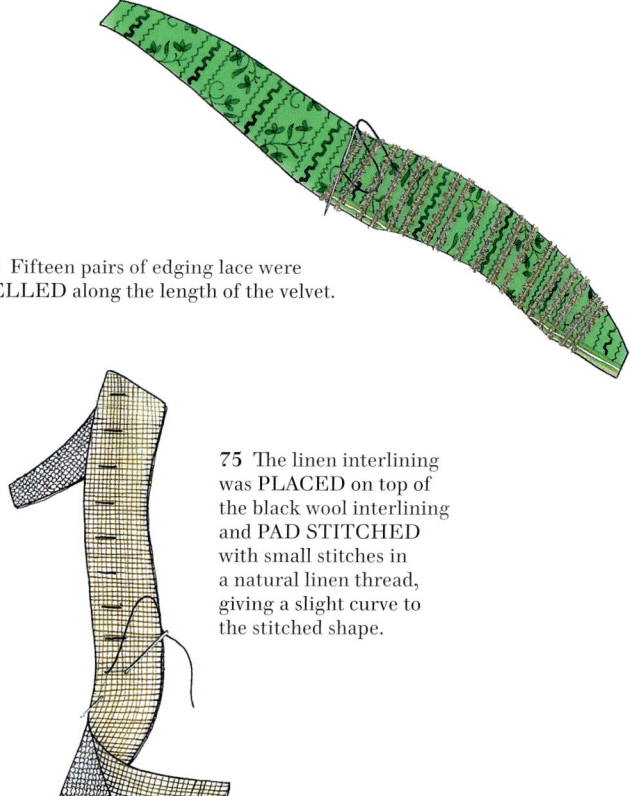

74 Fifteen pairs of edging lace were FELLED along the length of the velvet.

75 The linen interlining was PLACED on top of the black wool interlining and PAD STITCHED with small stitches in a natural linen thread, giving a slight curve to the stitched shape.

76 The WS of the velvet was PLACED over the linen interlining and *probably* BASTED.

69 The top-sleeve lining was then wrapped over the velvet top sleeve, WS together. The ⅜" seam allowance of the lining was FOLDED to the WS and then FELLED in green silk from the sleeve head to **H**. The sleeve was then TURNED THROUGH to the RS.

72 Two lengths of edging lace were FELLED onto the back of the sleeve, the first covering the seam, working along the front of the buttonholes and around the wrist edge. The second edging lace followed the same path, ³⁄₁₆" away from the first length, but was worked along the back of the buttonholes and around the wrist, finishing at **x**, where the raw ends were FOLDED under and STITCHED down.

Construction of the wings

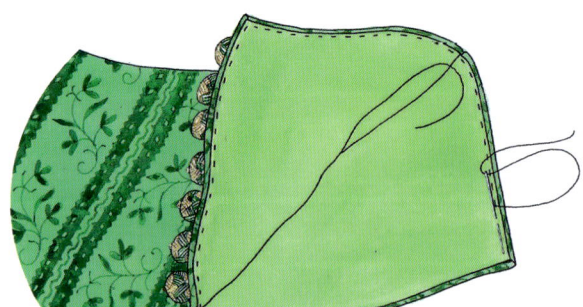

70 At the wrist opening the ⅜" seam allowance of the lining was FOLDED to the WS and RUNNING STITCHED to the velvet, close to the edge, in green silk thread.

73 With RS together, the velvet piecings of the wings were *probably* RUNNING STITCHED.

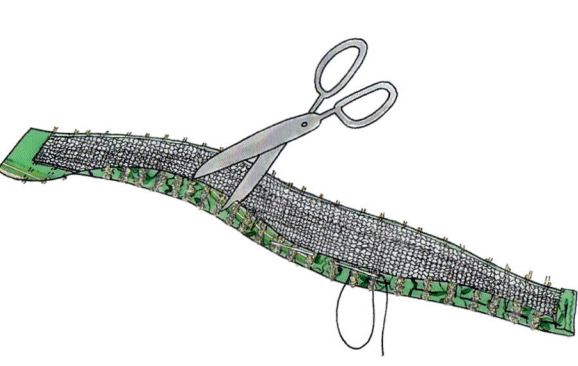

77 The ⅝" seam allowance of the velvet was FOLDED to the WS, clipped to make it lie flat, and RUNNING STITCHED onto the black wool in brown linen thread.

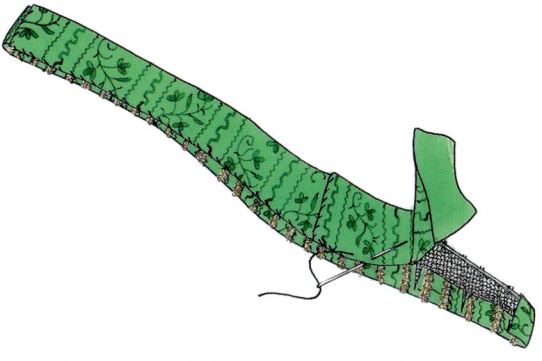

78 The wings were lined with scraps of velvet. The seam allowances were FOLDED to the WS and FELLED into place piece by piece rather than being seamed together. The raw edges at the armhole were *probably* BASTED.

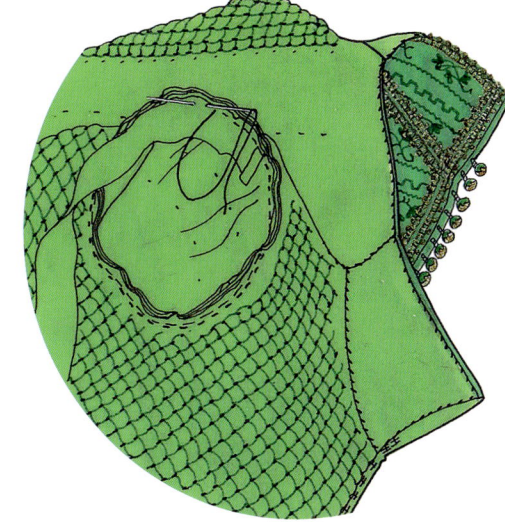

81 The raw edges of the armhole and sleeve seam were BOUND with strips of the silk lining, CUT 1¼" wide, and PIECED with a running stitch in green silk thread. The strip was PLACED inside the sleeve head, RS together, and RUNNING STITCHED around the armhole in green silk thread.

83 Two 4" lengths of binding lace were FOLDED into thirds lengthwise and FELLED in green silk thread, the finished width is ³⁄₁₆".

79 With RS together, the wing was POSITIONED inside the armhole. It was *probably* PINNED or BASTED and was RUNNING STITCHED with the brown linen thread, using a STAB STITCH.

84 A hole was PIERCED from the WS, on each front, as marked on the pattern, through all the layers. The binding lace was INSERTED through the hole from the WS, making a girdle loop of 1¼". The ends were FELLED down firmly on the WS in green silk thread. A length of green satin – not used previously in the construction – was made into two lacing loops, one FELLED to the quilting on each front.

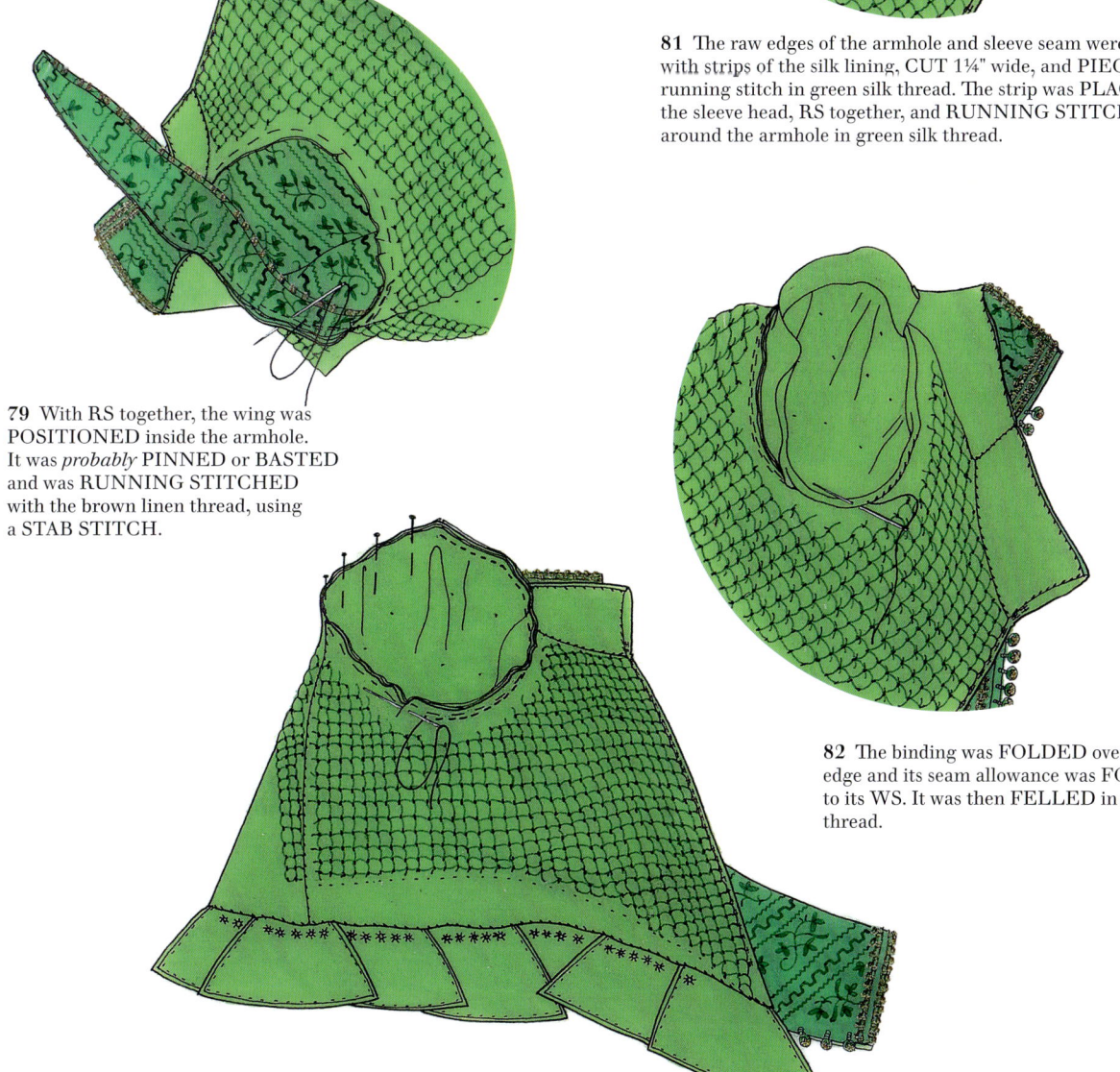

82 The binding was FOLDED over the raw edge and its seam allowance was FOLDED to its WS. It was then FELLED in green silk thread.

80 With RS together, the sleeve and doublet were *probably* PINNED and then RUNNING STITCHED with a ¼" seam allowance, working from the body into the sleeve, using brown linen thread. Around the sleeve head, where the wing sits, the RUNNING STITCH was stabbed, working in a single motion in and out through all the fabric layers.

85 Two holes were PIERCED with a bodkin, through all of the layers, at the centre fronts of the peak. They were then WHIPPED around in a green silk thread. Another pair of holes was made in the top edge of the front laps and WHIPPED as before.

Pattern by Claire Thornton

Sir Rowland Cotton's Suit
2A | Doublet of slashed silk satin

English, *c.* 1618 | V&A: T.28–1938 | Given by Lady Spickernell

Pattern by Melanie Braun

The suit of Sir Rowland Cotton, consisting of a doublet and a pair of matching trunk hose, was part of a small collection of historical men's clothing that included the sword girdle and hanger on page 80; they were all associated with the Cotton family of Etwall Hall, Derbyshire. They were given to the V&A by Lady Spickernell in 1938. John Nevinson, who accepted the gift on behalf of the textiles department, remarked that this suit was a rare example of its kind.[1] Janet Arnold was the first to connect this suit with a portrait sold at auction in 1961, which was then thought to have been painted by Daniel Mytens and to depict Sir Richard Cotton.[2] In 2010, a descendant of the Cotton family contacted the V&A. His genealogical research identified the sitter as Sir Rowland Cotton.[3] From 1961, the portrait remained in an unidentified private collection. In 2014 it came up for auction and was purchased by the Weiss Gallery in London (opposite).

The suit is made of several layers of silk fabrics: an outer layer of oyster-coloured silk satin, with an underlayer of blue silk. Rows of slashes, about two inches long alternate with three rows of small pinks, revealing a third layer of white silk, similar in quality to the blue. The suit is adorned with silver and silver-gilt filé edging lace and buttons. The doublet has a soft sea-green lining that is, in fact, a 'changeable' or shot blue and yellow silk, with a linen interlining forming its foundation. Sir Rowland's suit was well worn at the time. Stains of different kinds, for example, on the scye and crotch indicate this. The remaining lining is patched and repaired in several places in the sleeve-head and over the belly pieces. The suit was on display for many years and it has suffered severely from light exposure, as well as attempts to consolidate the disintegrating layers of silk. The white layer has completely crumbled and only a few fragments remain. At some point, a pink rayon backing was stitched and glued to the oyster satin in areas of weakness, a restoration treatment no longer acceptable. The sleeves are very damaged and their shape and construction can only now be conjectured.

Slashed silk satin doublet, *c.* **1620**
Courtesy of Perth Museum & Art Gallery, Perth & Kinross Council

When mounted, the fashionable silhouette of the suit can be clearly seen, with a narrow elegant waistline above the voluminous trunk hose. The style of the doublet is a transition between the green silk velvet doublet on page 26, padded with quilting, and the crimson silk grosgrain doublet on page 88, with cork belly pieces. Such rigid reinforcement of the lower front of a doublet was a new development. Here, the belly pieces are still quite soft, compared to those of the two later doublets in this book. Made of strips of baleen and pad-stitched linen, Sir Rowland's belly pieces form a concave curve at centre front, as can be seen in the portrait just above the sword girdle. The latter would have been held in place with a point threaded through the four eyelet holes at the bottom of the doublet peak.

Sir Rowland was knighted in 1618 and this oyster-coloured suit and portrait might have been specially made for this occasion. The painting illustrates the accessories that would have accompanied his suit: a circular cloak of plain oyster satin, lined with velvet, complementing his doublet and hose. The high-crowned hat with an elaborate hatband, plain gloves, delicate linen ruff and cuffs speak of Sir Rowland's wealth and taste, and complete the ensemble beautifully. As the son of a draper, he would have been familiar with fine fabrics and accessories. He left to his brother 'my best Cloake and my Coate that was lately made and is lyned with Plush and the new Spanish cloath to make a suite unto it.'[4] A doublet with a very similar slashing pattern, but more in the style of the grosgrain doublet on page 88, can be found in the collection of the Perth Museum and Art Gallery, UK.

1. V&A Nominal File Spickernell. Report by John Nevinson, 11 March 1938
2. Janet Arnold, *Patterns of Fashion 3: The Cut and Construction of Clothes for Men and Women 1560–1620*, London: Macmillan, 1985, p. 88
3. Letter from Jeffrey W. C. Dabbs, 27 June 2010
4. National Archives, PROB 11/166/473; transcribed by Sophie Pitman

Sir Rowland Cotton, *c.* 1618
Paul van Somer
The Weiss Gallery, London

Pattern by Melanie Braun

DETAILS
Right side (RS) details

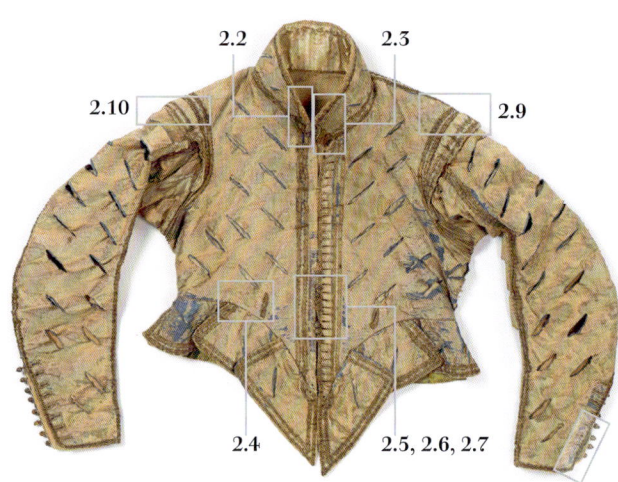

2.1 The front of the doublet, showing the remaining buttons and buttonholes, and the two pairs of eyelets at the bottom CF and the front laps.

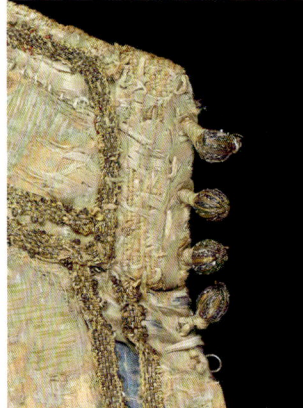

2.2 The edge of the RHS of the collar was bound with a strip of bias-cut silk satin, running stitched with linen thread.

2.3 On the LHS of the collar three loops of edging lace were pushed through pierced but unworked holes.

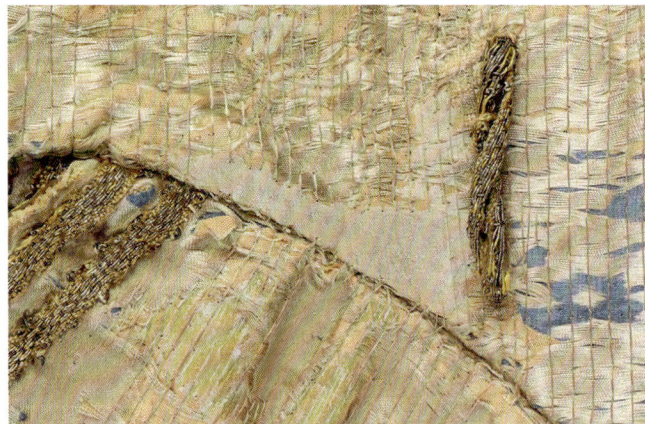

2.4 On each front there is a loop of edging lace to hold the girdle. It was pushed through unworked holes and secured on the WS to the belly pieces. The RHS is shown here.

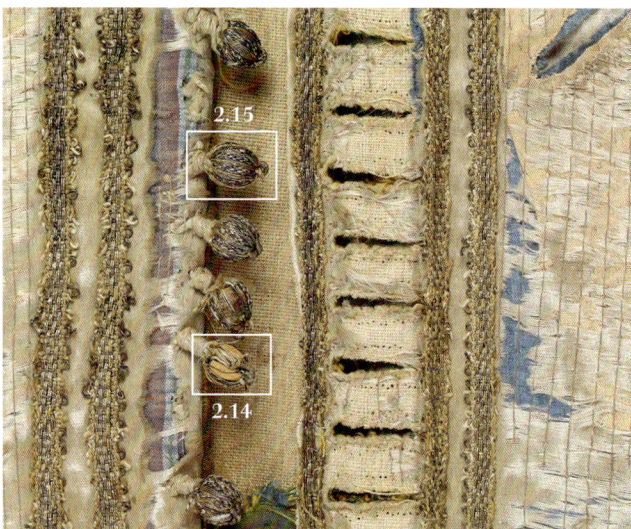

2.5 On the fronts the multi-coloured selvedges of the blue and white silk underlayers are visible under the buttons. These have been cut away on the LHS, so that no threads from the blue silk show when the buttonholes are cut. The wooden base of one button is shown in the box (2.14).

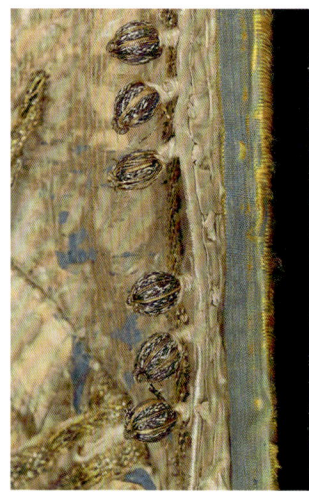

2.6 and 2.7 On both CFs a silk facing strip creates a fold to allow the closing of the doublet. The linen basting stitches holding the facing on the button side are visible in fig. 2.6. On the buttonhole side long running stitches in the same thread secure the lining and belly piece to the silk facing (seen in fig. 2.7).

2.8 A tear in the RHS undersleeve, which starts with one of the slashes, shown in the white box.

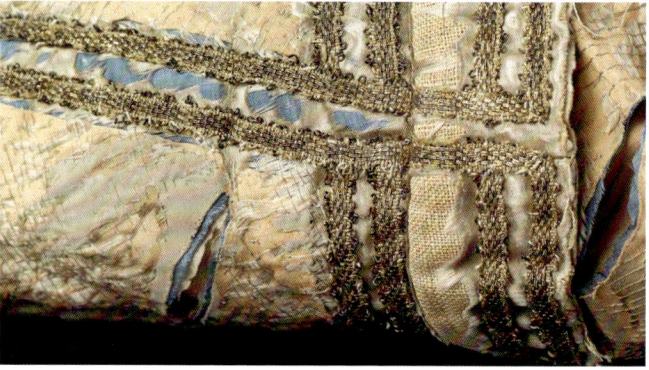

2.9 The LHS shoulder seam where the blue silk underlayer has been deliberately caught in the seam. Two rows of the lace were stitched around the armhole. The shoulder wing was cut in two pieces to fit smoothly into the armhole.

2.10 The silver and silver gilt of the edging lace on the sleeve are still untarnished. Also visible on the underside of the wing are its satin silk lining and the silk thread that stitched the lace to the wing.

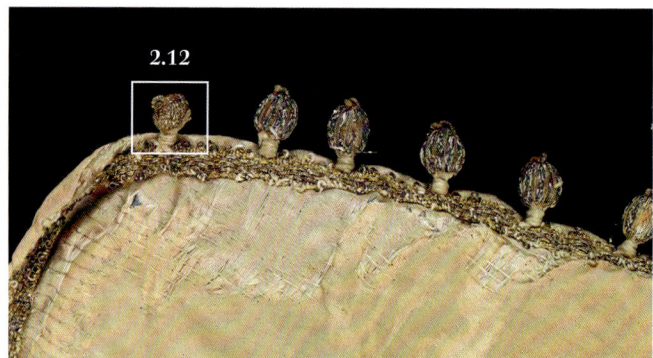

2.11 The sleeve buttons were stitched right on the edge of the sleeve openings, before the edging lace was applied. The button shank was made with doubled, white linen thread stitched through the silver and silver-gilt filé covering the wooden core of the button.

2.12 A button on the LHS sleeve that does not match the others, so it was probably a replacement.

2.13 The buttonholes were stitched on both sleeves with ivory silk twist, with 12 stitches per side.

50   **2A** | Doublet of slashed silk satin

Wrong side (WS) details

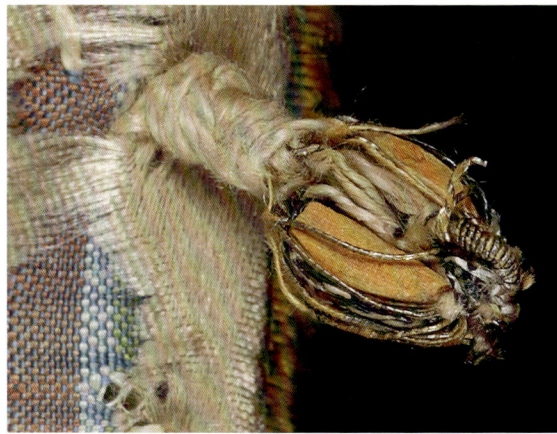

2.14 The doublet originally had 33 buttons down the CF; most are now missing or broken. This one reveals the wooden button core and the linen thread stitched through it to hold the metal purl at the top.

2.15 A close-up of a button on the CF. Its wooden core is covered with four strands of fine silver-gilt-wrapped yellow silk thread, alternating with a plait of four strands of thicker silver-wrapped white silk thread. The linen threads through the core are part of the button shank and the crossing purls of silver were added when the button was sewn on.

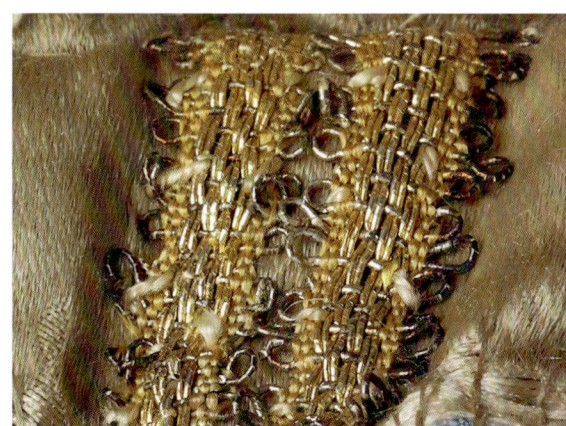

2.16 A close-up of the intact edging lace in fig. 2.10, showing its warp of silver-gilt-wrapped yellow silk and plain yellow silk, with a weft of silver-wrapped white silk that forms picots at the edge.

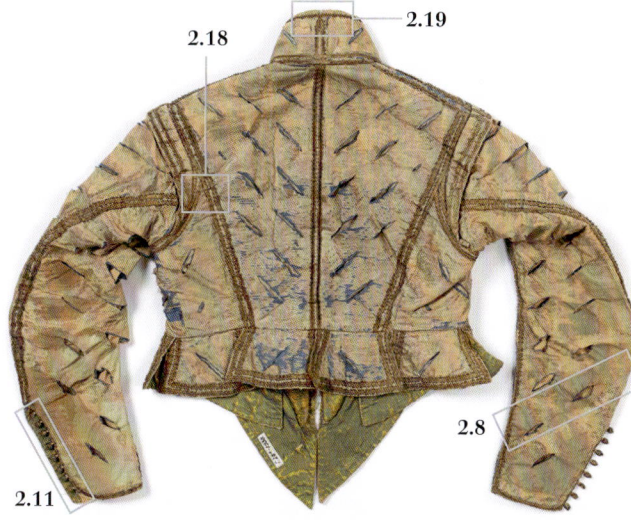

2.17 The back of the doublet, showing the two back laps meeting edge to edge at CB. The slashing and pinking of the two laps to the left and right of them go in the opposite direction. These two laps may have been removed to repair the waistband and their positions switched when they were sewn back.

2.18 The LHS where the two rows of edging lace that outline the armhole finish at the small 'step' of the side-back seam. Their ends were sewn into the side-back seam. All were stitched with white silk thread.

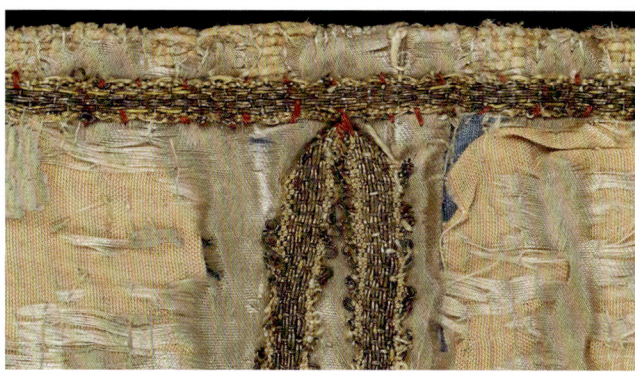

2.19 The CB of the collar at the top where the edging lace is mitred. The bottom edges of this lace were sewn into the seam attaching the collar to the doublet. The laces on the collar were sewn with red silk thread.

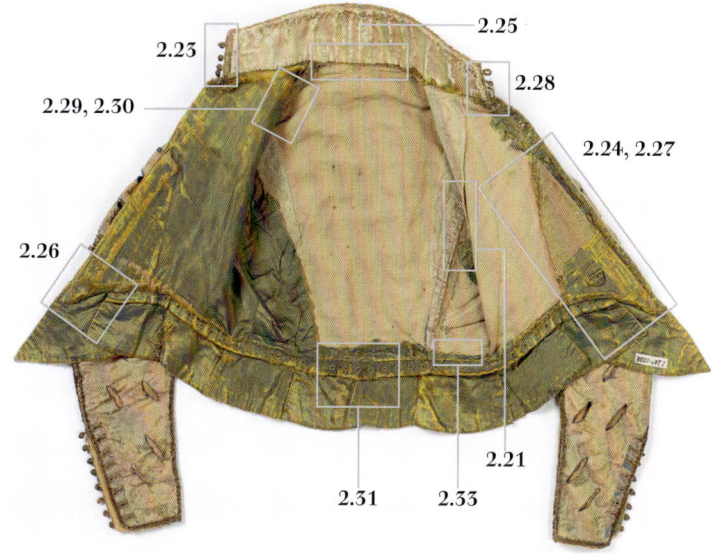

2.20 The doublet opened, showing its WS. The shot silk lining has worn and been cut away at the LHS back and front, revealing the interlinings.

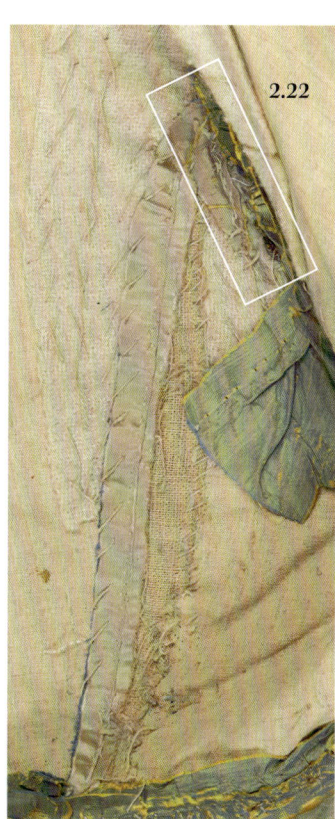

2.21 The side-back seam with small back stitches in white silk thread. The long pad stitches in the wool interlining at the back were sewn with linen thread, as were the fine whipping stitches that piece the linen of the front interlining. The LHS is shown.

2.22 A close-up of fig. 2.21. To the right of the image is an off-cut of oyster silk satin. It has been folded in half lengthways, laid over the side-back seam and stitched into the armhole, with linen thread. This both reinforces the seam and covers the raw ends of the edging lace stitched into it.

Pattern by Melanie Braun

Wrong side (WS) details   CONTINUED

2.23 The RHS of the collar. The buttons were stitched right at the edge of the collar with coarse linen thread. To the right of the buttons vertical running stitches in doubled linen thread hold a piece of reinforcement linen to the interlining. The collar was lined in white silk satin which is probably a later replacement.

2.25 The CB of the collar, showing the felling of it to the doublet in doubled linen thread. The seam allowances of both were glued first to prevent fraying; this is the very thin dark line in the centre. A thin strip of the green silk, lining the doublet, is trapped under the collar lining.

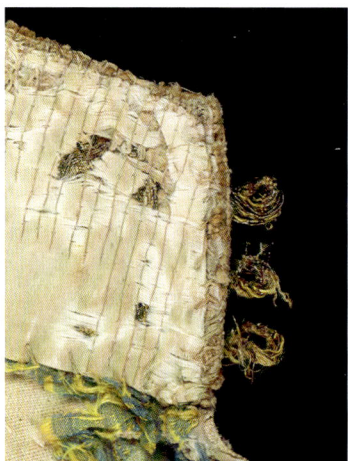

2.28 In the LHS front of the collar, holes in the satin lining reveal the ends of the edging lace that forms the button loops. The length of lace secured to the WS is almost as long as that used to form the loop on the RS. Here, the satin lining reaches right to the CF edge of the collar (compare with fig. 2.23).

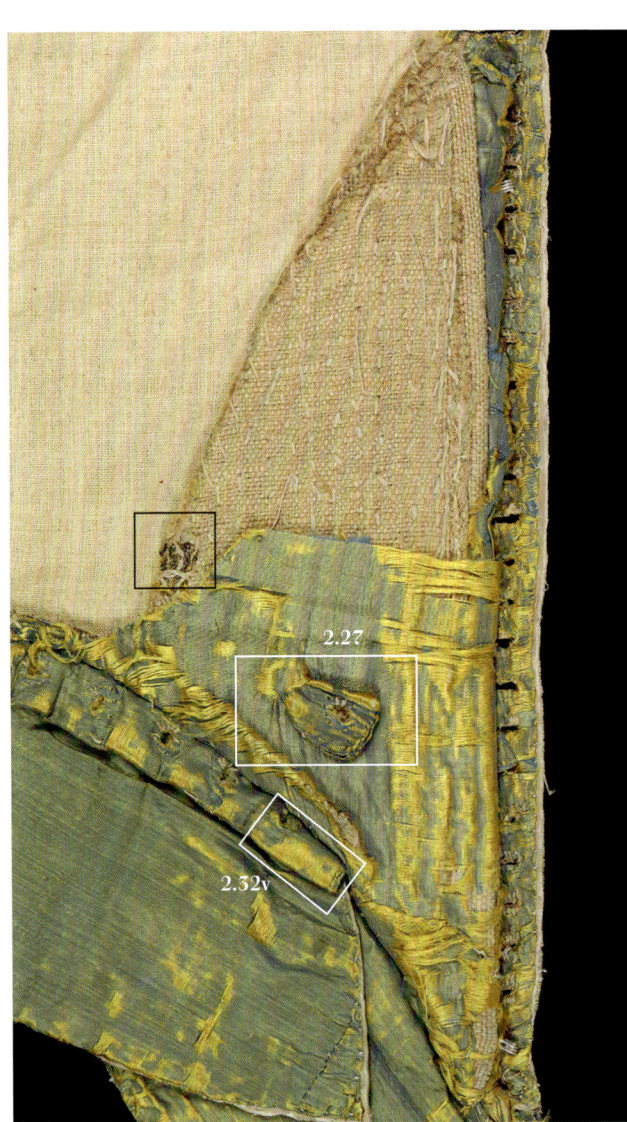

2.24 The LHS belly piece. The silk lining has worn away, revealing the linen layers that form it. Rows of pad stitching hold them together and strengthen the belly piece. The ends of the girdle loops were folded around the edge of the belly piece and stitched to it firmly, with linen thread, shown in the black box.

2.26 The RHS belly piece where the lining is patched over the peak. The eyelet at the very bottom of the CF is just underneath the tip of the belly piece, shown in the white box. The eyelet in the front lap is visible below it, shown in the black box.

2.27 The front lacing tabs have been stitched to the belly piece and pulled through an unworked eyelet in the lining. The LHS is shown. Only half its length can now be seen; the remainder is under the lining.

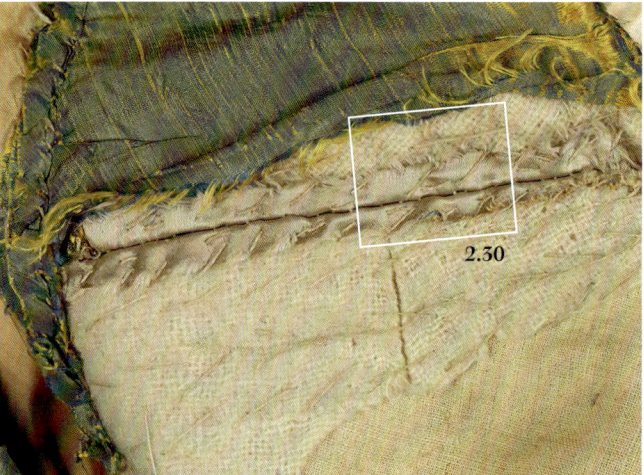

2.29 The RHS shoulder seam shows remains of the front lining at the top of the image and, below it, the pad stitches in the wool interlining at the back.

2.30 The RHS shoulder seam shows basting stitches holding the silk layers, and the felling stitches holding the seam allowances flat.

2A | Doublet of slashed silk satin

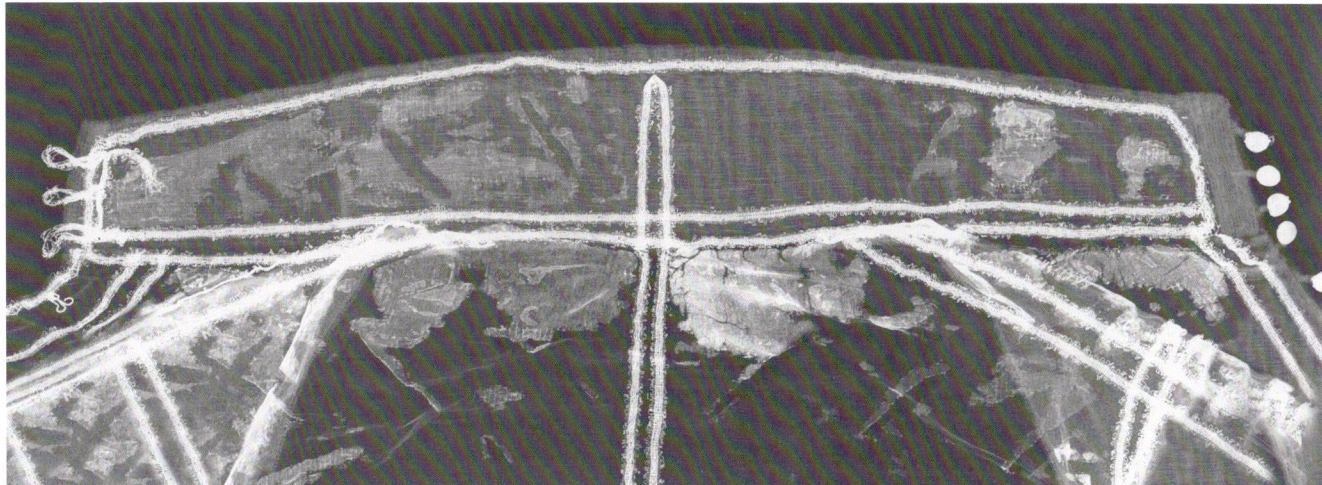

X-ray images
The greyish 'blobs' in these images are areas of early restoration work.

2.31 The lacing band at the CB with the laps turned up. The folded-up selvedge of the lacing band is visible on the right, providing support for the eyelets pierced just above it. The bottom of the image shows the CF, where the front edge of the lacing band lines up with the overlap of the first and second laps.

2.34 The collar and back of the doublet. The slashes in the silk are clearly visible, as are the metal edging laces outlining the doublet body and collar. The long end of the top button loop, sewn to the WS of the LHS collar, and hidden under its lining, can also be seen. There is an additional layer of interlining at the CB of the collar, between the shoulder seams.

2.32 The front edge of the lacing band on the LHS, showing the multiple folds of the selvedges that create a sturdy edge for the eyelets above.

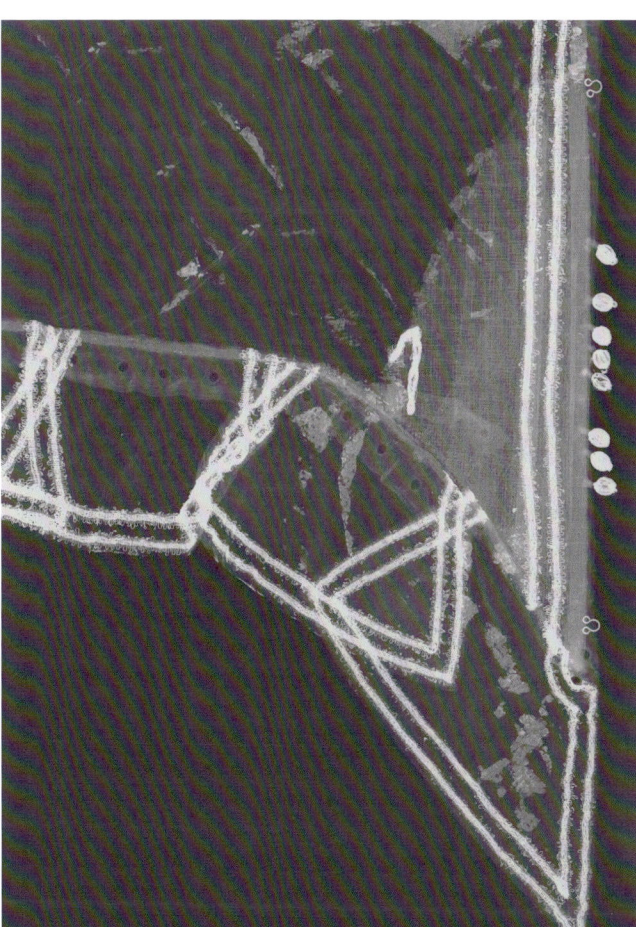
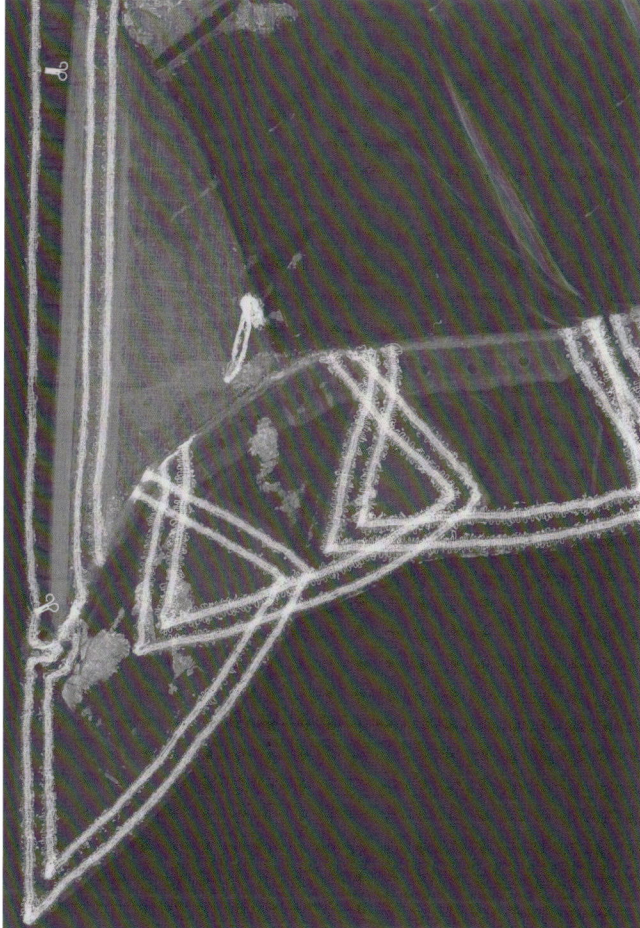

2.33 The seam allowance at the waist of the doublet body was cut to ⅛". The greyish residue on the raw edges is probably wax or glue applied to prevent fraying.

2.35 The CF of the doublet, showing the belly pieces and the girdle loops of metal edging lace. One of the two baleen strips inside each belly piece can been seen between the CF and the edging lace on the RHS, and on the LHS, between the edging laces at each end of the buttonholes. On the LHS, the belly piece curves away from the buttonholes along the CF, to allow enough space for buttoning up the doublet. The waistband with eyelets appears as a shadow underneath the top edge of the laps. The different weaves of the linen interlinings are also visible. The hooks and eyes visible here are a later addition to fasten the doublet while on display.

Pattern by Melanie Braun

PATTERN
Pattern of the oyster-coloured silk satin outer layer, and blue and white silk underlayers

SCALE 1:4

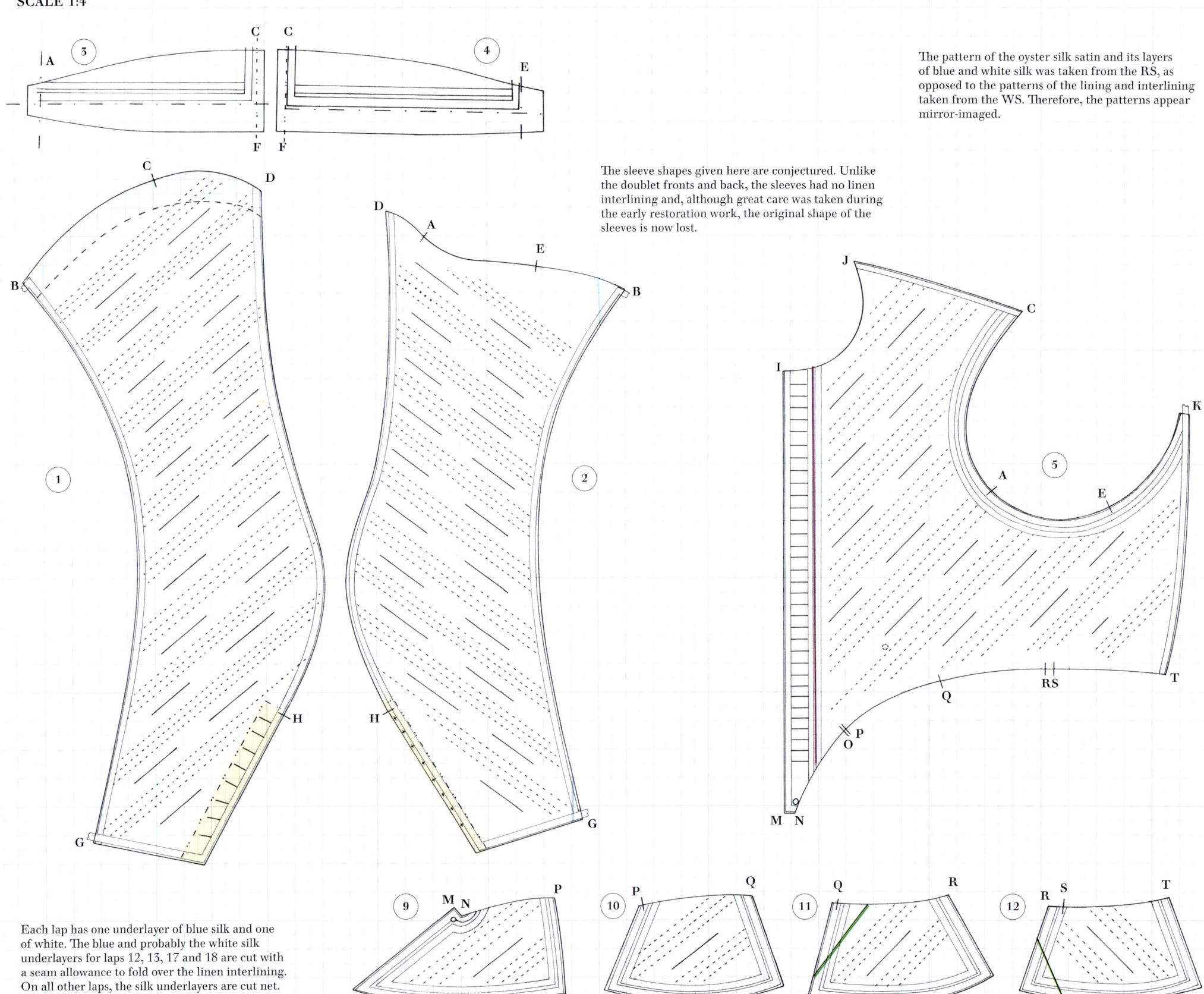

The pattern of the oyster silk satin and its layers of blue and white silk was taken from the RS, as opposed to the patterns of the lining and interlining taken from the WS. Therefore, the patterns appear mirror-imaged.

The sleeve shapes given here are conjectured. Unlike the doublet fronts and back, the sleeves had no linen interlining and, although great care was taken during the early restoration work, the original shape of the sleeves is now lost.

Each lap has one underlayer of blue silk and one of white. The blue and probably the white silk underlayers for laps 12, 13, 17 and 18 are cut with a seam allowance to fold over the linen interlining. On all other laps, the silk underlayers are cut net.

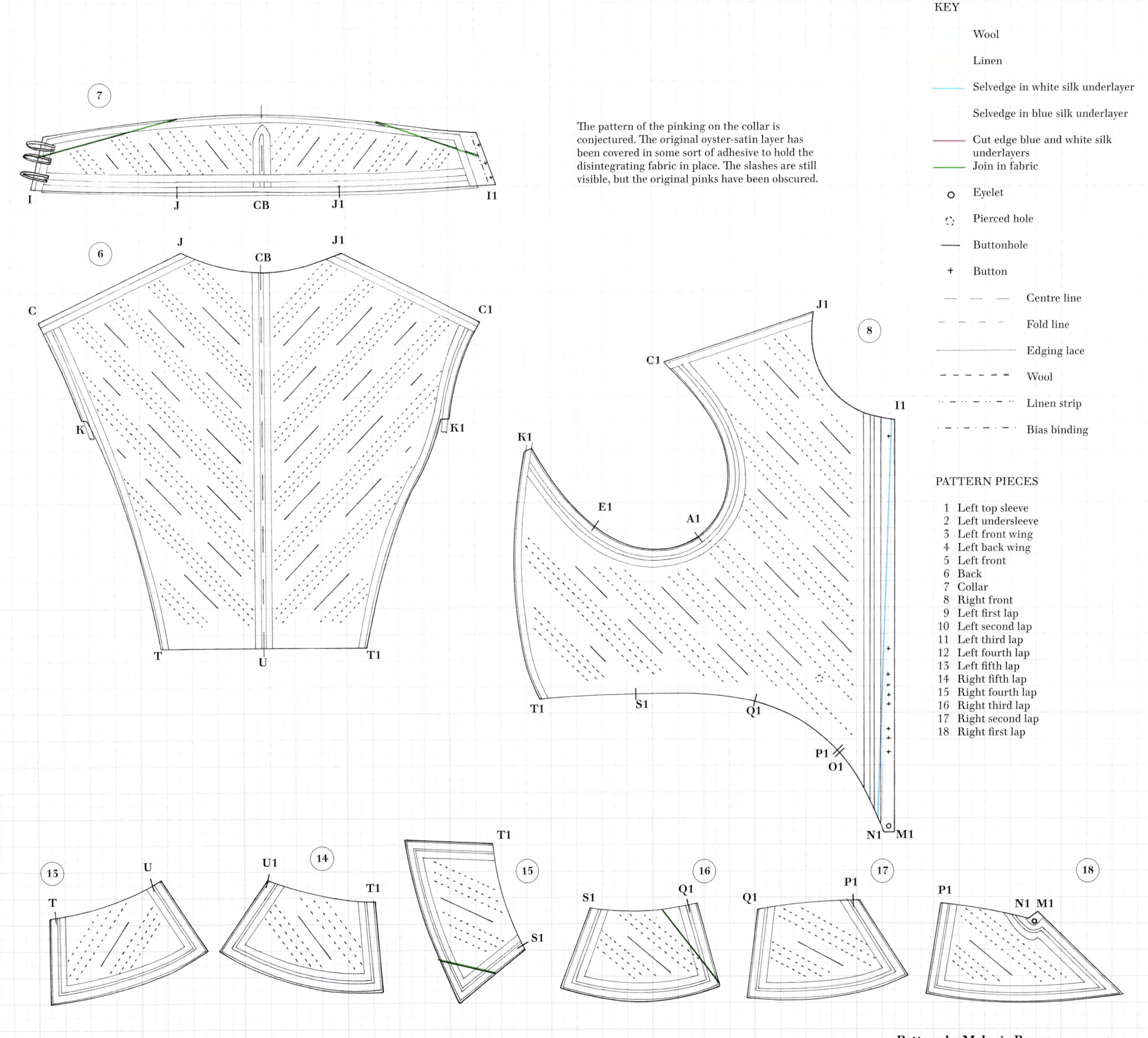

Pattern of the oyster-coloured silk satin outer layer, and blue and white silk underlayers CONTINUED

SCALE 1:4

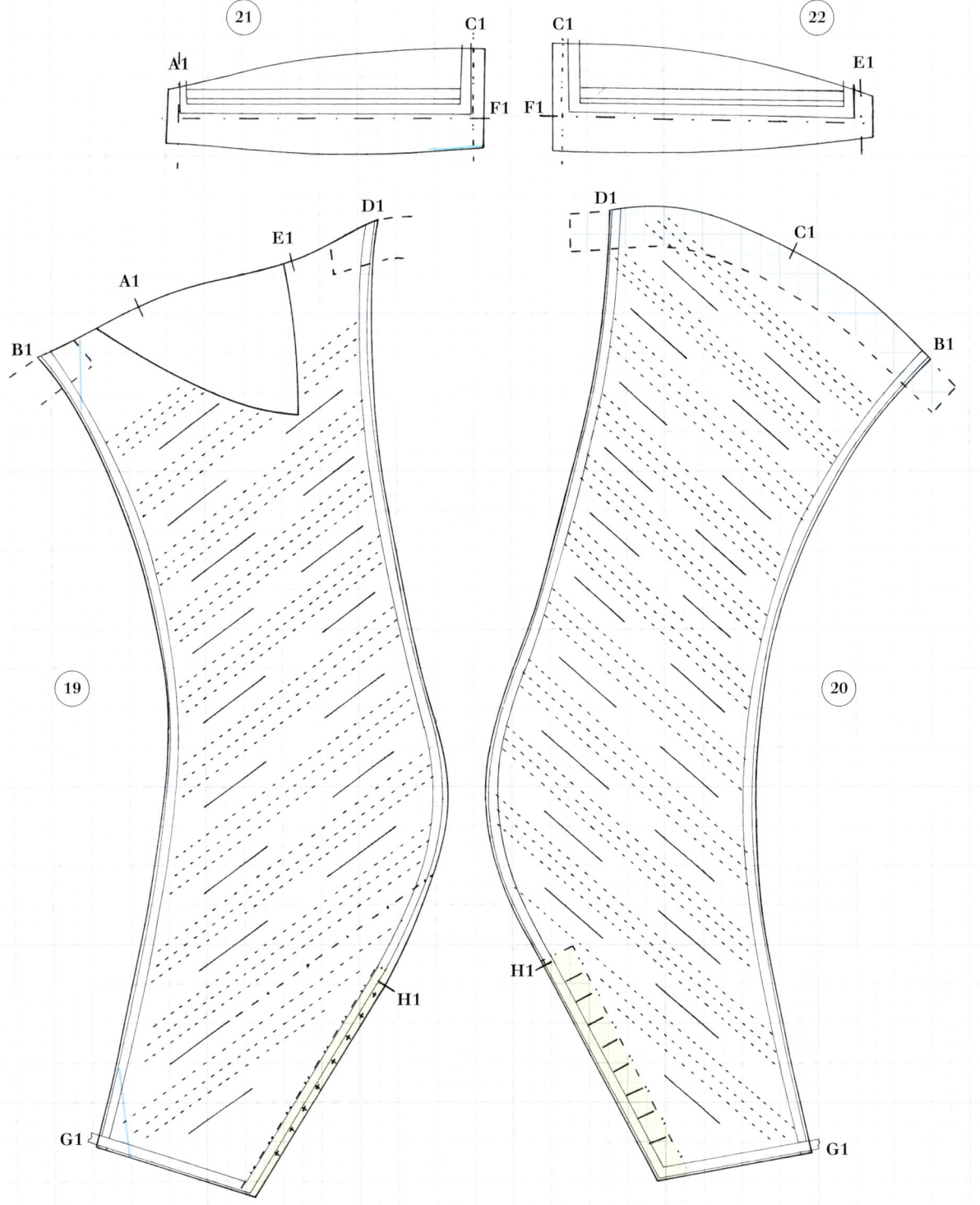

PATTERN PIECES

19 Right undersleeve
20 Right top sleeve
21 Right back wing
22 Right front wing
23 Right wing lining, oyster silk satin
24 Right top sleeve, green silk
25 Right undersleeve, green silk

KEY

Wool
Linen
Selvedge in blue and white silk
Selvedge in the oyster silk satin
Buttonhole
Button
Centre line
Fold line
Edging lace
Wool
Linen strip
Conjectured lining
Rip in fabric

Pattern of the green silk lining

SCALE 1:4

LIST OF MATERIALS

Oyster-coloured silk satin
Blue plain-weave silk
White plain-weave silk
White silk taffeta for the facing
White silk satin for lining the collar
Medium-weight linen
Medium-to-heavy-weight linen or hemp
Heavy-weight linen or hemp
Coarse linen buckram
Green changeable silk (blue warp/yellow weft)
White open-weave wool
Baleen
2 'S' ply linen thread
2 'S' ply silk thread, oyster-coloured
2 'S' ply silk thread, red
Silver and silver-gilt filé edging lace
49 silver and silver-gilt filé covered buttons

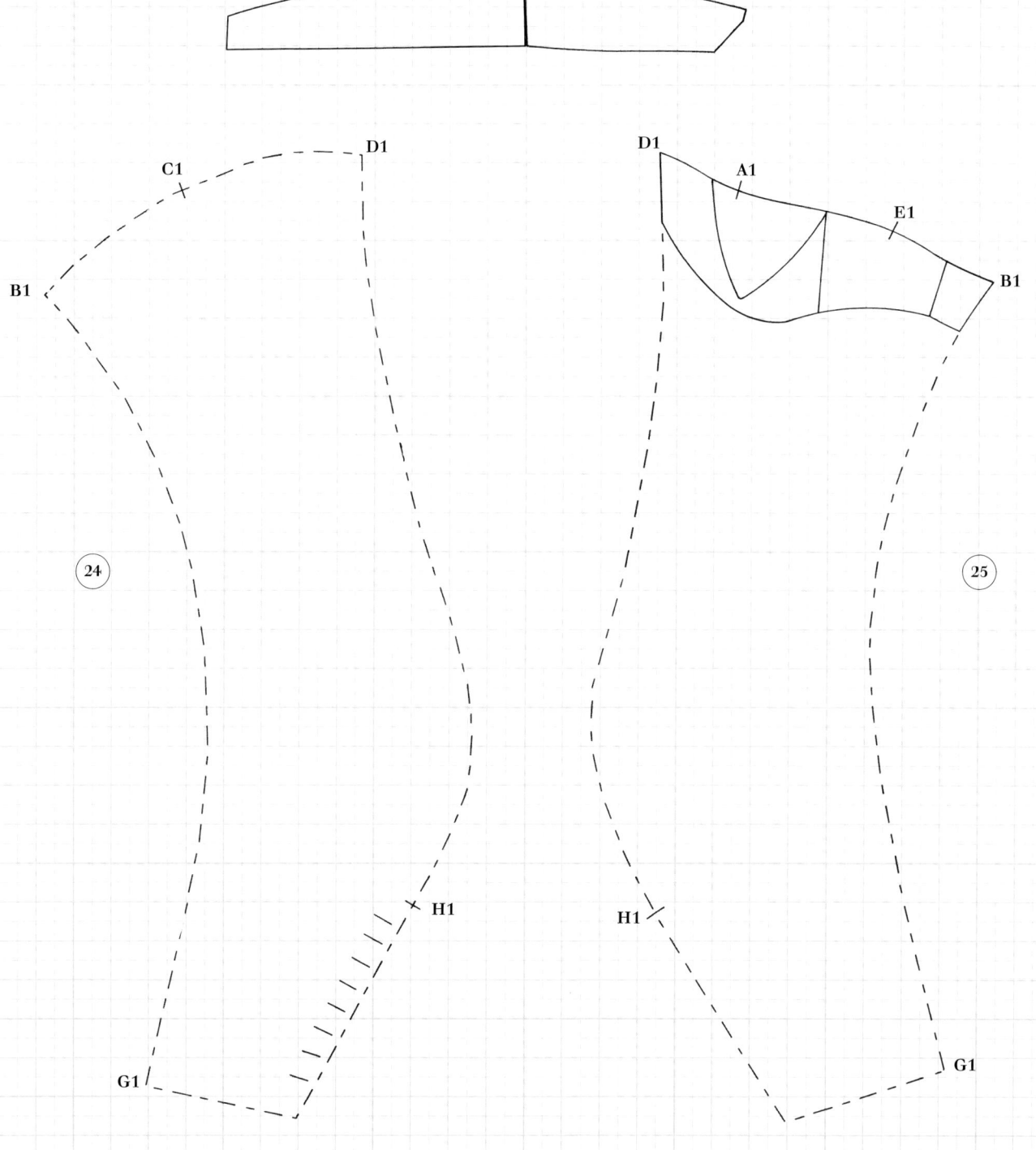

Pattern by Melanie Braun

Pattern of the green silk lining CONTINUED

SCALE 1:4

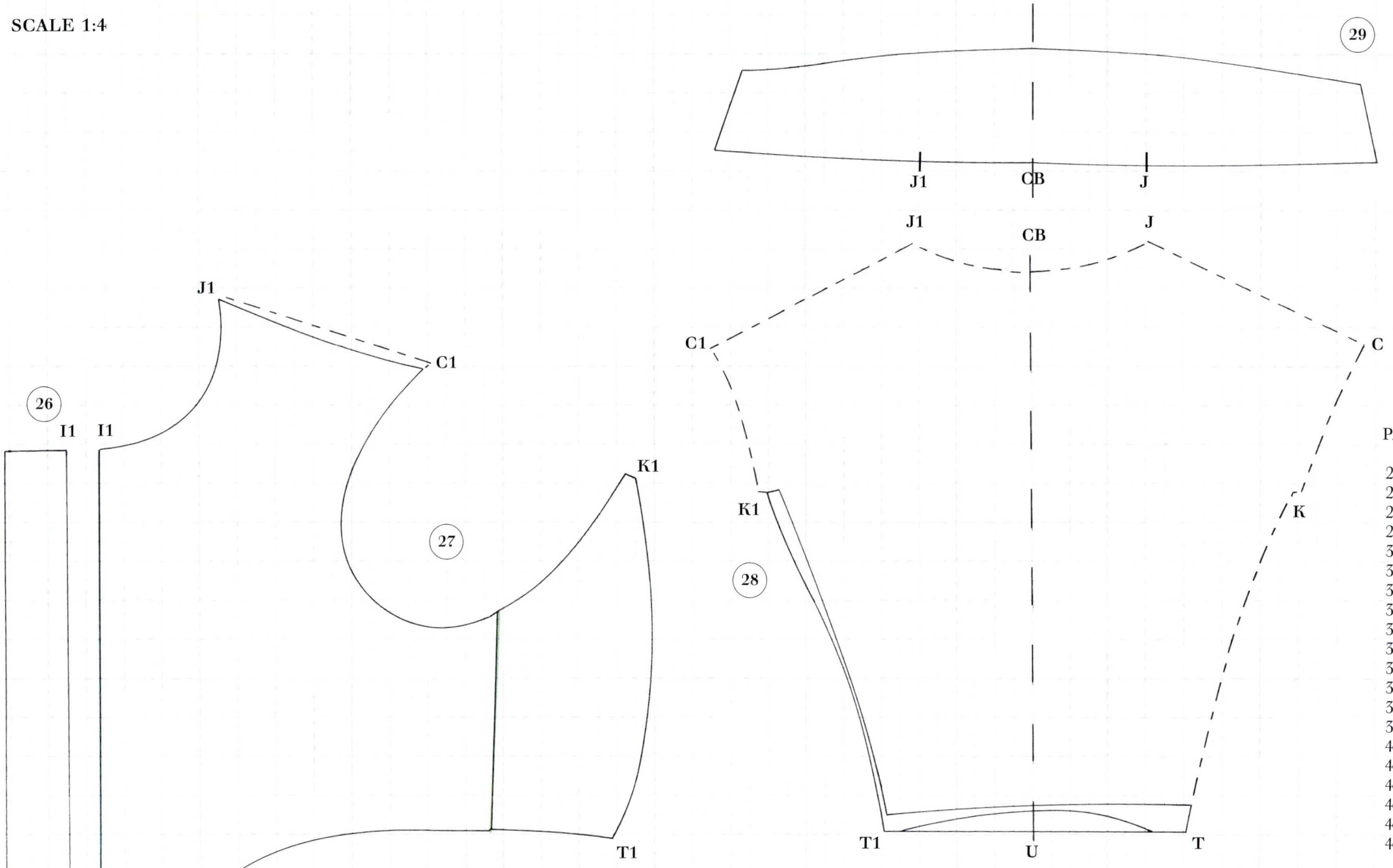

PATTERN PIECES

26 Facing, white taffeta
27 Right front lining
28 Back lining
29 Collar lining, white silk satin
30 Left front
31 Facing, green silk lining
32 Waistband
33 Right first lap
34 Right second lap
35 Right third lap
36 Right fourth lap
37 Right fifth lap
38 Left fifth lap
39 Left fourth lap
40 Left third lap
41 Left second lap
42 Left first lap
43 Left undersleeve
44 Left top sleeve
45 Left wing lining, oyster silk

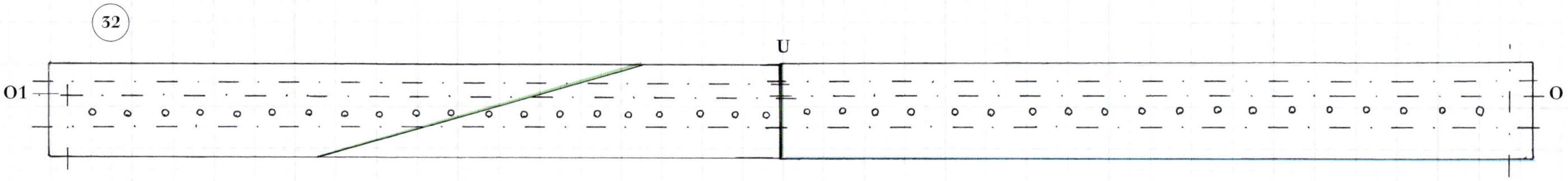

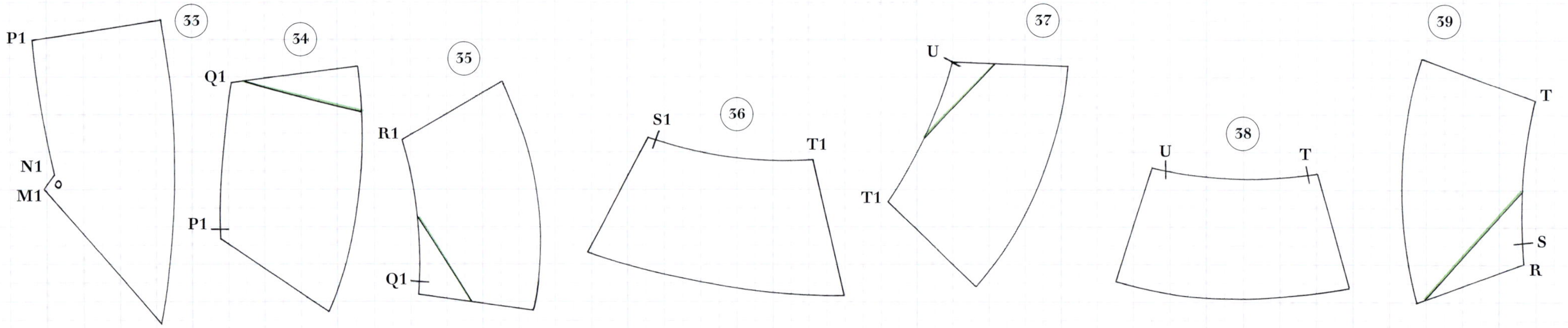

2A | Doublet of slashed silk satin

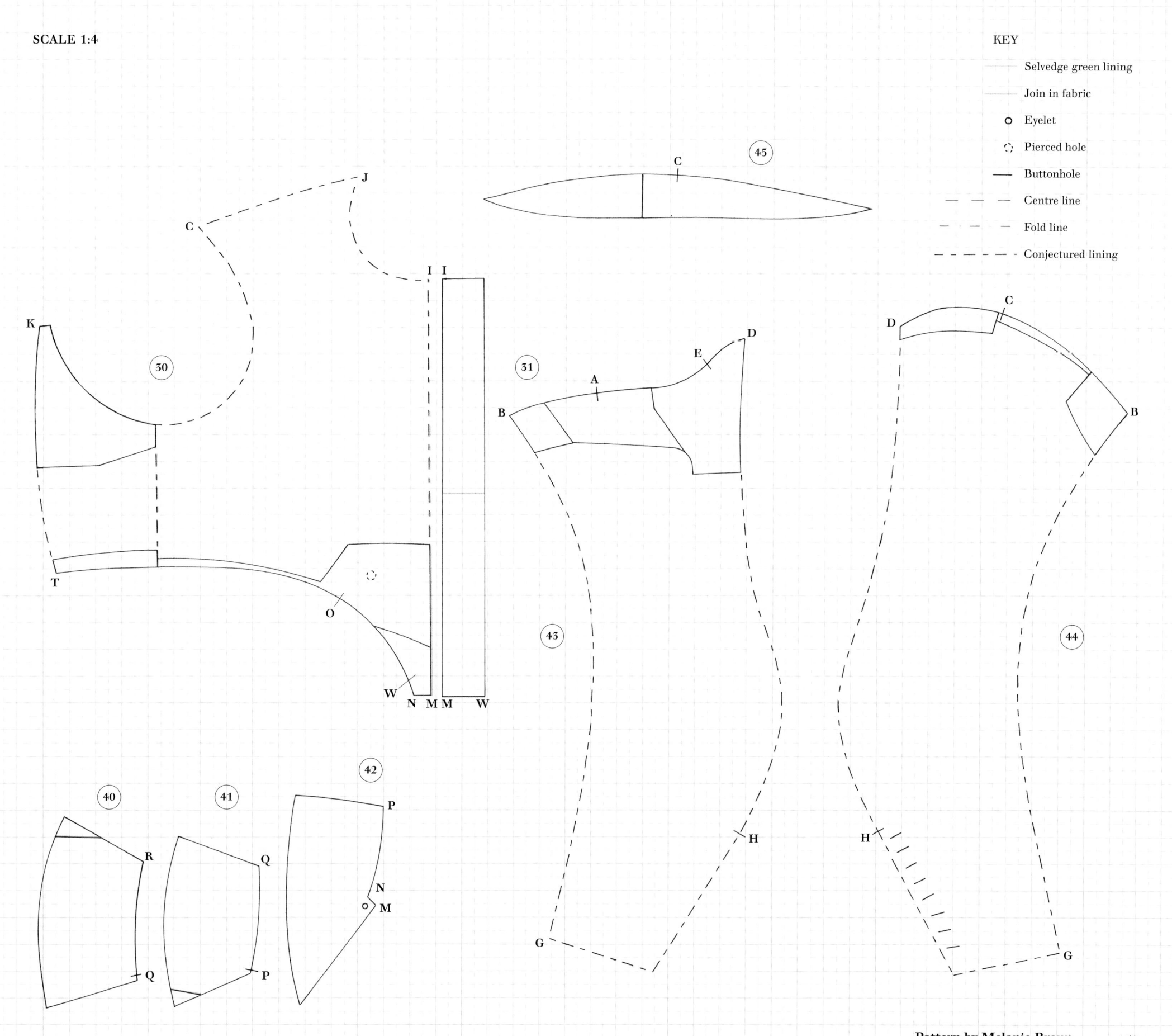

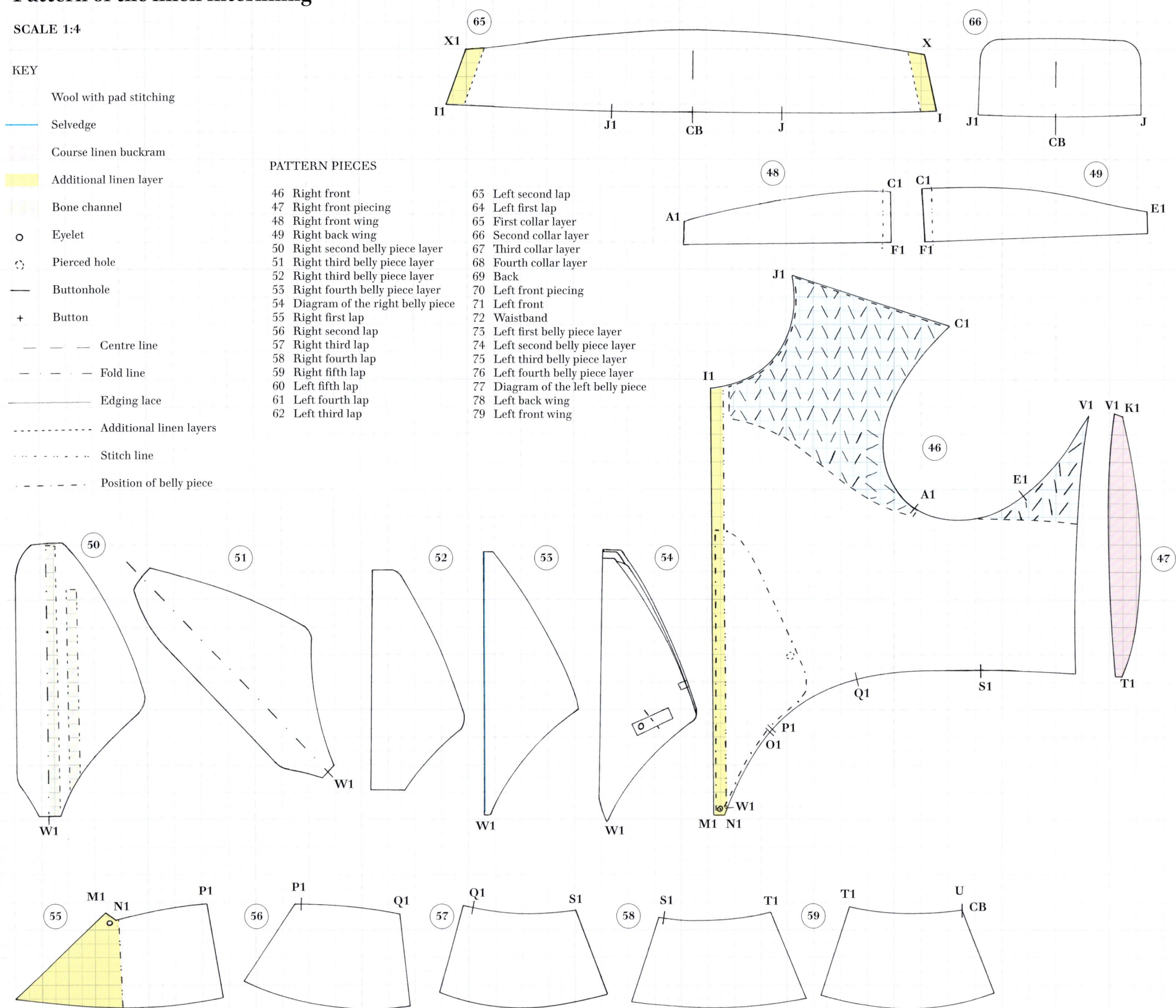

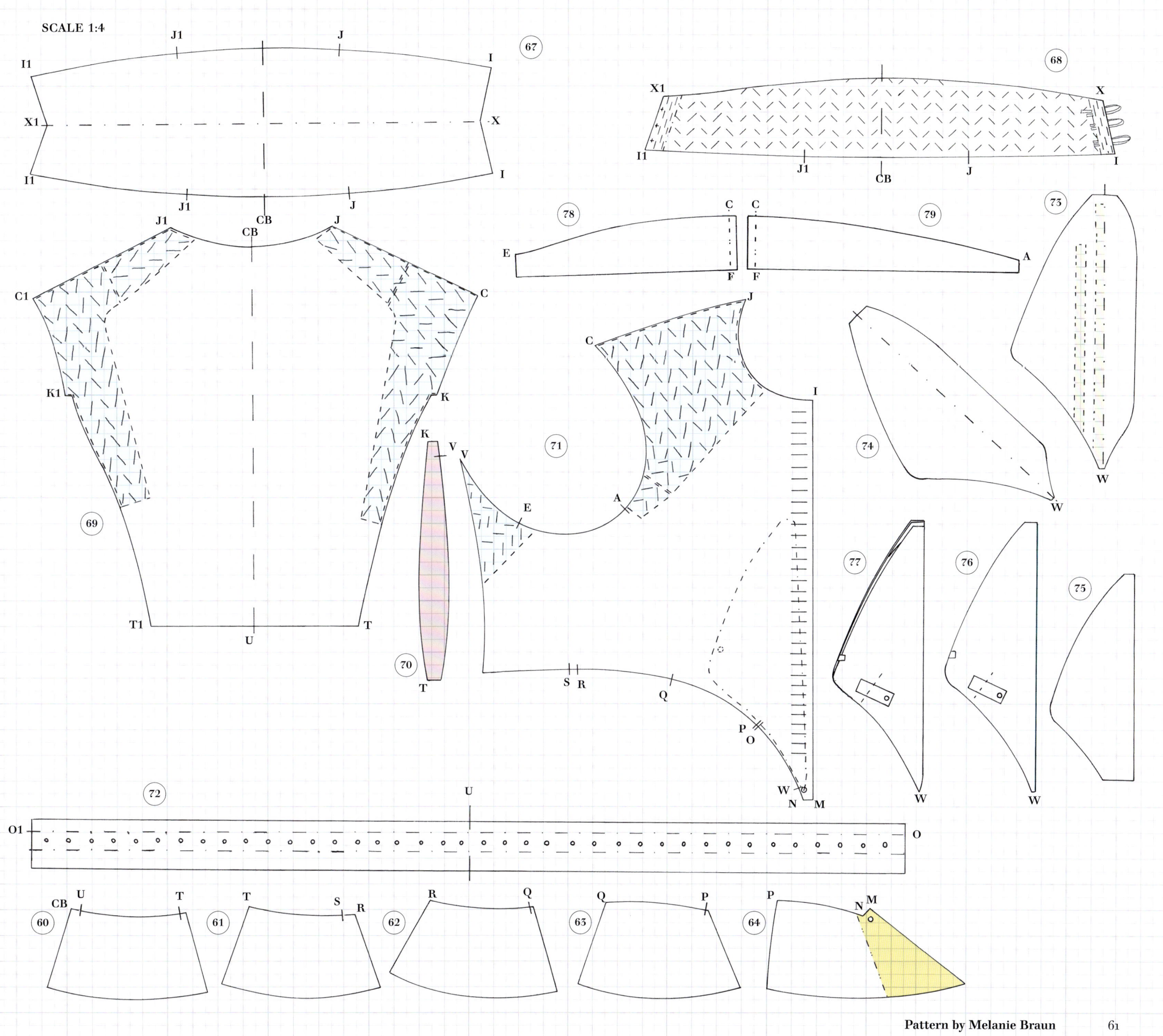

CONSTRUCTION
Construction of the doublet body

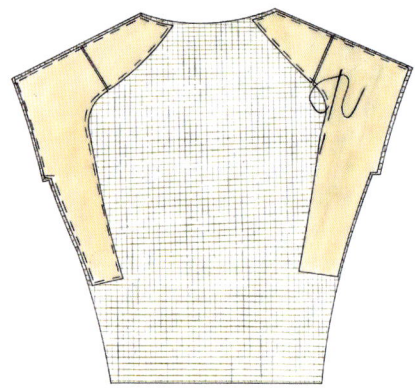

1 The wool and linen interlinings of the back were CUT net. The wool interlining was PLACED on the RS of the linen interlining of the back and BASTED to it around the edges.

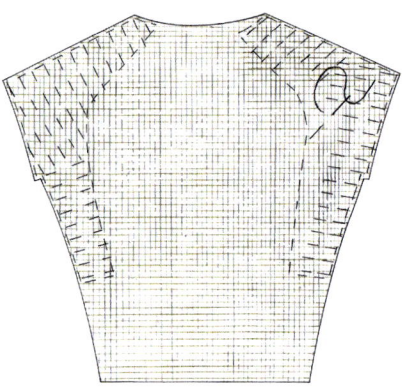

2 The wool interlining was PAD STITCHED from the WS of the linen, inside the basting stitches. While sewing, the shoulder areas were curved over the hand or knee, with the wool on the inside curve.

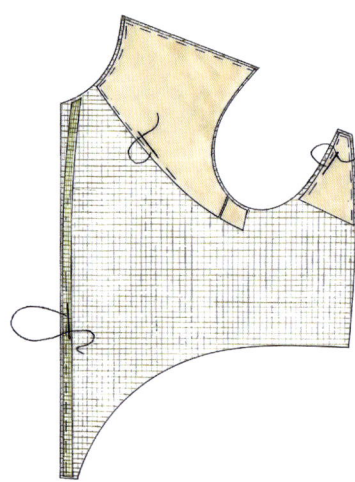

3 The two front interlinings were CUT net at CF, with a seam allowance of about ⅛" on all other edges. The wool interlining was PLACED on the RS of each front linen interlining and BASTED to it around the edges. On the RHS front, a linen strip, about ¼" wide, was RUNNING STITCHED to the CF to support the buttons when they were sewn on later.

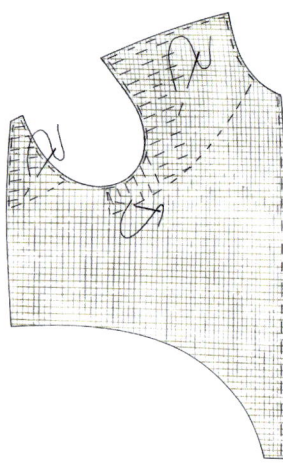

4 The wool interlinings were PAD STITCHED from the WS of the linen fronts, curving them over the hand or knee, with the wool on the inside curve.

For a fitting, the linen back and two fronts were *probably* BASTED together; the interlinings of the collar may have also been BASTED to the neckline. The doublet interlining may have been too tight, as another strip of linen was added to the side seam (see figs 2.21 and 2.22, page 51).

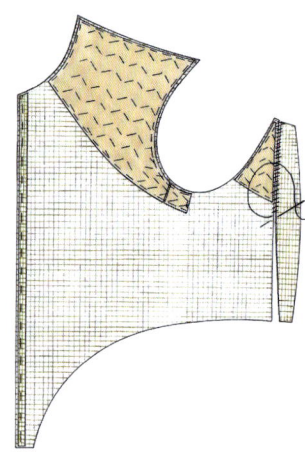

5 A small piece of coarse linen buckram was finely WHIP STITCHED, with linen thread, to each front at the side seam.

With the shape and size of the doublet now established, the silk layers of the fronts, sleeves, back and laps were CUT in the oyster silk satin, the blue silk and the white silk underlayers. The green silk linings were *probably* CUT as well.

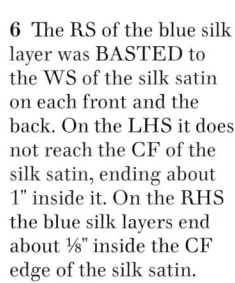
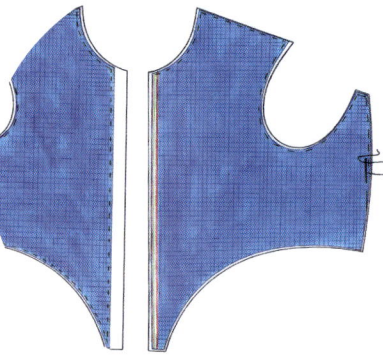

6 The RS of the blue silk layer was BASTED to the WS of the silk satin on each front and the back. On the LHS it does not reach the CF of the silk satin, ending about 1" inside it. On the RHS the blue silk layers end about ⅛" inside the CF edge of the silk satin.

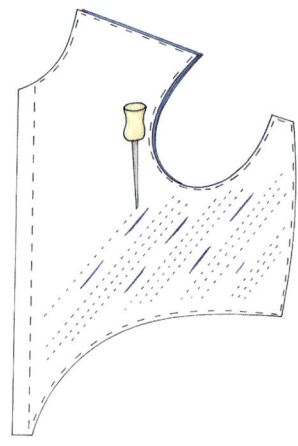

7 With WS together, the two fronts were SLASHED and PINKED, working from the RS through all the layers. (The decoration of the fronts is mirror-imaged.) The same was done for the back.

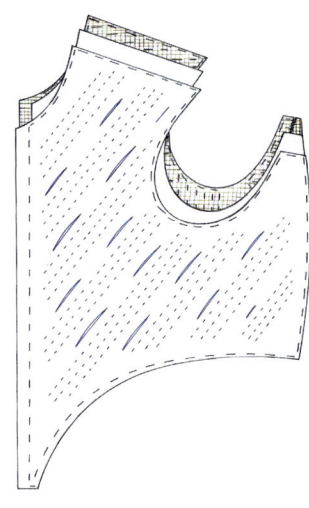

8 The WS of the slashed layer was PLACED on the RS of the white silk layer. The WS of the white silk layer was PLACED on the WS of the interlining. The same was done for the back.

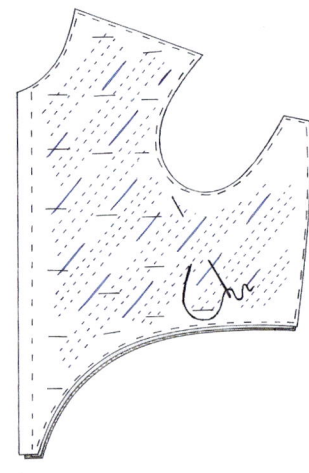

9 The three layers were BASTED together all over, *probably* using a large PAD STITCH on the fronts and the back.

2A | Doublet of slashed silk satin

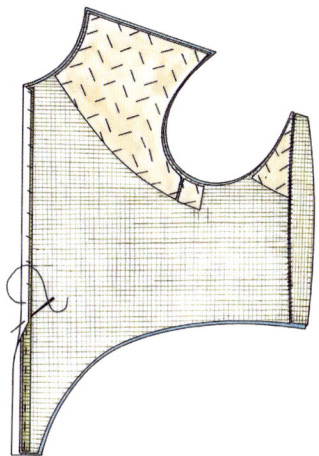

10 The CF seam allowances of just under ⅛" on both fronts were FOLDED to the WS and FELLED to the linen interlining.

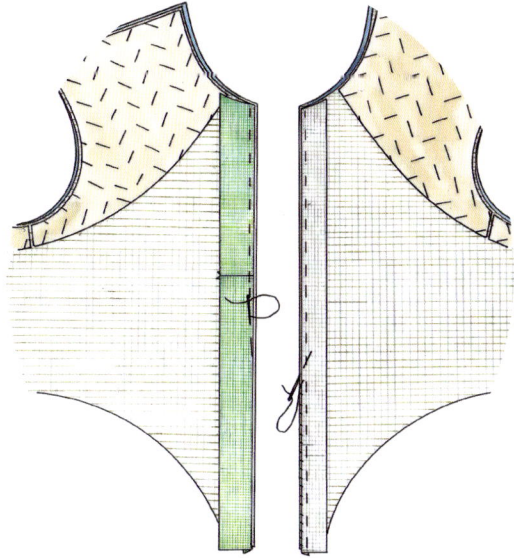

11 The green silk facing was BASTED to the WS of the LHS CF edge and then FELLED with small stitches to the silk satin. On the RHS the white silk taffeta facing was BASTED and FELLED to the CF edge. Both facings were left ¼" longer than the CF. These were later FOLDED to allow the doublet to be fastened.

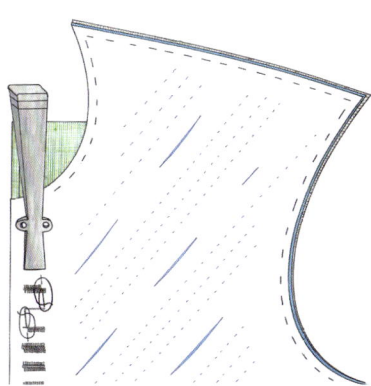

12 Thirty-three buttonholes were made on the LHS, about ¼" from the CF edge, each ¾" in length and ¾" to 1" apart. The buttonholes were *probably* CUT one at a time, to minimize stretching, and BUTTONHOLE STITCHED, working from left to right.

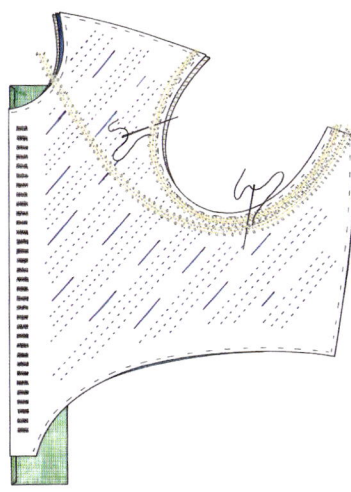

13 Two rows of the silver and silver-gilt edging lace were CATCH STITCHED to the net shape of the armhole about ⅛" apart.

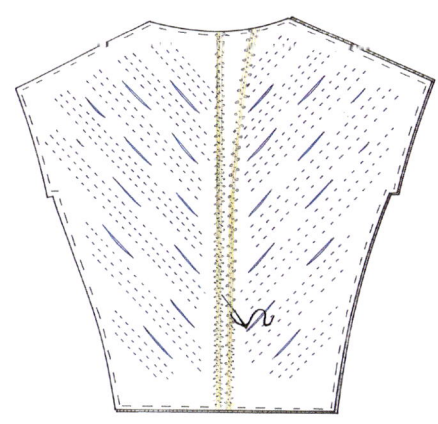

14 On the back, a length of edging lace was CATCH STITCHED to the left and right of the CB, leaving a gap of ⅛".

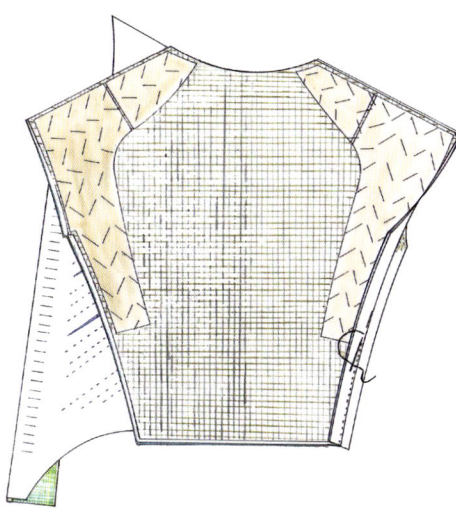

15 With RS together, the back was PLACED over the front. The side-back-seam allowance of the silk layers of the back was FOLDED to the WS along the edge of its net interlining. It was PRICK STITCHED to the seam allowance of the front, with white silk thread, stitching through all layers of the back and front. The back was sewn to the other front in the same way.

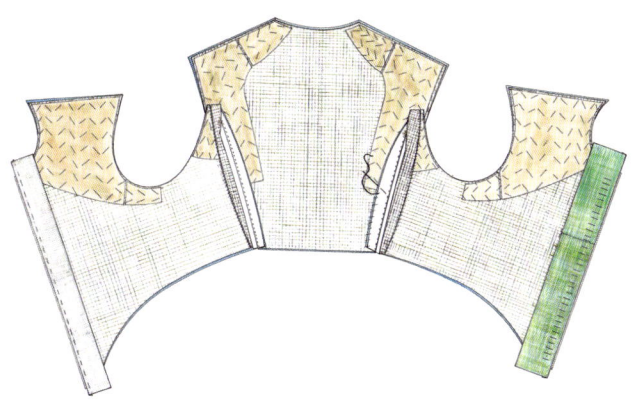

16 The seam allowances of the back were FELLED to the interlining.

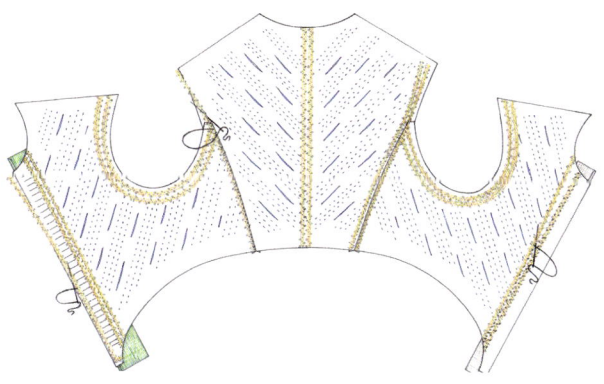

17 Edging lace was CATCH STITCHED to the RS of the doublet. On the CF of the LHS there are two lengths inside the buttonholes ⅛" apart, and a third length at CF: the first one covers the ends of the buttonholes. There are two lengths on each side of the side seams – on the front the lace just covers the side seam with the parallel lace about ⅛" away on the back. Both continue around the net shape of the back armhole. On the RHS front the two laces are 1" from the CF edge; the second one about ⅛" from the first.

Construction of the laps

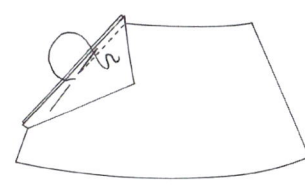

18 The piecings in the silk satin layer were *probably* RUNNING STITCHED together.

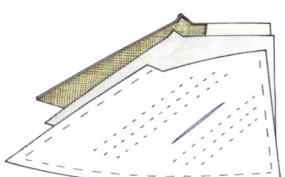

19 The extra layer of linen for the two front laps on each side was CUT net and PLACED on top of the linen interlining.

For all the laps: the WS of the silk satin layer was BASTED to the RS of the blue silk layer. They were PLACED, WS together, in pairs and SLASHED and PINKED. The interlinings for all the laps were CUT net. The RS of the white silk was PLACED on the WS of the blue silk. The WS of the interlining was PLACED on the WS of the white silk layer. All three layers were BASTED together.

Pattern by Melanie Braun

Construction of the laps CONTINUED

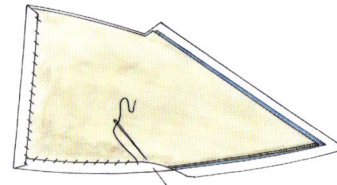

20 On all laps, the ⅛" seam allowances of the silk layers were FOLDED to the WS and FELLED to the interlining, on the sides and bottom.

21 Two rows of edging lace were CATCH STITCHED to the sides and bottom edges of all 10 laps: the first row on the outside edge, the second row about ⅛" from the first. On the two front laps, the lace continued around the square at the top front corner of each.

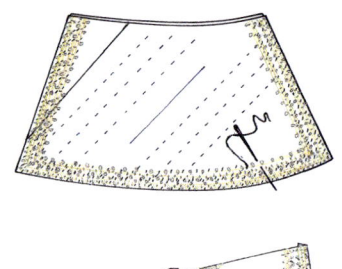
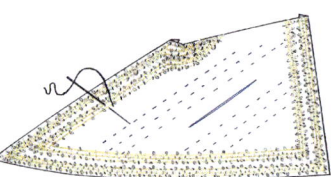

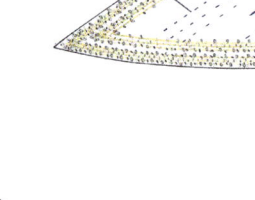

22a The green silk linings for the laps were PLACED on the lap interlinings, WS together. The ⅛" seam allowances of the linings were FOLDED to the WS and FELLED to the silk satin, with silk thread.

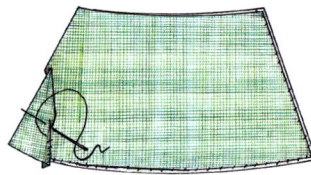

22b The piecings in the lining of laps 34, 35, 37, 39, 40 and 41 were joined with FELLING STITCHES while the outer edge of the laps was FELLED.

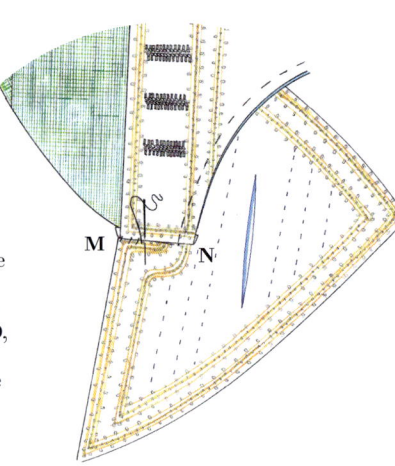

23a The seam allowance between M and N on the LHS doublet front was FOLDED to the WS. The front lap was PLACED beneath. This 'step' in the waist seam was FELLED, on the RS, with about four stitches. Keeping the thread, the doublet was TURNED to its WS.

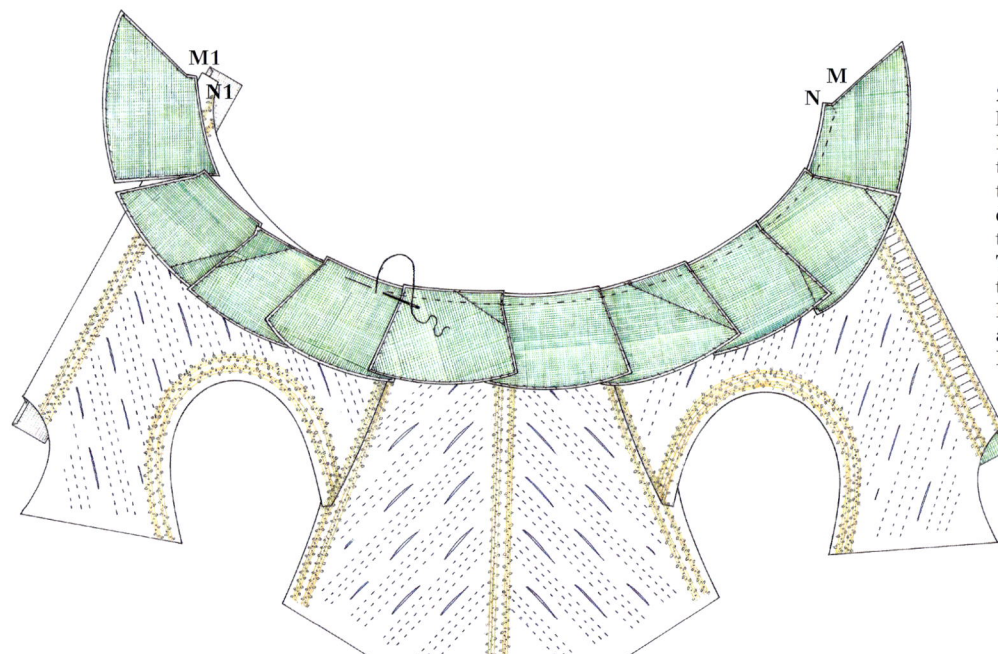

23b The top edge of the front lap and the next eight laps were BACK STITCHED, RS together, to the doublet. At point N1, the seam allowance of the RHS doublet front was FOLDED to the WS. The doublet was TURNED BACK to its RS and the 'step' in the waist seam was FELLED on the RS between N1 and M1, as it was done for the LHS, with about four stitches.

Construction of the waistband of eyelets

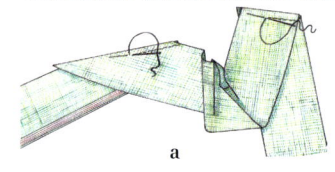
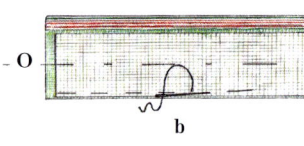
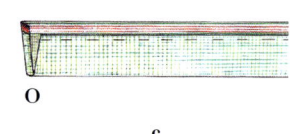
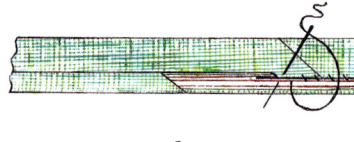

a　　　　　b　　　　　c　　　　　d

24a The piecings of the green silk strip for the lacing band were *probably* RUNNING STITCHED together. Part of one long edge of the waistband is a selvedge. **b** The linen interlining of the waistband was CUT net. With WS together, the interlining and green silk were BASTED together, leaving a seam allowance of ¼" on one edge.

c The waistband was first FOLDED lengthways, along the fold marked on the interlining pattern. **d** The seam allowance was FOLDED in by less than ⅛" and over the cut edge. The hem was FELLED to the green silk.

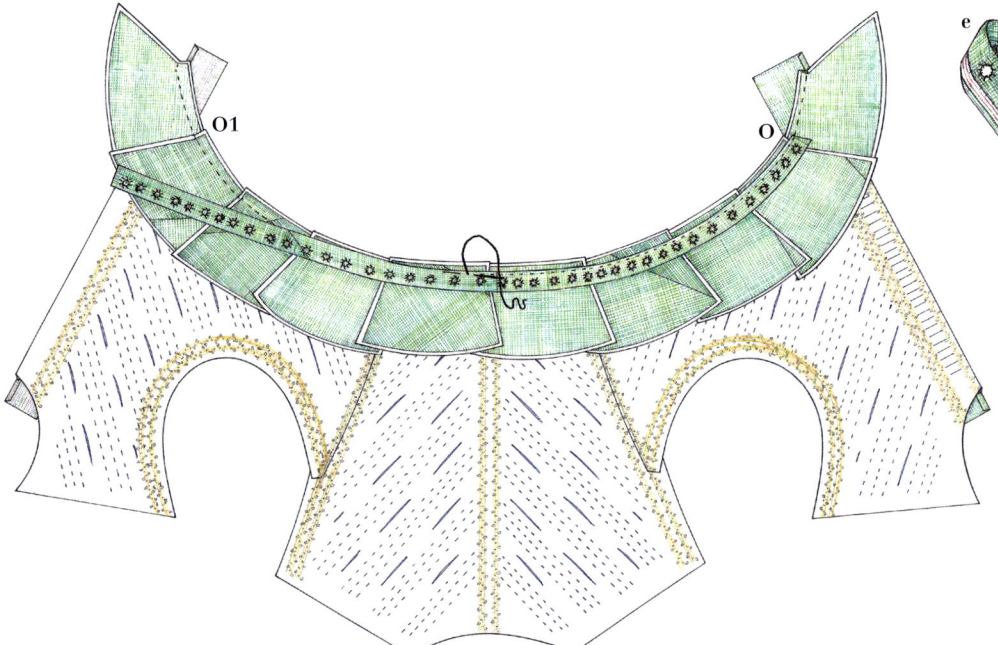

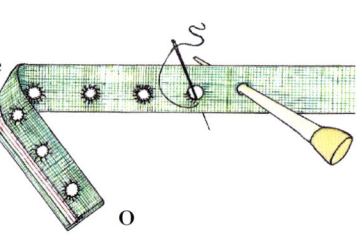

24e Forty holes, ⅝" apart, were PIERCED with a bodkin just above the waistband hem. They were then WHIPPED with silk thread.

25 The lacing band was HALF-BACK STITCHED to the WS of the waist edge of the doublet body, from O to O1, stitching through the back stitches in the laps underneath.

The seam allowances of the waist seam were TRIMMED to about ⅛" and GLUED or WAXED to prevent fraying.

2A | Doublet of slashed silk satin

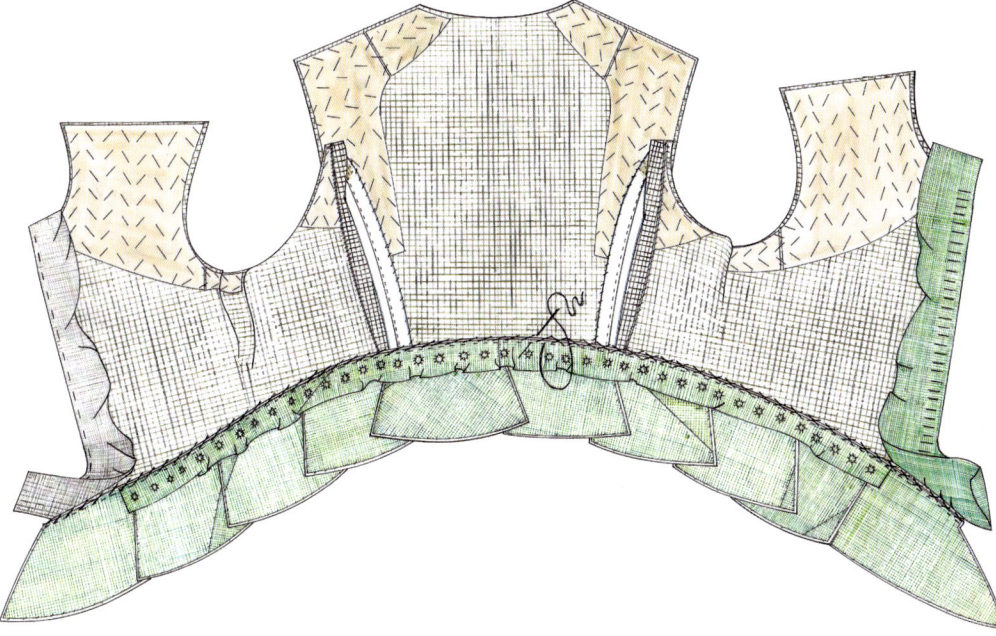

26 The waist seam allowances were FOLDED to the doublet interlining and FELLED, first with a row of stitches from right to left, and then with a continuous thread, from left to right.

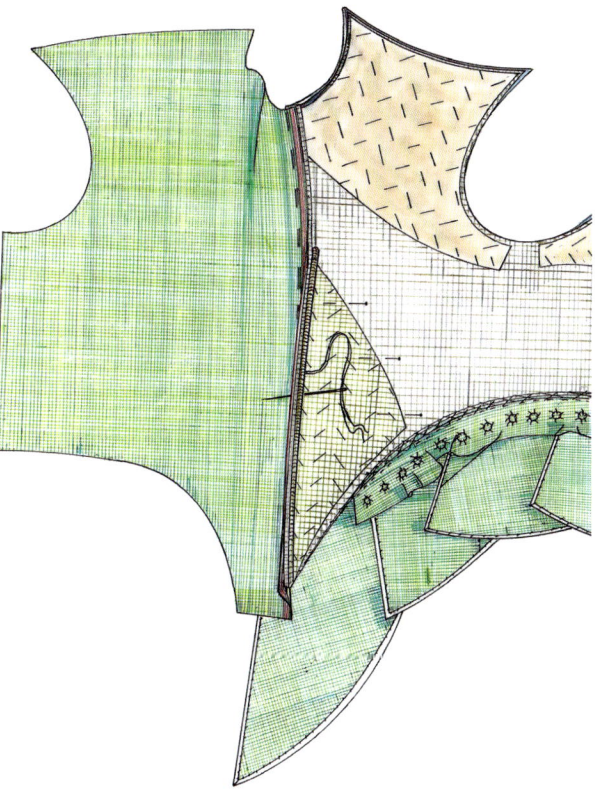

Construction of the belly pieces

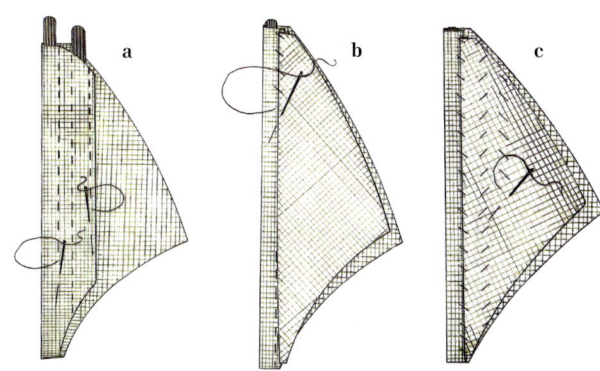

27a All the belly piece panels were CUT net. The front edges of the linen belly piece panels (numbers 50 and 73) were FOLDED to the WS. Three rows of RUNNING STITCHES were sewn parallel to the fold. A strip of baleen was INSERTED in each channel. **b** The front edges of the linen belly piece panels (numbers 51 and 74) were FOLDED to the WS. They were PLACED, WS together, onto the baleen panels, lining up with the running stitches closest to the folded edge. They were FELLED together at the folded edges, just behind the outside baleen strip. **c** The layers were PAD STITCHED together. **d** Linen panels (numbers 52 and 75) were PLACED closer to the folded edge of the baleen panel, lining up with the cut edges on the opposite side. The pieces were PAD STITCHED together. **e** Linen panels (numbers 53 and 76) were PLACED with their selvedges on the folded baleen edge and FELLED to the baleen panel. The panel was PAD STITCHED through all the layers. The first row of pad stitches inside the folded edge was worked between the two strips of baleen.

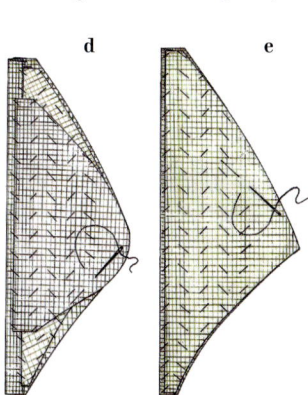

28 On both fronts the facings were FOLDED lengthways to their RS. The straight edges of the belly pieces were PLACED at the CF of the doublet fronts, the bottom point fitting between points M/M1 and N/N1, with the curved lower edge right on the seam allowance of the doublet waist seam. The top of the belly piece was set back from the CF, with about ½" more on the buttonhole side than on the button side to allow for buttoning up the doublet. The belly pieces were *probably* PINNED in place.

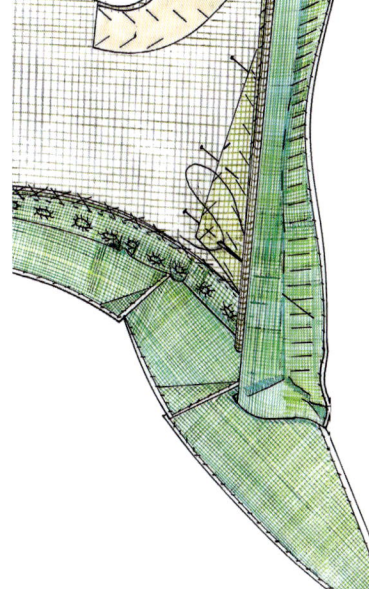

29 The facings at CF were UNFOLDED flat. Each facing was RUNNING STITCHED with a STAB STITCH to each belly piece down the centre of the facing's fold, from the RS, between the two strips of baleen with linen thread. The ¼" seam allowance of the bottom edge remained untouched.

30 The CF of the WS of the green silk lining was PLACED on the RS of the CF facing, along its fold. These two layers and the belly piece were RUNNING STITCHED together, along the crease, with doubled linen thread, stabbing the needle between the two strips of baleen. The stitching stopping at the bottom of the belly piece, leaving the bottom seam allowance on each CF facing.

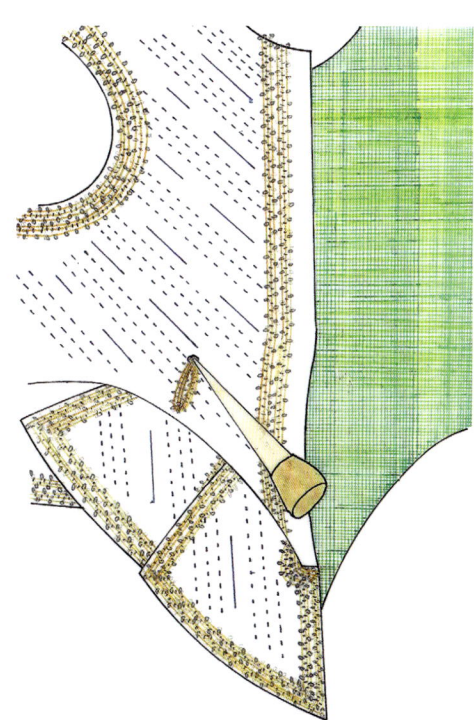

31 A hole was PIERCED in each doublet front and the ends of a 5½" length of edging lace were PUSHED from the RS of the doublet through to the WS, making the loop for the sword girdle.

Pattern by Melanie Braun

Construction of the belly pieces   CONTINUED

32a The interlining of the lacing tabs for the inside of the doublet were CUT net. It was PLACED on the green silk lining tab cut from the cabbage. The seam allowances of the green silk were FOLDED to the WS, on all sides, and BASTED to the interlining on two sides. **b** The lacing tab was FOLDED in half, lengthways, and FELLED, with small stitches, on three sides. **c** An eyelet was PIERCED with a bodkin and WHIPPED with silk thread on both tabs.

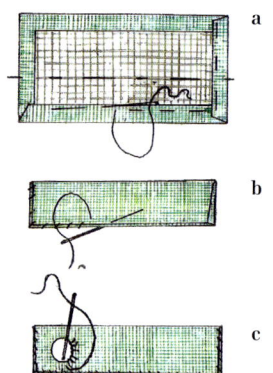

33 The unpierced end of the lacing tab was FELLED around three edges, with linen thread, to the belly piece. The ends of the lace from step 31 were FOLDED over the edge of the belly piece and FELLED to it with linen thread. The pinned edges of the belly piece were FELLED to the interlining, with linen thread, starting at the waist seam of the doublet.

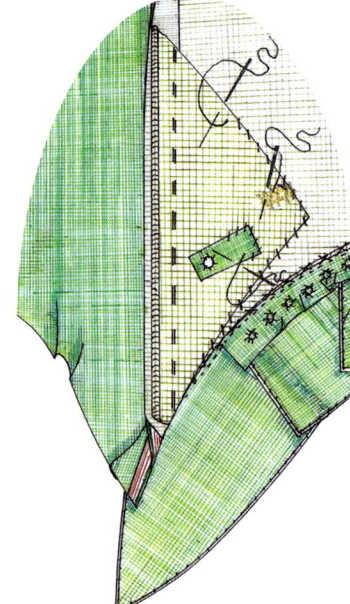

34 On both fronts, the bottom seam allowances of the facings were FOLDED to their WS, between points M/M1 and N/N1. These were FELLED, with small stitches, to the waist seam of the doublet, from M/M1 to N/N1 and only to the fold in the centre of the facing. The lining of the doublet remained unattached.

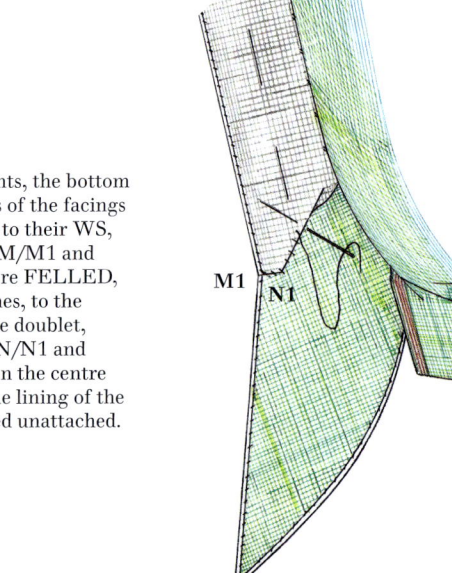

35 One eyelet was PIERCED, right at the bottom of each peak, and WHIPPED with silk thread. Below this pair, two more eyelets were PIERCED, one in the upper corner of each front lap and WHIPPED with silk thread.

36 Thirty-three buttons were sewn to the RHS. Working from the neckline down, the doublet and its lining were spread open and the top 10 buttons were STITCHED, ⅛" away from the CF edge, only to the interlining. From button 11 down, the remaining buttons were STITCHED, ⅛" away from the CF edge, through the white silk facing. **a** The buttons were STITCHED with linen thread, through the core of each button, adding a length of purl at the top (see figs 2.14 and 2.15, page 51). **b** These threads were then wrapped to make the button shank; the linen thread was carried over to the next button.

37 A hole was PIERCED, with a bodkin, in the front lining and the lacing tab was PULLED through to the RS of the lining. The piecings of the front linings were *probably* RUNNING STITCHED.

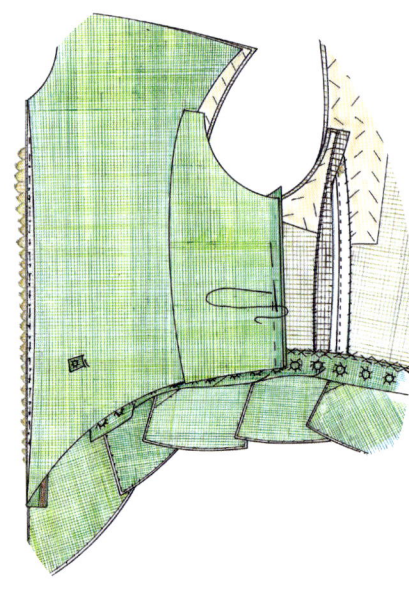

38 A rectangular off-cut of the oyster silk satin was FOLDED in half, RS together, and PLACED over the side seam at the back, covering the small bit of metal edging lace. It was then BASTED. With WS together, the back lining was FELLED to the seam allowances of the front of the side seams, covering the seam allowances of the doublet body.

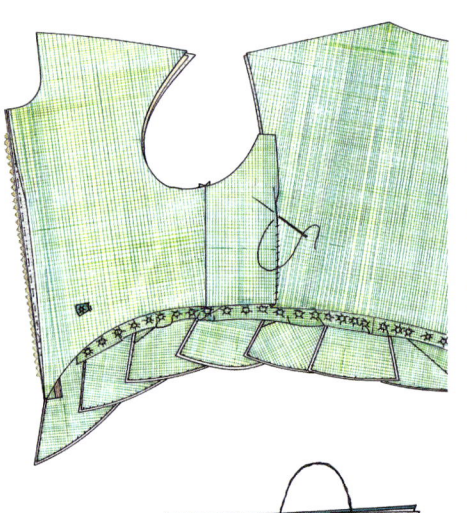

39 The side-seam allowances of the front linings were FOLDED to their WS, aligned with the side seams of the doublet beneath and FELLED to the back lining, with small stitches.

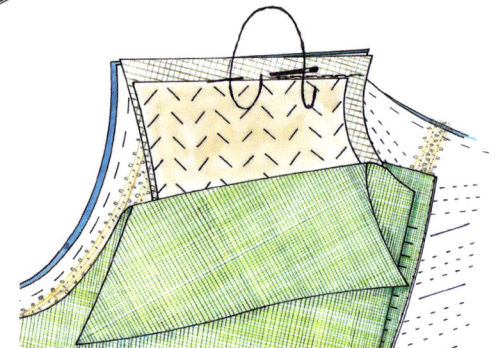

40 With RS together, the back and front shoulders of the doublet were BACK STITCHED, with the lining held out of the way. The LHS is shown; this was repeated for the RHS.

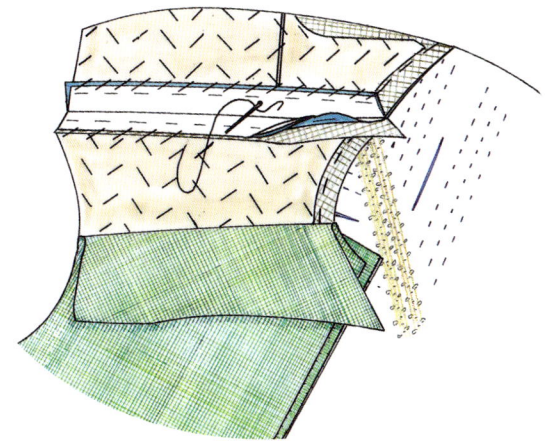

41 The seam allowances of both shoulders were OPENED and FELLED to the wool interlining with linen thread.

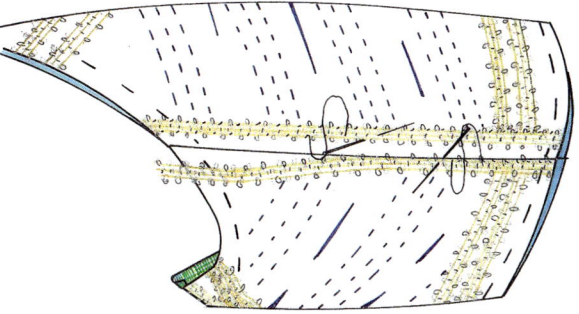

42 On the RS, two rows of edging lace were CATCH STITCHED to each shoulder: one length on the front shoulder covering the shoulder seam, the second ⅛" away from the first, on the back of the doublet.

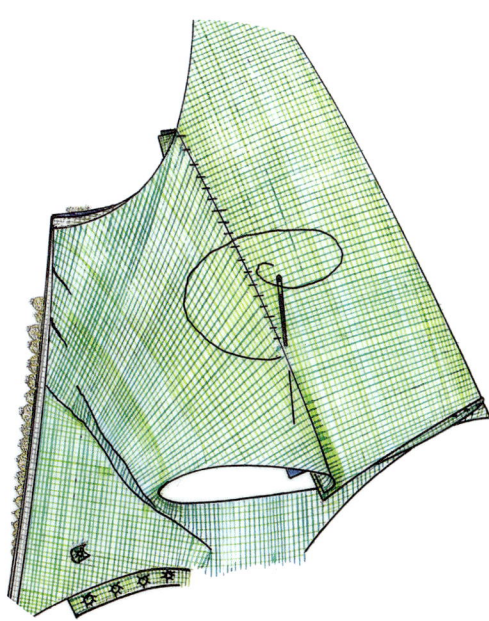

43 The seam allowances of the front linings were FOLDED to their WS and *probably* FELLED, along the shoulder seam, to the back lining.

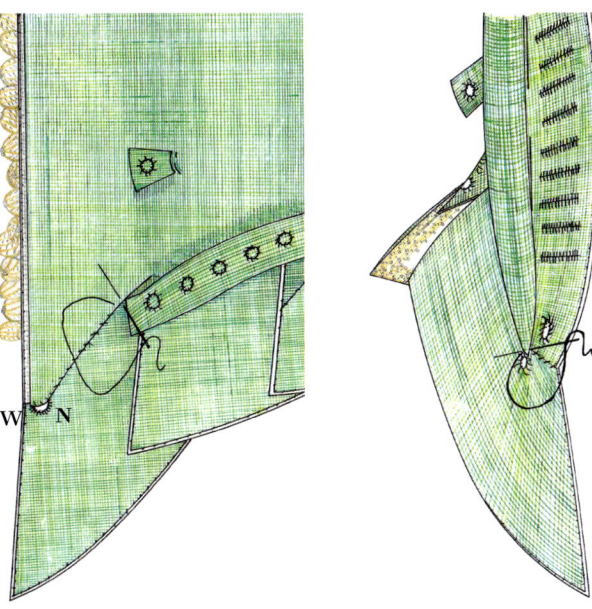

44 Following on from step 34, the seam allowance at the bottom of the lining at the RHS CF was FOLDED to its WS and FELLED to the remaining bottom seam allowance of the white facing, along the lower curve of the belly piece. From point N the lining was FELLED to the waistline of the doublet, stitching through the half-back stitches in the lacing band underneath. At the LHS CF, the bottom seam allowance of the lining was FELLED to the remaining bottom seam allowance of the green facing. This left both facings free of the belly pieces above the waist, so the points could thread through the eyelet holes.

Construction of the wings
The construction of the right wing is shown here

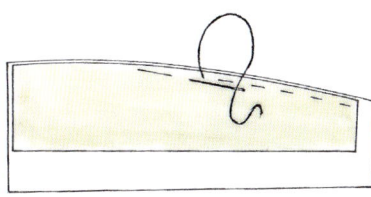

45 The four pieces of interlining for the wings were CUT net and the oyster silk satin wings were CUT from the cabbage. The RS of the interlining was PLACED on the WS of the satin wing, lining up the curved top edges. These were BASTED together.

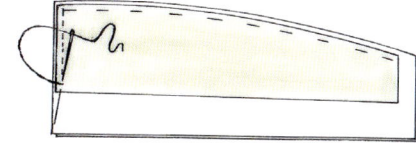

46 With RS together, the front and back wings were *probably* BACK STITCHED, along the shoulder seam, with a ⅛" seam allowance.

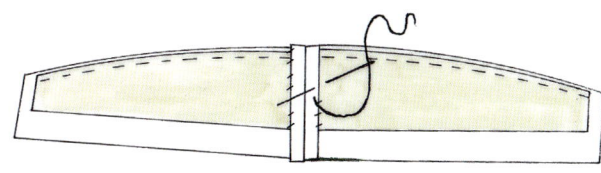

47 The seam allowances were FOLDED open and FELLED to the WS.

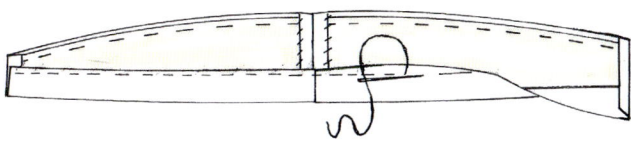

48 The seam allowances at the sides of each wing were FOLDED to the WS. The wide seam allowance at the bottom edge was FOLDED to the WS and RUNNING STITCHED to the interlining.

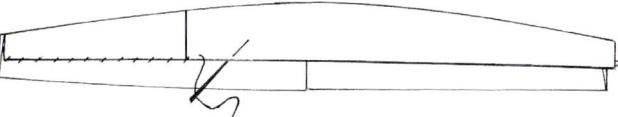

49 The oyster-satin lining piecings were RUNNING STITCHED. The linings were PLACED on the wings, WS together, lining up the curved edges. The seam allowances at the bottom of the linings were FOLDED to the WS and FELLED to the wing, with white silk thread.

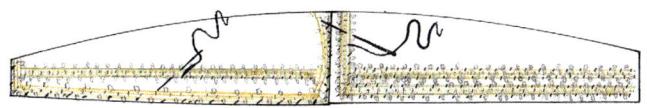

50 One length of edging lace was CATCH STITCHED to the front of the wing, down the shoulder seam and along the lower front edge. Another length was sewn ⅛" away from the first; two lengths of lace were sewn to the back of the wing in the same way.

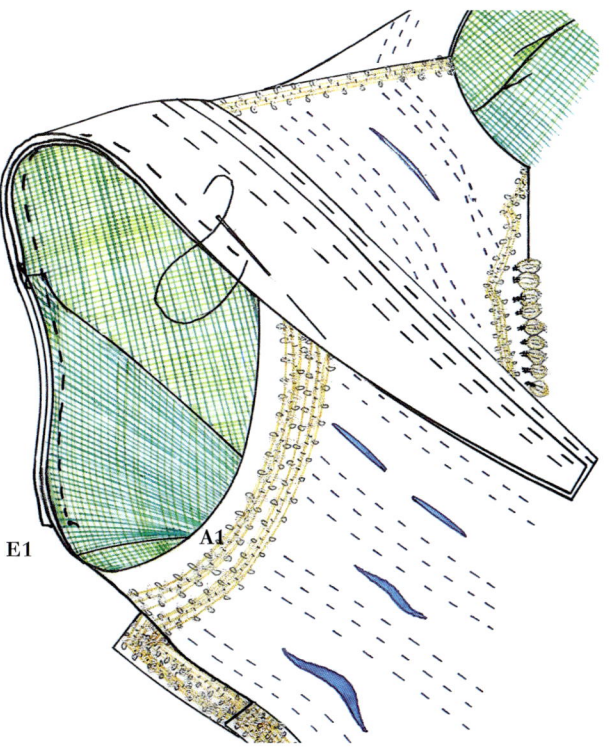

51 With RS together, the wings were PLACED around the armhole of the doublet and RUNNING STITCHED between points A/A1 and E/E1.

Pattern by Melanie Braun

Construction of the sleeves

52 The RS of the blue silk top sleeves were PLACED on the WS of the oyster-satin top sleeves and BASTED together around all edges. With WS together, the top sleeves were SLASHED and PINKED with a sharp blade (the decoration is mirror-imaged). The undersleeves were decorated in the same way.

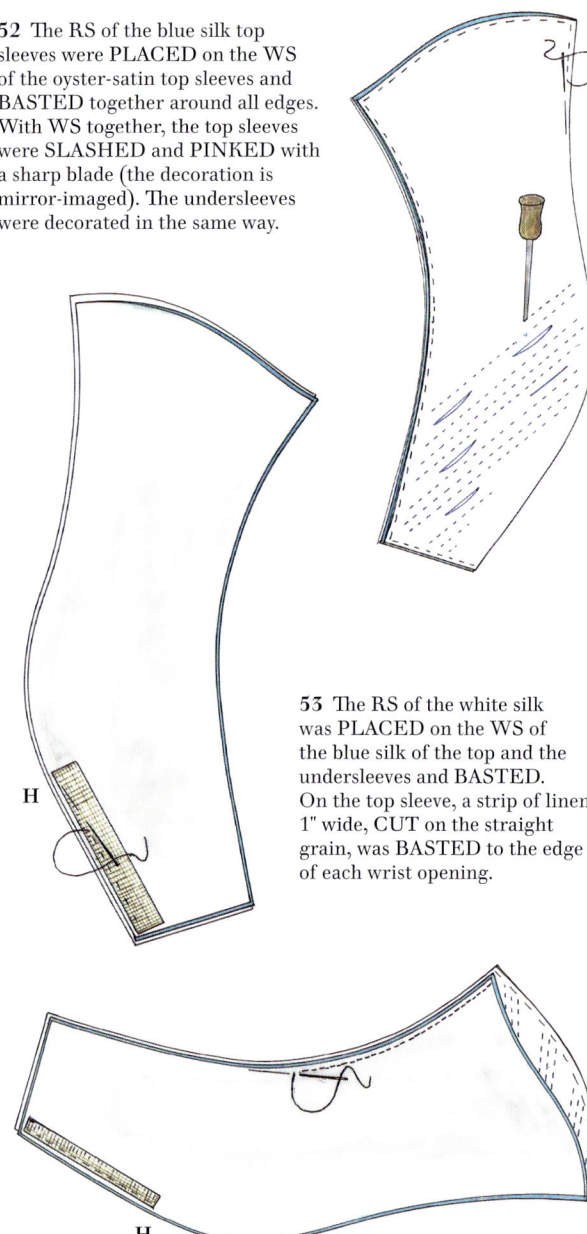

53 The RS of the white silk was PLACED on the WS of the blue silk of the top and the undersleeves and BASTED. On the top sleeve, a strip of linen, 1" wide, CUT on the straight grain, was BASTED to the edge of each wrist opening.

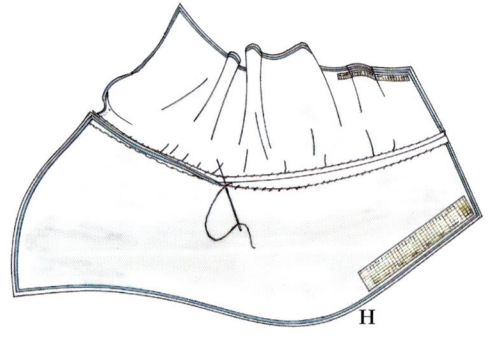

54 On the undersleeves, a strip of linen, ½" wide, CUT on the straight grain, was BASTED to the edge of each wrist opening. With RS together, each undersleeve and top sleeve was BACK STITCHED at the inside seam.

55 The seam allowance of the inside seam was OPENED and FELLED to the white silk.

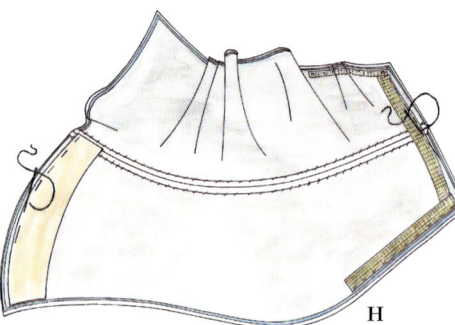

56 The wool interlining was BASTED to the sleeve head of each top sleeve. A strip of linen, ⅝" wide, CUT on the straight grain, was BASTED to each sleeve hem.

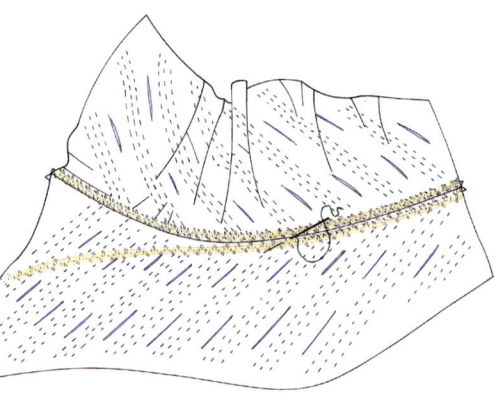

57 Two rows of edging lace were CATCH STITCHED, one on the top sleeve, covering the inside seam; the second, ⅛" away, on the undersleeve.

With RS together, the inside seam of each top and undersleeve lining was *probably* BACK STITCHED together, the seam allowance opened and FELLED.

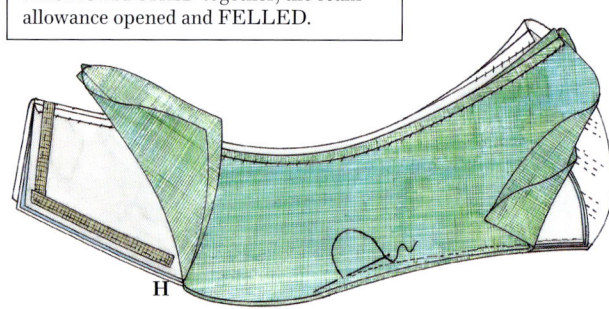

58 With WS together, the undersleeve lining was PLACED on the undersleeve. The outer sleeve seam was BACK STITCHED. From the sleeve head, the first 1½" of the seam was STITCHED just through the sleeve only (not the lining). Then the needle continued through all layers, including the lining, until about 1" away from the wrist opening, H and H1. The last inch was STITCHED through the sleeve only (not the lining).

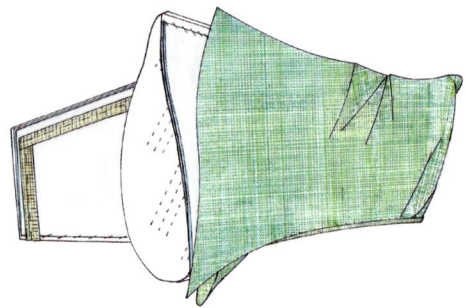

59 The sleeve was TURNED THROUGH to the lining.

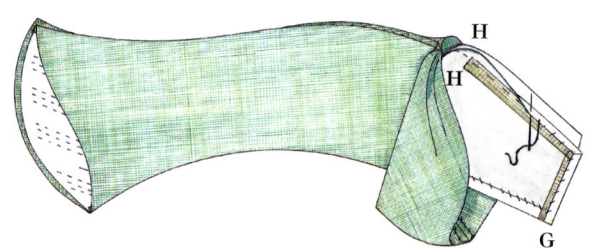

60 Starting at the top-sleeve wrist opening, the ⅛" seam allowance of the opening and hem was FOLDED to the WS and FELLED to the linen strips; it started from H over G to H.

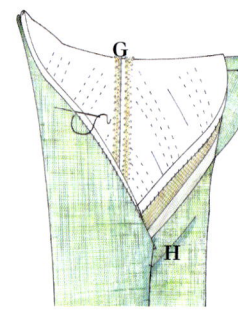 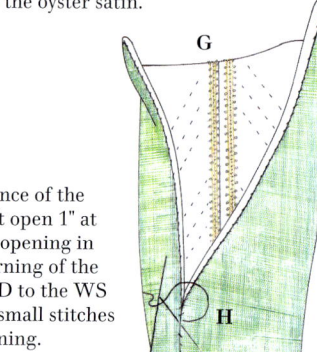

61 The seam allowance of the sleeve lining at the wrist was FOLDED to its WS and FELLED with small stitches to the oyster satin.

62 The seam allowance of the top-sleeve lining, left open 1" at the top of the sleeve opening in step 58 for easier turning of the sleeve, was FOLDED to the WS and FELLED with small stitches to the undersleeve lining.

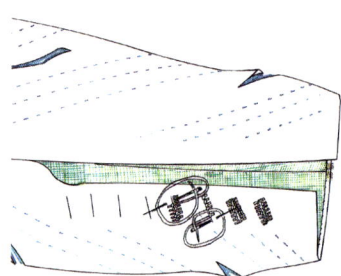 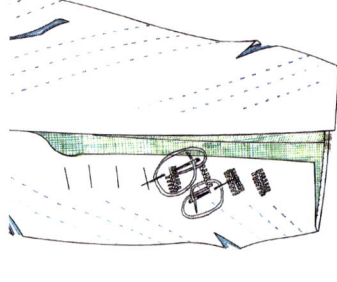

63 At the wrist opening of each top sleeve, eight buttonholes were made, about ¼" from the edge, each ¾" in length and ¾" to 1" apart. The buttonholes were *probably* CUT one at a time to minimize stretching and worked individually with BUTTONHOLE STITCH, from left to right.

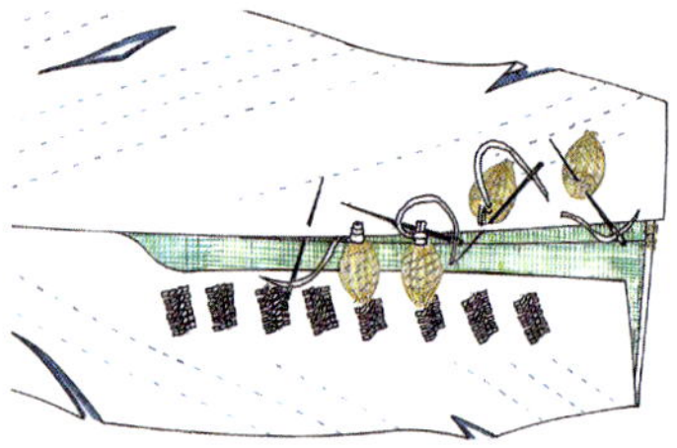

64 On each undersleeve, eight buttons were STITCHED through the edge of the wrist opening with a continuous thread, as done in step 36.

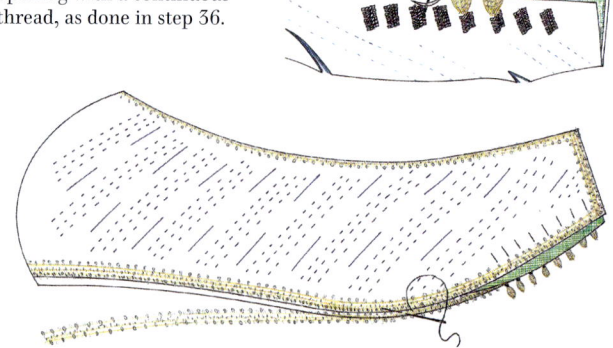

65 A length of lace was CATCH STITCHED from the sleeve head of the top sleeve down, covering the outer seam and ends of the buttonholes. It continued around the sleeve hem, passing the button shanks and up the outer sleeve seam, leaving a gap of ⅛" away from the first row.

66 With RS together, the sleeve was PLACED in the armhole and BACK STITCHED with linen thread, stitching through all layers of the sleeve, shoulder wings and doublet, keeping the sleeve lining out of the way.

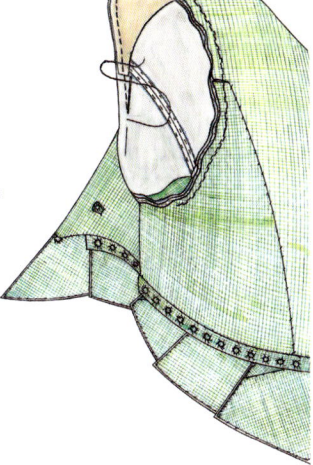

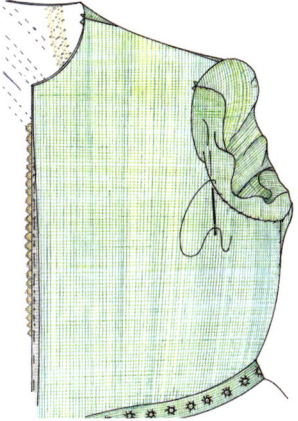

67 The seam allowance of the sleeve lining was FOLDED to its WS, aligned with the back stitches of the armhole seam, and FELLED to the lining of the doublet, with small stitches in linen thread.

Construction of the collar

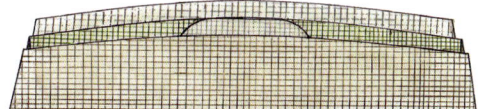

68 The four layers of the collar interlining were CUT net, from different weights of linen and PLACED on top of each other.

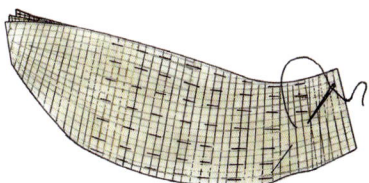

69 The layers of linen were PAD STITCHED together, beginning at the CB and working towards the front edges, shaping the collar over the hand.

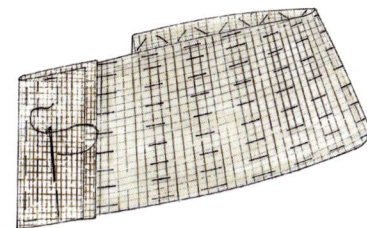

70 Small pieces, about 1¼" × 2", were CUT from the cabbage of a coarse linen. These were FOLDED in half lengthways and RUNNING STITCHED, with linen thread, to the CF edges of the collar to support the buttons and button loops. This also extended the collar by ½" and *probably* made up for shrinkage after the PAD STITCHING.

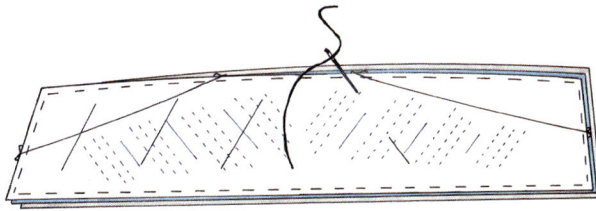

71 The silk layers for the collar were CUT from the cabbage. With RS together, the piecings of the oyster silk satin were *probably* RUNNING STITCHED. The seam allowances were OPENED. The RS of the blue silk was PLACED on the WS of the oyster silk satin and BASTED around all edges.

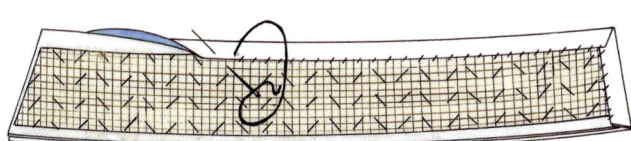

72 The collar was SLASHED and PINKED on the RS. The RS of the white silk was PLACED on the WS of the blue silk and all layers were BASTED, *probably* with PAD STITCHING.

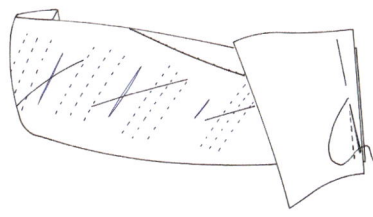

73 The WS of the silk layers were PLACED on the RS of the collar interlining. The seam allowances at the sides and top edge of the collar were FOLDED to the linen and FELLED.

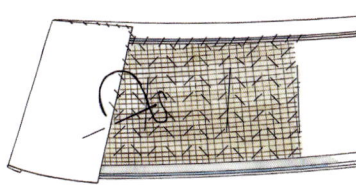

74 With RS together, a piece of oyster satin, 1½" × 2½", CUT on the bias, was RUNNING STITCHED, with linen thread, to the RHS CF edge.

75 The bias-cut piece was FOLDED to the WS of the collar. The seam allowance on the top edge of the piece was FOLDED to its WS and it was FELLED to the interlining at the top and side.

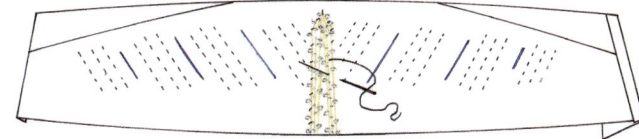

76 A length of edging lace was CATCH STITCHED to the CB of the collar in red silk thread. It was sewn from the bottom up, mitred at the top edge and sewn from top down, with a gap of ⅛" between the rows.

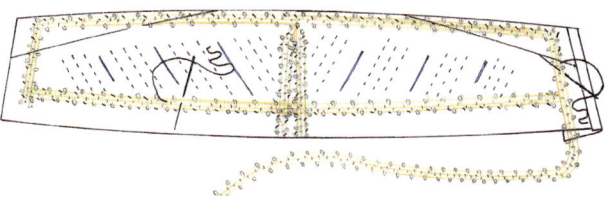

77 A length of lace was CATCH STITCHED along the net shape of the collar at the bottom. Another row of lace was STITCHED ⅜" from the LHS edge, along the top edge of the collar and ½" from the RHS CF edge. A length of lace long enough to reach back to the LHS was left to be STITCHED after the collar was sewn to the doublet.

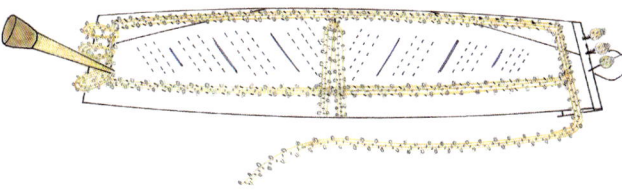

78 On the LHS, three holes were PIERCED with a bodkin. Three lengths of edging lace, each 5" in length, were PUSHED with a bodkin through all the layers to the WS to form the button loops. The ends of the lace on the WS were FELLED with linen thread. On the RHS, three buttons were STITCHED to the CF edge, as in step 36. The seam allowances at the bottom edge of the collar and neck of the doublet were TRIMMED and GLUED to prevent fraying.

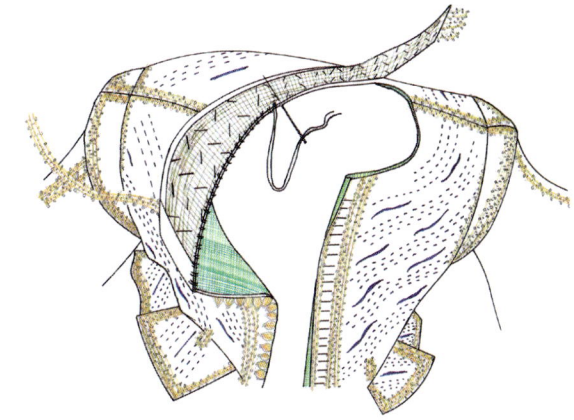

79 With RS together, the collar was FELLED to the neckline of the doublet, with doubled linen thread.

80 The seam allowance of the collar lining was FOLDED to its WS. The lining was FELLED to the collar around all edges.

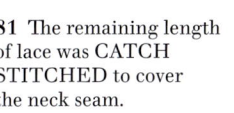

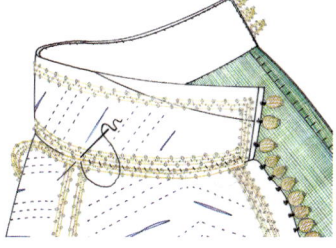

81 The remaining length of lace was CATCH STITCHED to cover the neck seam.

Pattern by Melanie Braun

2B | Slashed silk satin trunk hose with canions

English, *c.* 1618 | V&A: T.28A–1938 | Given by Lady Spickernell | Pattern by Melanie Braun

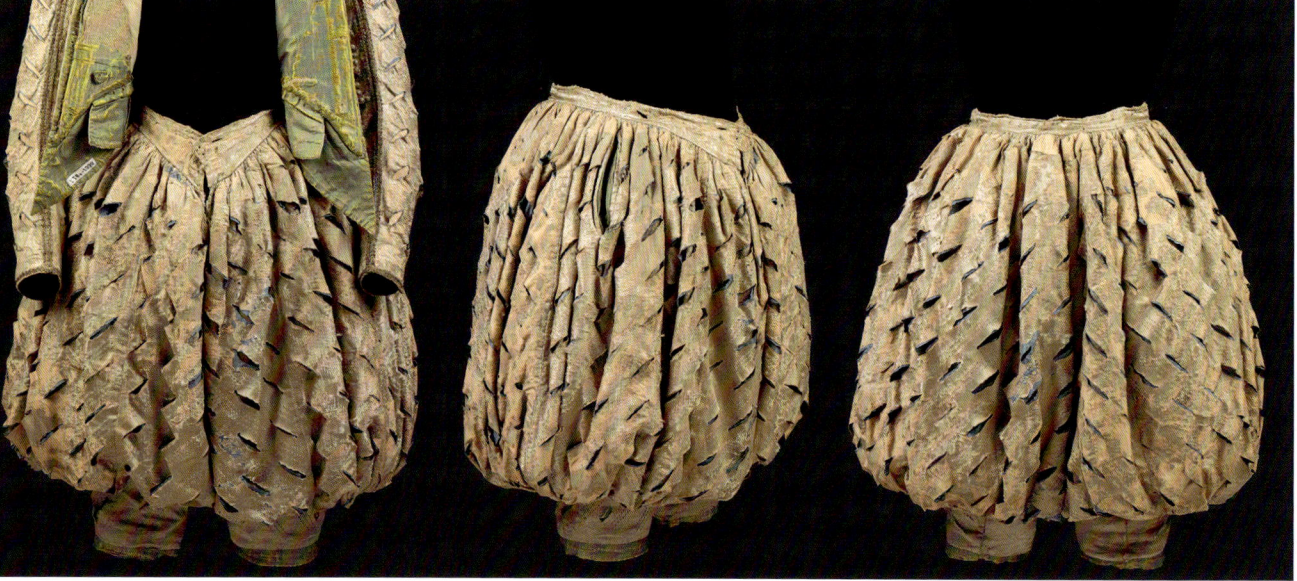

Above: Detail of Sir Rowland Cotton, *c.* 1618
Paul van Somer
The Weiss Gallery, London

Left: The Duc of Chevreuse, 1610
Frans Pourbus II
Collection of Earl Spencer, Althorp, Northamptonshire, UK/Bridgeman Images

Sir Rowland Cotton's suit is remarkable not only because its trunk hose with canions have survived, but also because there is a portrait showing them being worn. Few early 17th-century hose survive. In contrast, there are far more extant doublets, probably because their fabric was more difficult to recycle. The only other pair of trunk hose with canions, known in England, is at Grimsthorpe Castle in Lincolnshire.[1] Sir Rowland's hose are slashed and pinked, as is the matching doublet, and they are made of an oyster silk satin, with blue and white silk under layers. The white silk is different from that used in the doublet. The portrait and the x-ray images show that the side seams of the hose were once trimmed with the same silver and silver-gilt lace as the doublet. The hose have undergone extensive restoration; not all the stitching is original on them.

The full round shape of the hose is more clearly shown in the full-length portrait of the Duc of Chevreuse on the left. The voluminous hose in both portraits are in sharp contrast to the tight short-waisted doublets. This style of hose was described as 'round hose with canions', as recorded in the diary of Phillip Henlowe: 'For The Admirals Men: Layd owt for the company the 1 of febreyare 1598 to bye A blacke velluet gercken layd thicke wth black sylke lace & A payer of Rownd hose of paynes of sylke layd wth sylver lace & caneyanes of clothe of sylver at the Requeste of Robart shawe the some of . . .iiij li xs [£4 10s].'[2]

In 1611, Randle Cotgrave described them as 'Chausses a queue de merlus, Round breeches with strait cannions.'[3]

The pattern given by Martin de Anduxar (left) shows a basic shape for a pair of hose cut along the selvedge of the fabric, which could be adapted to any required style. The curve of the crotch seam and the length from waist to knee were the most important measurements for the tailor cutting a pair of trunk hose. The desired fullness could then be achieved by adding lengths of fabric, according to the taste of the client and how much fabric he could afford. The soft folds of Sir Rowland's trunk hose were supported by an open-weave wool interlining that was cut the same size as the silk layers and worked with them as one layer. Cutting the fustian lining shorter and smaller than the outer layers created the round shape of the hose.

There is a pair of pockets in the front panel of the hose with a second set of pocket openings in the back panels. The latter were stitched closed during restoration; stitch holes in the blue silk under layer and a cut in the wool interlining remain. Multiple sets of pockets were common in the 16th and 17th centuries. For example, the portrait of Sir Thomas Button (page 80) shows two sets of pockets. These held personal belongings and could also be used for stuffing the hose a little more. Sir Rowland's tailor may have cut four front panels by accident and made the pockets on each. When he realized his mistake, he unpicked one set. A wedge of oyster satin was then sewn from the centre back to the side seam as the back panels required more length than the fronts.

The front opening of the hose [codpiece] was fastened with five buttons, with corresponding holes worked on a buttonhole stand. The hose were closed at the waist with a point threaded through eyelets worked in pairs on either centre front. The point was probably tied to one eyelet and laced in a spiral movement, as on a woman's bodice, and closed with a half-bow. To fasten the hose to the doublet, 38 holes were pierced in the waistband but left unworked. A set of 19 points was laced through them and remained there, as illustrated in image 6 on page 11.

1. Janet Arnold, *Patterns of Fashion 3*, Basingstoke: Macmillan, 1985, p. 75
2. R. A. Foakes, *Henslowe's Diary*, 2nd edition, Cambridge: Cambridge University Press, 2002, p. 104
3. Randle Cotgrave, *A Dictionarie of the French and English Tongues*, London, 1611, fol. Q5 recto

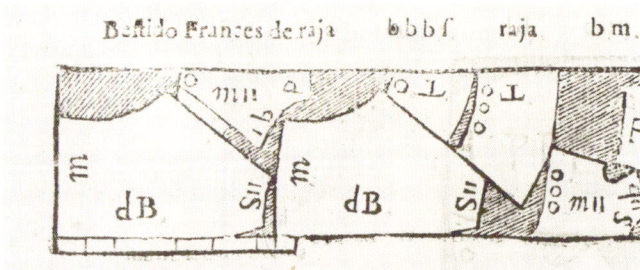

Detail: A Pattern for hose
Martin de Anduxar, *Geometria y trazas pertenecientes al oficio de sastres*, Madrid, 1640, p. 13

DETAILS
Right side (RS) details

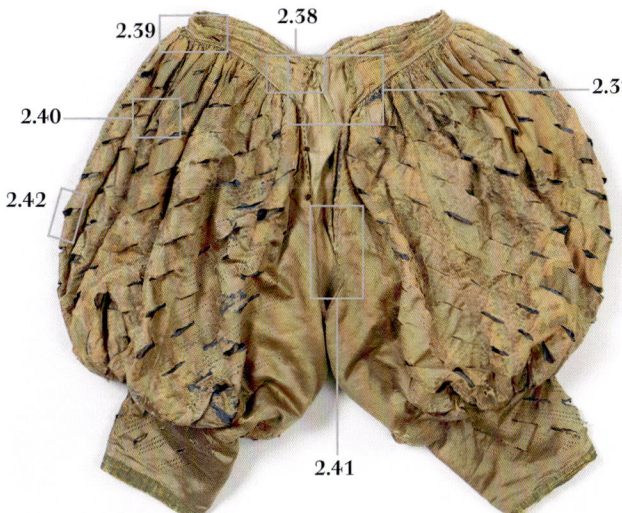

2.36 A front view of the trunk hose.

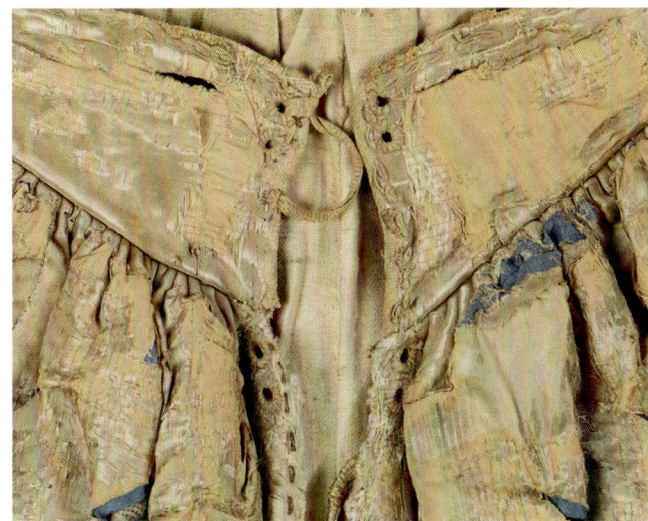

2.37 Detail of the waistband fronts. On the RHS, a length of tablet-woven silk lace remains, now stitched into a loop. This is probably the original point for lacing the waist. There is a pair of eyelets at the top of the waistband on each side, and another pair just below the waistband.

2.38 Detail of the tablet-woven silk point tied through the top eyelet on the RHS waistband.

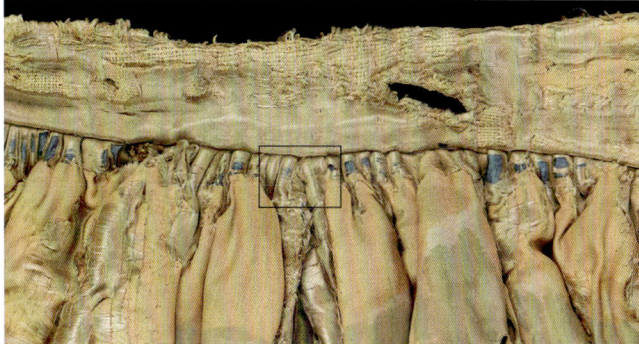

2.39 The top of the RHS pocket. The oyster-satin binding of the pocket is hidden in the gathers.

2.40 The bottom of the RHS pocket. The oyster-satin binding strips are stitched at an angle into the pocket side seams, creating an inverted pleat at the bottom of each pocket opening.

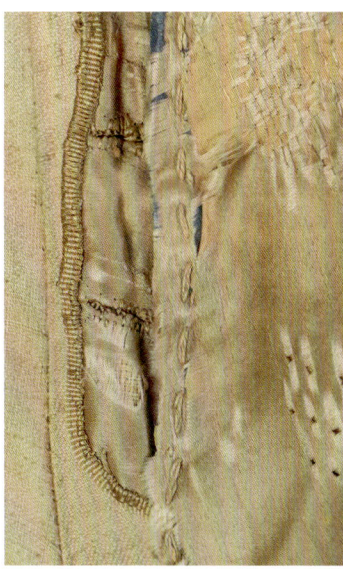 

2.41 The buttonhole stand is bound with a silk binding lace. The CF edge of the left leg was once bound with linen tape, before the buttonhole stand was added. The tape has worn away and only the running stitches that once held it are left.

2.42 At the RHS seam the imprint of the silver and silver-gilt edging lace is still visible although it has been removed.

2.43 A back view of the trunk hose.

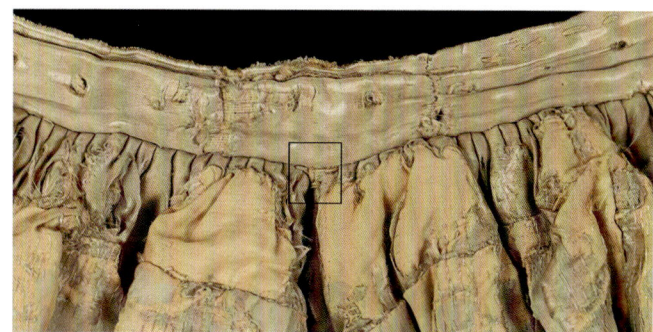

2.44 The waistband at CB, showing the even gathering stitches. The gathering threads were secured by stitching them a few times into the same spot, shown in the black box. There is a seam at the CB of the waistband in both the oyster silk satin and the interlining.

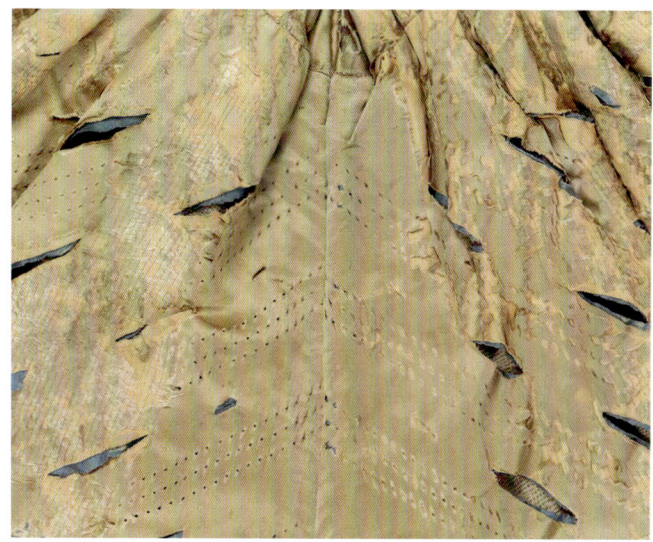

2.45 The pinking and slashing pattern at the seat of the hose where the pinking runs right into the seam. The wedges added at the back can be seen at the top of the image.

Pattern by Melanie Braun

Right side (RS) details CONTINUED

Wrong side (WS) details

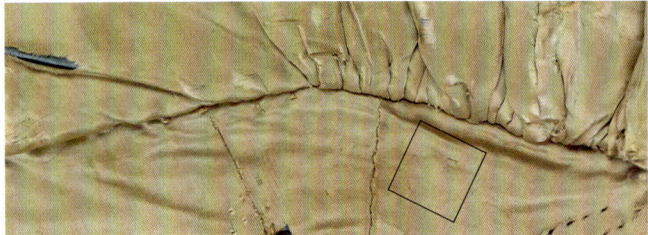

2.46 The back of the right canion. The bottom of each hose leg was gathered to fit the canions, with a portion on each inside leg left ungathered, to reduce bulk. The small basting stitches (shown in the black box) holding the silk underlayers remain.

2.47 The left canion. The seam of the canion runs down the back of the leg. The pinking and slashing are slightly different from that on the RHS canion, indicating they were not done together in two layers.

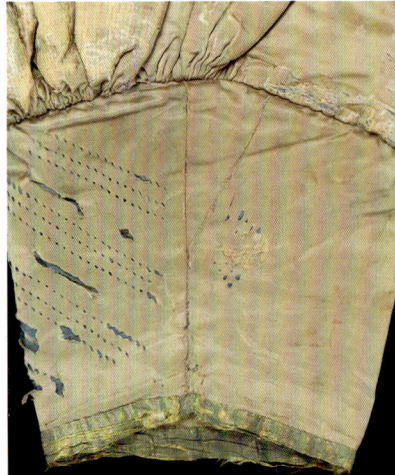

2.48 The right canion. A slash goes through the seam of the piecing, and was repaired with small felling stitches. The binding at the bottom of the canions would have always been covered by the top of the stockings.

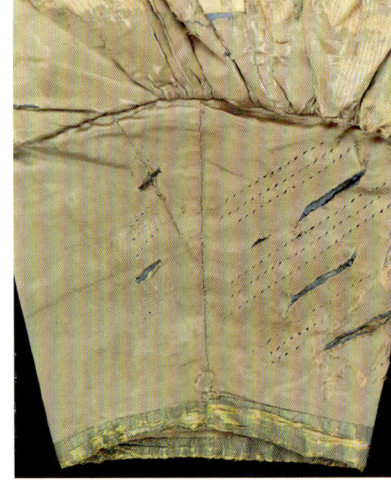

2.49 The front of the right canion. The canions are bound with a strip of the same shot green silk used to line the doublet, folded around the lower edge of the canion. The oyster-satin layer is shorter than the fustian lining, causing a ridge in the centre of the binding strip.

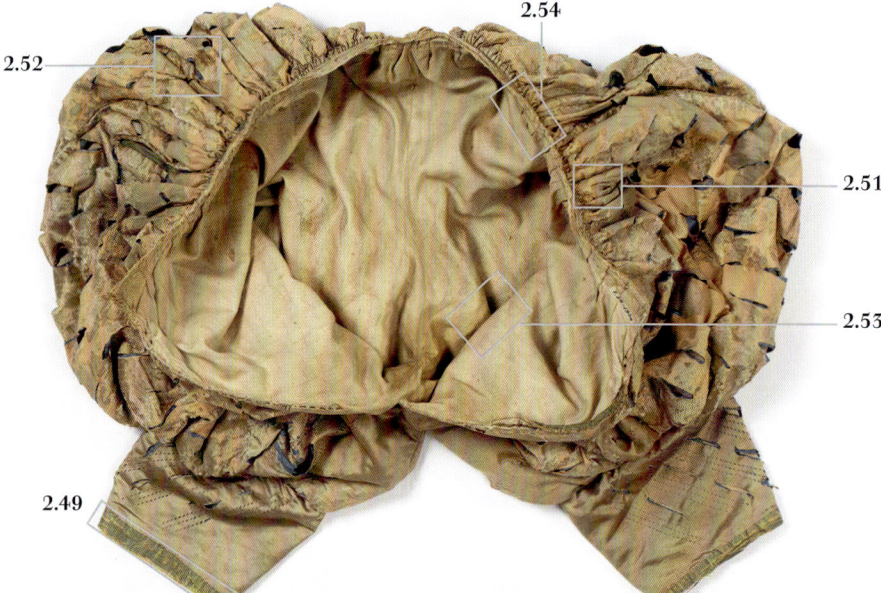

2.50 The WS view of the trunk hose. The stains on the inside of the hose indicate that they were well worn.

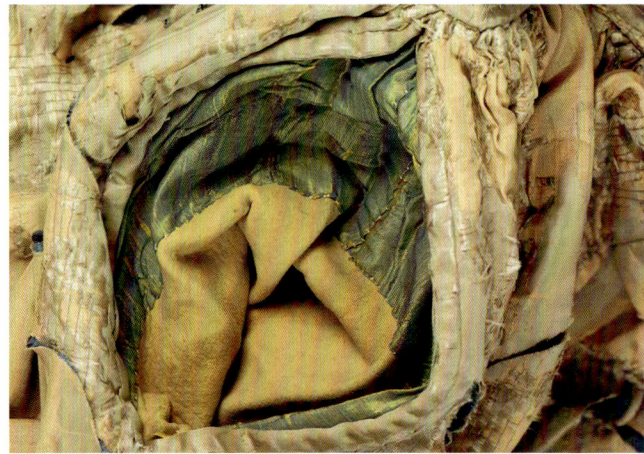

2.51 The LHS leather pocket bag was faced with the same green silk that lines the doublet. Leather was commonly used for pocket bags.

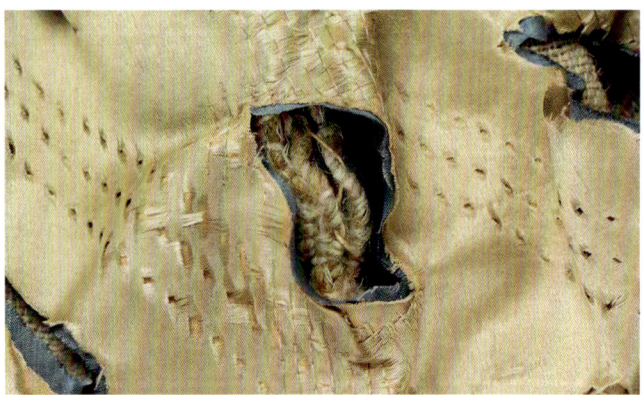

2.52 Looking through a slash near the RHS back pocket opening, the selvedges of the wool layer were loosely whip stitched together with linen thread.

2.53 The fustian lining of the leg was eased into the seam joining it to the canion.

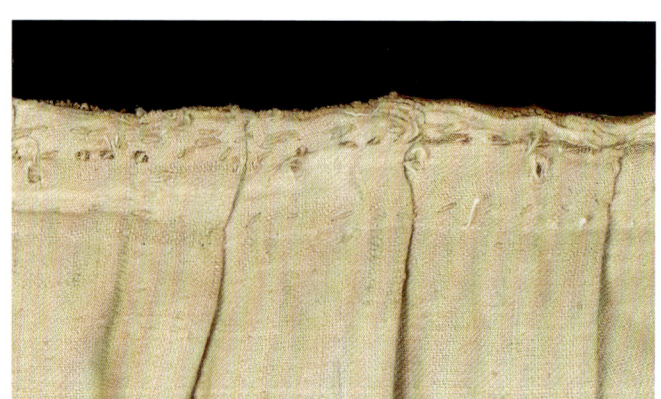

2.54 The fustian lining of the legs extends to the top edge of the silk waistband, where it was pleated to fit it. The lining was then running stitched at the top and bottom of the waistband.

72 | **2B** | Slashed silk satin trunk hose with canions

X-ray images
The greyish 'blobs' seen in all these images are areas of early restoration work.

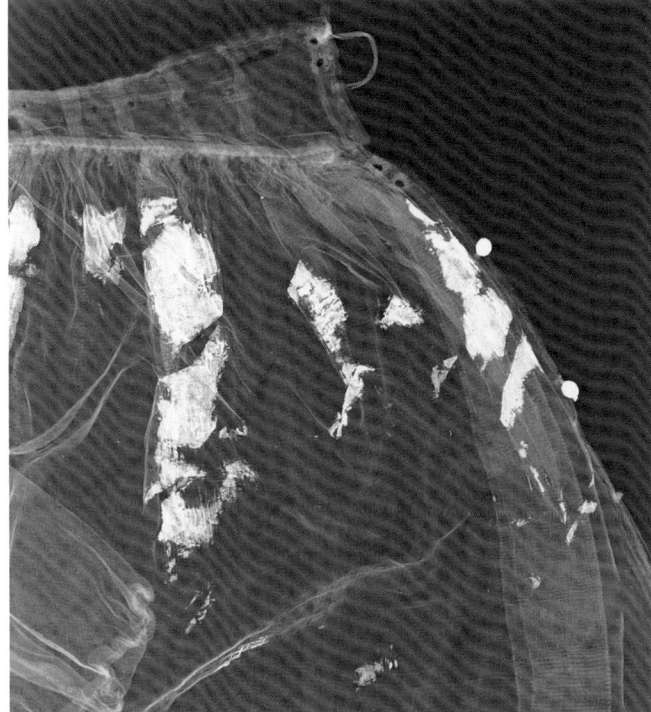

2.55 The CF of the trunk hose, RHS, where only two buttons out of five remain. The leather pocket bag can be seen in the bottom left of the image. The pleats in the fustian lining at the waistband appear as white lines.

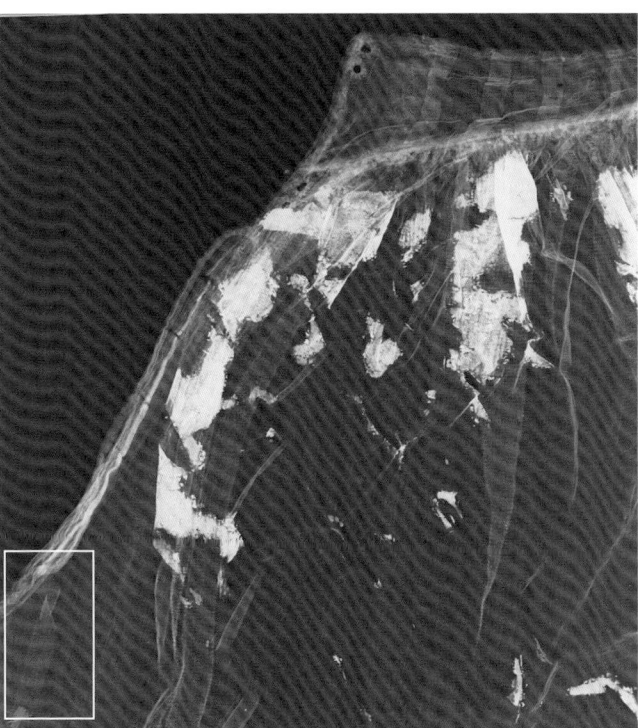

2.57 The CF of the trunk hose, LHS. Visible in the white box is a length of the linen binding tape that was left in the CF seam. Above the waistband seam, the bulk of the hose gathered into it appears as one dense line.

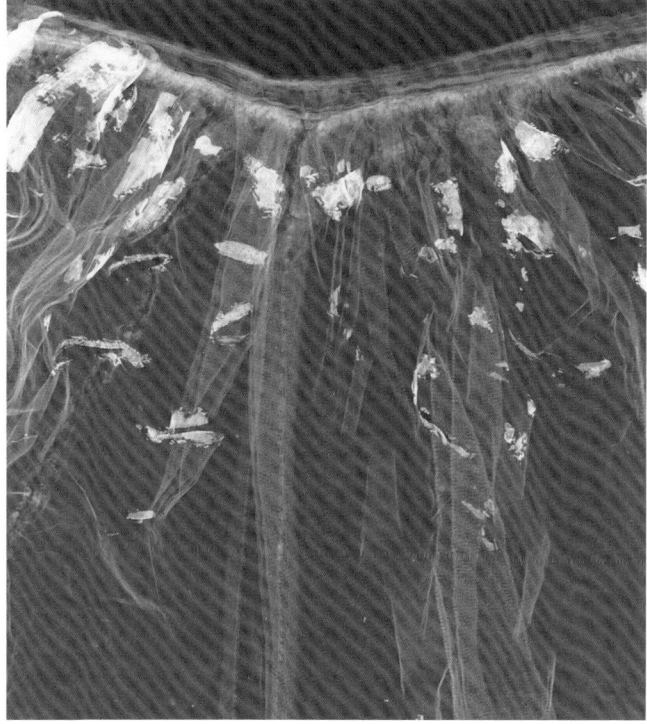

2.59 The CB of the trunk hose, from the RS, showing the back stitching of the crotch seam. To the left of this, the seam in the wool layer underneath is coming undone. The unworked eyelets are visible in the waistband.

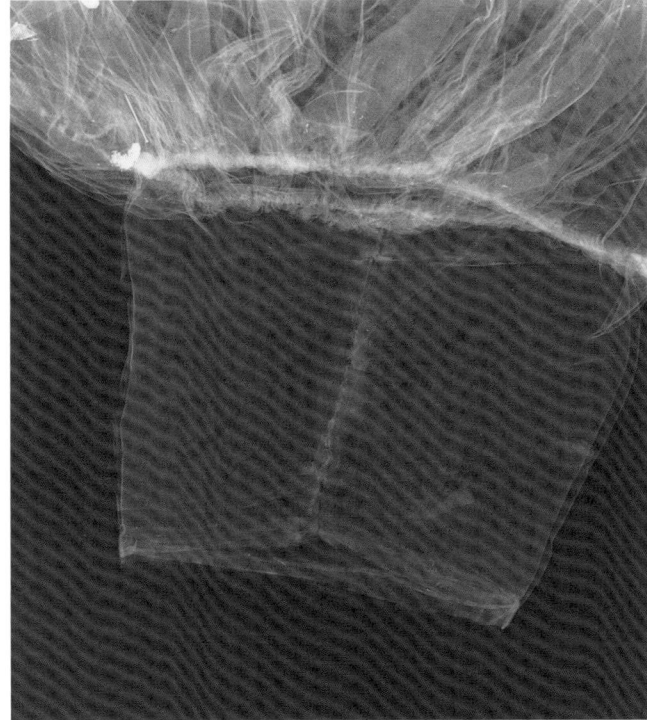

2.56 The back of the left canion. The inside leg of the hose is left ungathered, with the bulk of the fabric gathered at the back, front and outside seam.

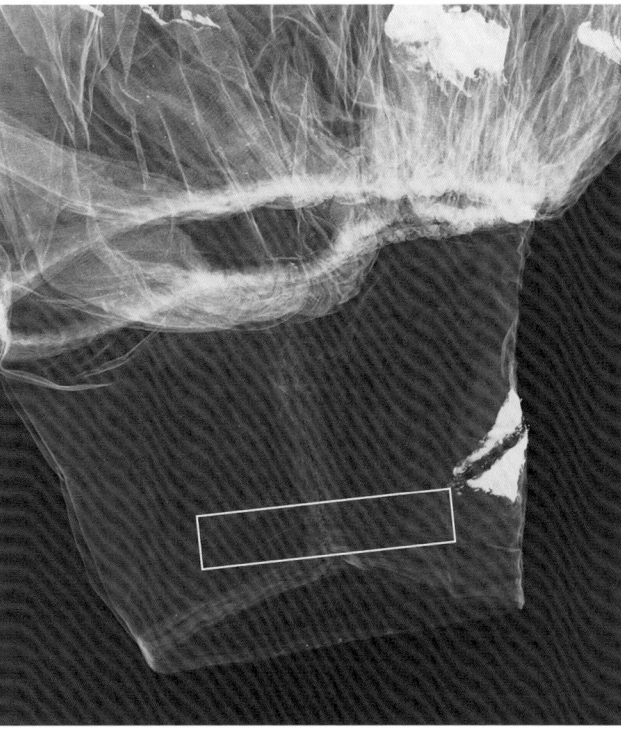

2.58 The back of the right canion. The blue and silk underlayers of the canions are unshaped rectangles of cabbage, the lower edges of which appear above the hem (shown in the white box).

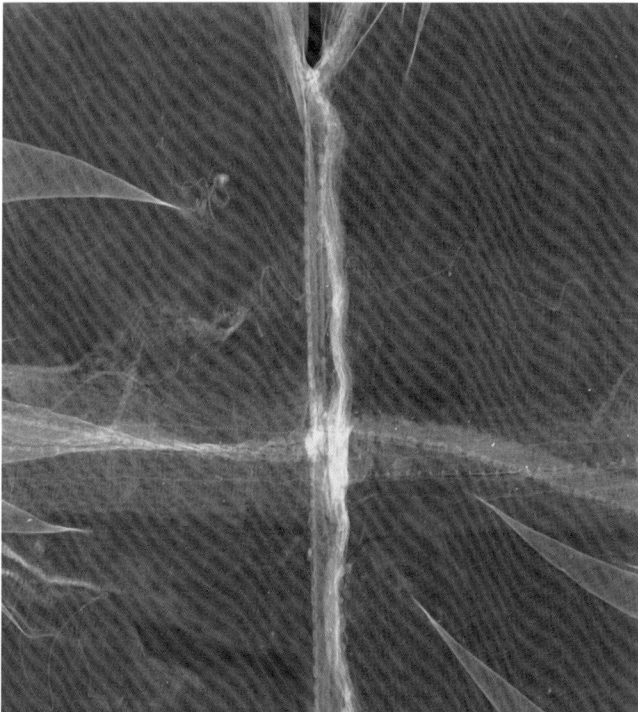

2.60 The meeting of the CB and CF seams and the inside leg seams at the crotch. These are all back stitched in both the silk layers and the fustian lining.

Pattern by Melanie Braun

PATTERN
Pattern of the oyster silk satin outer layer, the blue silk and white silk underlayers, and the wool interlining

SCALE 1:8

The pattern of the oyster satin and its layers of blue and white silk was taken from the RS, and the pattern of the fustian lining was taken from the WS. Therefore, the two patterns appear mirror-imaged. Pattern pieces are given as net shapes; a seam allowance of ¼" must be added.

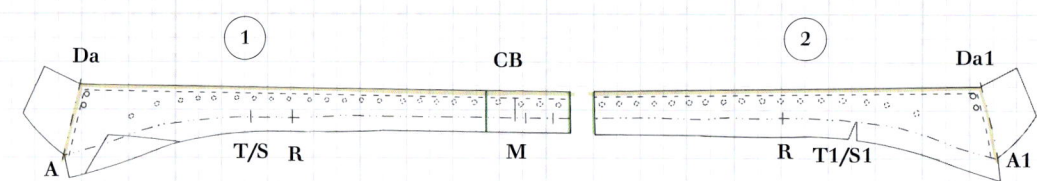

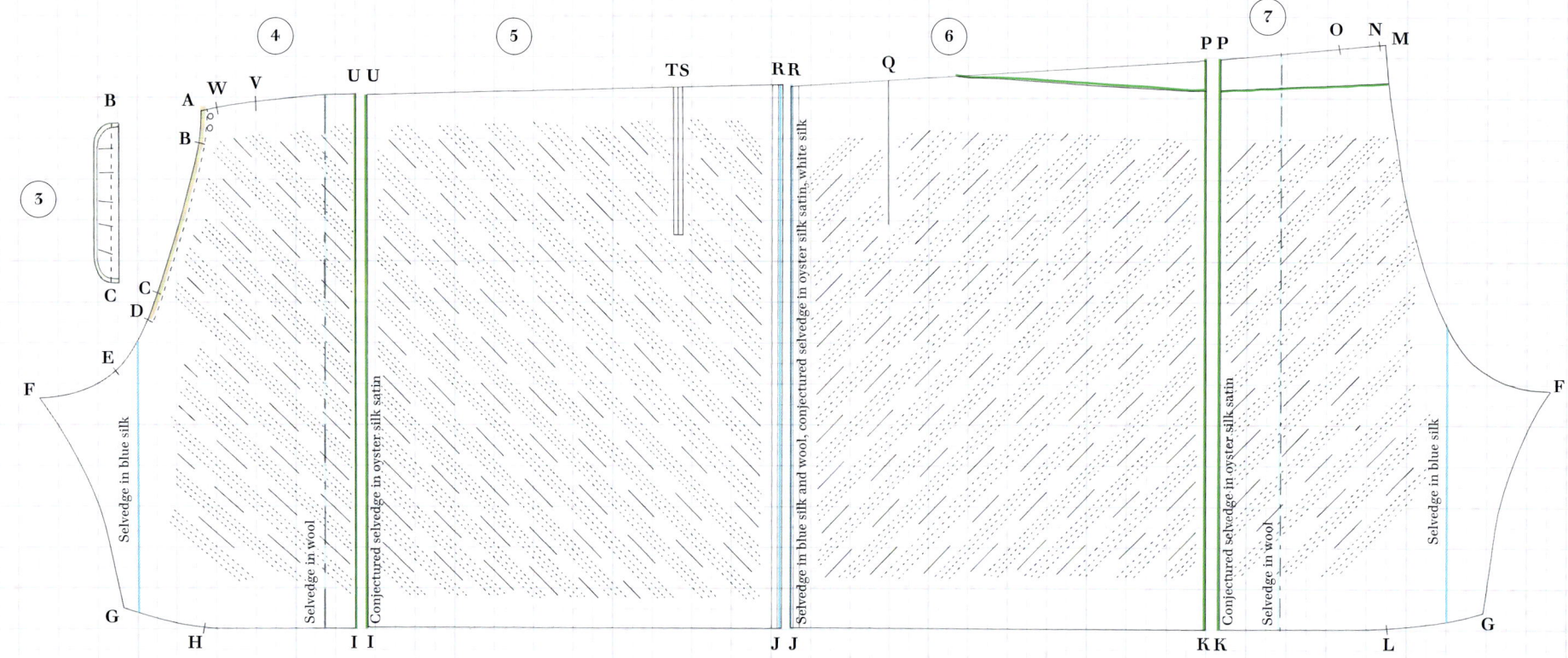

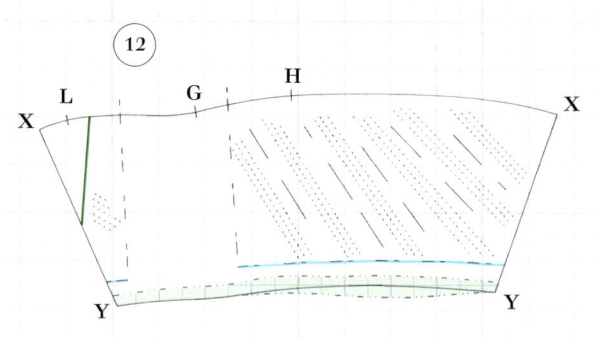

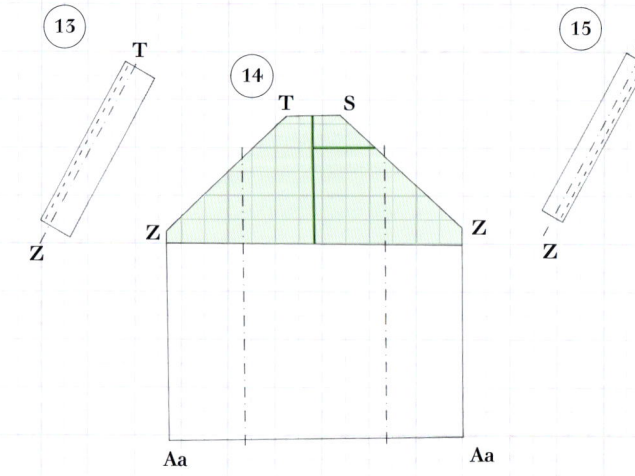

PATTERN PIECES

1. LHS waistband
2. RHS waistband
3. Buttonhole stand
4. Front left leg
5. Front side left leg
6. Back side left leg
7. Back left leg
12. Left canion
13. Left front pocket binding
14. Left pocket bag
15. Left back pocket binding

2B | Slashed silk satin trunk hose with canions

PATTERN PIECES

- 8 Back right leg
- 9 Back side right leg
- 10 Front side right leg
- 11 Front right leg
- 16 Right back pocket binding
- 17 Right pocket bag
- 18 Right front pocket binding
- 19 Right canion

SCALE 1:8

The hose are made of five layers: an oyster silk satin outer layer and one of blue silk, which are pinked and slashed together. These are backed with a white silk of slightly different weave from the white silk used for the doublet. There is an interlining of white wool and a lining of fustian (linen warp, cotton weft). The canions have only four layers: oyster silk satin, blue silk, white silk and fustian lining.

The blue and white silks are of a similar width, approximately 32", while the oyster silk satin is about 21"; unfortunately the only selvedge that could be found is hidden in the doublet wing. The selvedge is a very narrow green stripe which was probably pulling the fabric tied and was therefore cut off. The seam allowance of the hose shows a very clean straight cut edge. The width of the wool is about 24", but that of the fustian cannot be determined. The hose are sewn with three different threads: white silk, bleached and brown linen.

MATERIALS

Oyster-coloured silk satin
Blue plain woven silk
White plain woven silk
White open-weave wool
Green changeable silk (blue warp/yellow weft)
Bleached twill-woven fustian
Silk grosgrain binding lace
Linen tape
Leather for pocket bags
Silver and silver-gilt filé edging lace
Five silver and silver-gilt-filé-covered buttons
White silk thread, 2 'S' ply
Linen thread, 2 'S' ply
Brown linen thread, 2 'S' ply

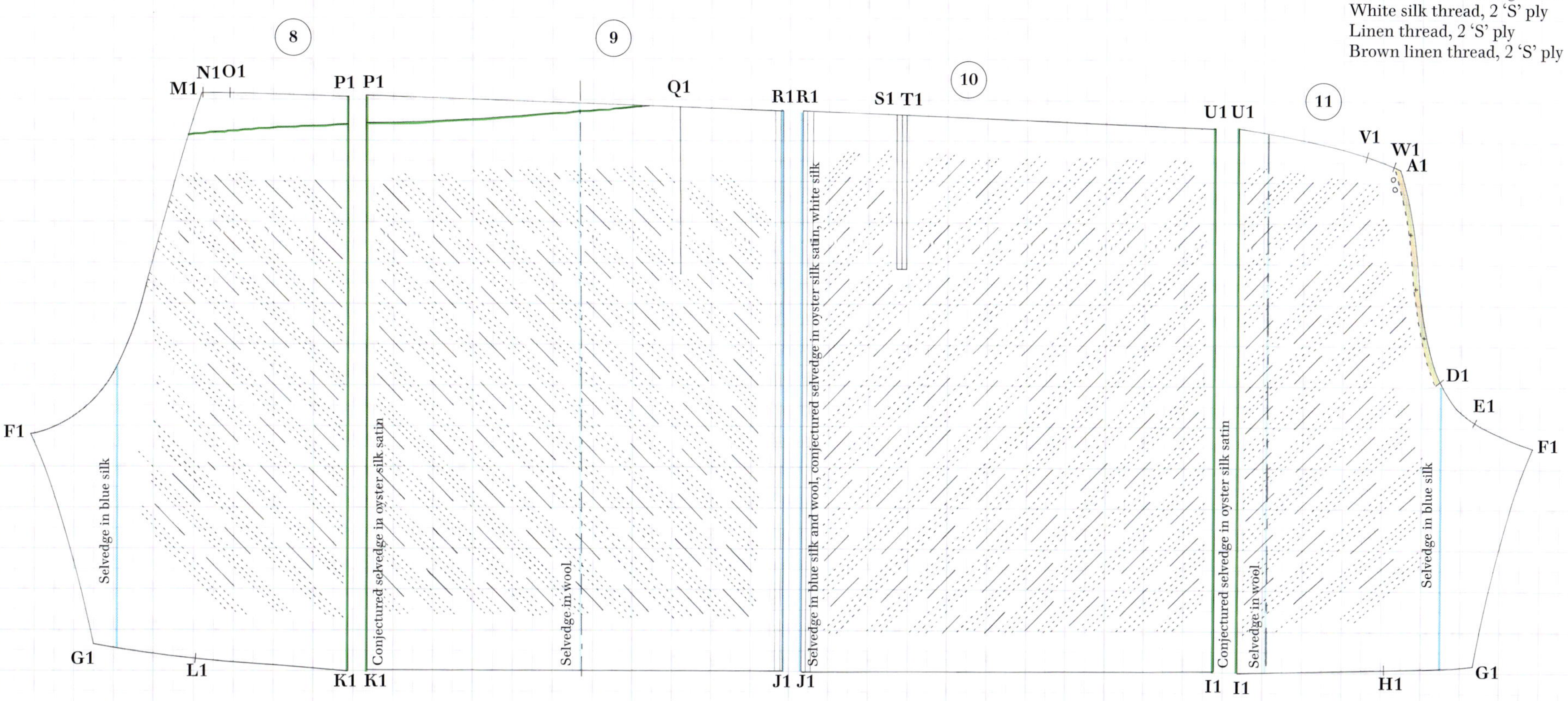

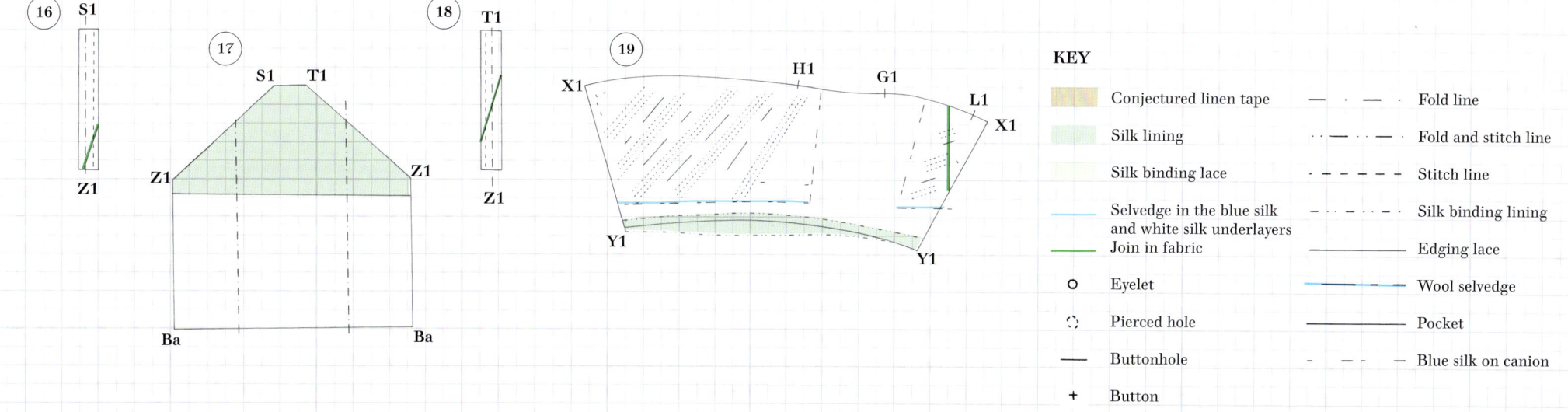

Pattern by Melanie Braun

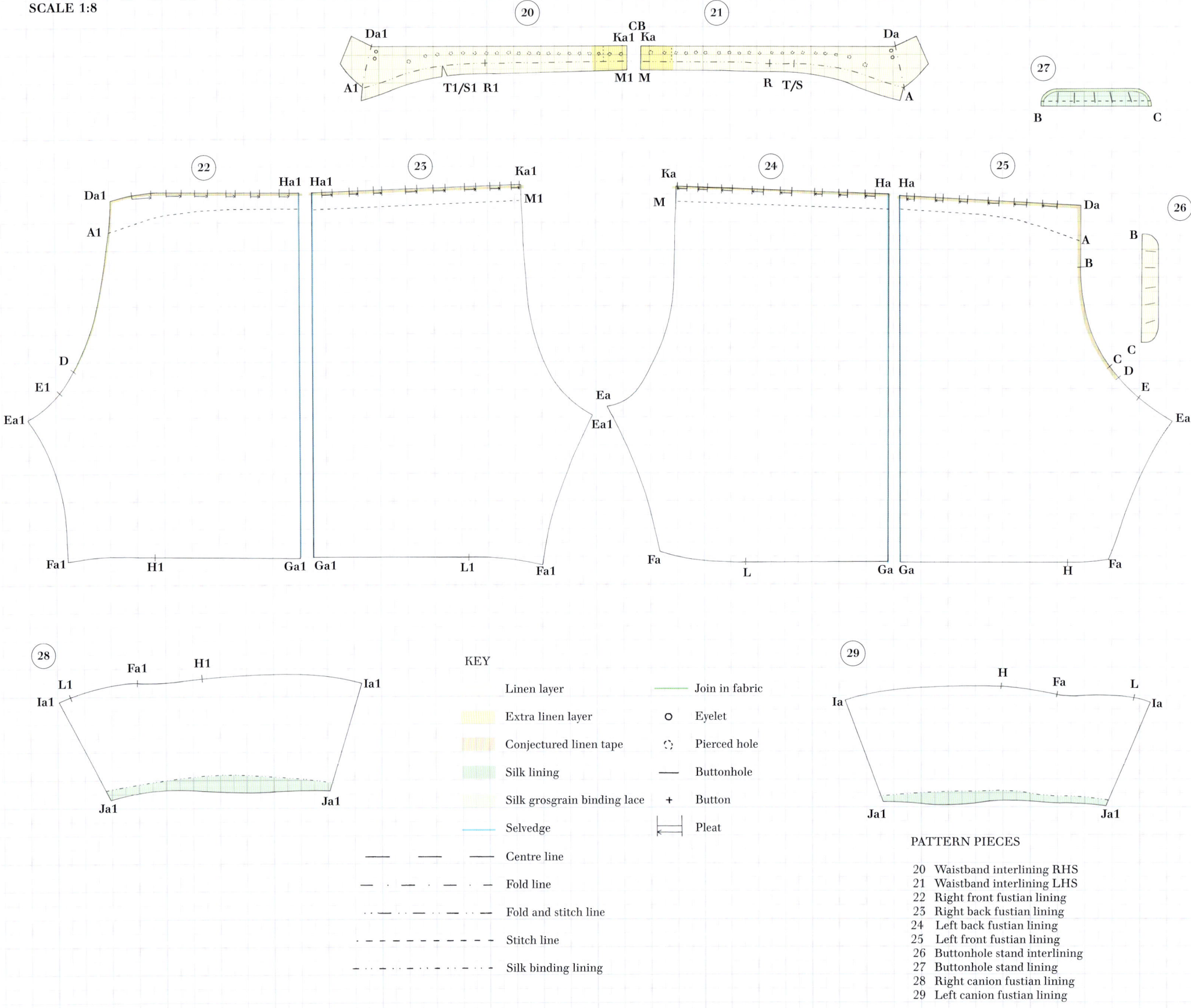

CONSTRUCTION

Construction of the hose

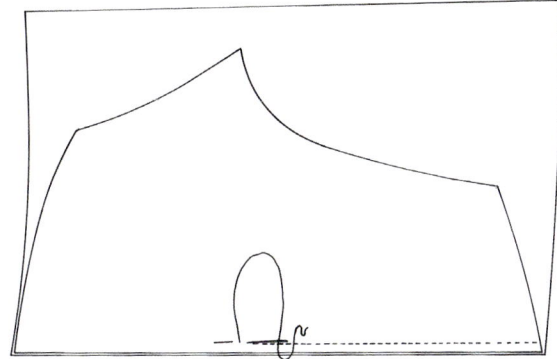

1 The two front panels of the oyster silk satin layer were *probably* HALF-BACK STITCHED together. The two back panels were sewn the same way and the wedges at the waist were *probably* HALF-BACK STITCHED afterwards.

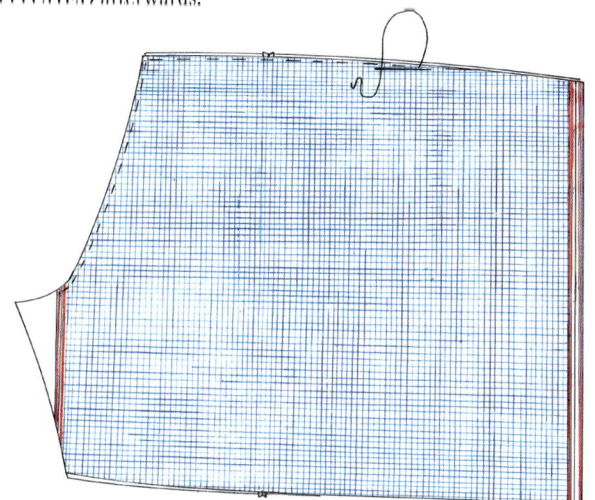

2 The RS of the blue silk layer of the front was PLACED on the WS of the oyster leg fronts and BASTED together. The same was done to the layers of the back legs.

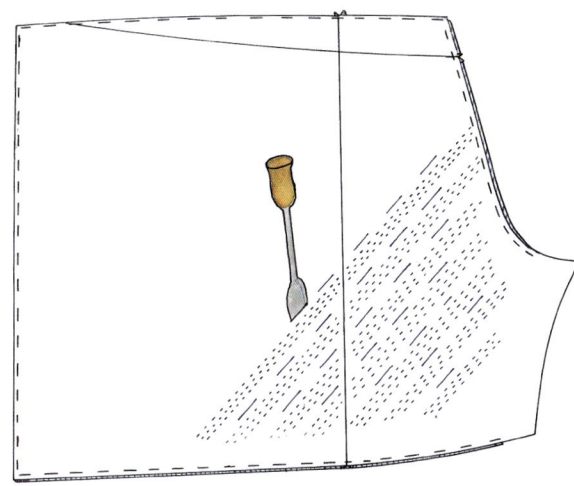

3 The front legs were PLACED blue sides together. They were SLASHED and PINKED through all layers, avoiding the seam and area of the pocket openings. A ½" gap was left next to the side-seam allowances. The same was done with the two back legs.

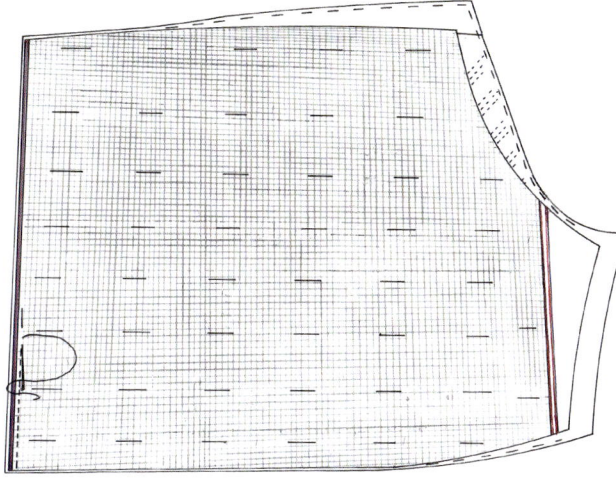

4 The RS of each white silk front layer was PLACED on the WS of each blue silk front and BASTED. The same was done to the back legs. With RS together, the front right leg and back right leg were *probably* HALF-BACK STITCHED together. The left leg was sewn in the same way.

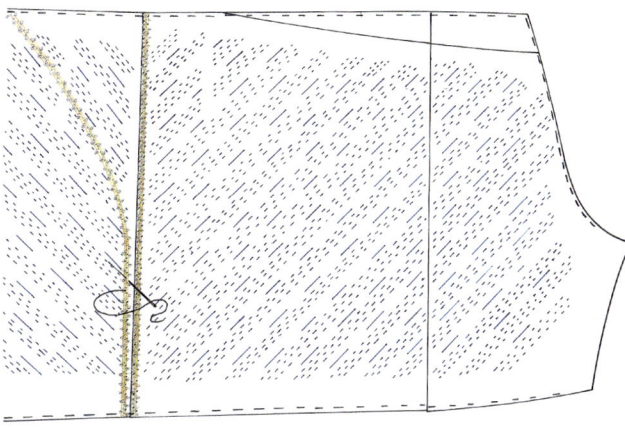

5 The side seams of each leg were opened. On the RS, two rows of silver and silver-gilt edging lace were CATCH STITCHED, the back row right next to the seam, the front row ⅛" away. This stitching also holds the seam allowances on the WS open.

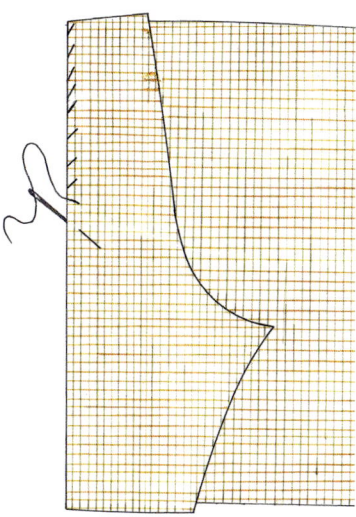

6 The edges – both selvedges and cut edges – of the wool interlining were loosely WHIP STITCHED together with linen thread. The RS of the interlining was then PLACED on the WS of the white silk of each leg and BASTED, *probably* with PAD STITCHES all over.

Construction of the pockets

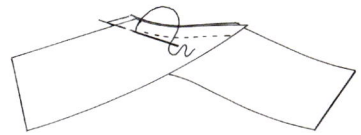

7 The binding strips of oyster silk satin for the RHS pocket were PIECED together with RUNNING STITCHES.

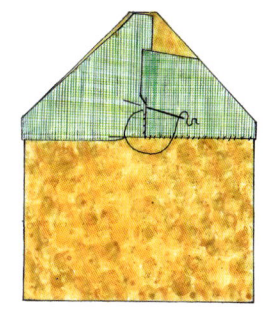

8 The pocket bags were faced only at the top. The green silk facings were FELLED to the leather bags along the lower edge. The piecings of the LHS silk facings were joined with FELLING directly to the leather.

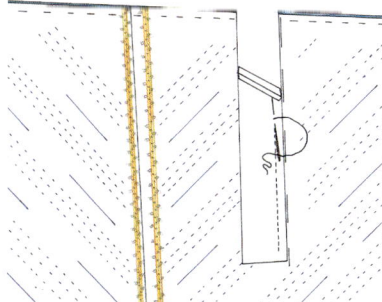

9 With RS together, the binding strips were PLACED one on each side of each pocket opening and BACK STITCHED, about ¼" away from the edge, along the length of each pocket opening.

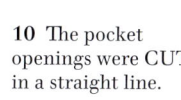
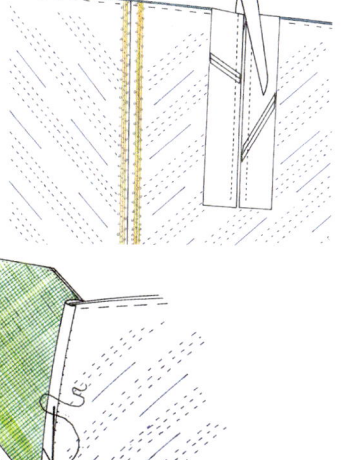

10 The pocket openings were CUT in a straight line.

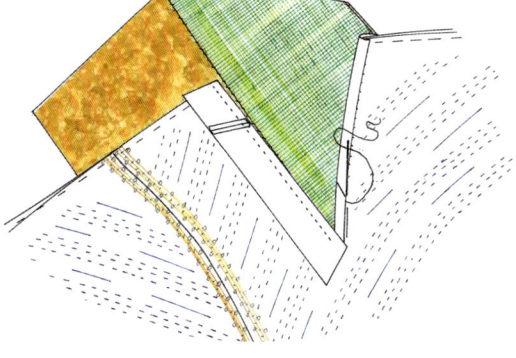

11 The oyster silk satin binding was FOLDED over the seam allowance to the WS. One triangular edge of the pocket bag was aligned with the seam allowance of the binding. From the RS, all layers – binding, pocket and hose – were PRICK STITCHED in the crease of the folded binding. This was done with all the pocket edges, making the open pocket bags stand away from the WS of the hose.

Pattern by Melanie Braun

Construction of the pockets CONTINUED

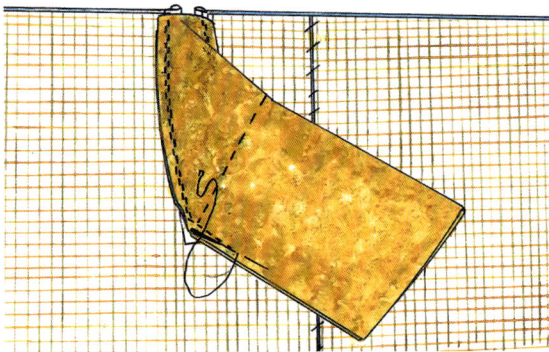

12 The side seam of each pocket bag was BACK STITCHED. The two satin binding strips were STITCHED into this seam at an angle, creating an inverted pleat on the RS at the bottom of each pocket opening (see fig. 2.40, page 71).

13 Each pocket bag was FOLDED in half at the bottom edge, with the side seam in the centre, and BACK STITCHED with linen thread.

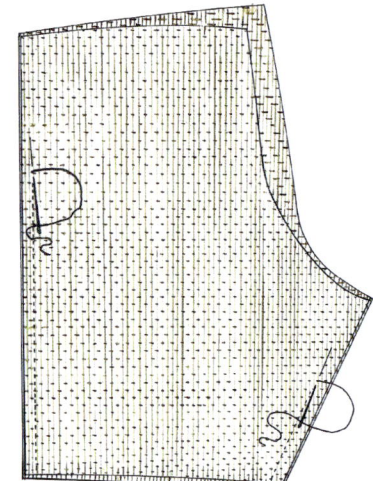

17 With RS together, each leg of the fustian lining was BACK STITCHED at the side seam. The seam allowances were opened and *probably* finger-pressed flat. At the bottom edge of each leg, two rows of RUNNING STITCH were *probably* sewn.

Construction of the hose CONTINUED

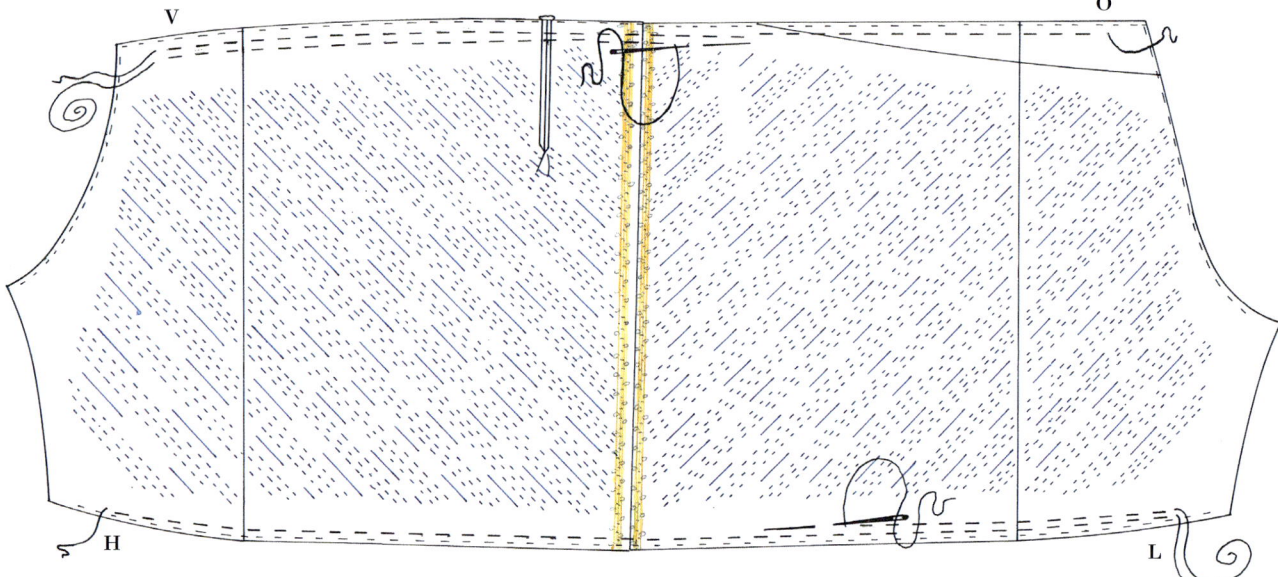

14 At least two rows of even RUNNING STITCHES, each about ⅛" apart, were sewn from V/V1 to O/O1 at the waistline of each leg. The binding strips of the pocket were OVERLAPPED slightly and the gathering STITCHED through them. At the bottom of each leg, two rows of even RUNNING STITCHES were sewn from L/L1 to H/H1, leaving the inside legs ungathered.

Construction of the canions

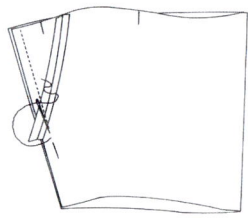

18 The oyster silk satin piecings of the canions were BACK STITCHED and the seams opened. The seam in the silk satin layer of each canion was BACK STITCHED. The fustian lining of each canion was sewn the same way.

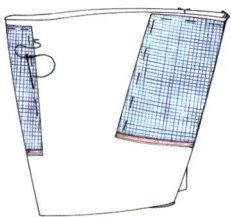

19 The RS of a piece of blue silk cabbage was PLACED on the WS of the oyster silk satin canion and BASTED. Each canion was PINKED and SLASHED in the round, *probably* with a piece of leather between the front and back. The inside leg was left undecorated.

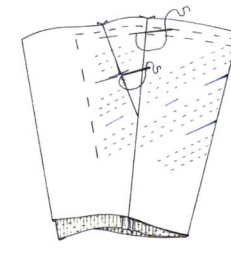

20 The RS of a piece of white silk cabbage was PLACED on the WS of the blue silk and *probably* BASTED. On the RS of the left canion, a slash cut through the seam of the piecing was repaired with small FELLING stitches.

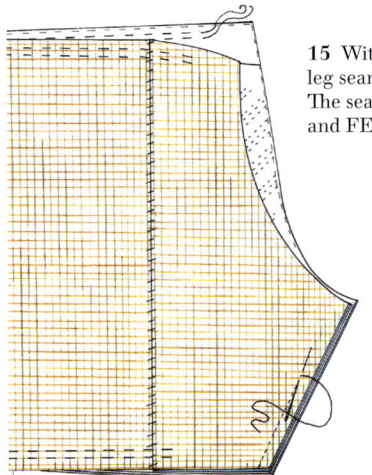

15 With RS together, each inside leg seam was BACK STITCHED. The seam allowances were opened and FELLED to the interlining.

16 With RS together, the legs were BACK STITCHED along the crotch seam from M/M1 through F/F1 to E/E1.

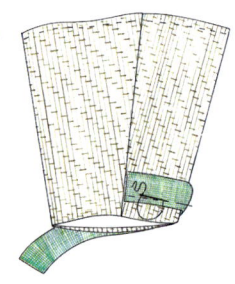 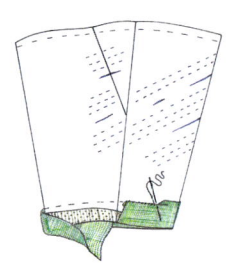

21 The WS of the lining was PLACED on the WS of the white silk and BASTED along the top and bottom edges. **a** With RS together, a binding strip of green silk, CUT on the straight grain, was RUNNING STITCHED to the fustian lining at the bottom edge. **b** The binding was TURNED OVER the canion hem and FELLED on the RS, with small stitches along the same line as the running stitch.

2B | Slashed silk satin trunk hose with canions

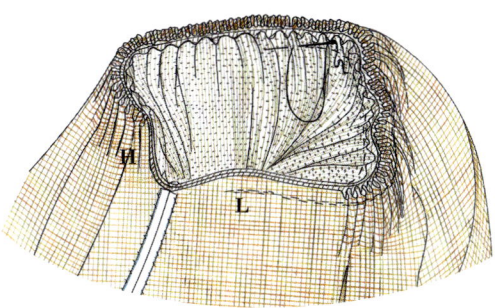

22 The running stitches at the bottom of the legs were PULLED tight to fit the canions; the ends of the gathering threads were SECURED with stitches. The lining of each leg was EASED at the bottom. The RS of each canion was PLACED on the RS of each leg. The RS of the lining was then PLACED on the WS of the canion and the three layers were BACK STITCHED together, with linen thread, leaving the area between L/L1 and H/H1 ungathered.

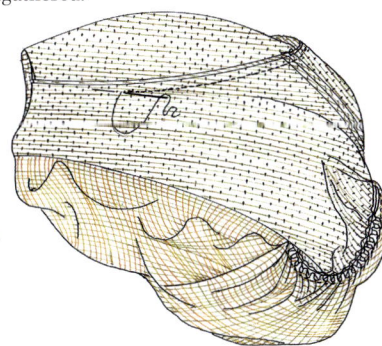

23 With RS together, the legs of the fustian lining were BACK STITCHED at the crotch seam, from M/M1 through F/F1 to E/E1.

Construction of the waistband

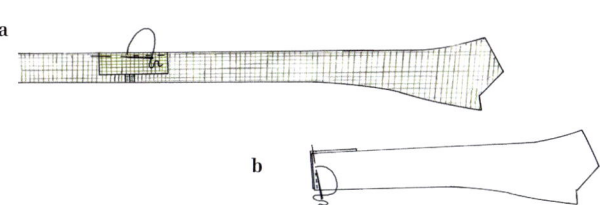

24a The linen interlining was BACK STITCHED at the CB seam and a small piece of linen BASTED over it, for reinforcement.
b The oyster-satin piecings were BACK STITCHED together. Then the two layers were *probably* BASTED all over with PAD STITCHING.

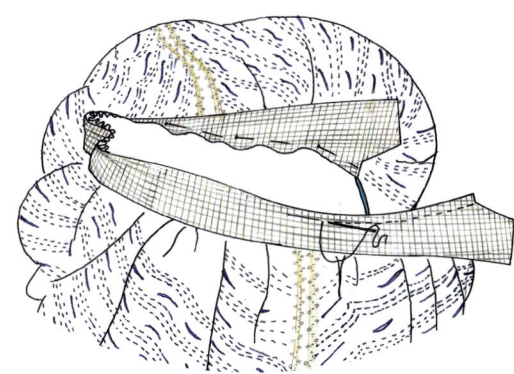

25 The rows of running stitch at the waistline of the hose were PULLED up to fit the waistband. The gathering threads were SECURED and a pleat in the CF and CB of each leg was made at V/V1 to W/W1 and O/O1 to N/N1. With RS together, the waistband was BACK STITCHED to the hose, keeping the lining out of the seam.

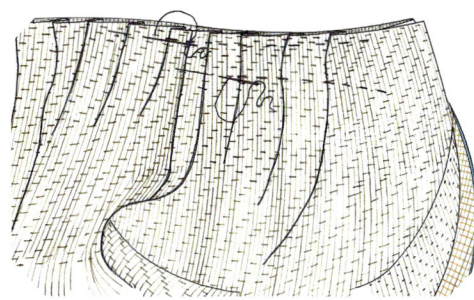

26 The top edge of the lining was pleated to fit the waistband. The lining was then RUNNING STITCHED at the top and bottom edges of the waistband.

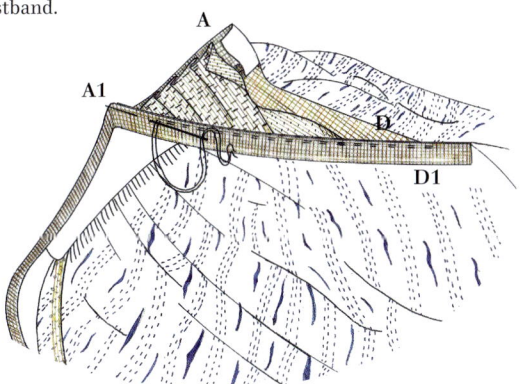

27 A length of linen tape was RUNNING STITCHED, with doubled linen thread from D1 through to A1, along the top edge of the waistband and lining edge, to A, and down the LHS CF to D, keeping the lining at the CF edges out of the seam.

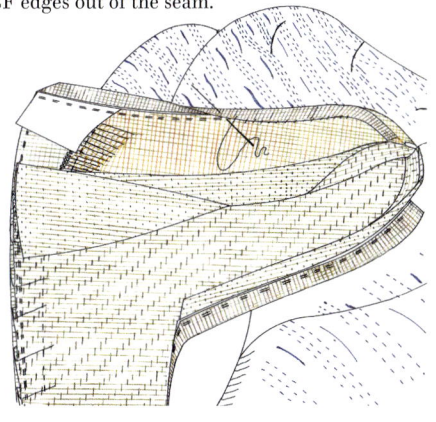

28 The linen tape was FOLDED to the WS and FELLED to the line of running stitches.

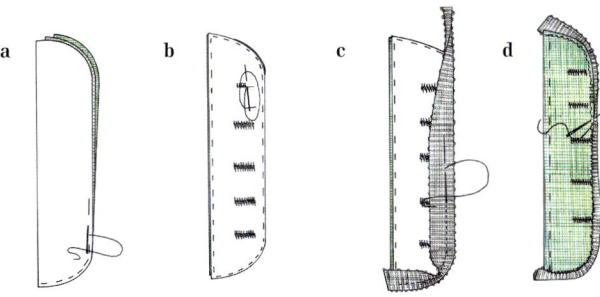

29a The three layers of oyster silk satin, linen interlining and silk lining for the buttonhole stand were BASTED together. **b** Five buttonholes were CUT and BUTTONHOLE STITCHED. **c** With RS together, a silk grosgrain binding lace was HALF-BACK STITCHED to the front edge of the buttonhole stand. **d** The binding lace was FOLDED to the WS and FELLED to the lining.

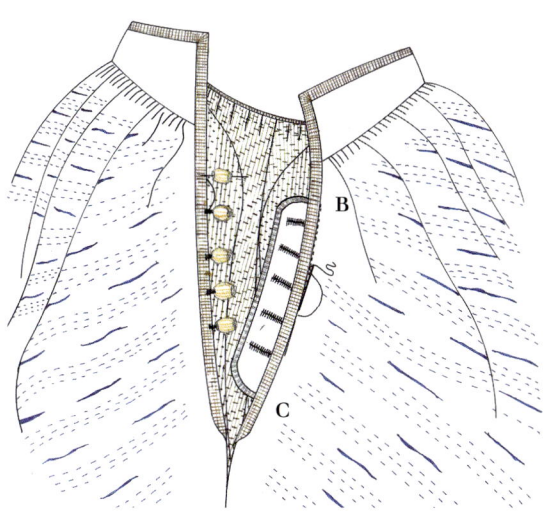

30 The buttonhole stand was PRICK STITCHED to the CF edge of the LHS leg, between B and C. On the RHS of the CF hose, five buttons were sewn, right on the CF edge, through the linen binding tape, as described in step 36.

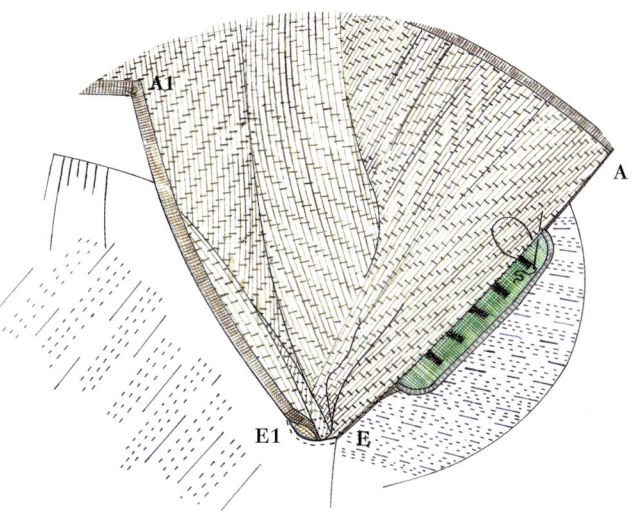

31 Each CF edge of the lining was FOLDED to the WS and FELLED from A/A1 to E/E1 to the linen tape.

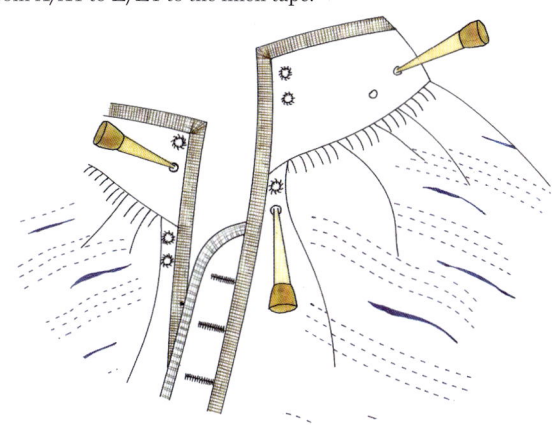

32 A pair of eyelets were PIERCED on each side of the CF waistband and then WHIPPED. Below the waistband, on each side, a pair of eyelets were PIERCED and WHIPPED with silk thread. Thirty-eight eyelets were PIERCED around the waistband.

Pattern by Melanie Braun

3 | Sword girdle and hangers

English, c. 1618 | V&A: T.35&A–1938 | Given by Lady Spickernell | Pattern by Jenny Tiramani

Above left
Detail of Sir Rowland Cotton, c. 1618
Paul van Somer
The Weiss Gallery, London

Above centre and right
Paper, cardboard and foamboard reconstruction of the sword harness mounted with reconstructions of a doublet and hose dating from c. 1615–20.

Left
Sir Thomas Button, 1615
English School
Collection of Lt. Col. Rhodri Traherne
Sir Thomas Button wears a green sword harness that matches his hose, making it a strong feature that stands out against his cream-coloured doublet. The doublet is decorated with oak-leaf motifs, as are the sword hangers opposite.

This finely embroidered sword girdle and hangers are also part of Lady Spickernell's gift to the V&A. Both girdle and hangers have foundations of two layers of leather, covered with embroidered green silk satin on the face and green silk velvet on the back. The embroidery of the girdle and the borders of the hangers is couched directly onto the satin, and the centres of both hangers have separate embroidered slips of oak leaves applied over leather shapes that make them three dimensional. Three widths of uncut, silk and metal fringe and one of cut fringe edge the set, which is all bound in a woven silk lace.

The girdle and hangers are now a shadow of their former appearance. The silver threads of the embroidery have tarnished and the front strap needed to hold the hangers in position is missing, together with one of the scabbard straps. The similarity between this set of girdle and hangers and the one worn by Sir Rowland Cotton in his portrait is remarkable. In the detail of the portrait shown above left, the metal fittings are identical in shape and size, the girdle depicted is similarly embroidered and it is bordered by silk and silver-gilt filé fringes in the same manner. The only aspect that does not match exactly is the design of the embroidery motifs. There are other examples of existing garments not depicted perfectly in the painted versions of them, perhaps because the artist had limited access to the actual girdle.

It is equally possible that Sir Rowland commissioned sword harnesses to be worn specifically with each doublet and hose made for him. In this case, it was perhaps part of an ensemble in green, a popular colour for hunting clothes. The choice of oak leaves for the embroidered slip motifs on the hangers adds to the association with outdoor pursuits in the oak forests of England. A surviving inventory for some of the clothing of Richard Sackville, 3rd Earl of Dorset gives details of the fabrics chosen to be worn together. In most cases the sword harness

matched the fabric of the doublet as in the following entry of 1619:

[1] Inprimis One Cloake of greene veluett embroadered fowre times about and lyned with vnshorne greene veluett embroadered with Ermyns
[2] Item one doublett of greene cloth of gold embroadered with golde
[3] Item one paire of greene veluett hose embroadered with gold and suteable to the Cloake
[4] Item one Hatband of greene Cipres embroadered with gold
[5] Item one Girdle and hangers of greene cloth of gold embroadered
[6] Item one paire of gloves with topps of greene cloth of gold imbroadered
[7] Item one paire of greene taffetie garters embroadered all over and edged about with a small edging lace of gold
[8] Item one paire of greene roses edged wth gold lace
[9] Item one paire of greene silke stockinges embroad'[1]

Both the spectacular metal-thread embroidery and the use of multiple fringes around the outside edges of this set contribute to a sense of luxury in three dimensions. Lining the set in green silk velvet could simply be seen as a luxurious choice but it had a practical use too; the softness of the velvet pile would have caused minimum friction and damage to the doublet and hose worn underneath. The frequency with which velvet linings were used is supported by other surviving examples and by accounts such as an inventory of goods made at the death of Henry Howard in 1614 which includes numerous examples including: 'A girdle and a paire of hangers of tawny satten imbrodered with seede pearle great and small, lined with tawnry velvett, 50s'.[2]

1. Peter and Ann MacTaggart, 'The Rich Wearing Apparel of Richard, 3rd Earl of Dorset', *Costume*, 14, 1980, pp. 41–55
2. George Ornsby, ed., *Selections from the Household Books of the Lord William Howard of Naworth Castle*, Publications of the Surtees Society, vol. 68, 1877, p. 122

Pattern by Jenny Tiramani

DETAILS
Right side (RS) details of the girdle

3.3, 3.1, 3.11v   3.6   3.2v   3.9   3.15v   3.14v   3.8   3.4   3.12v   3.5   3.7, 3.13v   3.3, 3.10, 3.16v

3.1 The ring at the left CF of the girdle.

3.2 The plain strap-end of the front girdle section.

3.3 The girdle fastened at centre front. A point made of silk ribbon, lace or loop-manipulated braid was threaded through or around the central ring to tie the girdle to the CF of the doublet.

3.4 The green silk fringe.

3.5 The green silk and silver-gilt filé fringe.

3.6 The buckle plate on the girdle. The section on the right was added later in the life of the girdle, possibly to make it longer or to replace a worn-through original section. The silk satin and embroidery differ slightly from the rest.

3.7 The buckle with a ring at the base to hook the hangers onto the girdle at the left waist. It was wrapped in green silk ribbon.

3.8 Detail of the girdle showing the couched embroidery with motifs outlined in silver-gilt filé, alternately filled and part-filled, and partially wrapped silver filé.

3.9 The buckle on the right-hand side of the girdle to hook on the front girdle strap, now missing. There are indentations in the slider, which are visible where the silk ribbon wrapping has unravelled.

3.10 The CF hook on the RHS of the girdle, seen in fig. 3.3, connected to the ring on the LHS of the girdle.

Wrong side (WS) details of the girdle

3.11 The back of the ring at the left CF of the girdle.

3.12 The lace binding the edges of the girdle has green silk warp threads, many of which have worn away to reveal the linen weft.

3.13 A triangular piece of green velvet was stitched to the back of the girdle to protect the doublet from rubbing against the ring.

3.14 The two leather layers may be seen where the velvet lining has come away. The reverse of the embroidery is visible here, worked through the green silk satin and a layer of linen.

3.15 A section of the back of the girdle where the velvet lining is still in good condition.

3.16 Side-back view of the CF hook on the RHS of the girdle.

The front strap and hook from the green velvet set surveyed here is missing. It was *probably* similar to this hook from the front strap of another girdle (V&A: T.36A–1938a) and hung from the buckle seen in fig. 3.9.

3 | Sword girdle and hangers

Details of the hangers

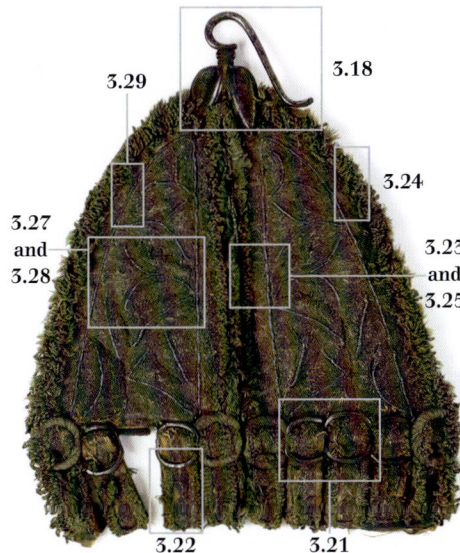

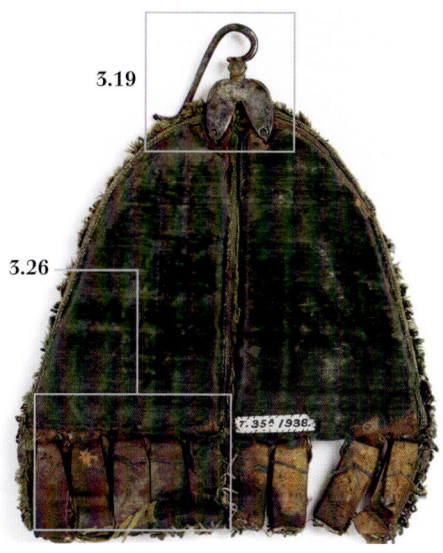

3.17 RS of the hangers. The buckles at both ends of each half of the hangers were wrapped in green silk ribbon, perhaps to protect the hose from damage.

3.18 RS of the hook. The two pieces of the hangers are joined together by the rivets of the central hook.

3.19 WS of the hook. The leather layer on the back was cut away to sink the hook bases flush with the surface of the hangers.

3.20 WS of the hangers. Originally the green velvet lining covered the leather straps where fragments of it remain stitched to the fold of the straps.

3.21 Hanger buckles. There is not enough room for the buckles to sit side by side, so they overlap slightly.

3.22 The ¼" wide fringe lace around the straps is continuous.

3.23 A length of green silk fringe that has come unstitched.

3.24 The silver-gilt filé and green silk fringe, ⅝" wide.

3.25 A view between the two halves of the hangers, which are connected only by the hook seen in 3.18 and 3.19.

3.26 Doubled blue linen thread stitched from strap to strap to hold them all in line. Fragments of the green velvet selvedge remain.

3.27 The lighting here shows the three-dimensional nature of the oak leaf slips, created by shaped leather pieces underneath them. The spines of the leaves are worked in a wide silver strip wrapped around several linen threads.

3.28 The three variations of embroidery threads on the oak leaf motifs: wrapped in the centre for the spine, partially wrapped two-plied threads on either side of it, and couched silk floss threads with silver coils twisted around them.

3.29 Detail of a motif on the border of each hanger. The centre of the motif has the appearance of a four-leafed clover.

Pattern by Jenny Tiramani

PATTERN
Pattern of the sword girdle and hangers

SCALE 1:2

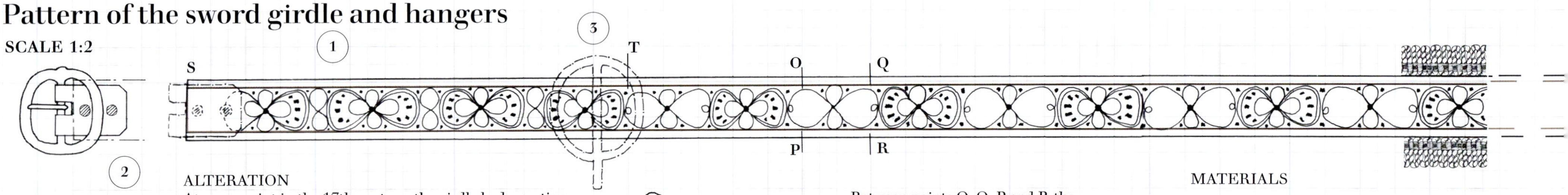

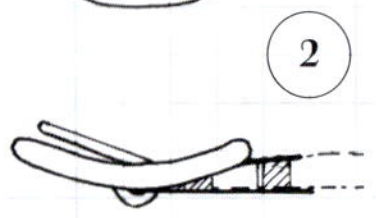

ALTERATION
At some point in the 17th century, the girdle had a section replaced from S to T, either to make it longer or because it was damaged. The new section was matched quite carefully but the fabrics, trimmings and embroidery design differ slightly from those of the original girdle.

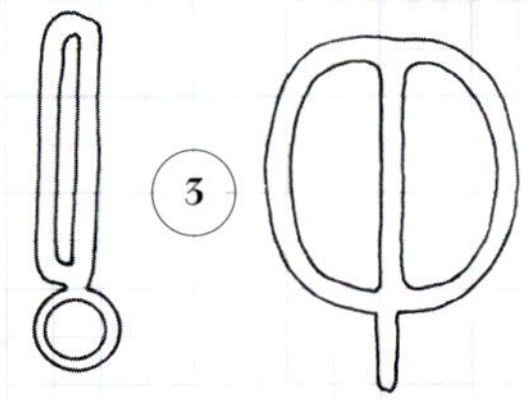

Between points O, Q, P and R the girdle is now misshapen, possibly due to the attachment of a dagger.

MATERIALS
Outer layer of girdle and hangers: green silk satin, interlined in bleached linen
Foundation of the girdles: natural leather
Lining of the girdles and hangers: deep green silk velvet, pile $\frac{1}{16}$" high
Gilt steel
Natural linen thread
Blue linen thread
Green silk thread

PATTERN PIECES
1. Long satin/linen, leather × two layers and velvet girdle piece
2. Long girdle buckle
3. Eye for front strap hook
4. Velvet buckle guard
5. Eye for hangers
6. Long girdle RHS CF hook
7. Short girdle LHS CF ring
8. Short satin/linen, leather × two layers and velvet girdle piece
9. Short girdle end
10. Front short leather hanger piece × two
11. Back short leather hanger piece × two
12. Hangers hook
13. Front satin/linen hanger piece
14. Back satin/linen hanger piece
15. Front long leather/velvet lining hanger piece
16. Back long leather/velvet lining hanger piece
17. Conjectured hanger strap
18. Conjectured hanger strap hook
19.
20.
22. } Hanger scabbard buckles
|
28.
21. Conjectured hanger scabbard buckle

LAYERS OF THE FRONT HANGER

LAYERS OF THE BACK HANGER

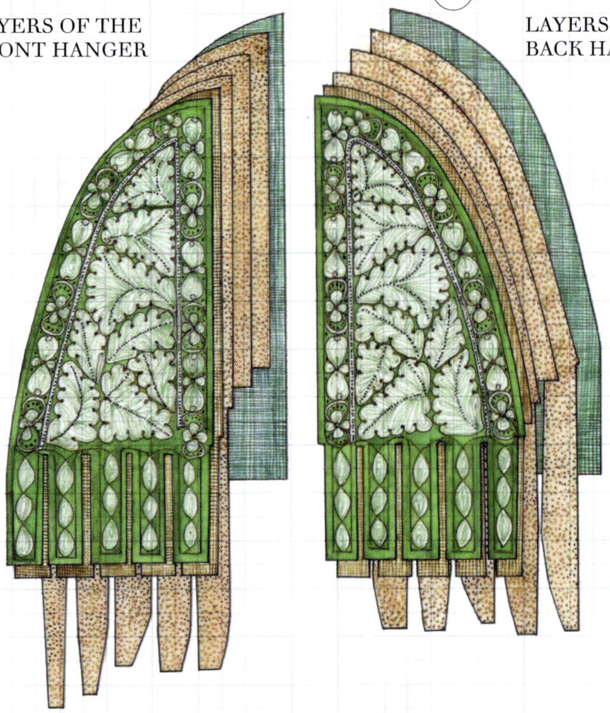

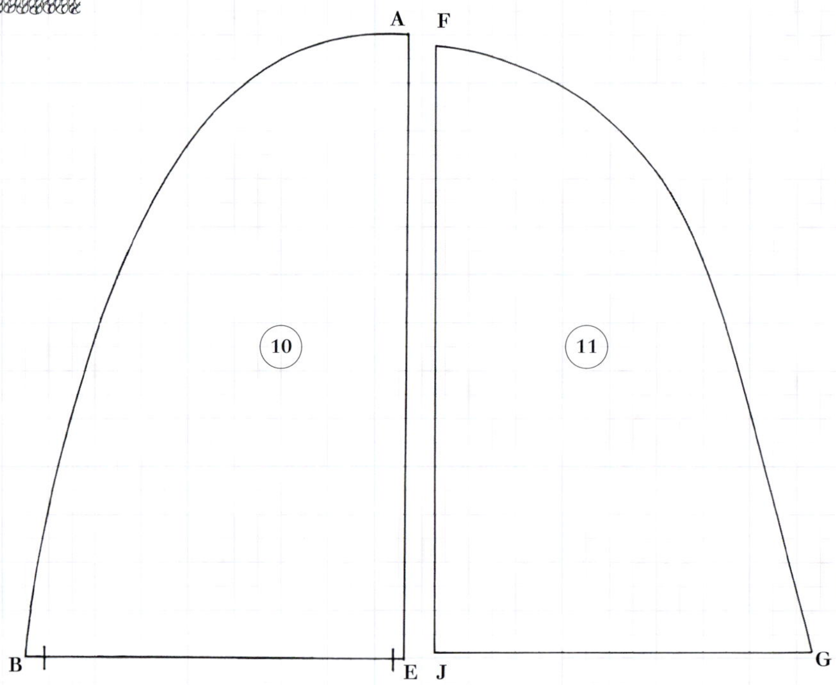

LAYERS KEY
- Dark green silk velvet
- Leather
- Linen
- Embroidered green silk satin

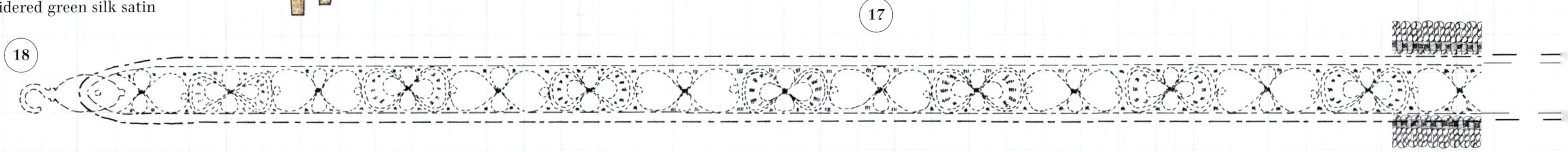

BINDING LACE AND FRINGES

SCALE 1:1

WIDE UNCUT FRINGE LACE 1
12 warp in green silk
4 warp in silver-gilt filé
1 weft in green silk partially wrapped in silver-gilt filé [A–B–C and F–G–H]

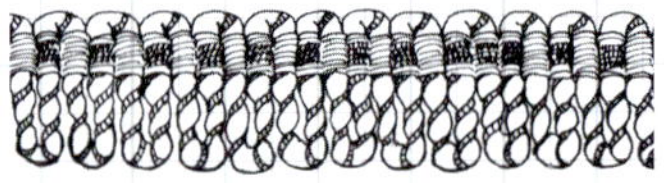

WIDE UNCUT FRINGE LACE 2
12 warp in green silk
4 warp in silver-gilt filé
1 weft in green silk partially wrapped in silver-gilt filé [A–E–D and F–J–I and all edges of pattern pieces 1 and 8]

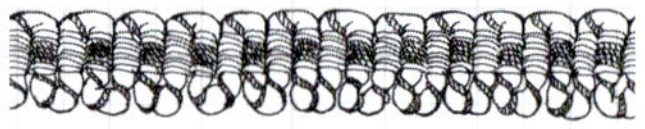

NARROW UNCUT FRINGE LACE 3
28 warp in green silk
1 weft in natural [C–D–E and H–I–J]

CUT FRINGE LACE 4
28 warp in green silk
1 weft in green silk [B–A–E and J–F–G and all edges of pattern pieces 1 and 8]

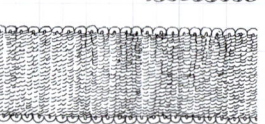

BINDING LACE
28 warp in green silk
1 weft in natural linen [B–A–E and J–F–G and all edges of pattern pieces 1 and 8]

3 | Sword girdle and hangers

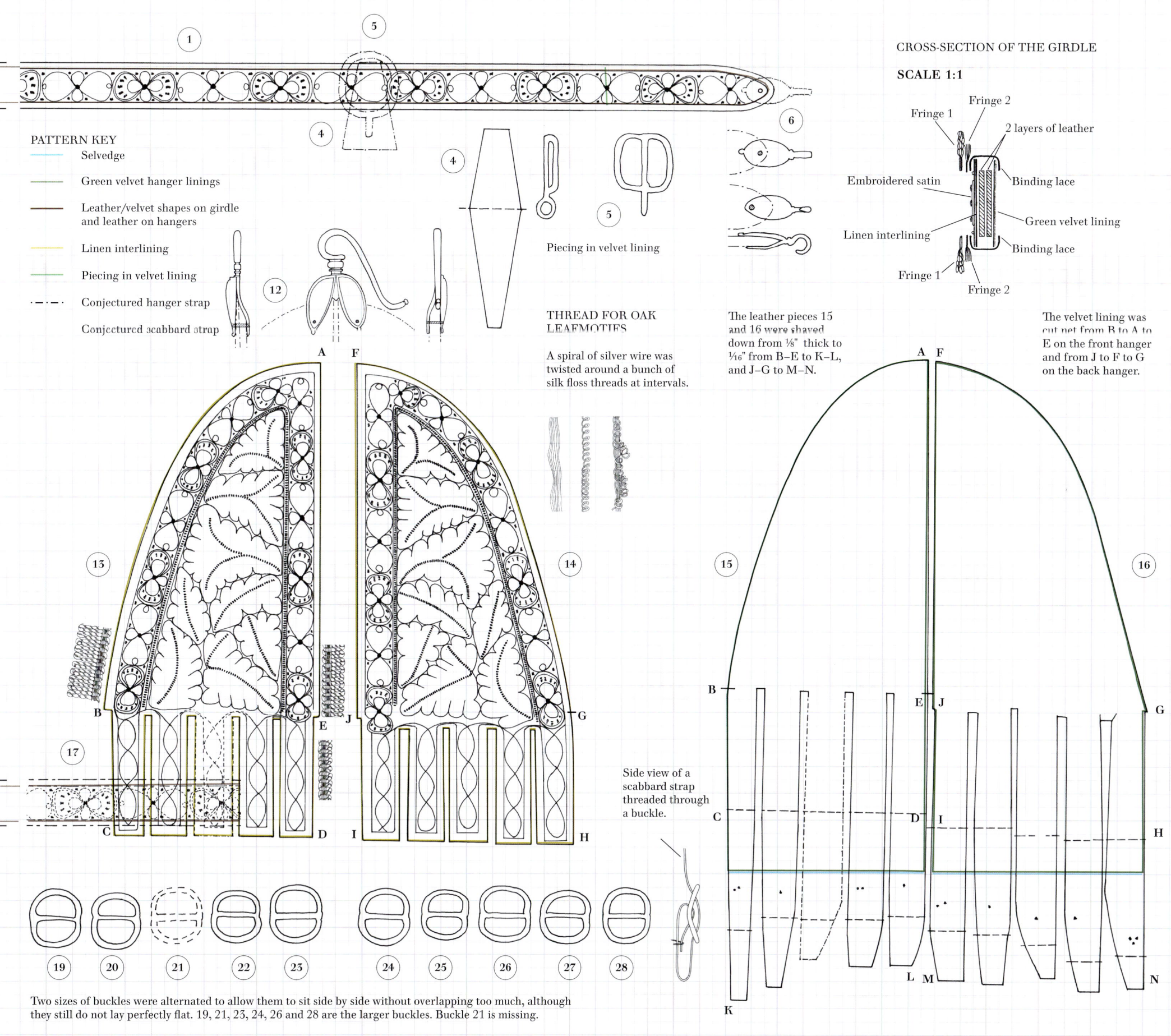

CONSTRUCTION
Construction of the hangers

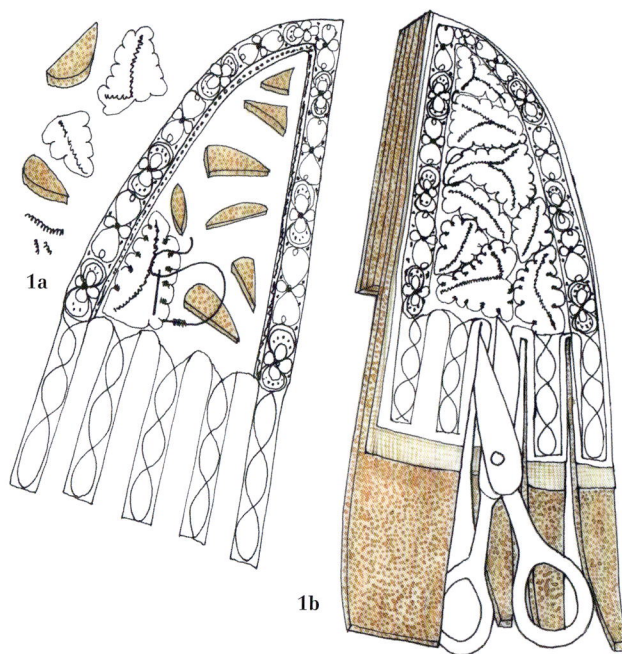

1a The borders and scabbard straps of the hangers and the girdle were embroidered through the green silk satin over the layer of linen, *probably* stretched on a frame. Leather shapes were GLUED to the embroidered satin, *probably* while still in the frame. Each oak leaf slip was PLACED over a leather shape and COUCHED to the satin ground with short lengths of purl in between the lobes of the leaf. **b** The leather layers for the hangers were GLUED together. The back hanger was TURNED OVER, so the long leather piece was uppermost. The embroidered satin/linen was GLUED to the RS of each hanger. Slits were CUT between the scabbard straps.

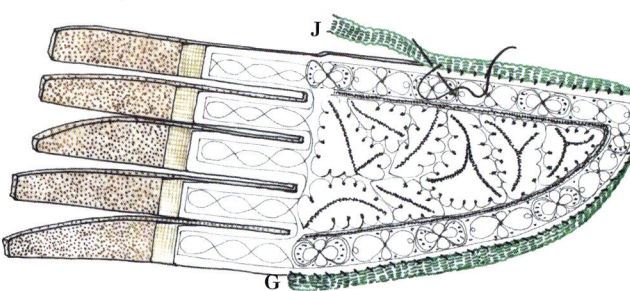

2 A length of green silk binding lace was FELLED to the RS of each hanger with green silk thread from G to J.

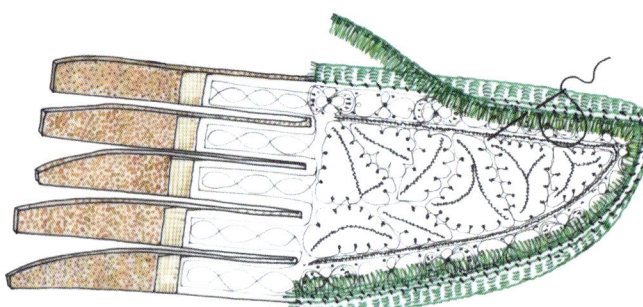

3 A length of fringe 4 was FELLED close to where the binding lace was STITCHED to the hanger from point G to point J in green silk thread.

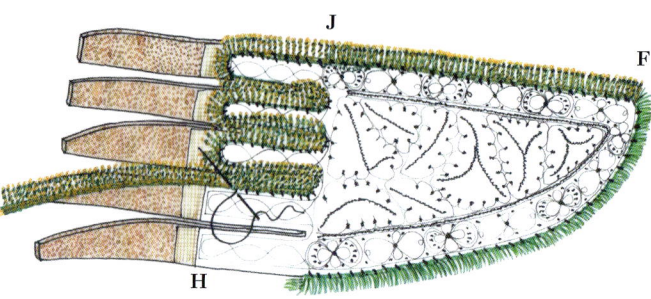

4 Having PUSHED the previous fringe over the outer edge, a length of fringe 2 was FELLED from F to J. A length of fringe 3 was FELLED from J to H with green silk thread.

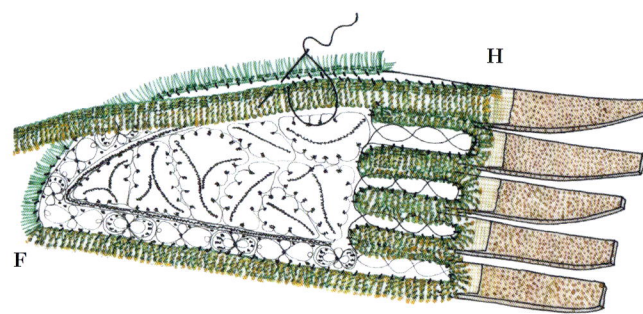

5 A length of fringe 1 was FELLED to the outer edge of the hanger next to where the green silk fringe was STITCHED, from H to F.

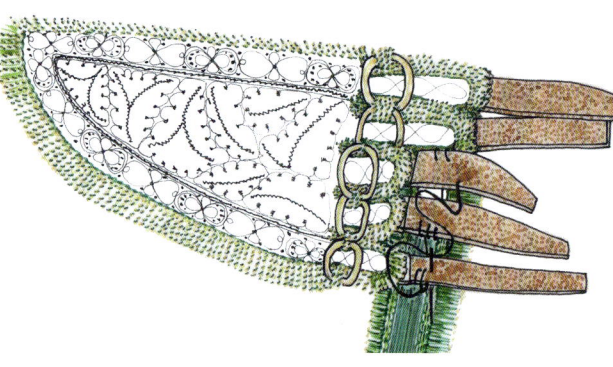

6 The metal buckles were THREADED onto the scabbard straps and the front hanger strap was STITCHED to the back of three scabbard straps of the front hanger. Only fragments of thick natural linen thread and stitch holes remain on the scabbard straps; the front strap is missing.

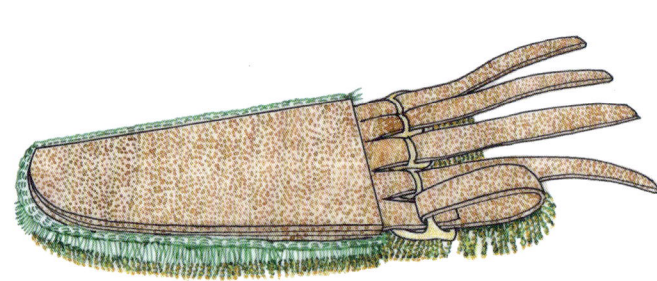

7 The ends of the scabbard straps were THREADED back through the middle bar of the buckles (the back hanger is shown here).

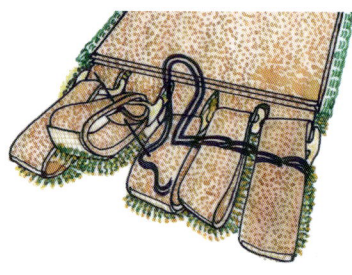

8 The leather on either side of the metal buckle was WHIPPED together in thick doubled blue linen thread continuously across all the straps, *probably* with a triangular glover's needle.

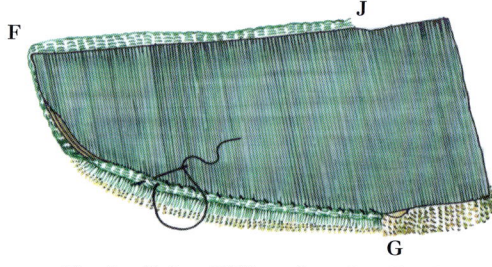

9 The green silk velvet lining, CUT net from G to F to J, was PLACED onto the back of the hanger. The other edge of the binding lace (step 2) was pulled over it and FELLED down.

10 The seam allowance of the velvet lining was FOLDED and WHIPPED to the edges of the outer scabbard straps and FELLED to the lower edge of the folded straps with thick natural linen thread.

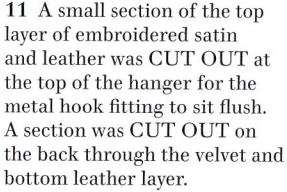

11 A small section of the top layer of embroidered satin and leather was CUT OUT at the top of the hanger for the metal hook fitting to sit flush. A section was CUT OUT on the back through the velvet and bottom leather layer.

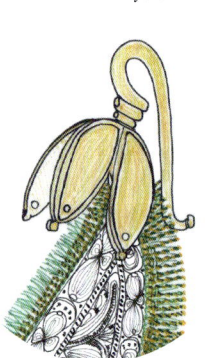 

12 The hangers were INSERTED between the front and back plates of the hook and RIVETED on, joining them together.

Construction of the girdle

The construction of the short and the long parts of the girdle are the same. Only the fittings on each end are different.

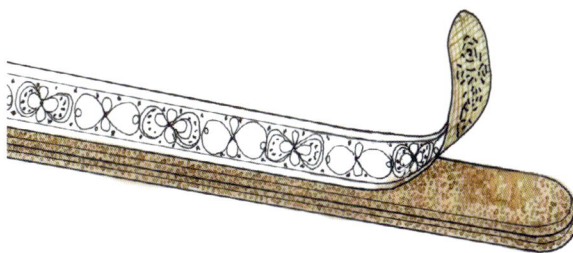

13 The two layers of leather and the layer of embroidered green satin were PLACED together. There is no sign of glue on them now, although they would *probably* have needed gluing together originally.

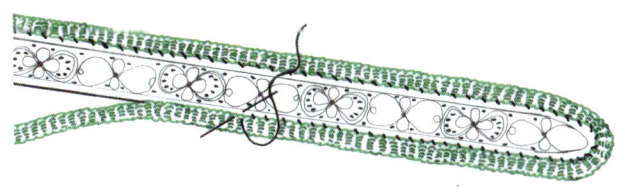

14 A length of green silk binding lace was FELLED to the RS of the girdle with green silk thread.

15 The green silk velvet lining, CUT net, was PLACED over the leather on the back of the girdle.

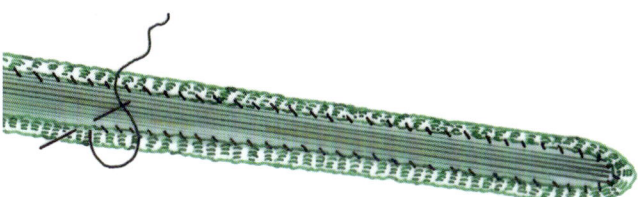

16 The binding lace was FELLED down to the velvet on the back.

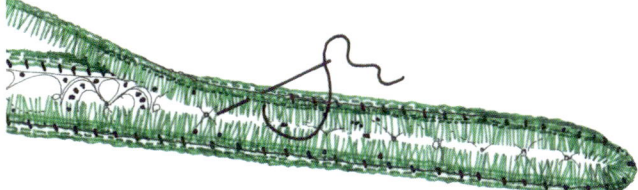

17 On the RS a length of fringe 4 was FELLED down on the RS edge of the binding lace.

18 A length of fringe 2 was FELLED down, next to fringe 4.

19 The CF end of the short girdle piece was INSERTED between the front and back plates of the LCF ring and RIVETED on.

20 The strap end was PLACED on the other end of the short girdle piece and RIVETED onto the topside. This girdle piece was complete and ready to be buckled to the long girdle piece.

21 The end of the long girdle piece was INSERTED between the front and back plates of the buckle and attached with two rivets. The RCF hook was RIVETED to the other end of the piece. Then the two ring fittings were THREADED onto the long girdle piece.

22 A triangular piece of velvet was BACK STITCHED behind girdle buckle five.

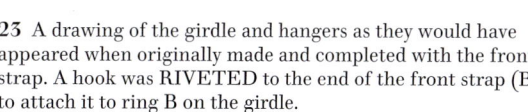

23 A drawing of the girdle and hangers as they would have appeared when originally made and completed with the front strap. A hook was RIVETED to the end of the front strap (B) to attach it to ring B on the girdle.

Pattern by Jenny Tiramani

4 | Crimson silk grosgrain doublet

English, *c.* 1620 | V&A: 268–1891   *Pattern by Jenny Tiramani*

The South Kensington Museum purchased this doublet, along with an 18th-century gown, a pair of 18th-century shoes and a pair of cushion covers, for £5 in 1891. The doublet was originally thought to have been part of the wedding suit of George Ashby (b. 1629), High Sheriff of the county of Leicester, who married in 1652. However, the style of the doublet dates from a generation earlier. The waistline is raised well above the natural waist of the wearer, leaving only 4½" from waist to armhole at the sides, and such high-waisted doublets were considered a Dutch fashion in England at the time, according to a character in John Webster's play *The White Devil* of around 1610. The character of Flamineo, Secretary to the Duke of Bracciano, describes his sister's husband Camillo as being 'unable to please a woman that, like a Dutch doublet, all his back is shrunk into his breeches'.[1]

This doublet is a superb example of tailoring. Both the pattern drafting and the construction demonstrate the art and craft of an early 17th-century tailor being practised at the very highest level. There is a refinement to the style eminently suitable for a gentleman with the subtle use of a decorative lace of silver filé and crimson silk to decorate the doublet and 53 buttons to fasten the fronts and sleeves.

The extant account book of two brothers, John and Richard Newdigate, written between 1618 and 1620, contains entries for many of the items required for the construction of a doublet such as this one, which also has pasteboard in the collar, silk taffeta facings, wool foundations in the shoulder wings and canvas interlining.[2]

Item 3 yards Turkie grogeron [for] dublet for Mr Richard	0 15 0
Item 22 yards gallonie binding, 2*oz*. dimi. at ii*s*. iiii*d*.	0 5 10
Item 1*oz*. styching & sowing silke	0 2 0
Item dimi. ell taffatie for fasing	0 6 3
Item dimi. yards bayes for sleeves	9
Item dimi. yard canvas to peece the lynig	6
Item past bord for the coller	1

Grosgrain was a term used in this period for both worsted and silk fabrics with a thicker weft than warp, giving a horizontal rib to the fabric. The rich unfaded red colours of both the grosgrain and the taffeta lining suggest their silks were dyed with costly insect dyes such as cochineal. Features such as the eyelet holes and buttonholes now stand out in contrasting yellow silk thread which was originally rich pink or red. The colour has now almost completely gone in places, suggesting the dye was fugitive.

The x-ray images of the doublet revealed the presence of cork, used to create the almost rigid triangular shapes over the belly area of the centre fronts. Until this discovery there was scarce evidence of cork being used in clothing until the appearance of cork rumps for women in the 1770s. To find cork used inside a tailored garment as early as 1620 poises the question of whether this was commonly used or whether it was an experiment by the tailor who made it. The cork would have been imported into England where bottle stoppers were made from it at this time. It was produced in Mediterranean countries such as Portugal, Spain and Italy and may have been a common reinforcement material for clothing in these places. Although the doublet has an English provenance, the presence of cork may indicate that it was made abroad.

On the other hand, the 1652 inventory of a country mercer, Thomas Harris's shop in Charlbury, a small town in Oxfordshire, records '14lb. of corke at 3*d*. per lb.' in a list that includes many other items used in tailoring among the more general household goods he sold. Harris stocked 'Hookes & iues for briches [at] I : 6' of the kind needed to fasten together this doublet and its breeches, 'loope lace at 14*d*', '7lb. & ½ of whallbone at 5*d*.' and various canvases such as those used for the foundation of this doublet.[3]

While the quality of this doublet suggests the work of a London tailor, the inventories of other country mercers demonstrate that the fastenings, threads, interlinings and reinforcements used in tailoring were widely available throughout rural England.

1. http://www.gutenberg.org/ebooks/12915
John Webster, *The White Devil*, c. 1610, Act I, Scene I, Line 34
2. Vivienne Larminie, ed., *The Undergraduate Account Book of John and Richard Newdigate, 1618–21*, Camden Miscellany XXX, 4th series, vol. 39, 1990, p. 267
3. D. G. Vaisey, 'A Charlbury Mercer's Shop, 1632', *Oxoniensia*, vol. XXXI, 1966–67, pp. 107–16

Portrait of a gentleman, traditionally identified as Henry, Prince of Wales, *c.* **1620**
Anglo-Flemish School
Oil on canvas
Private collection
Photograph © Christie's Images/ Bridgeman Images

The doublet depicted here is worn in the same way as the V&A doublet would have been. There is a sword girdle around the waist and decorative ribbon points tied through the eyelet holes at the top of the laps. The wrist bones of the wearer are exposed and the ends of the doublet sleeves are probably turned back to support the lace and linen cuffs. A high, stiff collar on the doublet was necessary to support the falling band. This suit of matching doublet, hose and cloak has metal laces that not only outline the seams and edges, but also fill the internal areas with a pattern of diagonal lines. The ground fabric is silk satin, a more luxurious choice than the subdued silk grosgrain of the V&A doublet.

Pattern by Jenny Tiramani   89

DETAILS

Right side (RS) front details

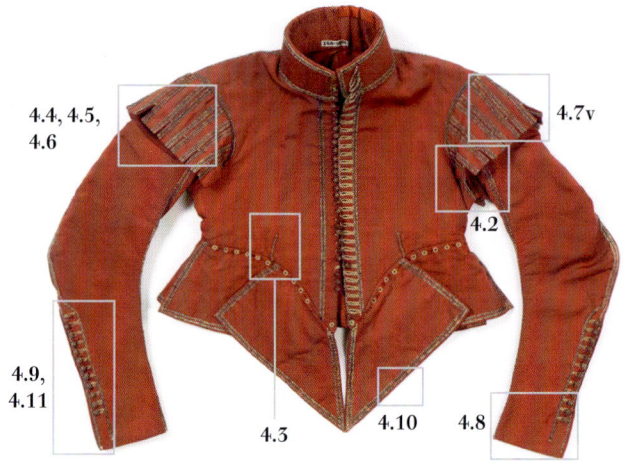

4.1 A front view of the doublet.

4.2 The creases under the left arm from when it was worn were caused by the shallow sleevehead, necessary to enable free movement of the arms in such a tightly fitting garment.

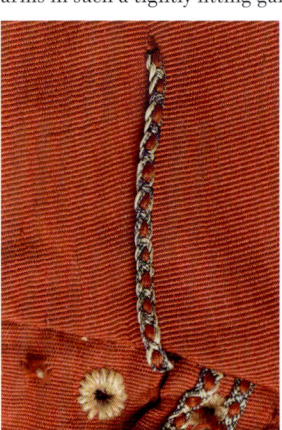

4.3 A loop of the silk and silver lace to hold the girdle in place on the waist.

4.4 Silk thread bars connect the wing sections below the point at which they are stitched together.

Shoulder wing details

4.5 Detail of the wing sections whipped together and the ends secured by thread bars. The right wing is shown.

4.6 Underneath the right wing several piecings with green and white striped selvedges were used for the wing lining to reduce the bulk of the turned edges.

4.7 The black linen interlining of a section of the wing is visible here, together with the seam allowance of the red grosgrain basted to it.

Sleeve details

4.8 The edge of the section of the sleeve-end intended to be turned back is prick stitched. The silk taffeta lining would have been visible here through a fine, transparent linen cuff.

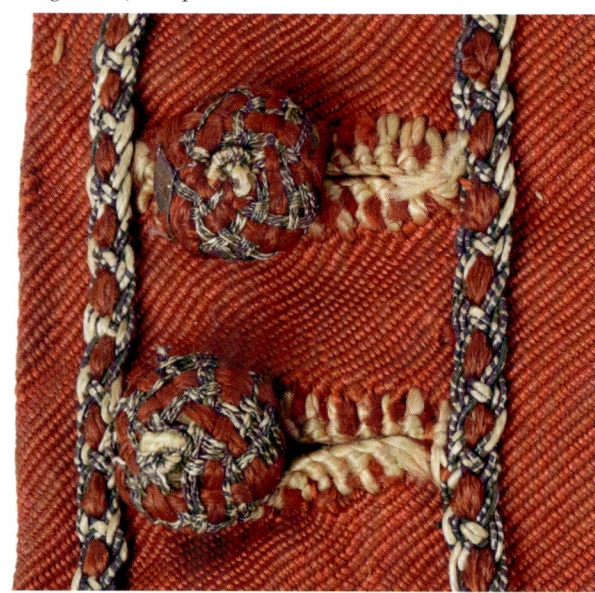

4.9 The buttonholes had to be worked on the bias grain of the curved sleeves, resulting in many frayed threads and an untidy appearance. The buttons have a five-pointed star motif worked in red silk threads.

4.10 The edging lace at the base of a lap where the silver wrapping of the filé has worn away, revealing the white silk core. The red silk thread running through the four-way filé plait has also worn away.

Back body details

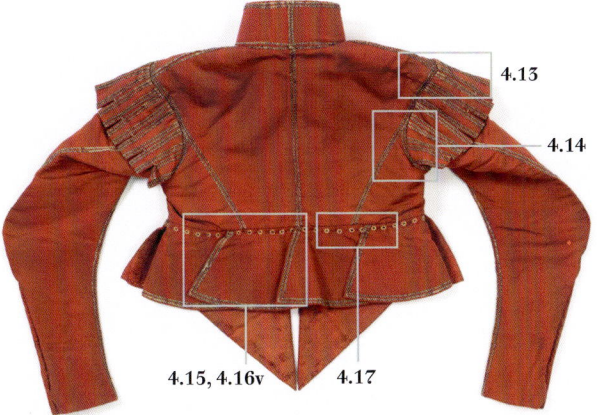

4.12 A back view of the doublet.

Lap details

4.15 The lap to the left of CB overlaps the one on the left and is overlapped by the lap at the right of CB.

4.13 There is a point at the end of the shoulder seam, accentuated by the outlines of the laces.

4.16 The WS of the lap shown in fig. 4.15. The chevron shapes made by the long diagonal threads of the back of the pad stitches are clearly visible through the thin taffeta lining.

4.11 The edging laces stop short of the wrist end of the sleeve.

4.14 The side-back seam is hidden by the lace sewn on top of it. The armhole seam is not covered by the lace, as it was sewn on before the sleeve was sewn into the armhole.

4.17 Some of the eyelet holes were stitched through two adjacent laps. The pierced, unworked holes are clearly seen here inbetween the worked eyelet holes.

Pattern by Jenny Tiramani

Wrong side (WS) details

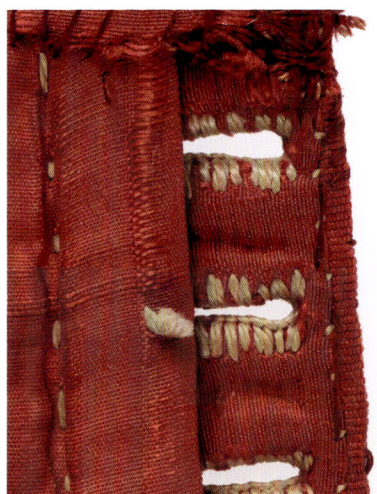

4.18 The doublet laid open.

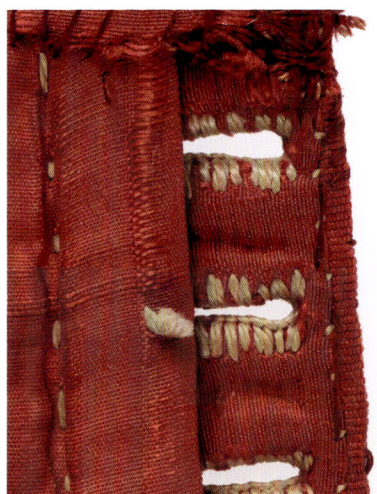

4.19 The point where the collar meets the left front.

4.20 The peak of the RHS belly piece where the lining has worn, revealing the cork and linen layers.

4.21 The selvedge of the lining covering the belly piece on the LHS.

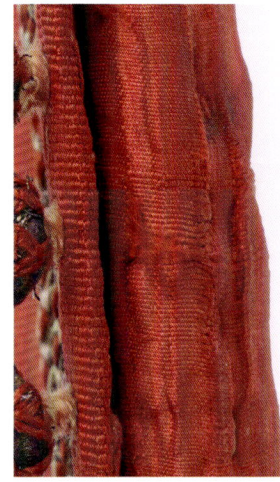

4.22 The belly piece is nearly ½" thick in total.

Wrong side (WS) belly piece details

4.23 The WS of the left-hand side of the doublet.

4.24 The WS of the right-hand side of the doublet.

4.25 The eyelet on the lacing tab has been put under considerable strain when tied to that on the RHS and has distorted, breaking some threads around the hole.

4.26 In addition to the distortion of the hole, the lining on this lacing tab has been worn away.

4 | Crimson silk grosgrain doublet

Body details

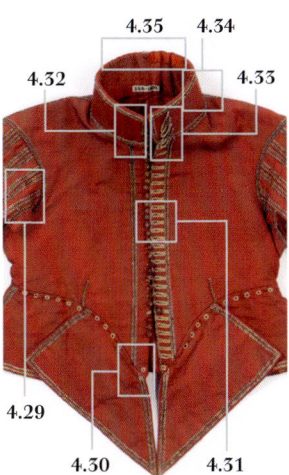

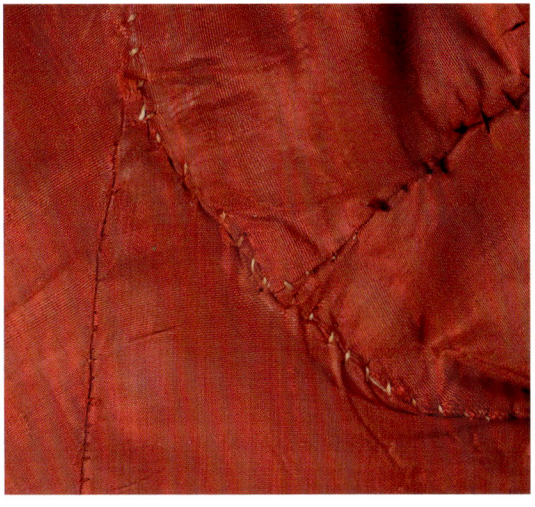

4.27 A front view of the body.

4.28 The left sleeve lining felled onto the lining of the doublet body.

Collar details

4.32 The RHS of the collar.

4.33 The loops on the LHS of the collar. The pasteboard inside the collar makes it too rigid for buttonholes.

Waistband details

4.36 The waistband sits directly on top of the laps, inside the waist of the doublet.

4.37 One of the iron eyes on the WS of the waistband.

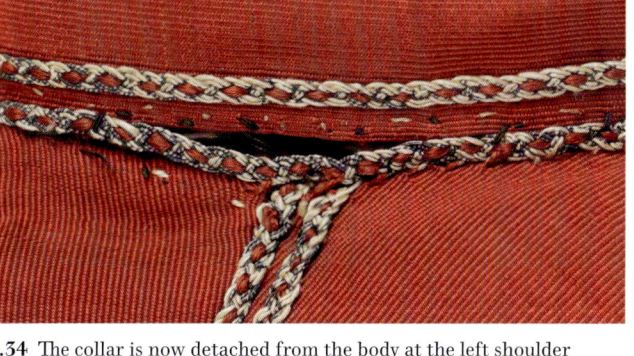

4.29 The seam has come undone under the right wing and the tiny seam allowance of the grosgrain is visible.

4.34 The collar is now detached from the body at the left shoulder seam; the rigidity of the collar and sharp curve of the neckline created a weak point.

4.38 An eye seen from the topside of the waistband, where two selvedges of the taffeta have been pieced by whipping them together.

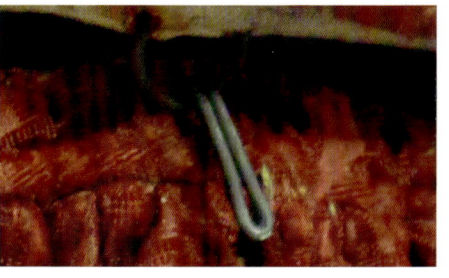

4.30 There is one eyelet hole at the CF waist of the body and another at CF on the lap. The RHS is shown.

4.31 The buttonholes were worked on the straight grain and they are very neat; there are no frayed threads as in fig. 4.9. On grosgrain fabric the splits had to be cut exactly on the grain to achieve such straight edges.

4.35 The collar lining has worn away in places, revealing the layer of soft 2:1 twill wool interlining that would have cushioned the wearer's neck from the hard pasteboard within the collar. Long running stitches basting the seam allowance of the grosgrain to the wool are still in place.

4.39 An iron hook and eye on a doublet and hose, 1612, Historisches Museum Hannover. The length of the hook ensured that the doublet and hose did not easily become uncoupled.

Pattern by Jenny Tiramani

Right side (RS) x-ray images

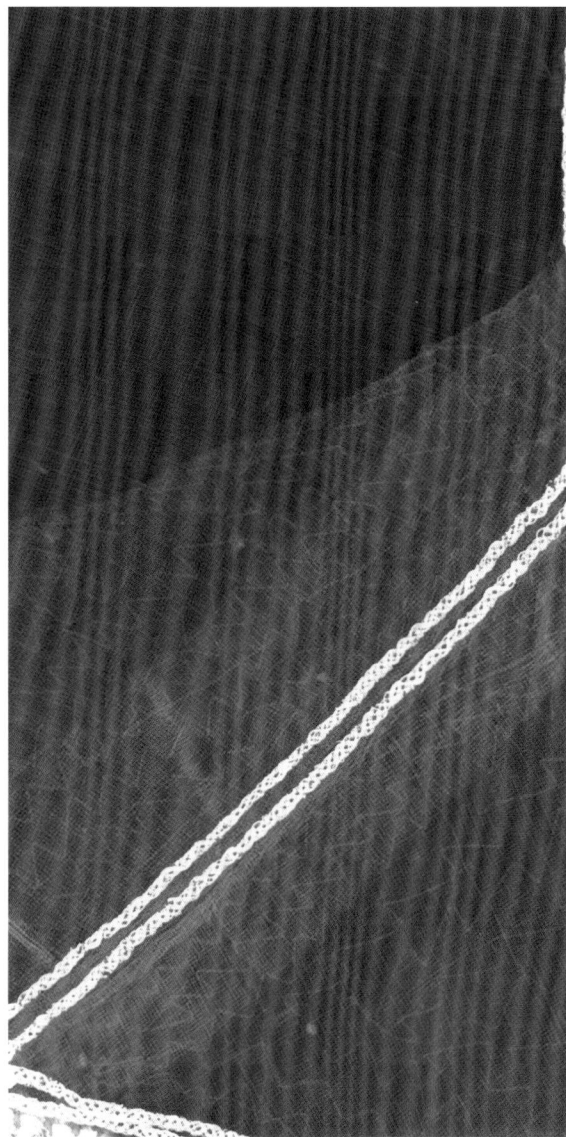

4.40 The pad stitching of the folded interlinings on the left shoulder.

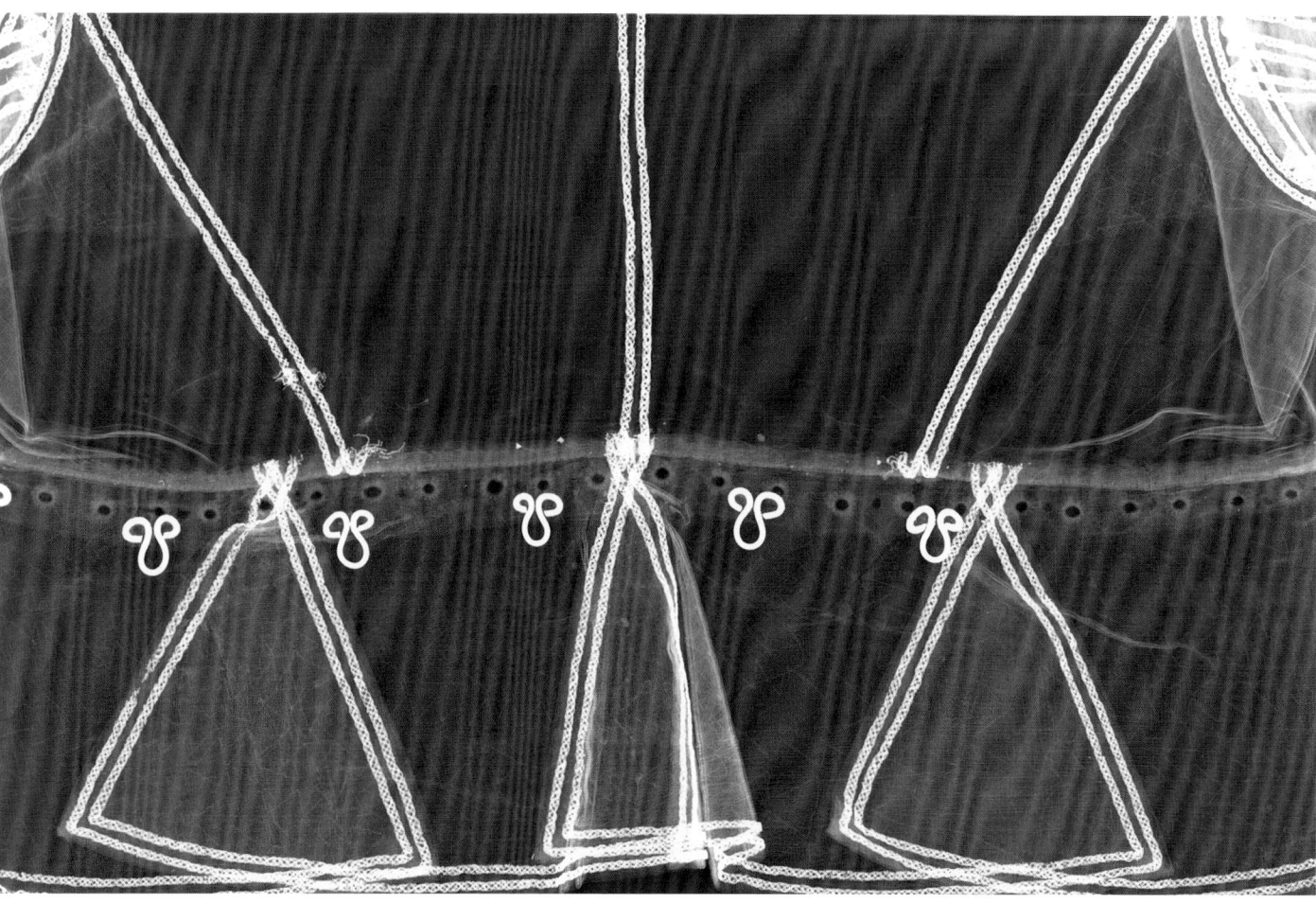

4.42 The back laps where the zig-zag path of the pad stitching across them is visible. The silver of the filé in the lace and the iron eyes appear as bright white here.

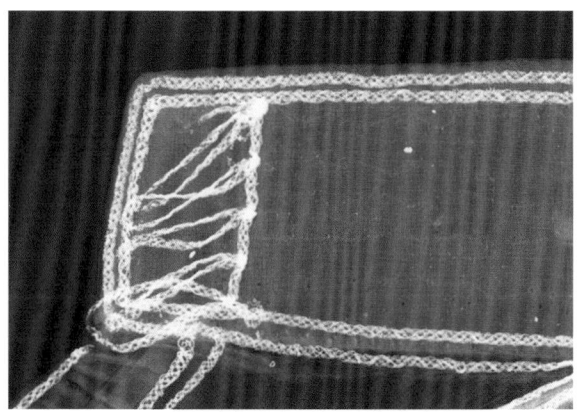

4.41 The loops on the left collar were made from a continuous length of the edging lace used on the rest of the doublet.

4.43 The piecings of the linen interlining at the wrist end of the left sleeve.

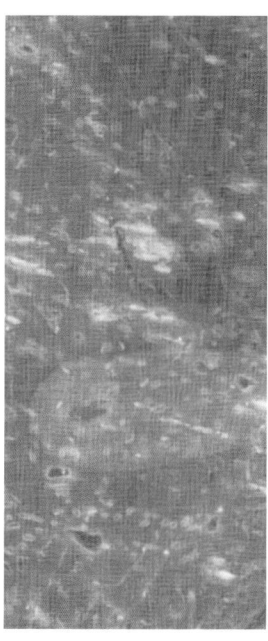

4.44 Detail of the layer of cork inside the belly piece.

4 | Crimson silk grosgrain doublet

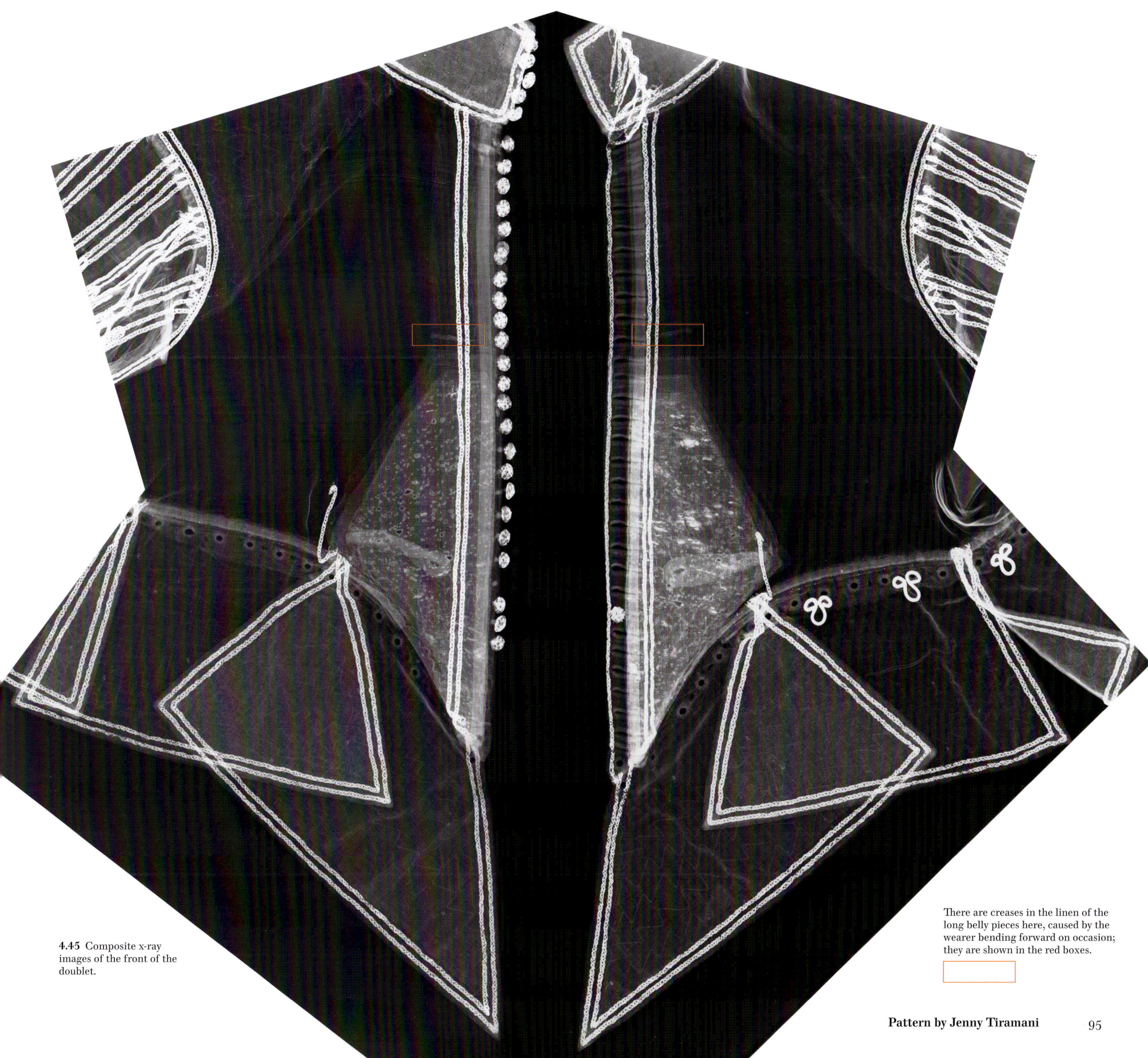

4.45 Composite x-ray images of the front of the doublet.

There are creases in the linen of the long belly pieces here, caused by the wearer bending forward on occasion; they are shown in the red boxes.

Pattern by Jenny Tiramani

PATTERN
Pattern of the crimson grosgrain layer

SCALE 1:4

MATERIALS

Main fabric
Crimson silk grosgrain

Lining of body, laps, collar and front facings
Crimson silk taffeta

Lining of wings
Crimson silk grosgrain

Interlining of body, laps, belly pieces, collar and wrist edges
Plain woven linen

Interlining of wing sections
Black stiffened linen

Interlining of wing
Red twill-woven wool

Interlining of collar
Pasteboard plain woven white wool

Decoration
Silver filé and crimson silk plaited lace

Buttons
Wooden bases wrapped in silver filé and crimson silk

Threads
'S' 2 × plied red silk
'S' 2 × plied linen

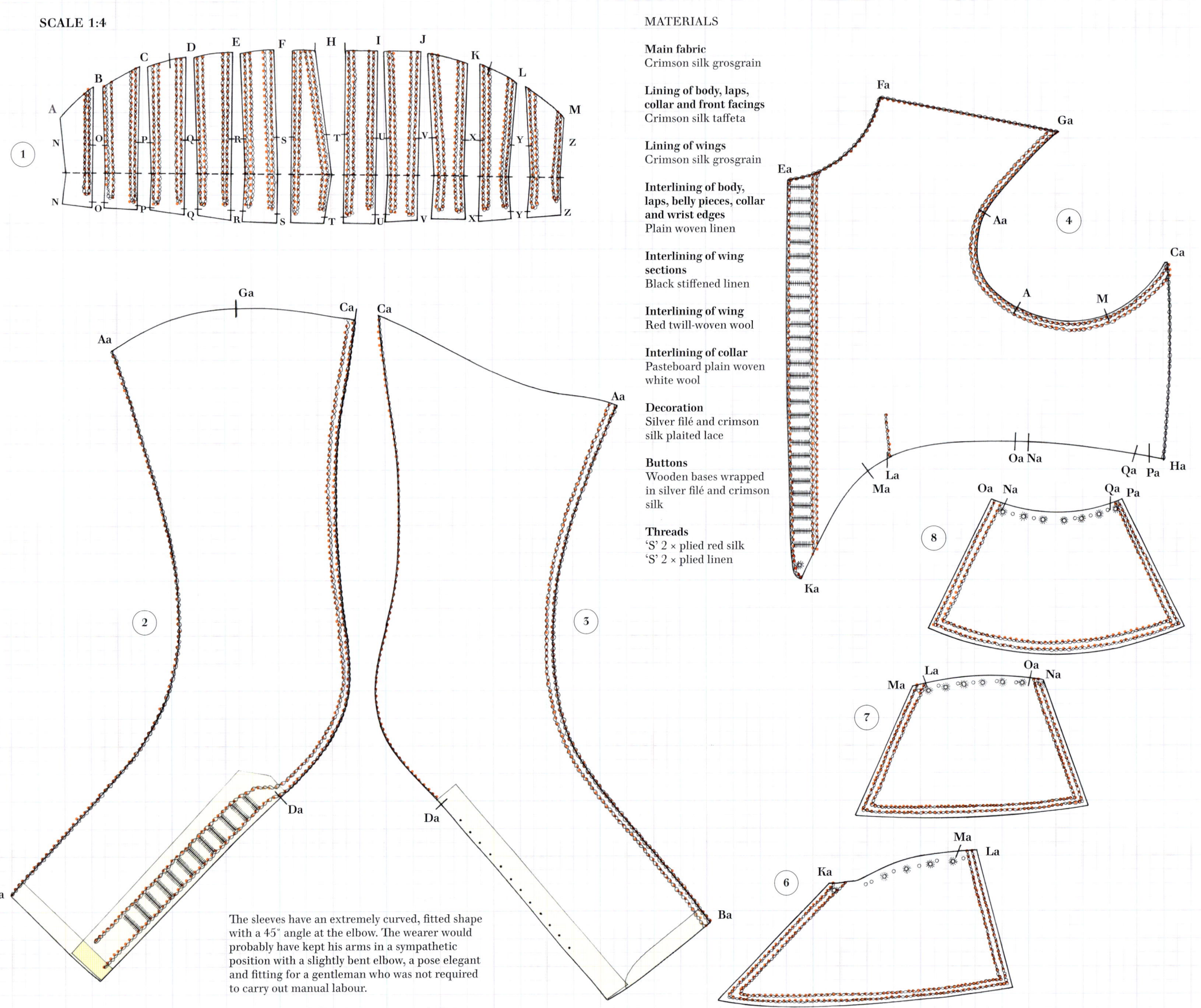

The sleeves have an extremely curved, fitted shape with a 45° angle at the elbow. The wearer would probably have kept his arms in a sympathetic position with a slightly bent elbow, a pose elegant and fitting for a gentleman who was not required to carry out manual labour.

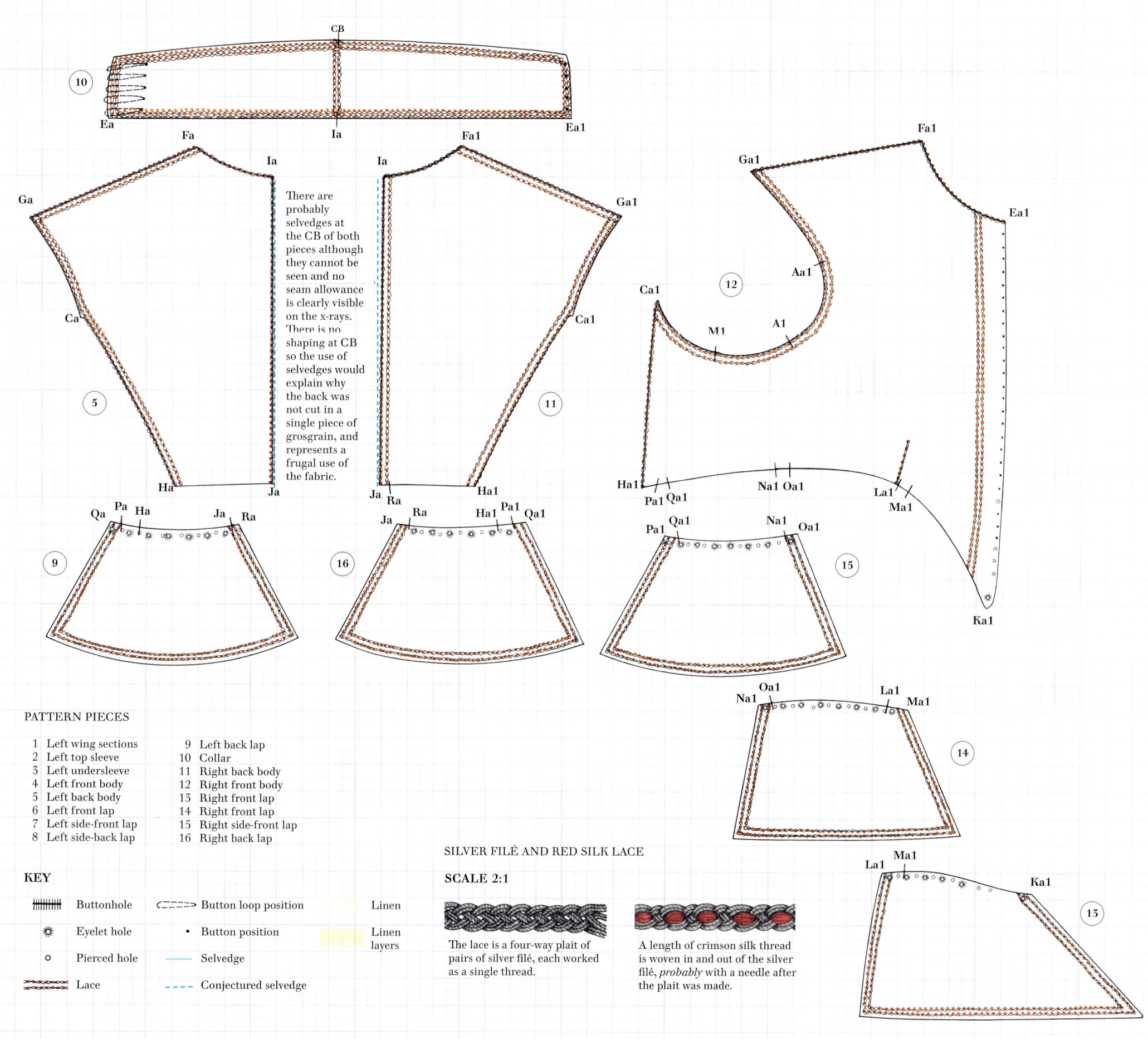

Pattern of the crimson grosgrain layer CONTINUED

Pattern of the linen canvas foundation
Pattern shown from the WS

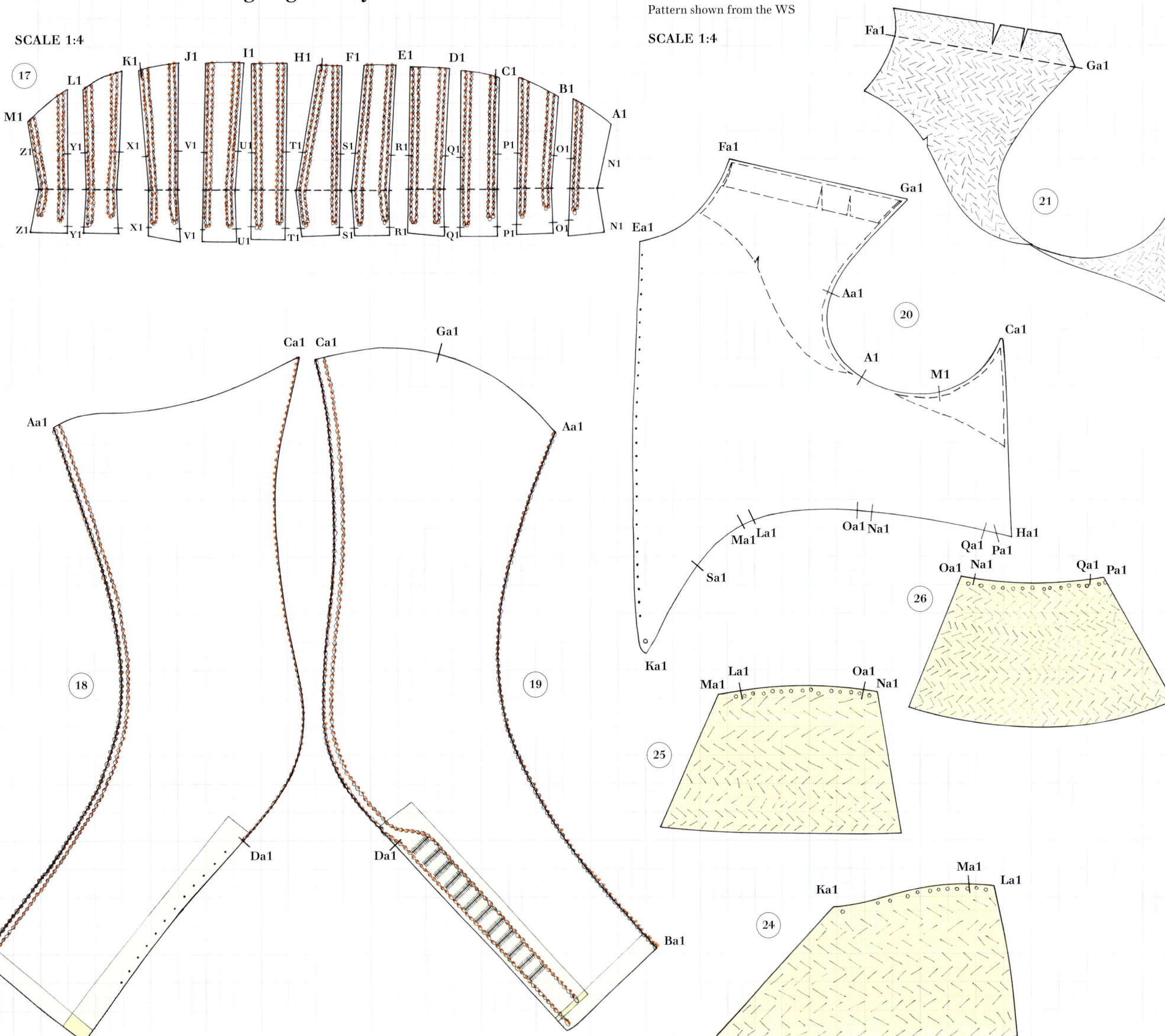

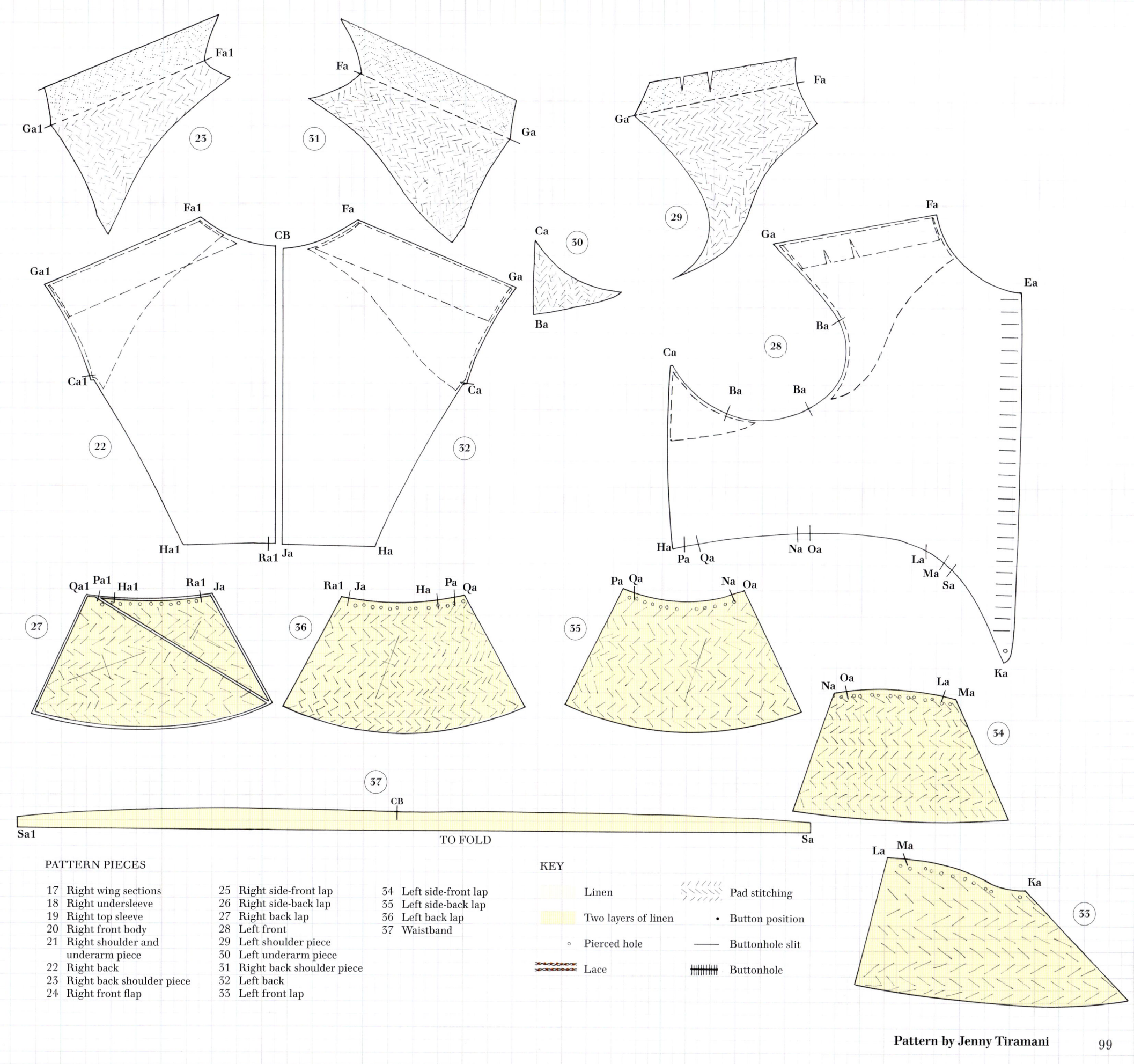

Pattern of the wing lining and interlinings

SCALE 1:4

All the wing sections of pattern pieces 1 and 17 are interlined with a layer of black stiffened linen, cut net.

Layers of the doublet fronts (left side shown)

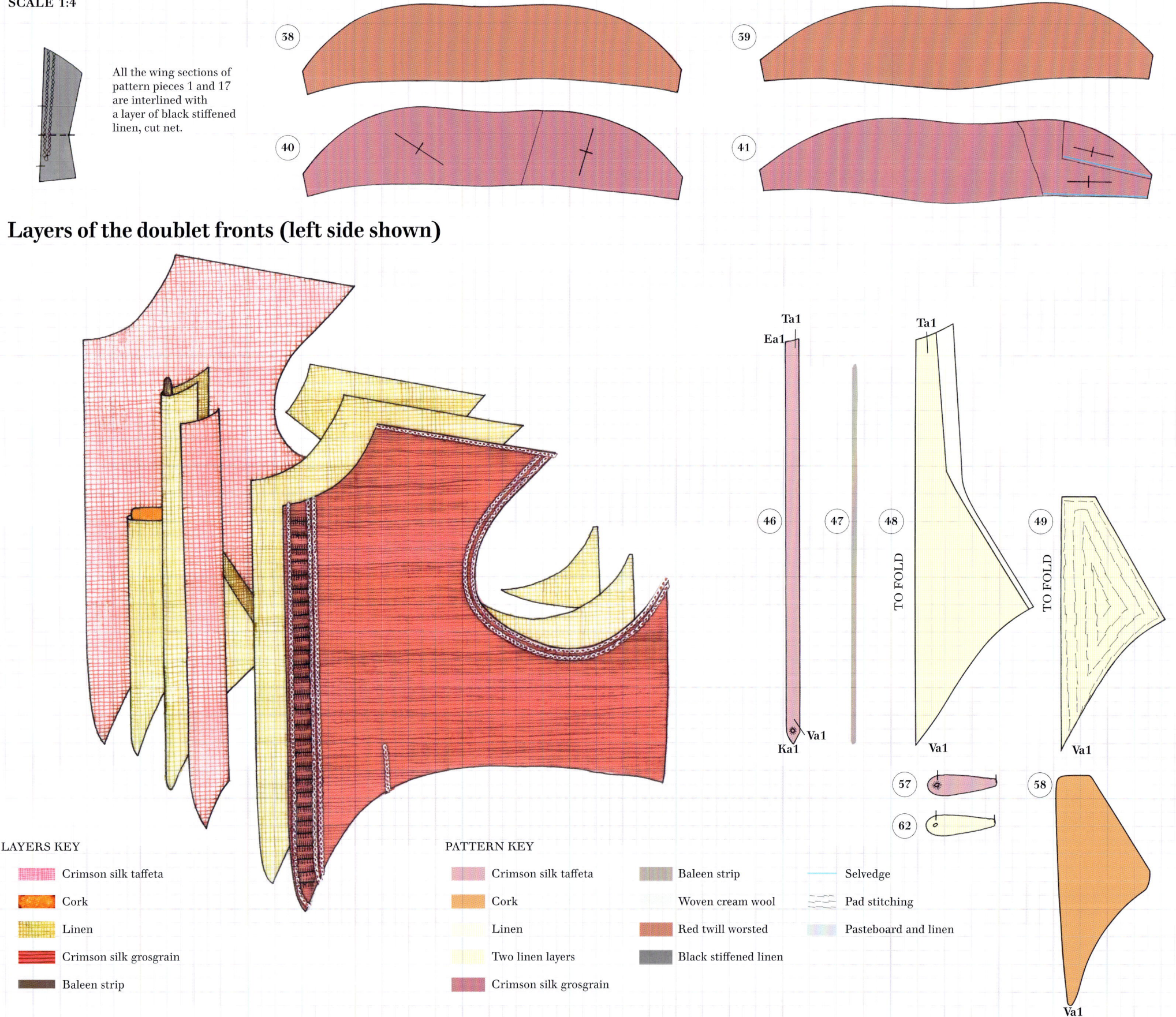

LAYERS KEY
- Crimson silk taffeta
- Cork
- Linen
- Crimson silk grosgrain
- Baleen strip

PATTERN KEY
- Crimson silk taffeta
- Cork
- Linen
- Two linen layers
- Crimson silk grosgrain
- Baleen strip
- Woven cream wool
- Red twill worsted
- Black stiffened linen
- Selvedge
- Pad stitching
- Pasteboard and linen

100   4 | Crimson silk grosgrain doublet

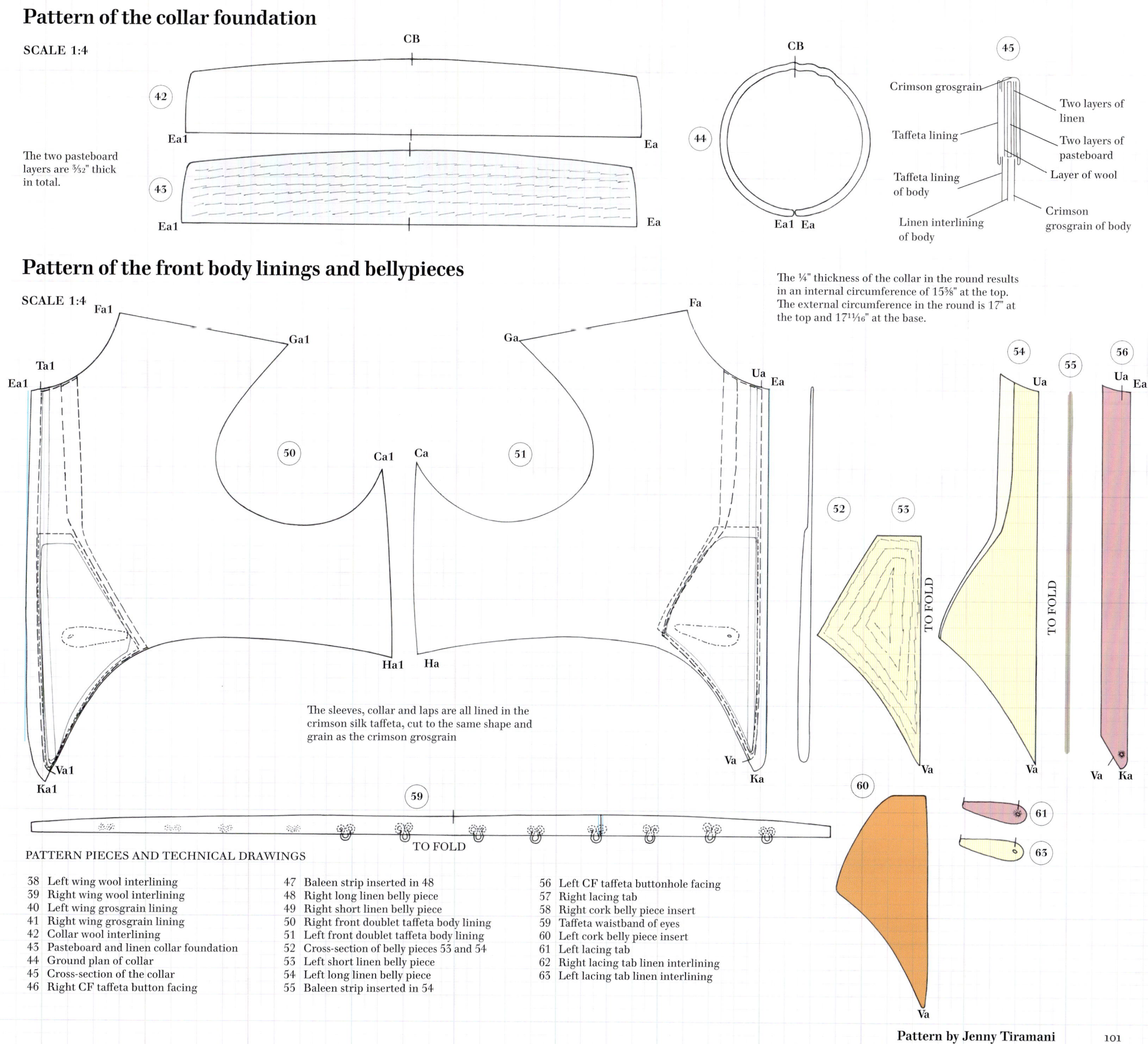

CONSTRUCTION
Construction of the body of the doublet

The whole body of the doublet was interlined in a net layer of partially bleached linen.

1 A second layer of linen was CUT for the front shoulder area and the underarm. Two slits were CUT in the top portion of the front piece.

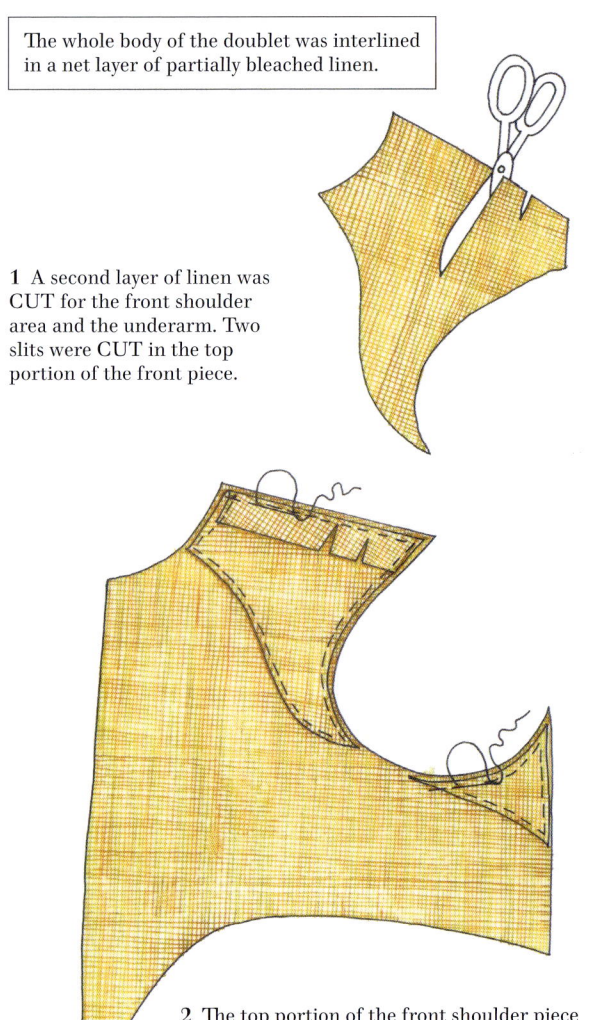

2 The top portion of the front shoulder piece was FOLDED back and PLACED on the WS of the interlining. The second layer pieces were BASTED to the linen interlining. The right front is shown.

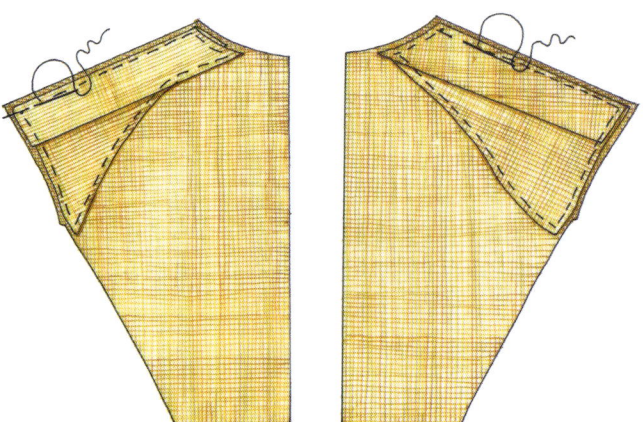

3 The top portions of the back shoulder pieces were FOLDED back and PLACED on the WS of the interlining. These were BASTED to the linen interlining.

4 The shoulder areas of the backs were PAD STITCHED from the RS while curving the linen in the hand or over the tailor's knee to shape it.

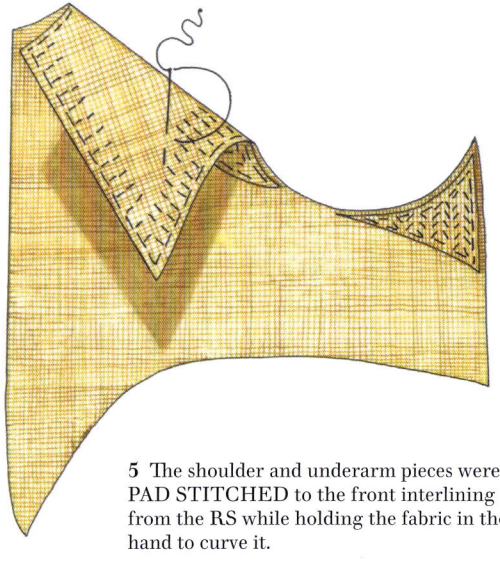

5 The shoulder and underarm pieces were PAD STITCHED to the front interlining from the RS while holding the fabric in the hand to curve it.

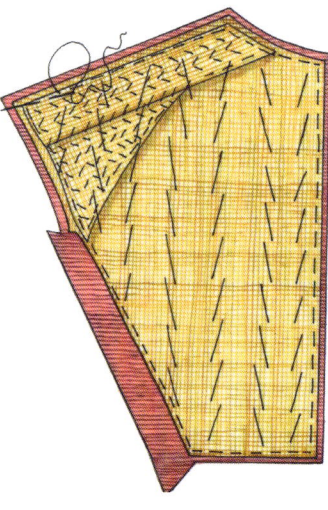

6 The RS of the interlining of each back was BASTED to the WS of the crimson grosgrain. The right back is shown. Each front was prepared in the same manner.

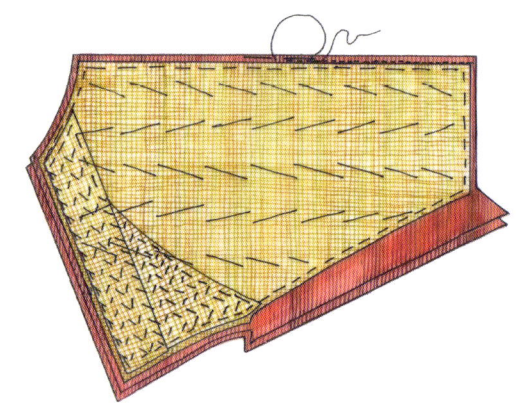

7 The CB seam was BACK STITCHED in red silk thread.

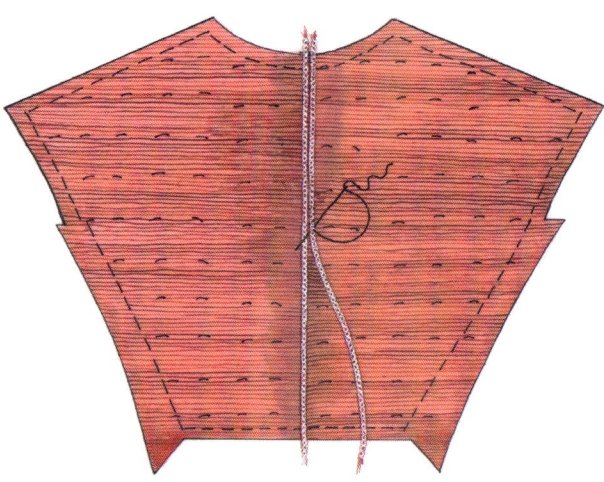

8 A length of the red silk and silver edging lace was CATCH STITCHED on top of the CB seam and a second row was STITCHED ⅛" from the first, on the right back.

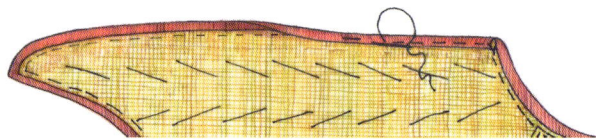

9 On both fronts the ¼" CF seam allowance of the grosgrain was FOLDED and BASTED to the interlining. The right front is shown.

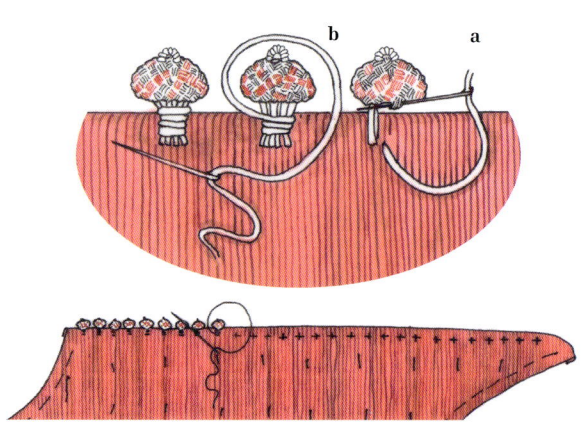

10 On the right front the button positions were marked down the CF and STITCHED ⅛" from the edge. **a** A shank was formed by stitches worked through the silver and red silk threads wrapped round the wooden core of the button. **b** The thread was twisted around the shank to make it stiff.

4 | Crimson silk grosgrain doublet

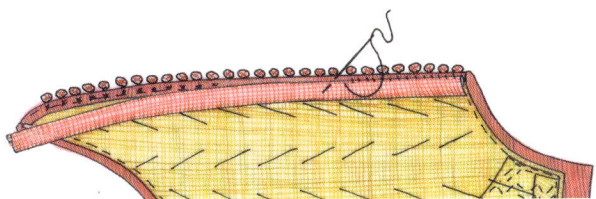

11 A taffeta facing was BASTED and FELLED ⅛" from the folded edge of the WS of the right front.

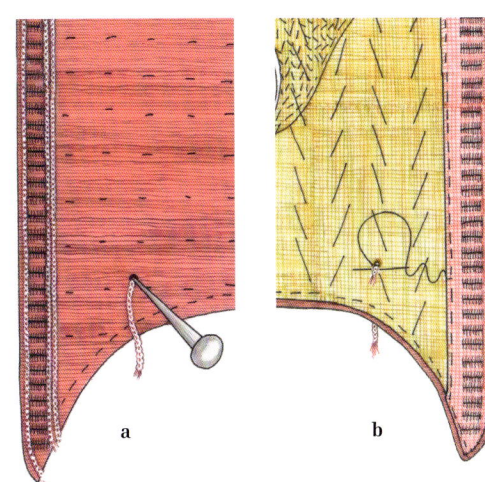

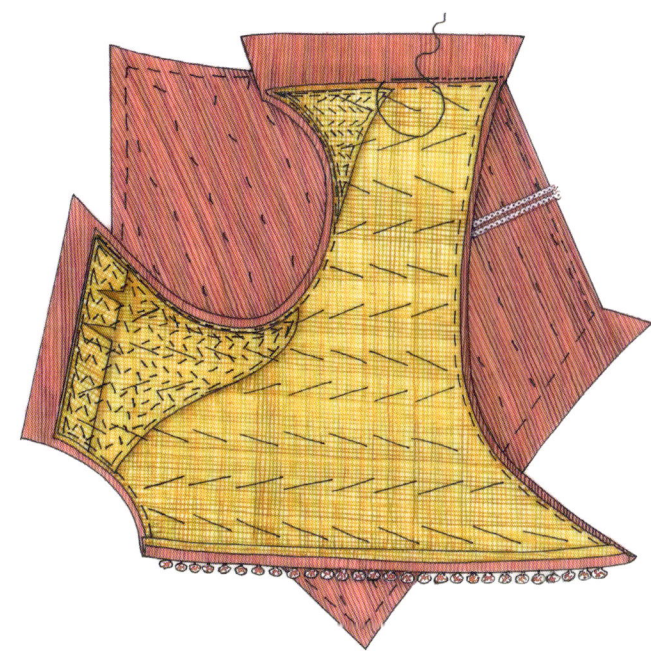

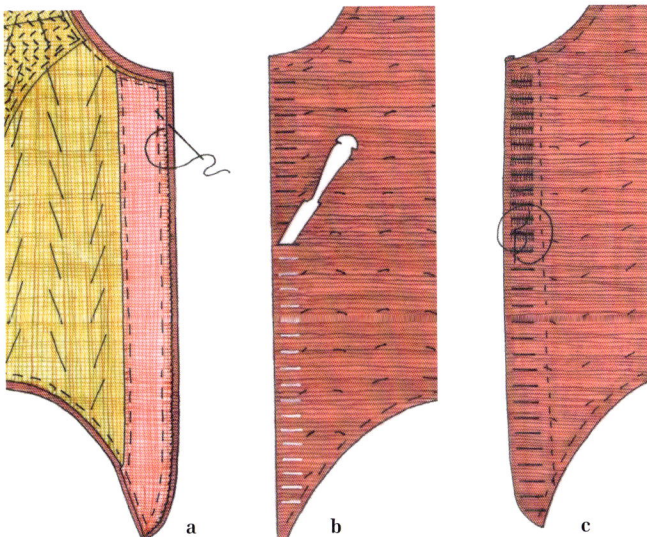

12a On the LHS front, a taffeta facing was BASTED and then FELLED ⅛" from the folded edge at CF. **b** The 28 buttonhole positions were MARKED and CUT. **c** The buttonholes were WORKED in red silk thread from left to right. See fig. 4.31, page 93, for a detail of the BUTTONHOLE STITCH.

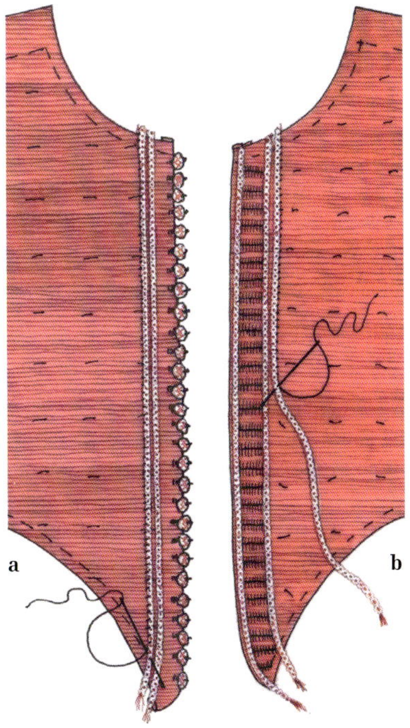

14a A hole was PIERCED on both doublet fronts. A short length of lace was PUSHED through each hole, left front shown. **b** The lace was WHIPPED in place on the WS of the pierced hole and at the waist end. This created a loop to hold a sword girdle, keeping it on the waistline while on the left side. It also supported the weight of the hangers, sword and scabbard.

15 With RS together, the side seams were BACK STITCHED in red silk thread, the right front and back are shown.

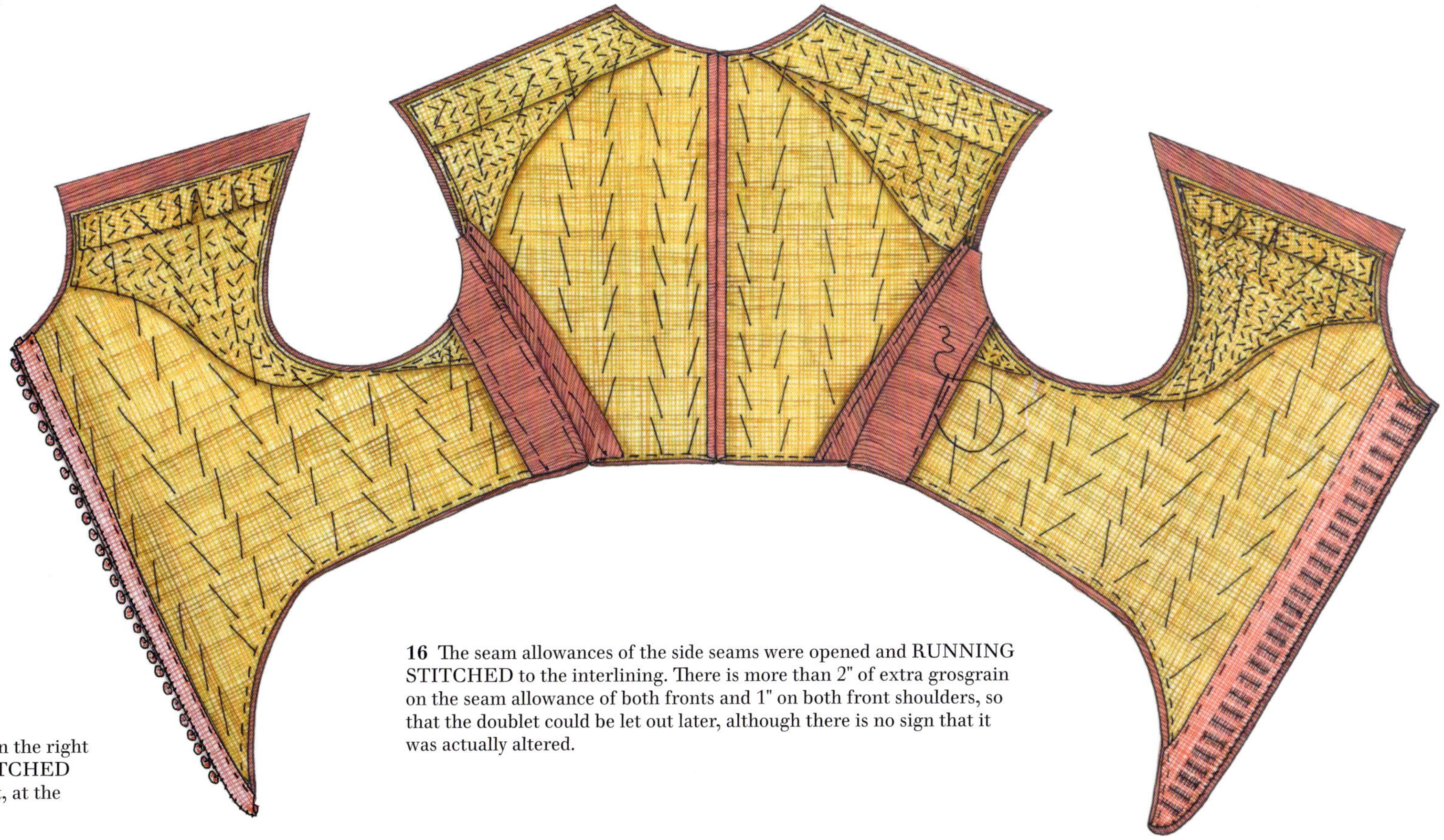

13a Two lengths of the lace were CATCH STITCHED down the right front 1½" from the buttons. **b** One length was CATCH STITCHED 1⁄16" from the CF edge of the left front and two more ⅛" apart, at the other side of the buttonholes covering their ends.

16 The seam allowances of the side seams were opened and RUNNING STITCHED to the interlining. There is more than 2" of extra grosgrain on the seam allowance of both fronts and 1" on both front shoulders, so that the doublet could be let out later, although there is no sign that it was actually altered.

Pattern by Jenny Tiramani

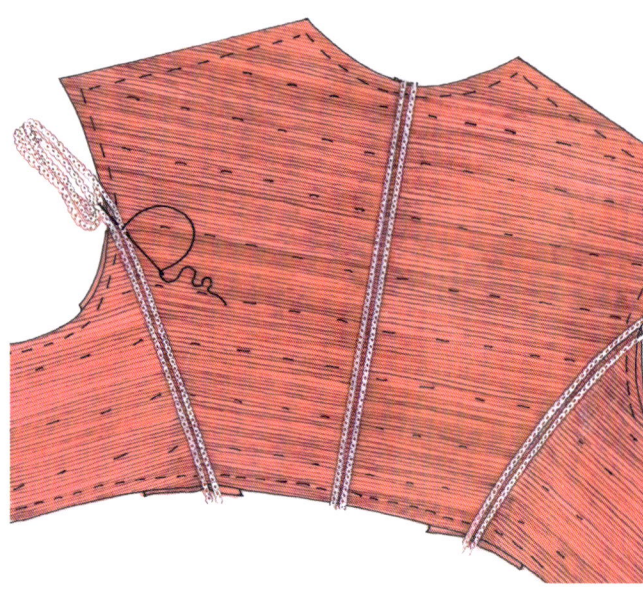

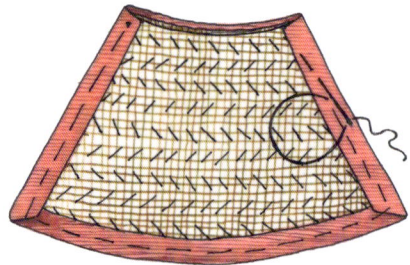

19 The seam allowance of the grosgrain was FOLDED over the net shape of the linen interlining on the sides and bottom and then BASTED to it.

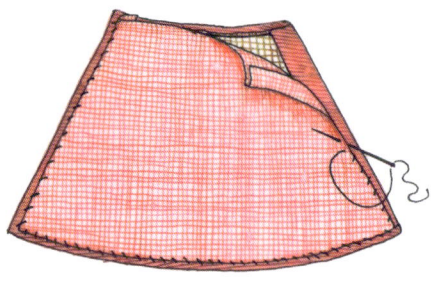

21 The seam allowance of the taffeta lining was FOLDED to the WS on the sides and bottom. It was FELLED to the WS of the lap about 1/16" from the edge.

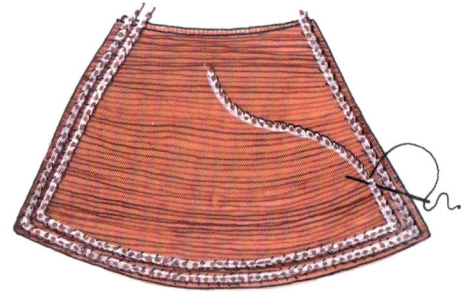

17 A long length of the lace was CATCH STITCHED over both side seams and a second length STITCHED 1/8" from the first on the right and left backs of the body. There are no joins in these laces at the shoulders, so the lengths were long enough to stitch all around the armholes once the shoulders were joined.

20 Two lengths of the edging lace were CATCH STITCHED to each lap, 1/8" apart and 1/8" from the edge on the sides and bottom.

22 The raw edges at the top of each lap were *probably* BASTED together.

Construction of the laps

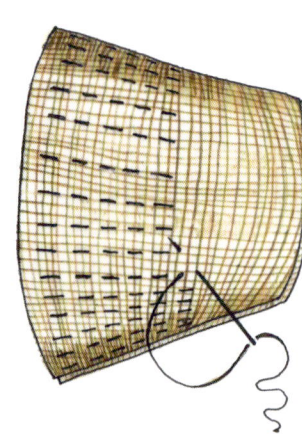

18 Two layers of stiffened linen were PAD STITCHED together with linen thread, in rows of stitches worked across the laps, with linen thread, curving them in the hand as they were STITCHED.

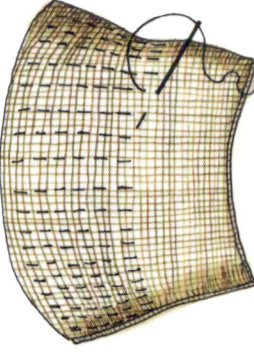

The short stitches were worked from the RS of the laps in parallel rows so that the long diagonal threads on the WS could be pulled slightly to create the curve. The stitches varies from nine rows of large PAD STITCHES on each front lap to 14 rows of small stitches on the side-back laps.

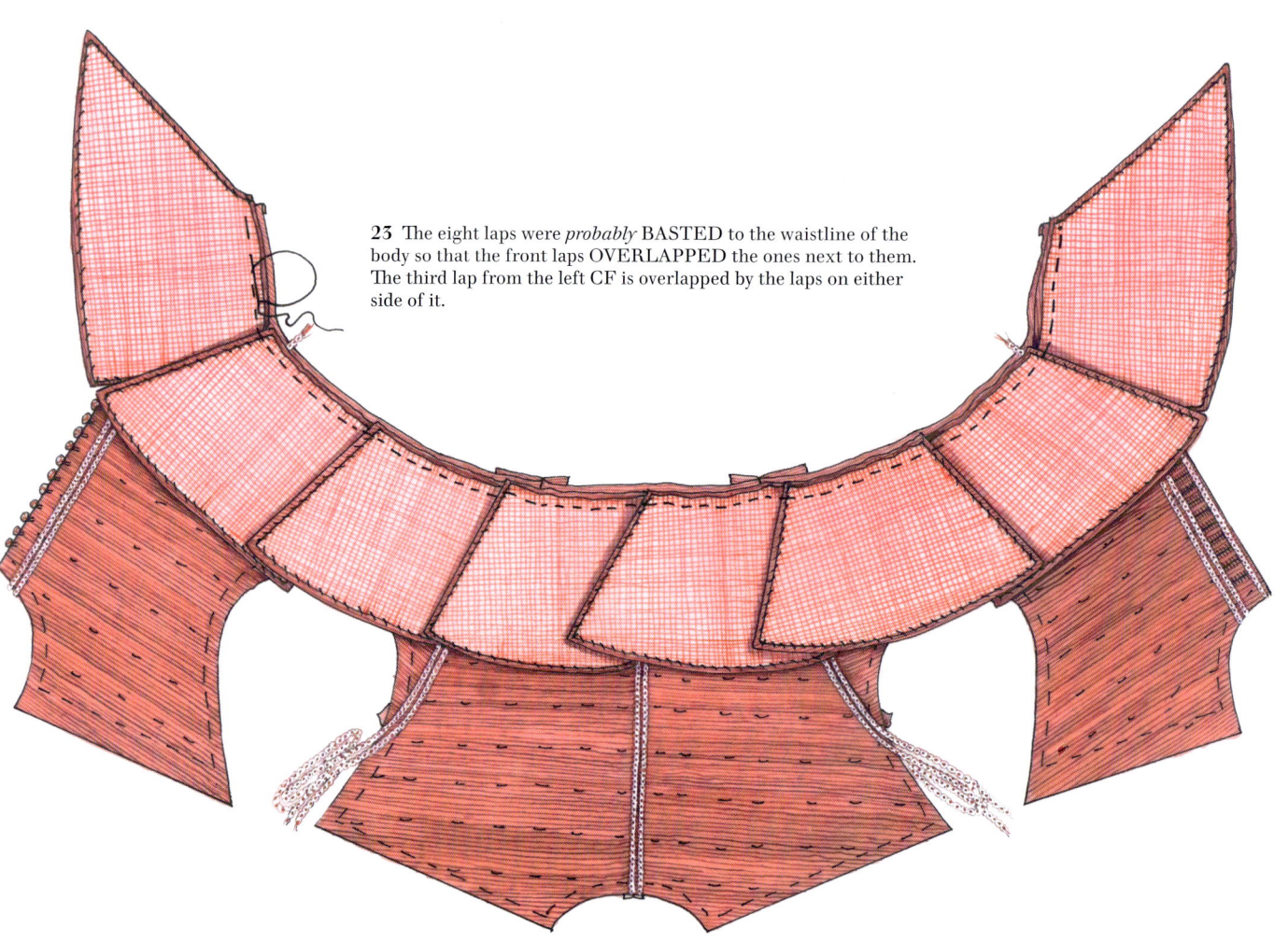

23 The eight laps were *probably* BASTED to the waistline of the body so that the front laps OVERLAPPED the ones next to them. The third lap from the left CF is overlapped by the laps on either side of it.

4 | Crimson silk grosgrain doublet

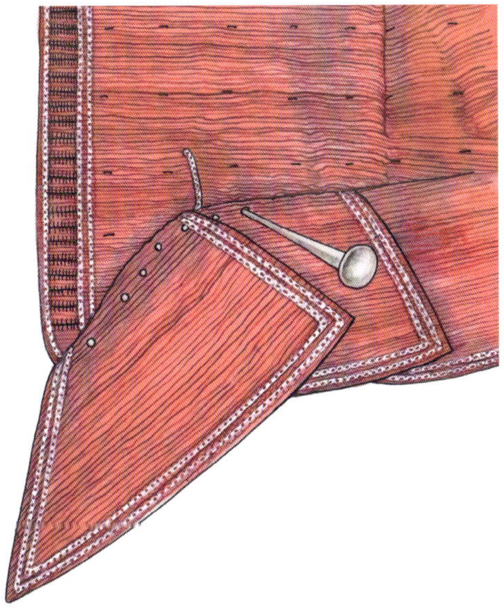

Construction of the waistband of iron eyes

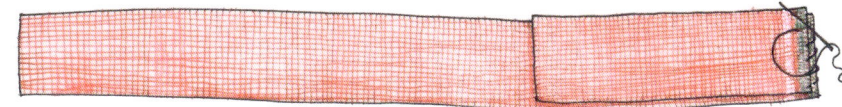

26 The selvedges of two pieces of the red silk lining fabric were WHIPPED together to make a strip long enough for the waistband.

27 A length of linen interlining, CUT net, was BASTED to the WS of the silk. The waistband was FOLDED in half and *probably* BASTED together.

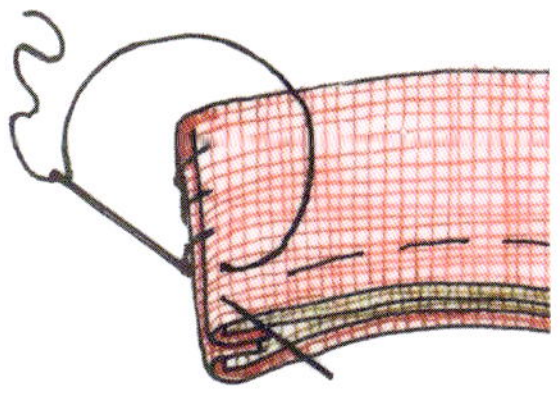

28 The ends of the waistband were FOLDED in and WHIPPED together in red silk thread.

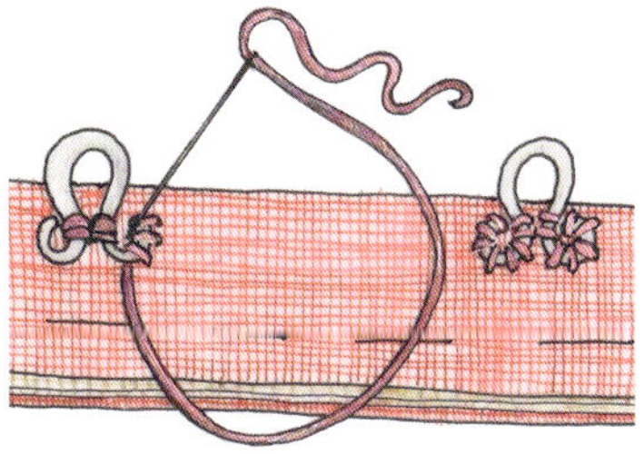

29 Twelve iron eyes were WHIPPED with STAB STITCHES to the waistband in red silk thread. They were *probably* spaced out by eye as the distances between them vary.

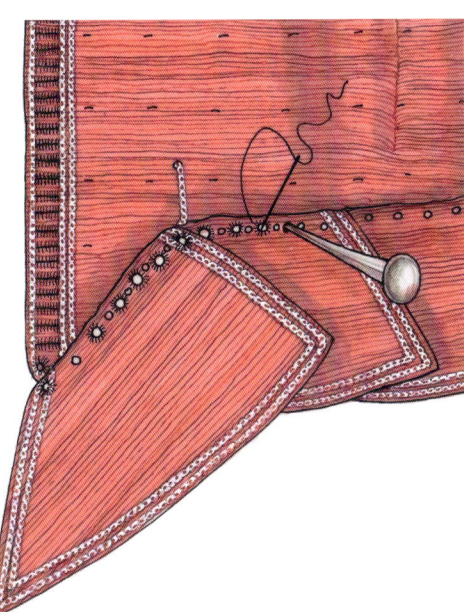

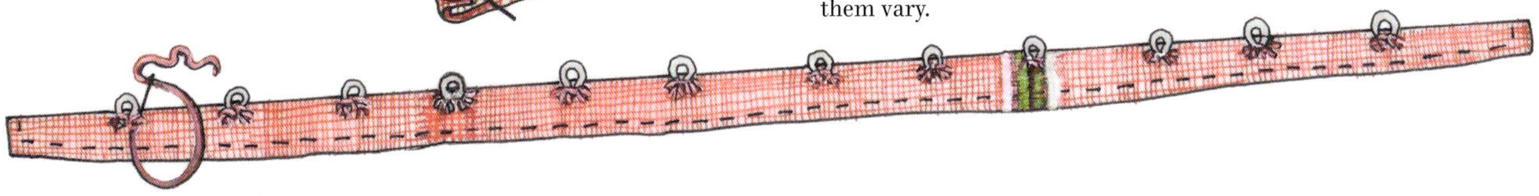

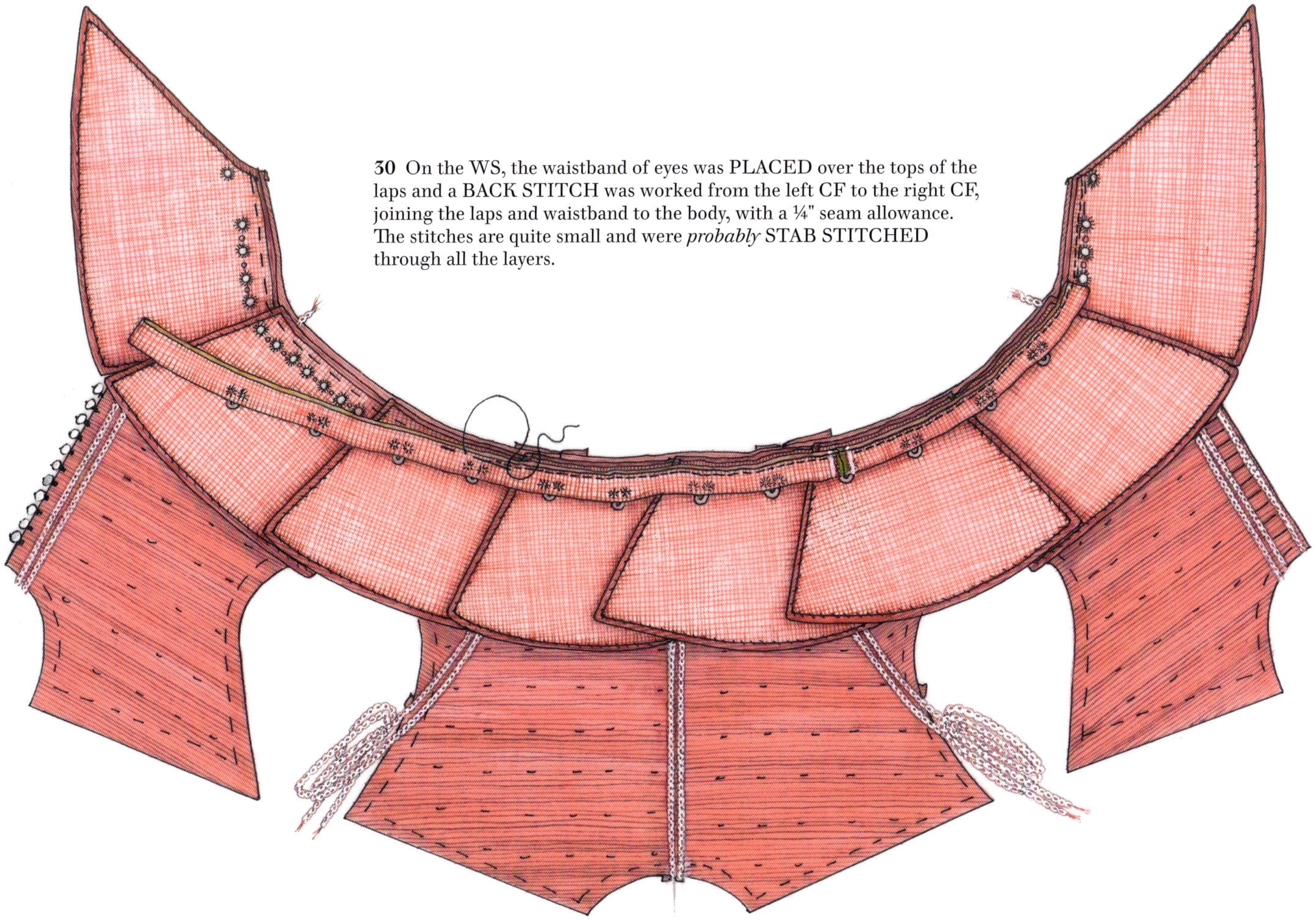

24 Forty-nine holes were PIERCED with a bodkin all the way around the doublet through the layers of the laps near the waist. They are unworked holes that were never whipped around their edges with thread. The holes were possibly used for a fitting with points temporarily THREADED through them before the waistband of eyes was added.

25 Another series of 48 holes was PIERCED between the unworked ones. These were WHIPPED all around their edges with red silk thread in small neat stitches. When worn, the unworked holes would have been hidden by decorative ribbon points THREADED through the worked holes. The presence of two sets of holes is puzzling. Was it a mistake?

30 On the WS, the waistband of eyes was PLACED over the tops of the laps and a BACK STITCH was worked from the left CF to the right CF, joining the laps and waistband to the body, with a ¼" seam allowance. The stitches are quite small and were *probably* STAB STITCHED through all the layers.

Pattern by Jenny Tiramani

Construction of the waistband of iron eyes

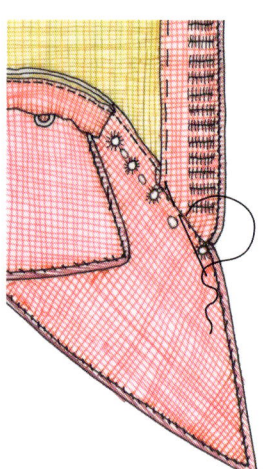
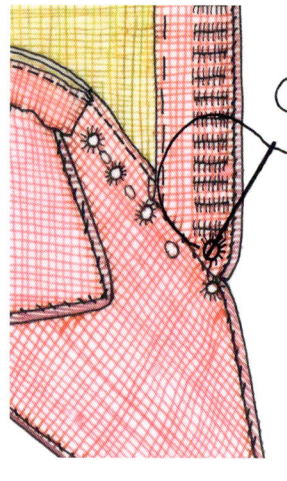

31 The lower edge of the taffeta facing on each front was FOLDED to its WS and FELLED onto the front lap.

32 On both fronts, an eyelet hole was PIERCED with a bodkin in the peak of the doublet and WHIPPED in red silk thread.

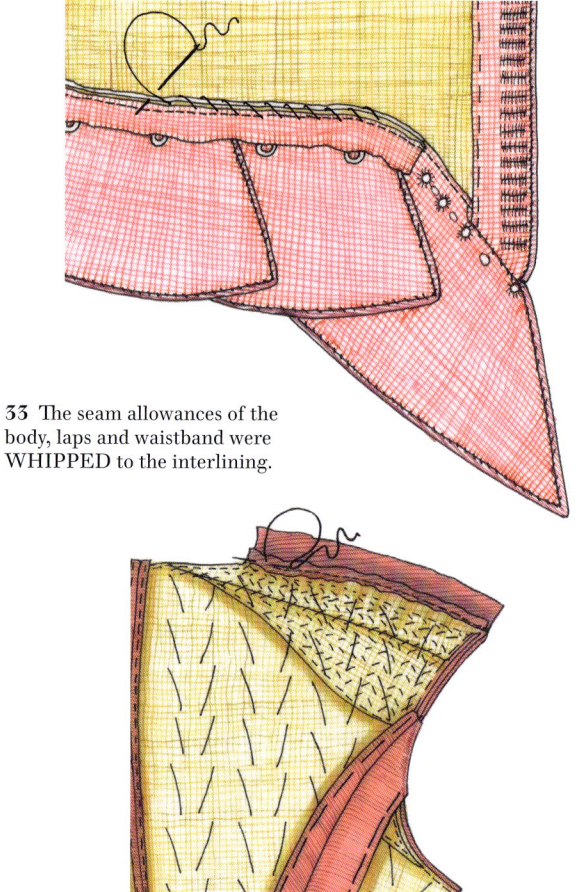

33 The seam allowances of the body, laps and waistband were WHIPPED to the interlining.

34 With RS together, the back shoulder seams were EASED and then BACK STITCHED to the front shoulders, with red silk thread. The seam allowances on the fronts are 1" wider than the back-seam allowance of ¼".

CONTINUED

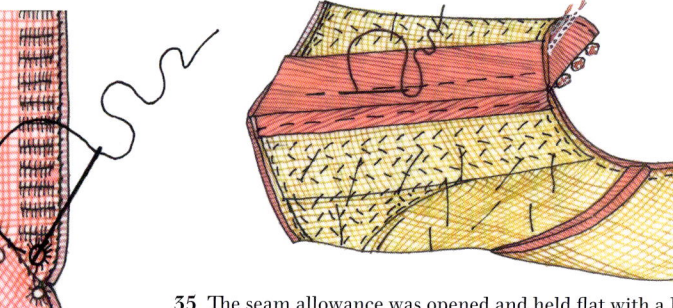

35 The seam allowance was opened and held flat with a RUNNING STITCH in linen thread.

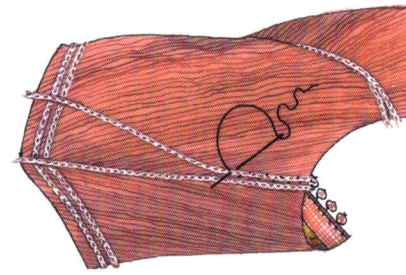

36 A length of lace was CATCH STITCHED over the shoulder seam with a second length ⅛" away on the back.

37 The lace that covered the side seam was CATCH STITCHED to the net shape of the armhole, with a ¼" seam allowance. A second lace was STITCHED ⅛" from the first and both laces were finished off neatly where they met at the top of the side seam.

Construction of the wings

The construction of the right wing is shown here.

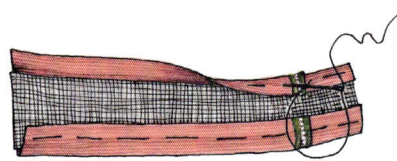

38 The seam allowances of the grosgrain for each wing section were FOLDED to the WS and BASTED to the linen interlining. Small scraps of the grosgrain were pieced together on some of the sections. Shown here is a wing section, with a selvedge used at the join between two piecings.

39 A length of lace was CATCH STITCHED ⅛" from both edges of the wing sections with about 1" of lace past the fold line. The lace was TURNED BACK in a loop and CATCH STITCHED ⅛" from the first length.

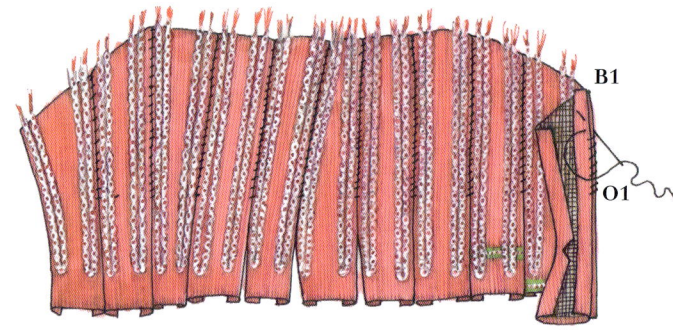

40 The 11 sections of the wing were WHIPPED together from L1 to Y1, K1 to X1, J1 to V1, I1 to U1, H1 to T1, F1 to S1, E1 to R1, D1 to Q1, C1 to P1 and B1 to O1, in red silk thread.

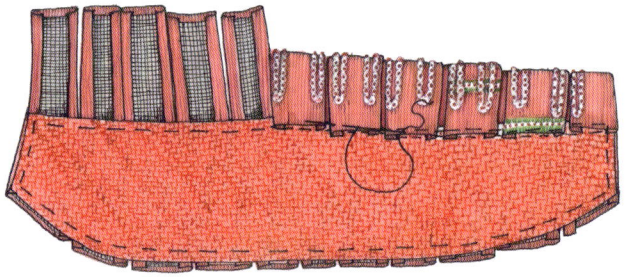

41 A layer of red worsted interlining was PLACED on the WS of the upper part of the wing. The loose ends of the 11 wing sections were FOLDED to the WS, just overlapping the edge of the worsted, and BASTED into position.

42 A thread bar was worked in BUTTONHOLE STITCH between each loose section of the wing.

43 The whole upper portion of the WS of the wing was lined in piecings of grosgrain, covering the seam allowances of the 11 sections. Some of the piecings were left with raw edges or selvedges were used to reduce the bulkiness of the wing. The long vertical seam was FELLED in both directions to secure the loose threads of the weave.

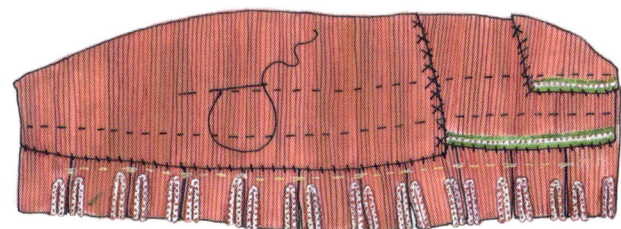

44 Two rows of RUNNING STITCH in red silk thread were worked across the wing, catching the lining, worsted and buckram together.

45 All the layers were *probably* BASTED together along the top edge, slightly PULLING the thread to ensure that the wing could be EASED into the armhole.

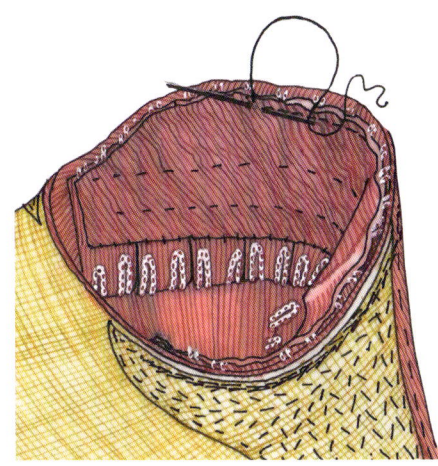

46 With RS together, the wing was *probably* BASTED into the armhole. It was then BACK STITCHED in red silk thread.

Construction of the belly pieces

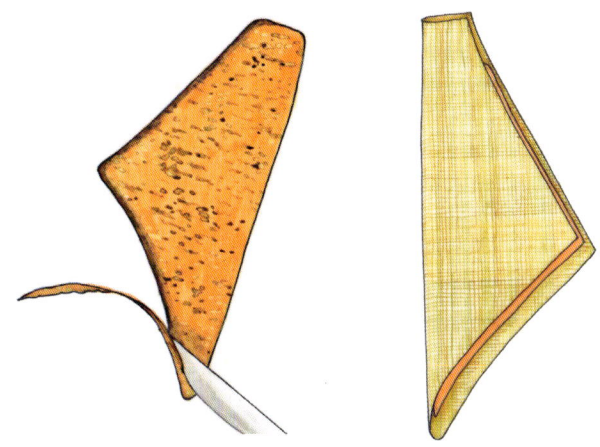

47 A piece of cork (a vertical slice from the tree bark) was CUT into a triangular shape about ¼" thick for each short belly piece. They were SHAVED down to a soft round edge. The cork shapes were WRAPPED in linen.

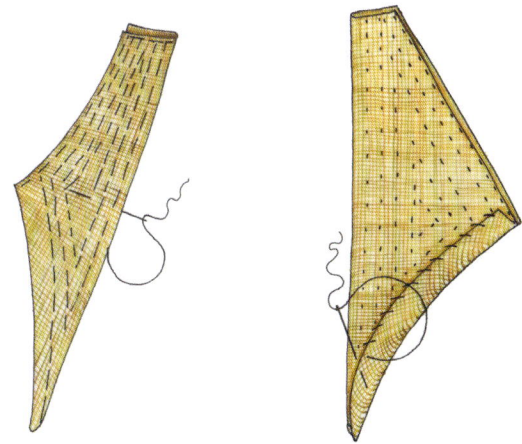

48 Rows of PAD STITCHING were worked through the linen and cork. The lower edge of the linen was FOLDED up and FELLED onto the shape.

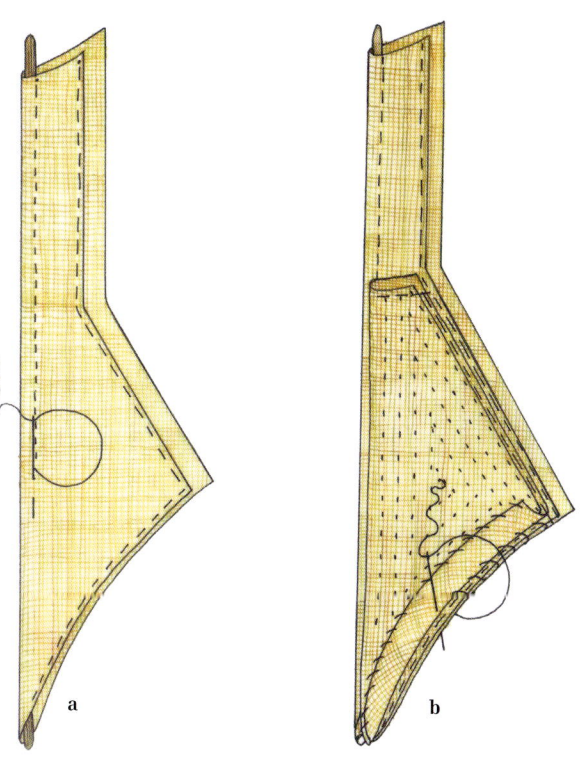

49a A length of baleen was INSERTED in the fold of the long belly piece linen shape and a line of RUNNING STITCHES worked beside it. The outer edge of the long belly piece was RUNNING STITCHED together. **b** The short and long belly pieces were WHIPPED together along the lower edge.

Construction of the body lining

50 The belly piece was PLACED on the WS of the taffeta lining of each front. The selvedge of the lining was FOLDED over and FELLED to the belly piece 2" from the CF edge. The right front is shown.

Pattern by Jenny Tiramani

Construction of the body lining
CONTINUED

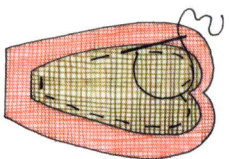

51 The net shape of the linen interlining of the lacing tab was *probably* BASTED to the taffeta lining.

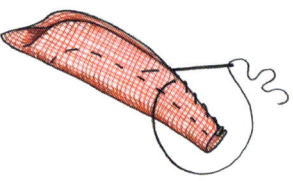

52 The tab was FOLDED lengthways. The seam allowance of the taffeta was FOLDED to the WS and the edges WHIPPED together.

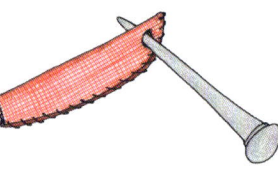

53 A hole was PIERCED in the curved end of the lacing tab with a bodkin.

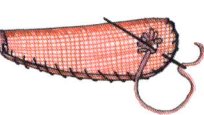

54 The edges of the hole were WHIPPED with red silk thread.

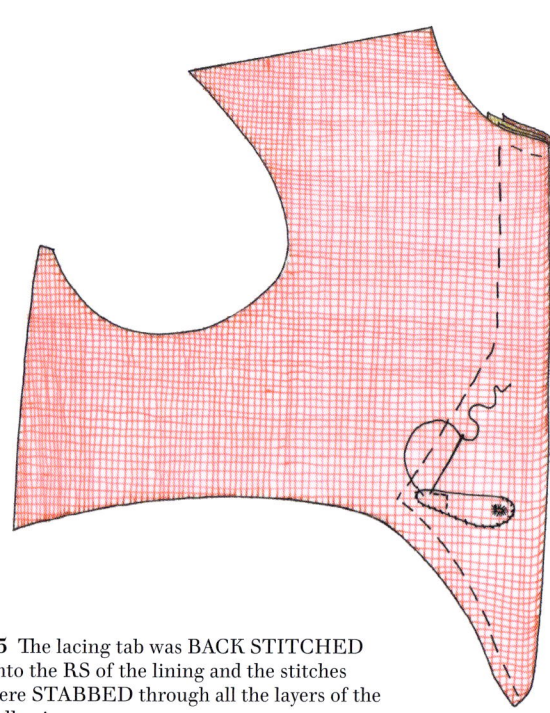

55 The lacing tab was BACK STITCHED onto the RS of the lining and the stitches were STABBED through all the layers of the belly piece.

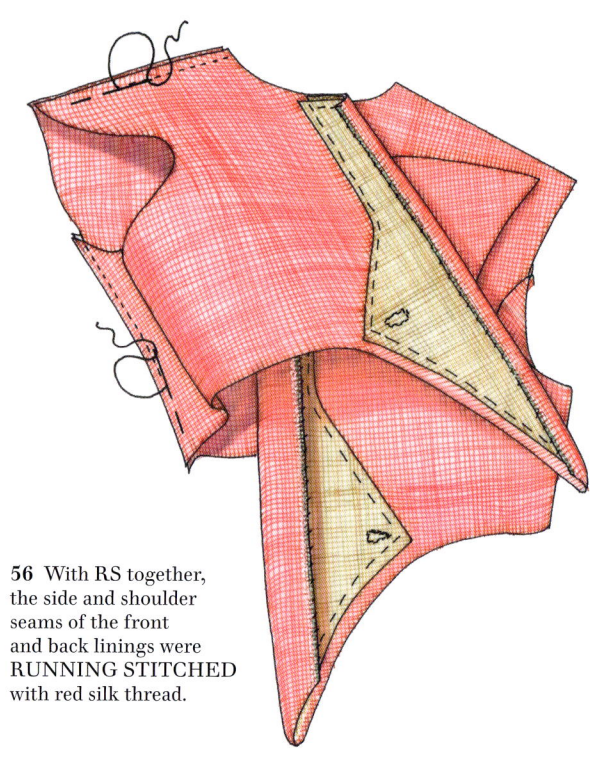

56 With RS together, the side and shoulder seams of the front and back linings were RUNNING STITCHED with red silk thread.

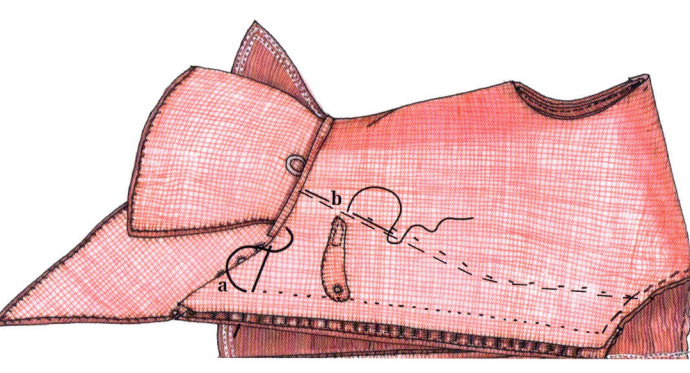

57a The doublet and the lining were PLACED WS together. A row of PRICK STITCHES was STABBED through to the RS holding the lining and belly pieces to the body along the inside edge of the buttonholes. On the RS the stitches are hidden by the lace that has been STITCHED over the ends of the buttonholes. **b** A row of PRICK STITCHES was worked around the inner edge of the belly pieces, just catching threads of the WS of the grosgrain. The RHS is shown.

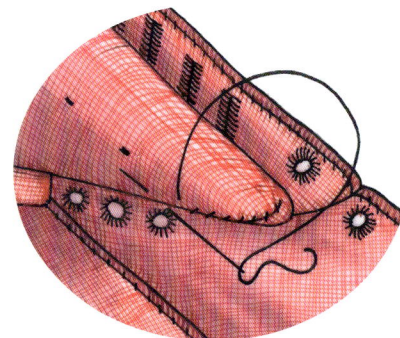

58 At the bottom of the belly piece the seam allowance of the taffeta was FOLDED to the WS and FELLED.

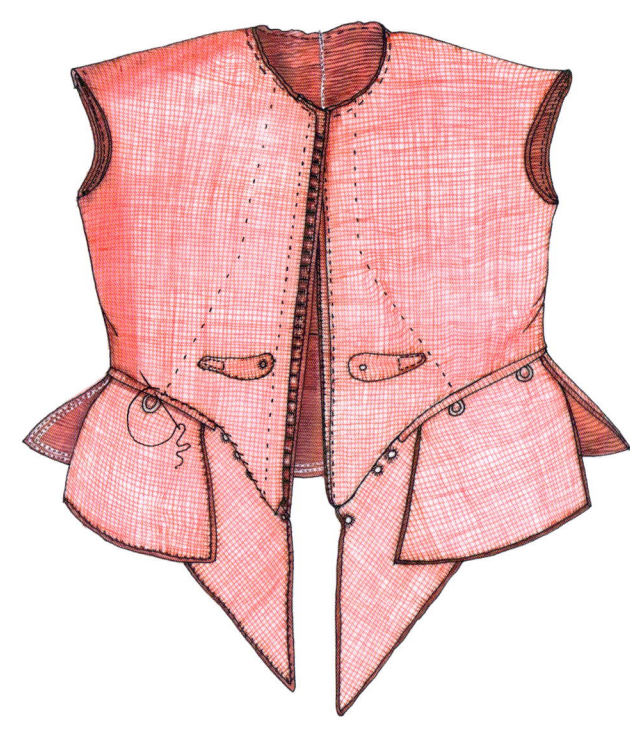

59 The felling of the body lining was continued all around the waist, over the seam allowance of the waistband of eyes.

Construction of the sleeves
The construction of the left sleeve is shown here.

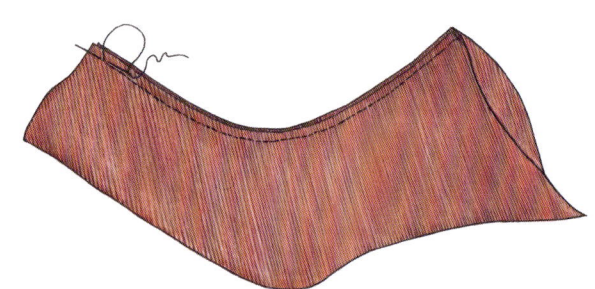

60 With RS together, the inside seam of the grosgrain top and undersleeves was RUNNING STITCHED in red silk thread.

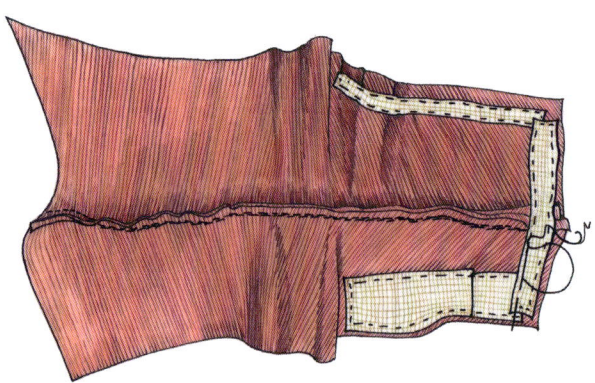

61 Pieces of linen interlining were BASTED to the wrist end and opening of the sleeve to strengthen the areas where the buttons and buttonholes were to be STITCHED. Some basting stitches remain. On the right sleeve the pieces were PLACED on the wrist first.

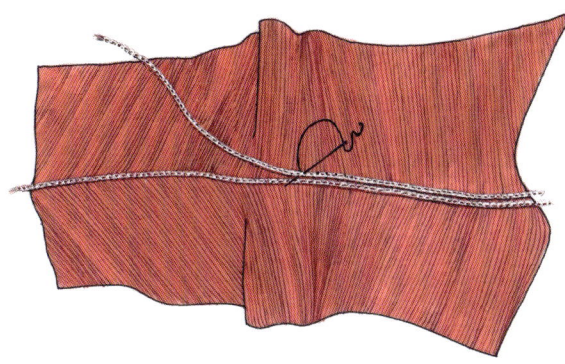

62 A length of edging lace was CATCH STITCHED over the inside seam. A second length was STITCHED ⅛" from the first, on the undersleeve.

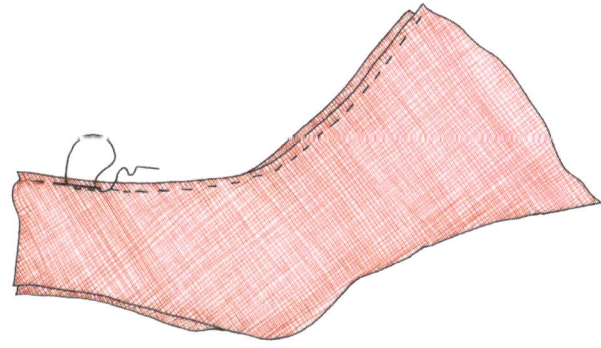

63 With RS together, the inside seam of the taffeta lining was RUNNING STITCHED together.

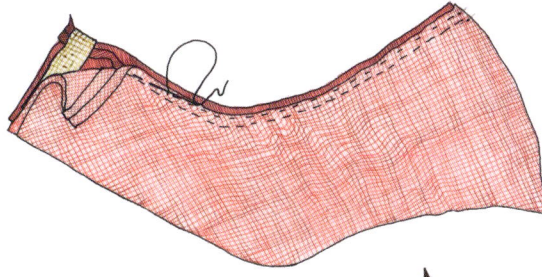

64 The WS of the sleeve and sleeve lining were PLACED together and the seam allowance of the top-sleeve lining was RUNNING STITCHED to the seam allowance of the top sleeve, just inside of the seams sewn in steps 60 and 63.

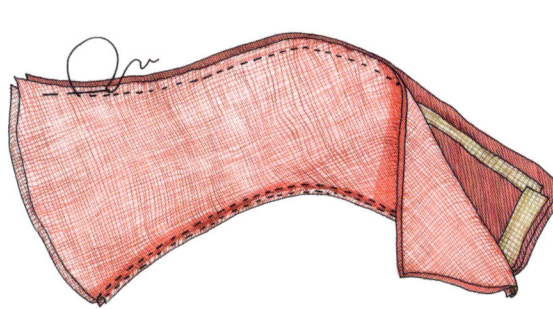

65 The outside seam was RUNNING STITCHED through all layers of the sleeve and lining.

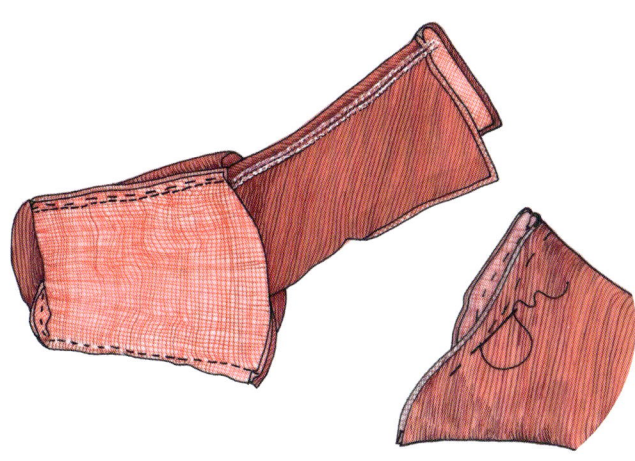

66 The sleeve and lining were TURNED THROUGH to the RS and the seam allowance of the sleeve and lining were *probably* BASTED together.

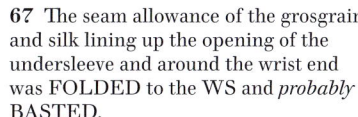

67 The seam allowance of the grosgrain and silk lining up the opening of the undersleeve and around the wrist end was FOLDED to the WS and *probably* BASTED.

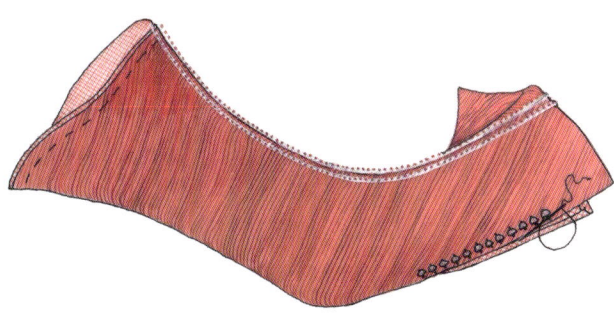

68 Twelve buttons were STITCHED ³⁄₁₆" from the edge, as in step 10.

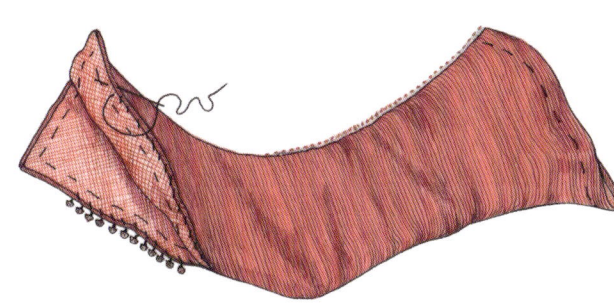

69 The lining was FELLED to the grosgrain along each side of the opening in the outside seam to the planned position of the last buttonhole and to the last button.

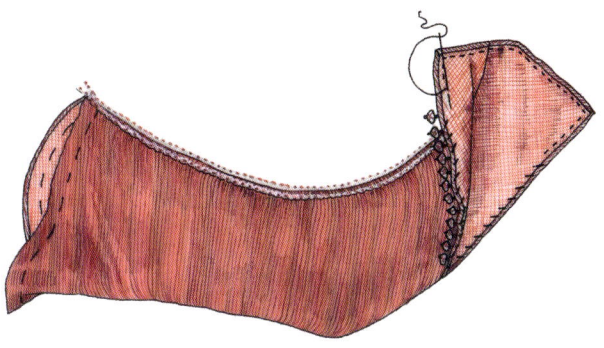

70 The remainder of the wrist end was PRICK STITCHED to the grosgrain with small stitches. This is the portion of the sleeve that was designed to be TURNED UP and to support a linen wristband.

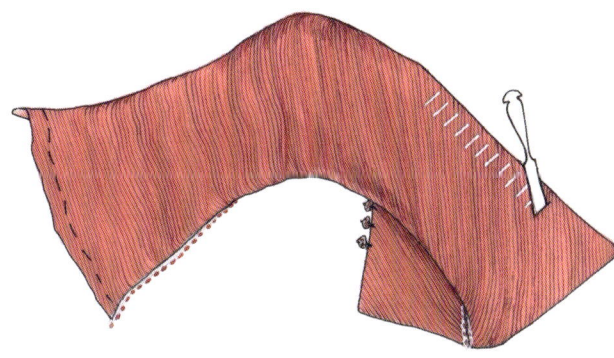

71 Twelve buttonhole positions were *probably* MARKED with chalk or threads on the top sleeve. The slits were CUT with a cutter.

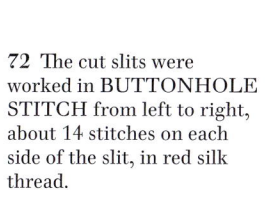 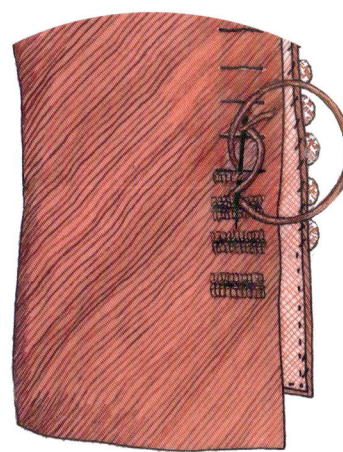

72 The cut slits were worked in BUTTONHOLE STITCH from left to right, about 14 stitches on each side of the slit, in red silk thread.

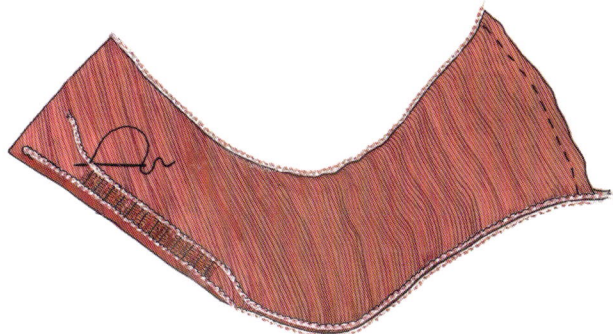

73 A length of lace was CATCH STITCHED over the outside seam. A second length was CATCH STITCHED ⅛" from the seam on the top sleeve. Both laces cover the ends of the buttonholes and stop just short of the wrist.

Pattern by Jenny Tiramani

Construction of the collar

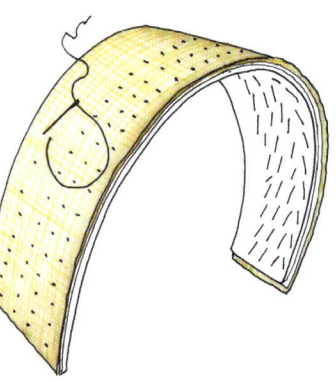

74 Two layers of pasteboard, and two layers of linen on the outside of them, were PAD STITCHED together, curving them in the hand, to make the foundation for the collar.

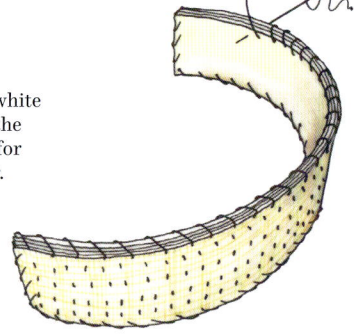

75 A layer of thick, soft white wool was WHIPPED to the inside of the foundation, for the comfort of the wearer.

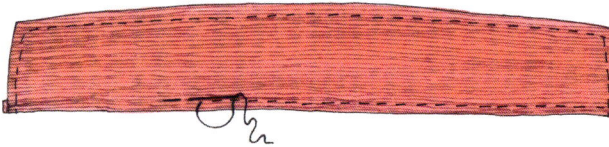

76 A line of BASTING was *probably* worked on the net shape of the grosgrain and the lower edge FOLDED to the WS and BASTED to give a clean edge for whipping to the body in step 79.

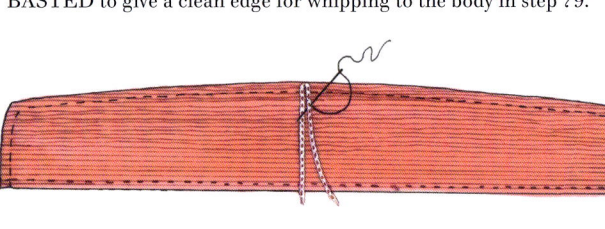

77 A length of lace was CATCH STITCHED at the centre back of the grosgrain and looped round for the second row of the RHS.

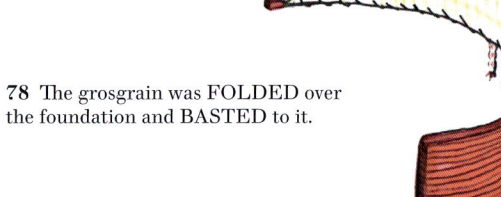

78 The grosgrain was FOLDED over the foundation and BASTED to it.

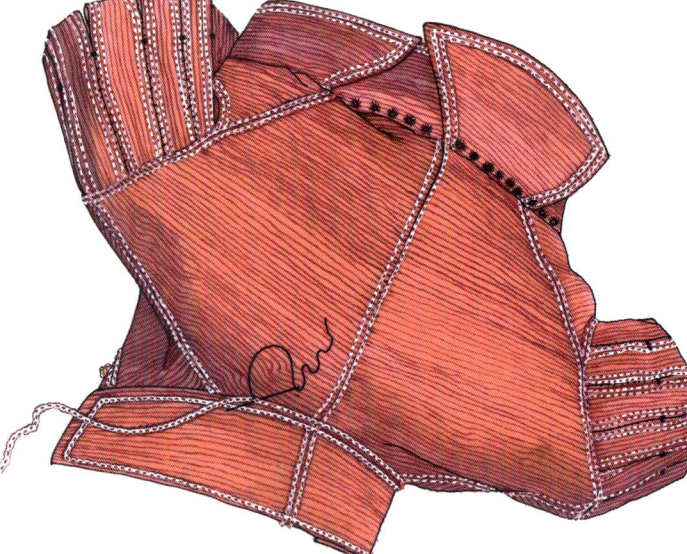

79 The lower edge of the collar was FELLED to the body.

80 Two rows of lace were CATCH STITCHED around all the edges of the collar in one continuous length; one line covered the seam at the neck.

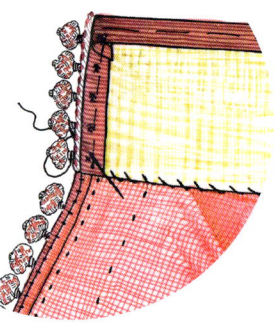

81 Five buttons were STITCHED through all the layers of the collar as in step 10.

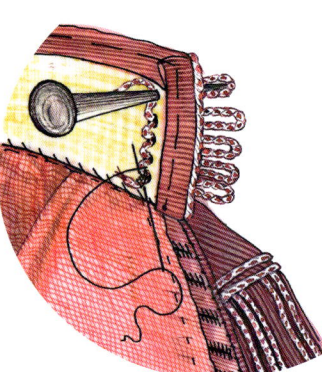

82 Five holes were PIERCED with a bodkin on the left front of the collar. Five button loops were made with one continuous length of lace PUSHED through the holes and WHIPPED in place on the WS.

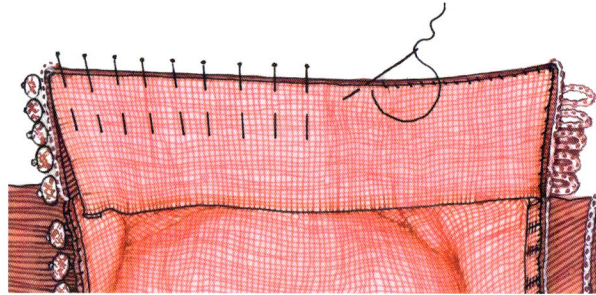

83 The seam allowances of the collar lining around the top and side edges were FOLDED to the WS. The lining was FELLED to the collar in red silk thread.

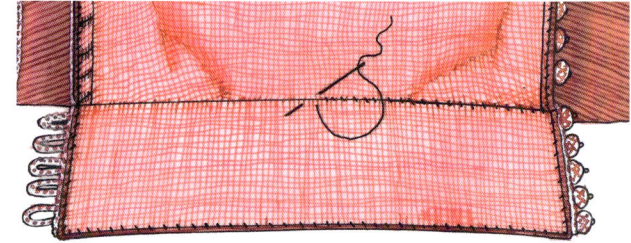

84 The bottom edge of the lining was FOLDED to the WS and FELLED to the neckline of the doublet.

It is impossible to tell whether the collar or the sleeves were attached first. It is equally possible that steps 85 and 86 were completed before steps 74 to 84.

Half-scale reconstruction

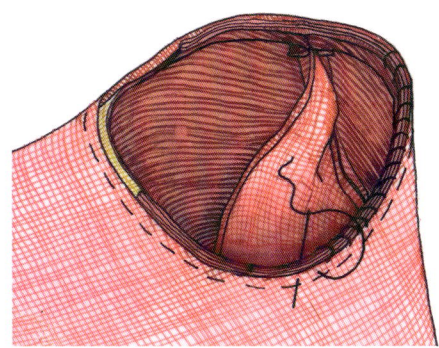

85 With RS together the grosgrain sleeve was WHIPPED to the armhole, with the sleeve lining PUSHED down out of the way.

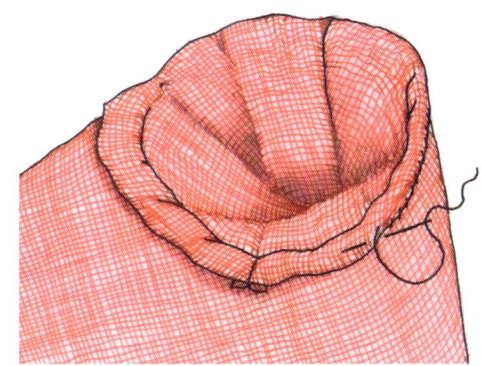

86 The top seam allowance of the sleeve lining was FOLDED to the WS and FELLED around the armhole with red silk thread.

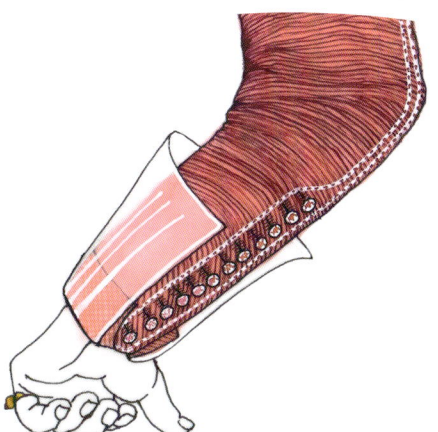

87 The sleeve with the wrist end TURNED BACK and a fine, darted linen cuff worn over it. The edges of a cuff would *probably* not have met, so that the doublet buttons were visible. Numerous sitters in contemporary portraits are shown styling their doublets and cuffs in this way, such as that of William van Heythuysen (*c.* 1625) by Frans Hals in the Alte Pinakothek, Munich. https://en.wikipedia.org/wiki/Willem_van_Heythuysen#/media/File:Frans_Hals_-_Willem_van_Heythuyzen_-_WGA11076.jpg

88 A ribbon point THREADED through the eyelet holes of the lacing tabs on the belly pieces.

89 The point through the lacing tabs TIED in a half-bow.

90 A point is shown here THREADED through the centre front eyelet holes ready to fasten to the sword girdle. Another point is THREADED through the left front lap (see illustrations on page 12).

91 Ribbon points at centre front and on the left front lap both TIED in bows.

Pattern by Jenny Tiramani

5 | Slashed doublet of stamped ivory silk satin

Possibly English, 1625–30 | V&A: T.59–1910

Pattern by Luca Costigliolo

James Hamilton, 1st Duke of Hamilton, *c.* **1629**
Daniel Mytens
Scottish National Portrait Gallery, Edinburgh

This beautiful doublet was found in a farmhouse at Whaddon in Dorsetshire together with a small group of 17th-century clothes. The entire collection was purchased by the V&A in 1910 for £105 from H. Fetherstonhaugh Frampton, Esq. The doublet is made of ivory satin, which has now discoloured to a yellowish grey, and the sleeves are damaged around the elbows. It is lined with a pink silk satin that was dyed with safflower, a particularly fugitive dyestuff. It was once an intense shade of carnation pink, but is now almost completely faded to beige, even though the lining would have been protected from light during display.[1] The wrist openings once fastened with eight wooden buttons covered in ivory silk thread, of which only four remain on each sleeve; no buttons remain on the front.

The doublet is stamped with floral motifs interspersed with leafy branches. Stamping was a cheap and effective technique used to decorate fabric; it was done with metal stamps purposely crafted with many different patterns, heated and pressed against silk fabrics to leave a permanent impression. Six different sizes of these stamps were used to decorate the doublet, arranged all over the garment in vertical double rows. On the body and sleeves, the motifs are placed diminishing in size, from the shoulders to the waist and wrists. The entire garment is lavishly decorated with strips of ivory satin, sewn in pairs on the gaps left between the rows of stamped motifs. These are cut on the bias, pinked on each side and couched lengthwise with spiral-plied ivory silk threads. The upper part of the sleeves and torso have long vertical slashes bound with ivory silk edging lace, a fashion that was very popular between 1620 and 1640. In *The Academy of Armory* (1688), Randle Holme describes a 'slashed doublet' as 'when both sleeves, and back, and fore-body, are cut like unto long slices, or fillets'.[2] When the doublet was worn over a full shirt, the slashes would spread apart, creating a series of vertical openings through which lace insertions or delicate embroidery on the shirt would show. Although the shape of the pattern suggests a fitted sleeve, the upper part is slashed into six panes and spreads almost like a puffed sleeve while the fastened forearm remains fitted. This style of sleeves, slashed into eight parts rather than six, can be seen in the portrait of Charles I (opposite). The sleeves in the portrait of James Hamilton (left) look similar, but are made of panes cut separately and then sewn together.

From the chest to the bottom of the peak, the fronts of the doublet are stiffened by large belly pieces made with bents. These are skilfully arranged and stitched together to create two panels that, although rigid, retain some flexibility. The bents are covered by a layer of loosely woven wool to prevent their rough edges from damaging the lining or poking the wearer. Each belly piece has a lacing tab, stitched at waist level, drawing the front edges together and pushing them outwards, which gives the front of the doublet a pointed, rather than flat, shape. When the 43 buttons, of which only the stiff linen thread shank remains, were fastened, they would have stood up straight, enhancing the centre front line. This pointed effect echoes the shape of

contemporary armour breastplates, and is particularly visible in the portrait of James Hamilton (opposite), whose cloth-of-silver doublet also has sectioned shoulder wings, similar in proportion to those of the ivory doublet. The wings extend the shoulder line without raising it, creating a silhouette with wide sloping shoulders. This shape is accentuated by the stiff high collar that provided support for a falling band (left) or a falling ruff (right), and together with the belly pieces, forced the wearer to stand with his back in an upright posture.

The high waistline is encircled by eight laps, stamped and decorated like the rest of the doublet, each pierced with eyelet holes near the waist seam. Inside the doublet, there is a waistband with eyelet holes underneath the laps. The two sets of eyelets do not match. The hose were laced to the doublet through the eyelets on the internal waistband, with points that could be tied and untied when necessary. The eyelets in the laps were for purely decorative bows tied with a more precious set of ribbon points, unsuitable for fastening. A girdle, perhaps of a contrasting colour, would have been worn above the bows, following the curved waistline to the bottom of the peak. The girdle was held in place with a girdle loop on each front, made of plaited ivory silk, of which only fragments now remain. To prevent the girdle from moving up, a matching set of eyelets was worked in the peak of the doublet and at the top edge of the first lap, for a ribbon point to tie the girdle in position at centre front (see portraits).

The body of the doublet is very short; from underarm to waist measures only 4½ inches. At first this might give the impression that the doublet was worn by a man of short stature and large build. However, the chest measures 38", the width of the shoulders across the back is 15¾" and the sleeves are 26" in length, proportions indicating a wearer who, today, would be considered to be of medium build. As the portraits show here, and many others confirm, such a high waist was the height of fashion in the 1620s, a style that Randle Holme calls 'Short waisted'.[3] Both back seams appear to have been let out, using the front-seam allowances. This appears to be contemporaneous alteration, possibly done by the same tailor because the wearer had put on weight, or at a slightly later stage when the doublet had been given to someone else, or been bought on the secondhand market.

1. Rosa Costantini, PhD student, Royal Institute for Cultural Heritage, Brussels. Presentation of her preliminary research on pink dyestuffs at Dye Analysis Study Day at V&A Museum, 20 November 2015
2. Randle Holme, *The Academy of Armory*, 1688, Book III, chapter III, p. 96
3. Ibid, p. 95

Charles I, King of England, *c.* **1629**
Daniel Mytens
Metropolitan Museum of Art, New York
Gift of George A. Hearn, 1906 (06.1289)
© 2016. Image copyright The Metropolitan Museum of Art/Art Resource/Scala, Florence

Pattern by Luca Costigliolo

DETAILS
Right side (RS) details

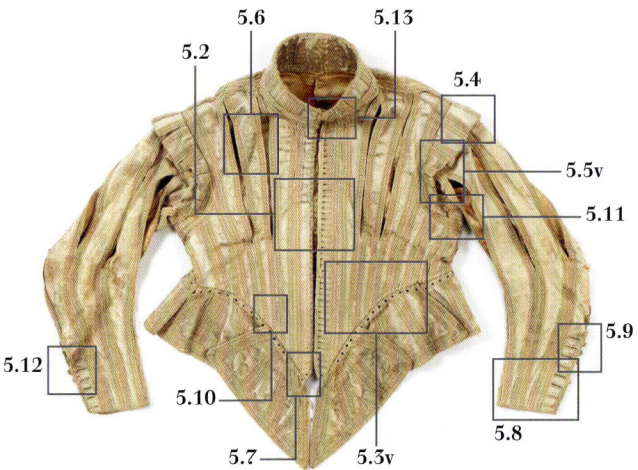

5.1 A front view of the slashed doublet lying flat.

5.2 The RHS edge at CF is bound with a strip of edging lace to create a firm base for the buttons.

5.3 The eyelets on the top edge of the laps are worked through all the layers, including the decorated satin strips, with a 2 'S' ply silk thread.

5.4 The sections forming the wings are held together at the top by bars worked in 2 'S' ply silk thread beneath the decorated strips of satin.

5.5 Underneath the right shoulder wing the laps are caught together with long stitches in thick 2 'S' ply white linen thread.

5.6 Four of the six different sizes of stamps used to decorate the doublet.

5.10 The girdle loops were formed with plaited ivory silk which has almost completely disintegrated; only fragments of each end remain on both fronts.

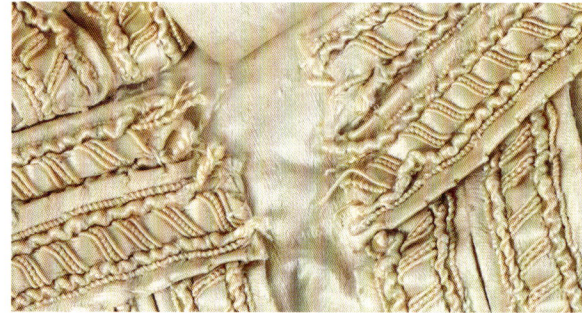

5.11 Probably due to the alteration of the side seams, the strips of decoration are roughly cut and set apart in the underarm area where they would not be seen.

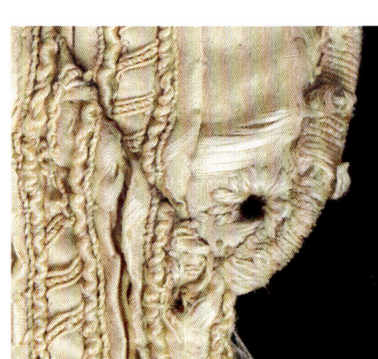

5.7 An eyelet, for a ribbon point to fasten the doublet and secure the girdle, is worked in the peak of the doublet and another at the top of the lap at CF.

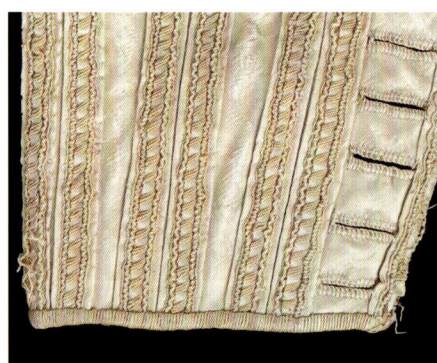

5.8 The edging lace that binds the wrist and other parts has an ivory silk warp and a thick linen weft.

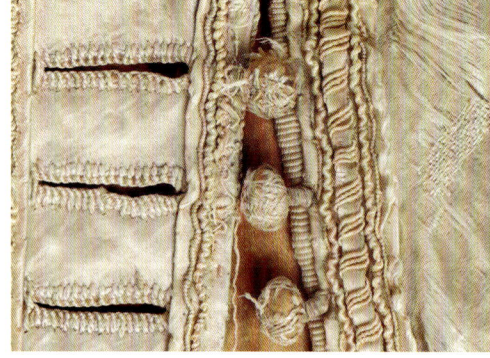

5.9 The edging lace that binds the wrist is carried up to bind the undersleeve edge of the wrist opening to create a firm base for the buttons.

5.12 The buttons are covered with a 2 'S' ply silk thread.

5.13 The remnants of the button loops in the collar are made with plaited silk, now almost completely disintegrated.

Wrong side (WS) details

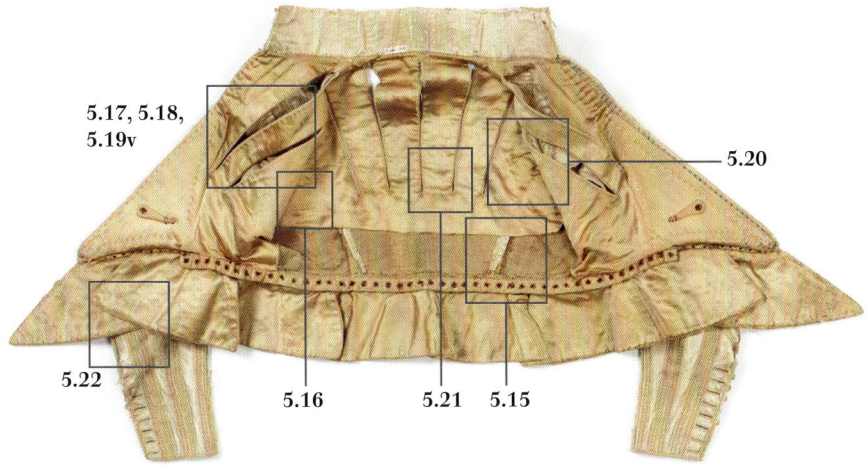

5.14 A front view of the slashed doublet lying open.

5.15 The side-seam allowances are held open with running stitches. Visible right in the seam are the basting lines outlining the back panel, shown in the white box.

5.16 The pad stitches, shown in the white box, on the extra pieces of canvas are worked in a thick 2 'S' ply linen or hemp thread. The long basting stitches holding the piece to the main canvas interlining can be seen along its curved edge.

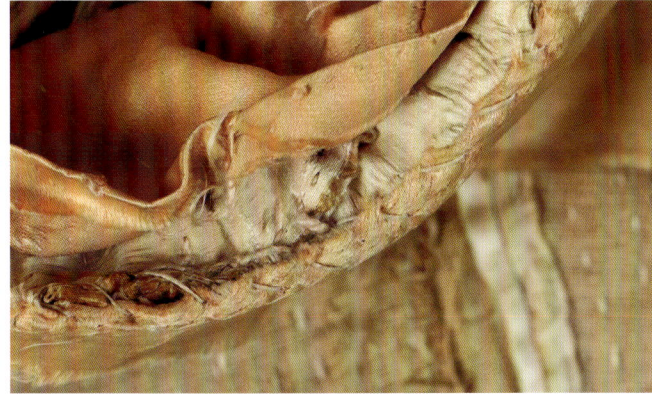

5.17 The sleeve was whipped around the armhole with a strong doubled, white linen thread. The original colour of the lining can still be seen on the top seam allowance of the sleeve.

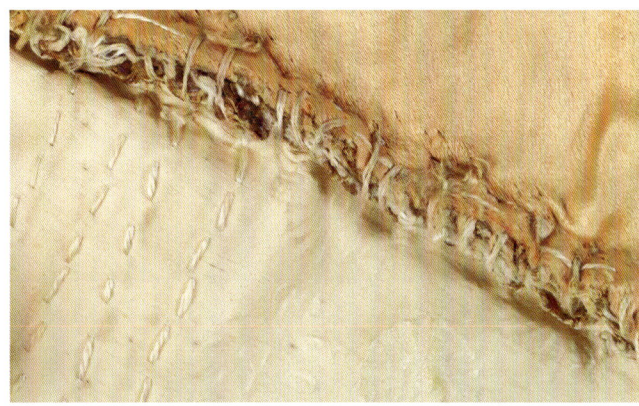

5.18 The seam around the armhole is whipped more closely in the area where the layers of the shoulder wing make it thicker. The seam allowance is only ⅛" deep.

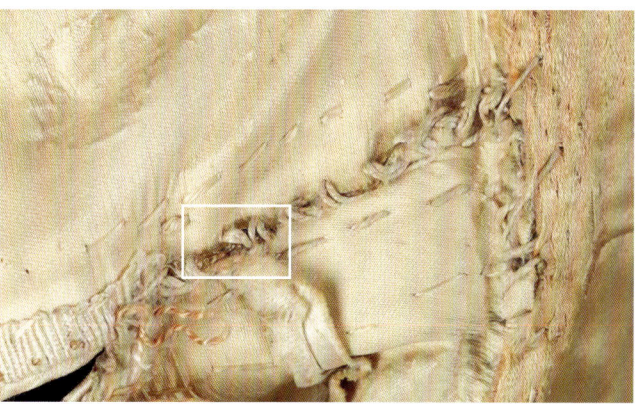

5.19 The sleeve seams consist of two raw edges strengthened with glue and then whipped together with strong doubled, white linen thread. Remnants of the glue can still be seen, shown in the white box.

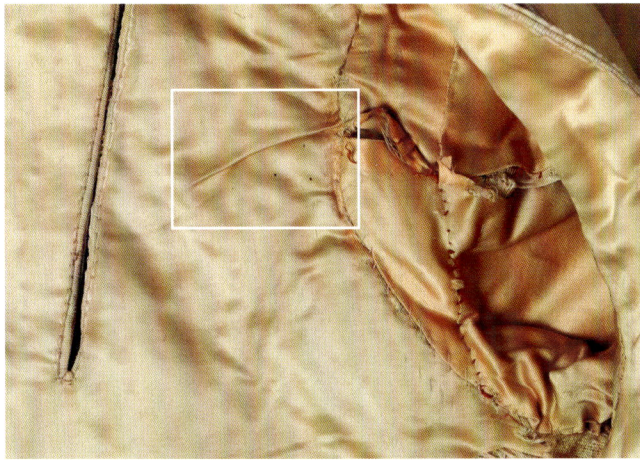

5.20 On the LHS only, a pleat is made in the back lining, shown in the white box, *probably* to accommodate a protruding shoulder blade.

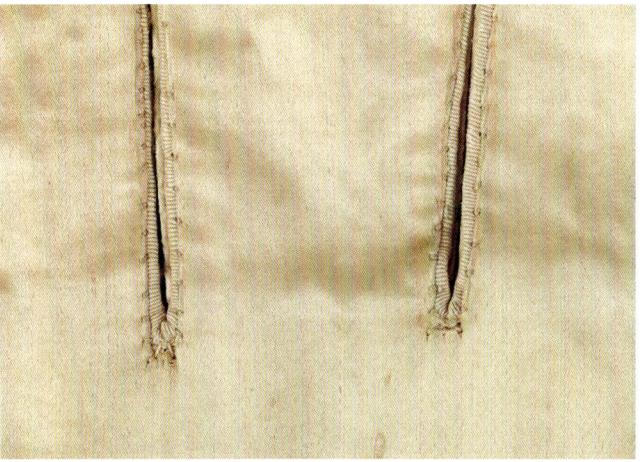

5.21 The lining is felled to the edging lace binding of the vertical slashes with a 2 'S' ply, pink silk thread. There are about six to seven stitches per inch.

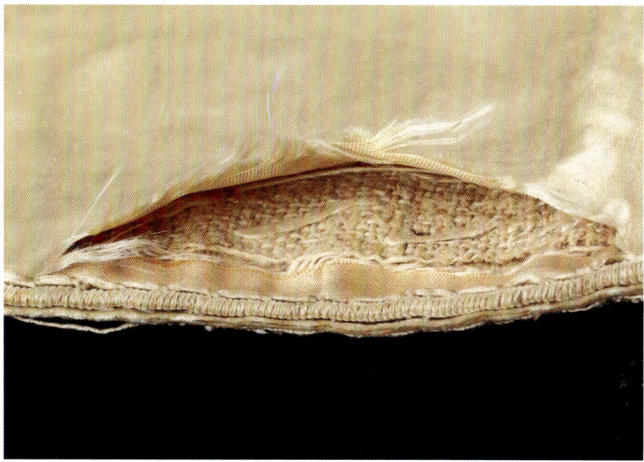

5.22 An extra layer of canvas is pad stitched to the interlining of the four front laps. Unlike the pad stitching elsewhere, the rows of stitches in the laps are all worked in the same direction.

Pattern by Luca Costigliolo

Wrong side (WS) details CONTINUED

5.23 The LHS belly piece.

5.24 The RHS belly piece.

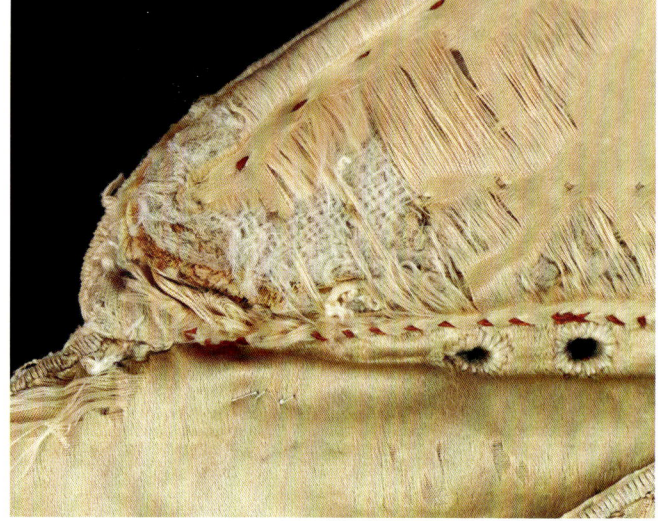

5.25 The layer of wool, covering each side of the belly pieces, can be seen in the areas where the satin lining has disintegrated. The wool is glued and pad stitched through the bents.

5.26 The lining was felled along the bottom edge of the belly piece with a 2 'S' ply red silk thread. There are about seven stitches per inch.

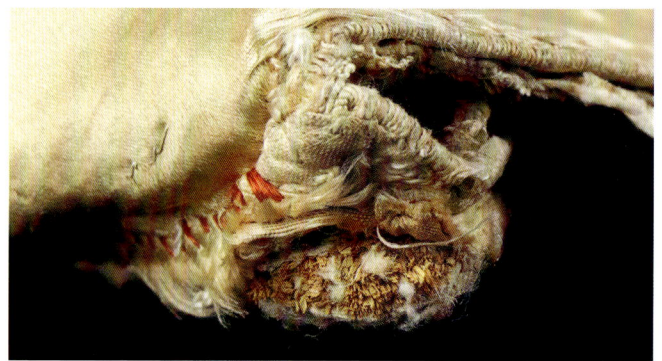

5.27 The bents forming the belly piece can clearly be seen in places where the wool covering and the satin lining have worn away. The use of bents make the belly piece stiff but slightly flexible.

X-ray images

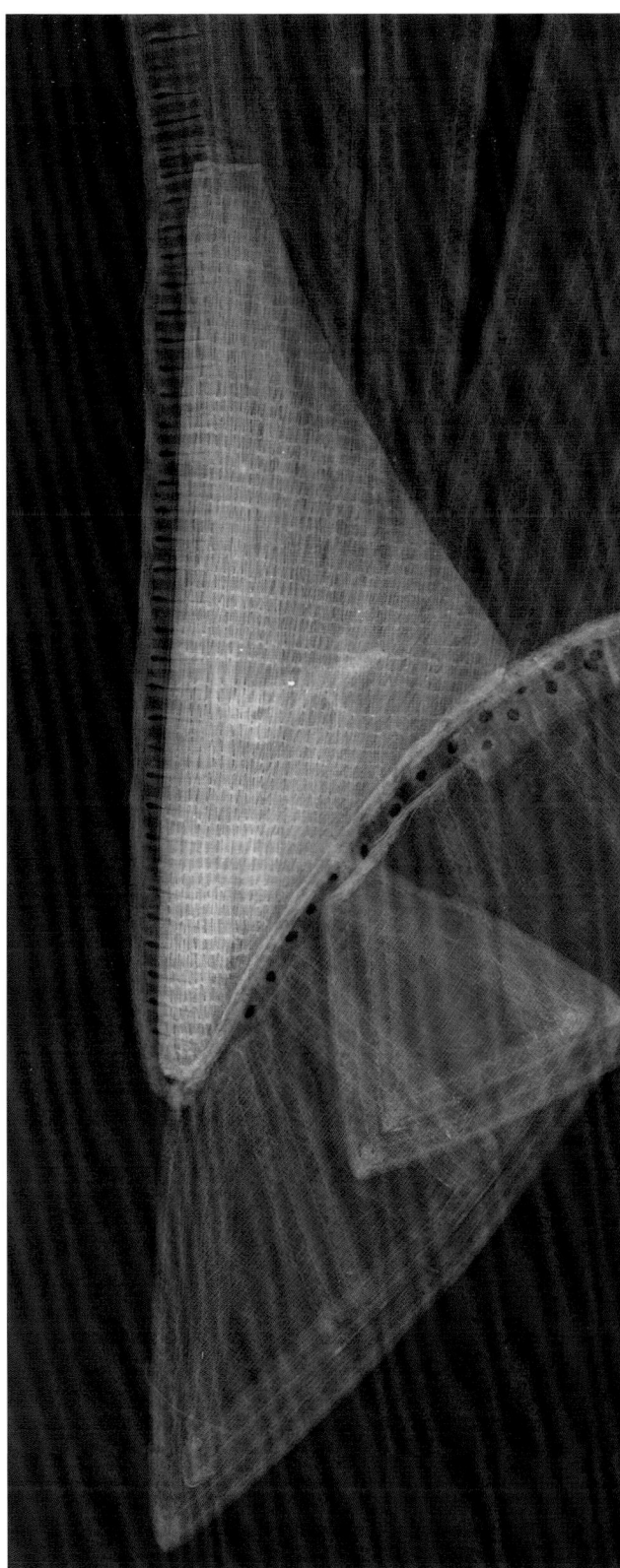

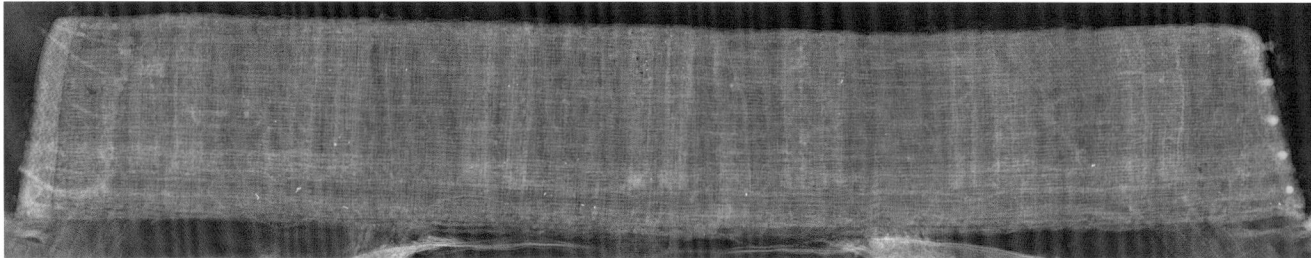

5.29 An x-ray image of the collar. The pad stitching holding the three layers of canvas stiffened with glue can be seen. The remnants of the button loops are visible on the left side, as well as the shank of the buttons on the right edge.

5.30 The extra pieces of canvas pad stitched to the interlining on each side of the armhole are cut net, avoiding any extra bulk in the shoulder seam.

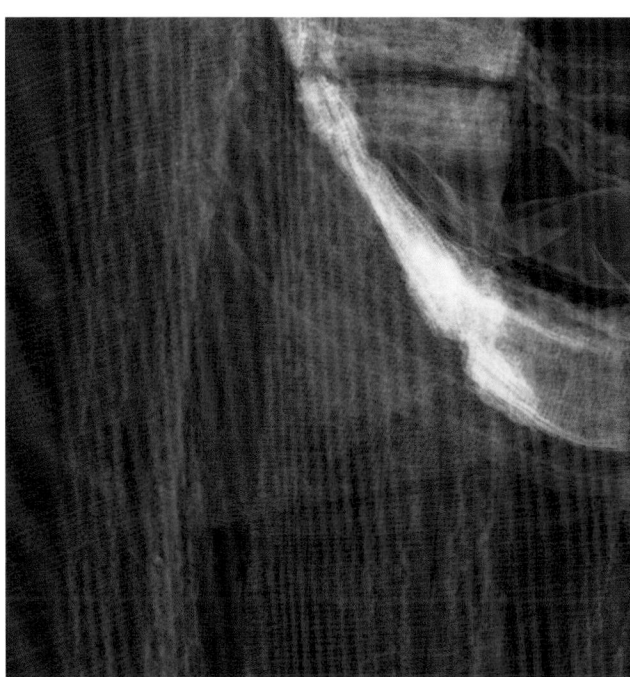

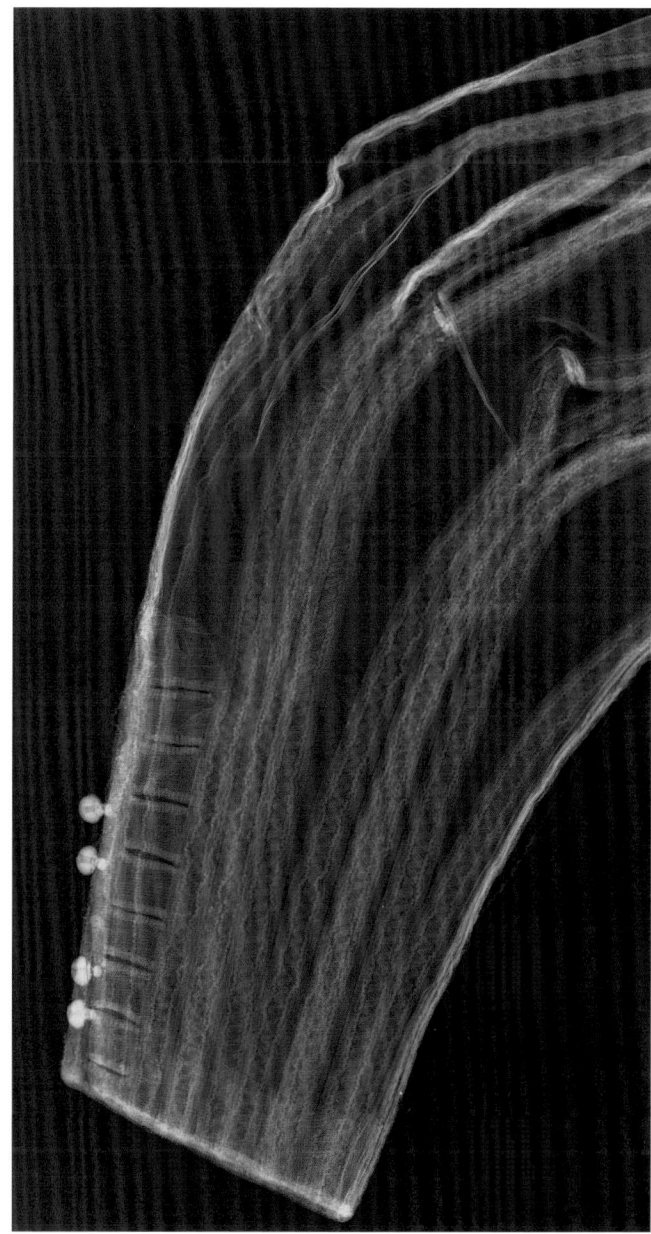

5.28 A composite of two x-ray images of the LHS of the doublet, showing the layers of the front. Extra pieces of stiffened canvas pad stitched to the front laps can be seen. The bents in the belly piece are arranged vertically and stitched horizontally.

5.31 The RHS of the doublet, showing the extra pieces of canvas pad stitched to the interlining of the body at the back of the armhole. The overlap of the finer piece of canvas that was added to the front to enlarge the side seams can also be seen at the centre of the image.

5.32 To stabilize the satin, cut on the bias below the elbow, strips of canvas cut on the straight grain are placed along the wrist and the buttonhole edge of the wrist opening. The buttons are sewn with white linen thread, worked continuously from one button to the next, which can be seen, hidden between the layers of fabric.

Pattern by Luca Costigliolo

PATTERN
Pattern of the stamped satin layer

SCALE 1:4

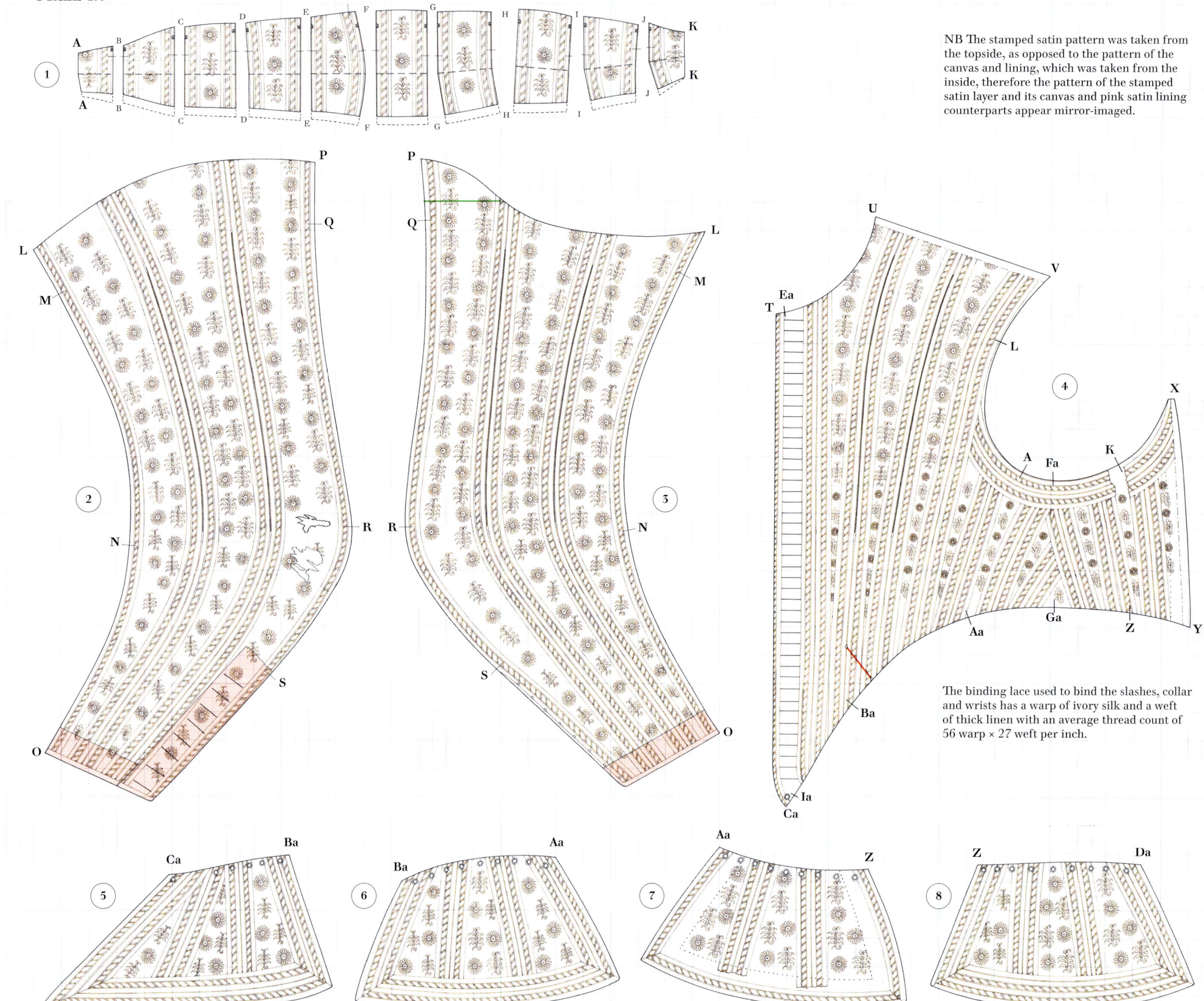

NB The stamped satin pattern was taken from the topside, as opposed to the pattern of the canvas and lining, which was taken from the inside, therefore the pattern of the stamped satin layer and its canvas and pink satin lining counterparts appear mirror-imaged.

The binding lace used to bind the slashes, collar and wrists has a warp of ivory silk and a weft of thick linen with an average thread count of 56 warp × 27 weft per inch.

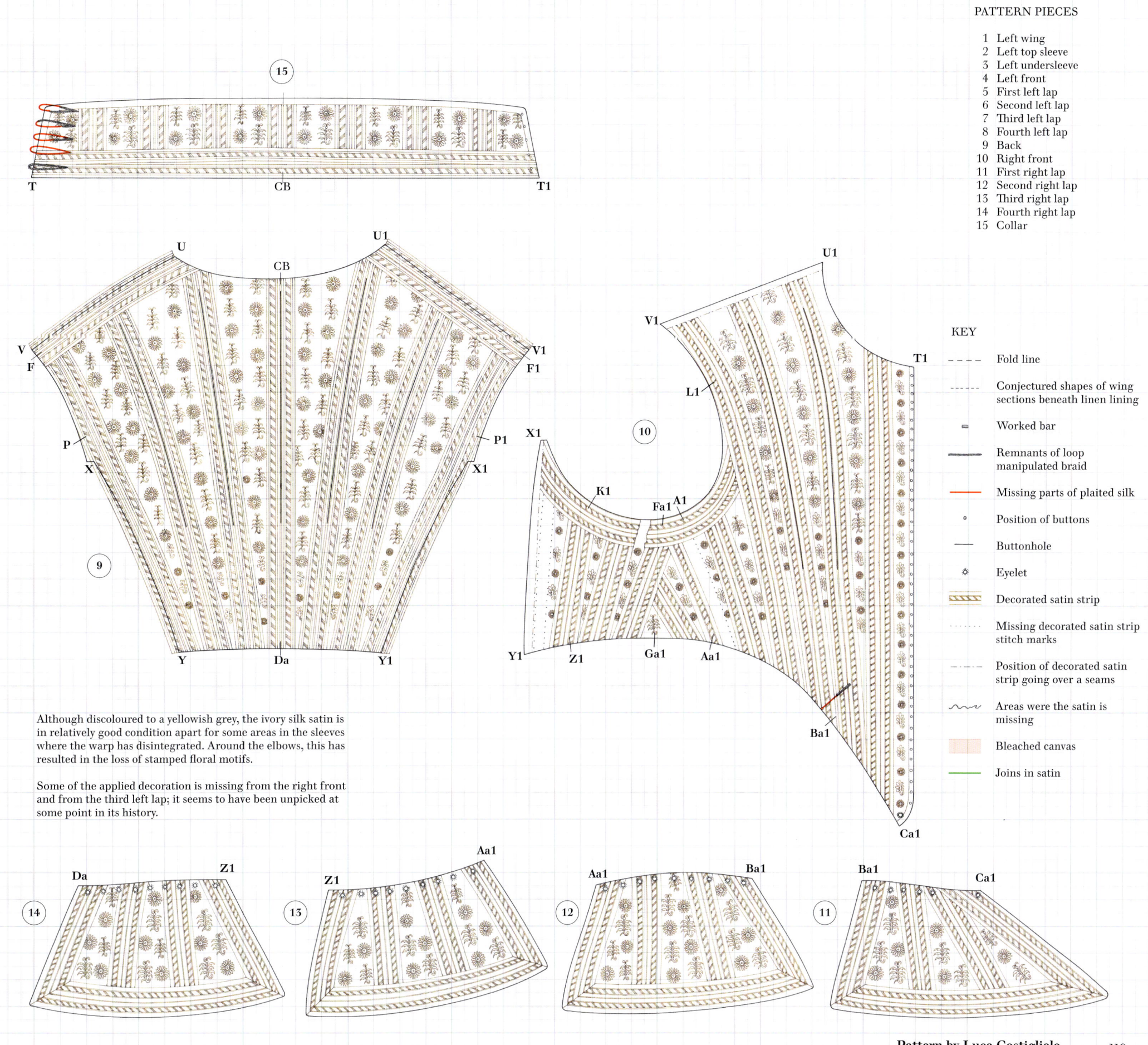

Pattern of the stamped satin layer CONTINUED
SCALE 1:4

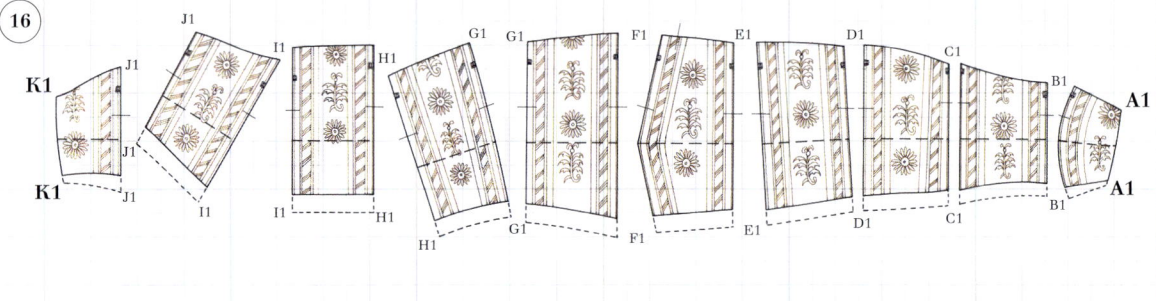
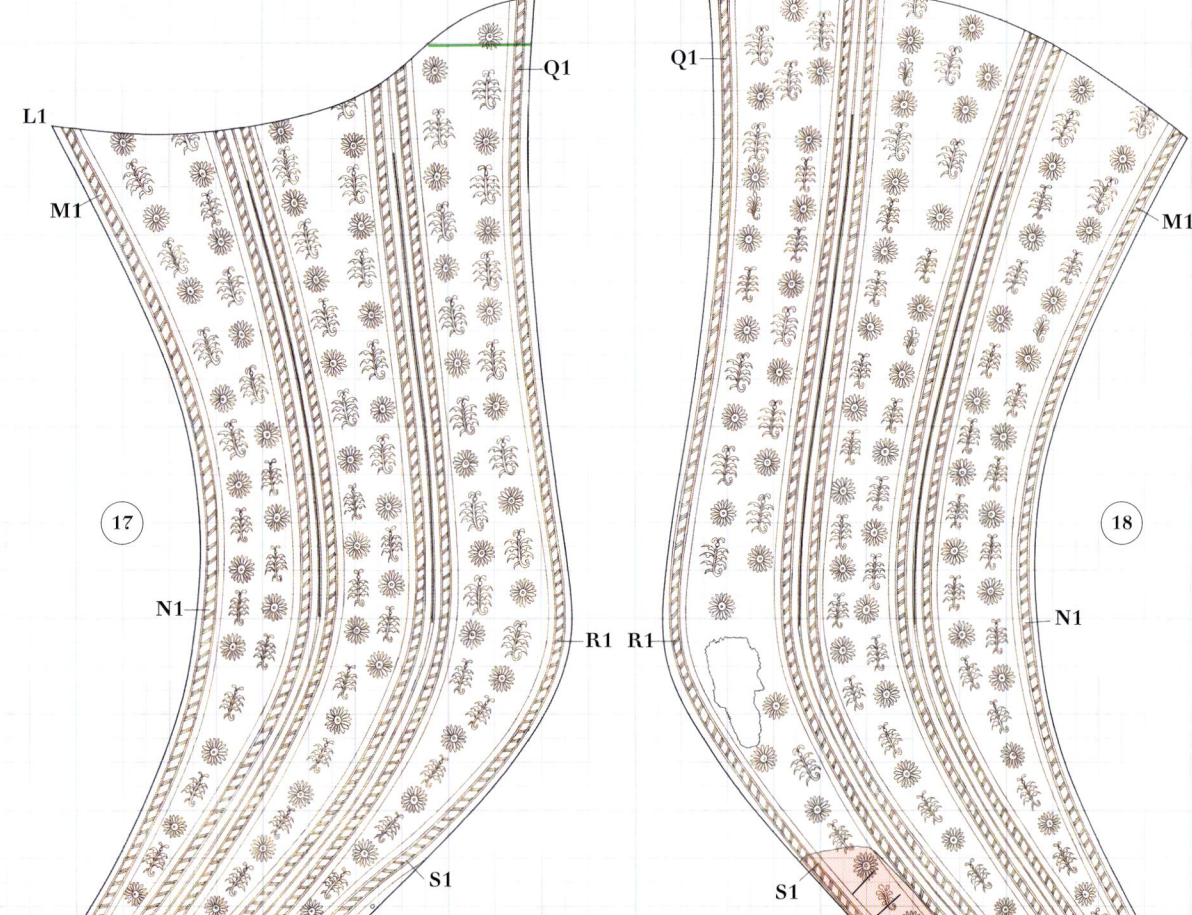

Pattern of the lining and belly pieces
SCALE 1:4

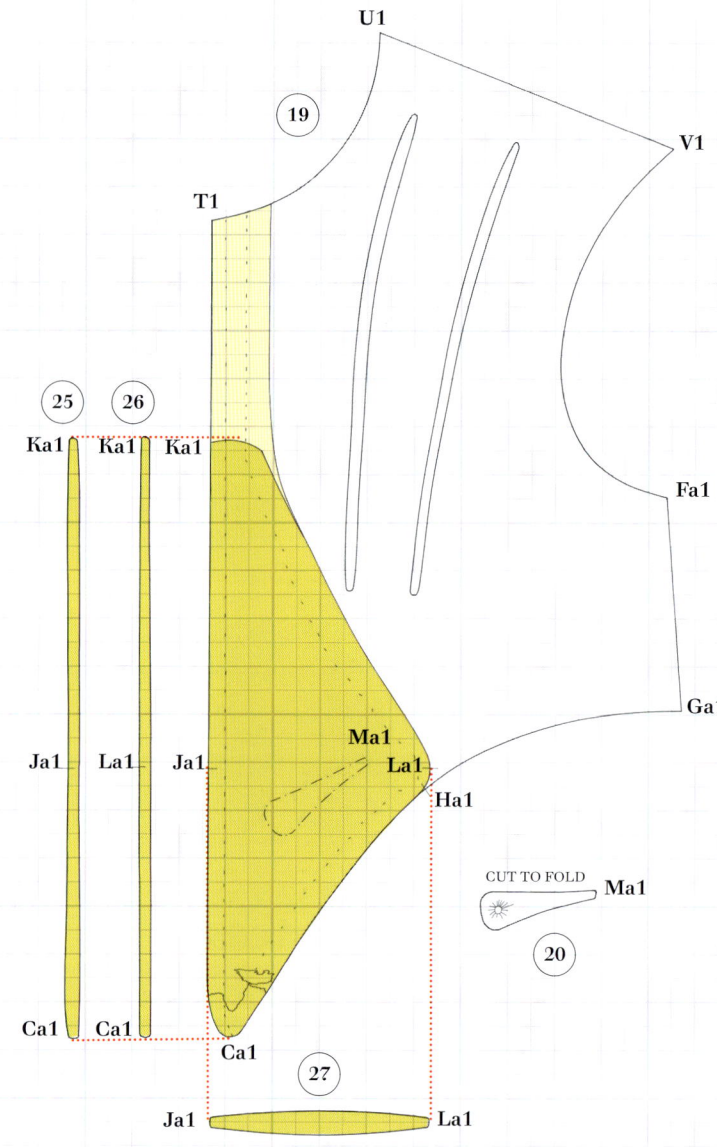

The thickness of the belly pieces varies between the two fronts. On the LHS, the middle part is ½" and tapers at each end to ¼" (pattern piece 27). On the RHS, the middle part is ½", tapering to ⅜" at centre front and ¼" on the side edge (pattern piece 30). The bents used to stiffen it are golden in colour and resemble the stalks of great millet, a cereal plant still used in broom-making in many European countries.

STAMPED MOTIFS
SCALE 1:1

FASTENINGS DETAILS
SCALE 1:1

 Actual size of the plaited silk used for the collar and girdle loops.

Actual size of the silk covered wooden buttons.

5 | Slashed doublet of stamped ivory silk satin

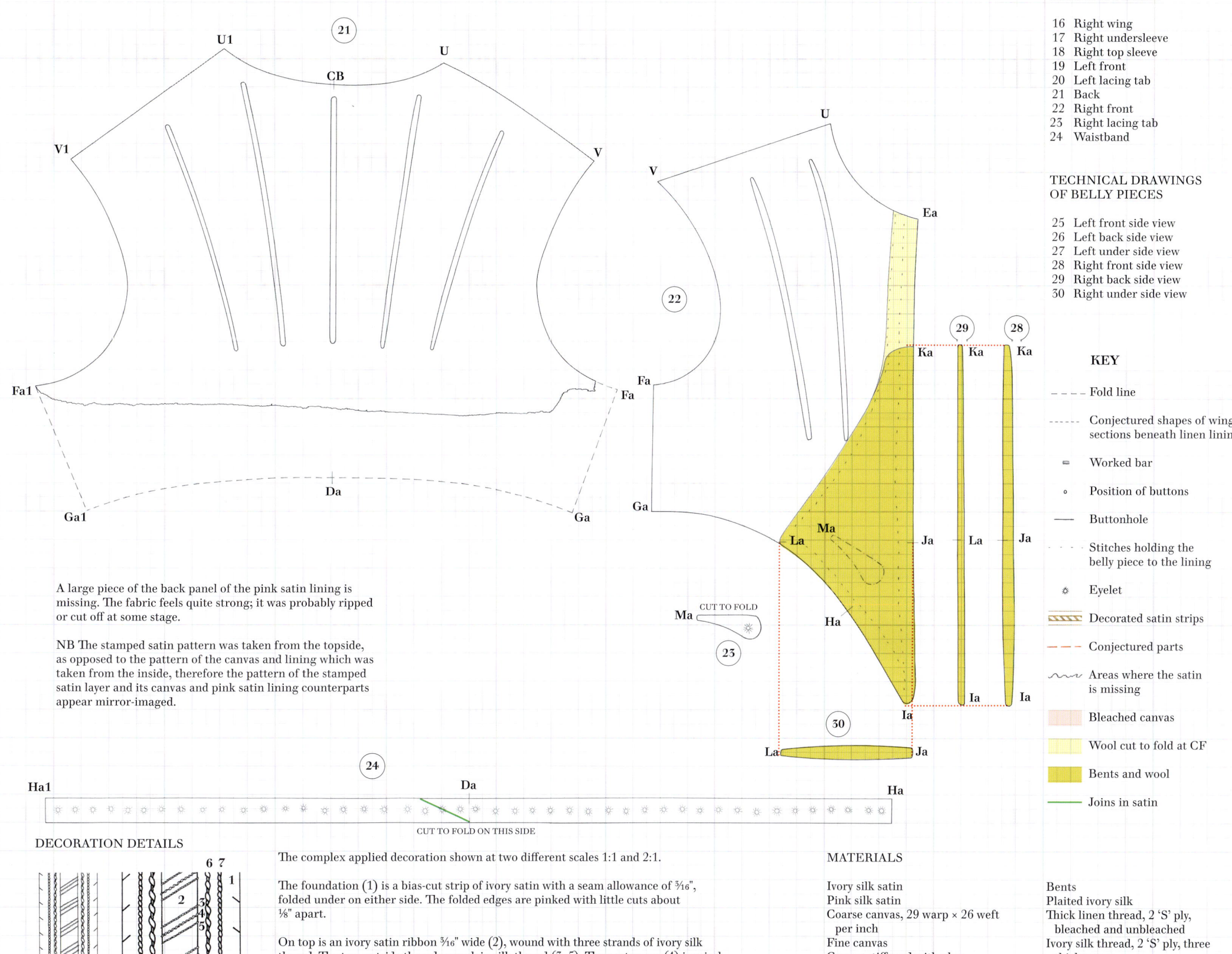

Pattern of the lining

SCALE 1:8

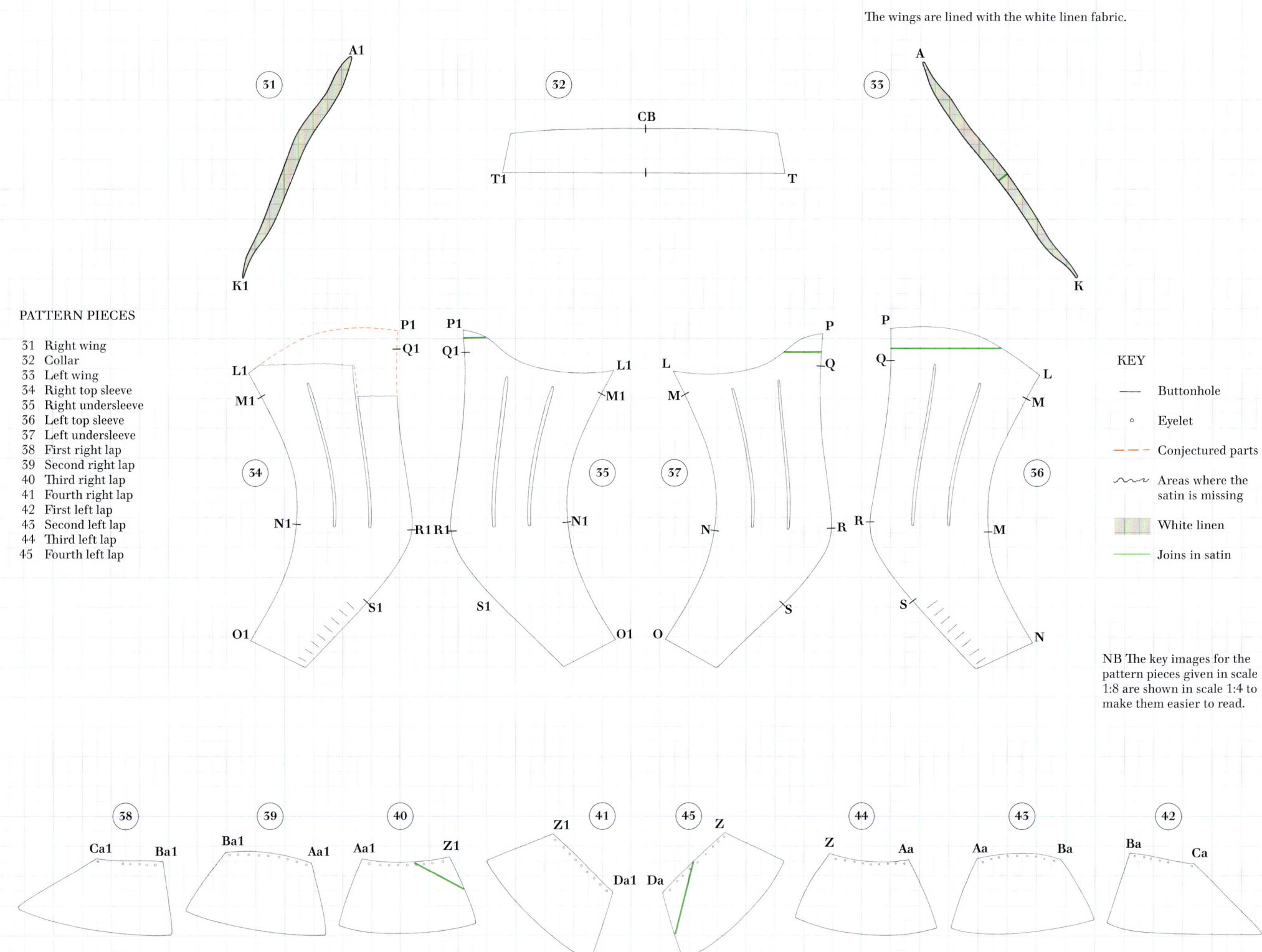

Pattern of the canvas interlinings

SCALE 1:8

The body of the doublet is interlined with coarse canvas. The extra pieces of interlining on the body, front laps and collar are made from the canvas stiffened with glue.

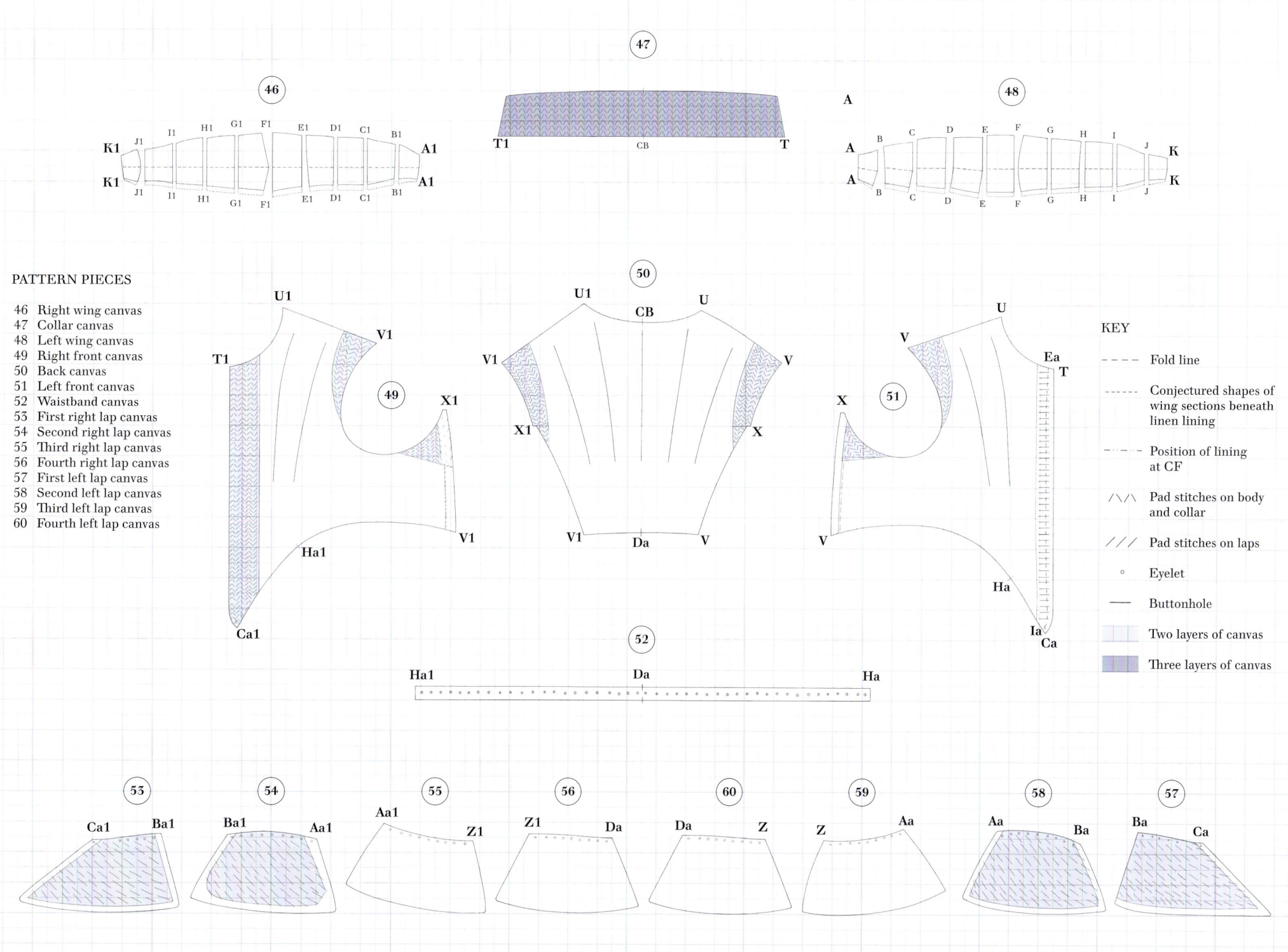

PATTERN PIECES

- 46 Right wing canvas
- 47 Collar canvas
- 48 Left wing canvas
- 49 Right front canvas
- 50 Back canvas
- 51 Left front canvas
- 52 Waistband canvas
- 53 First right lap canvas
- 54 Second right lap canvas
- 55 Third right lap canvas
- 56 Fourth right lap canvas
- 57 First left lap canvas
- 58 Second left lap canvas
- 59 Third left lap canvas
- 60 Fourth left lap canvas

KEY

- ---- Fold line
- ------ Conjectured shapes of wing sections beneath linen lining
- -·-·- Position of lining at CF
- /\/\ Pad stitches on body and collar
- /// Pad stitches on laps
- ○ Eyelet
- — Buttonhole
- Two layers of canvas
- Three layers of canvas

Pattern by Luca Costigliolo

CONSTRUCTION
Construction of the body

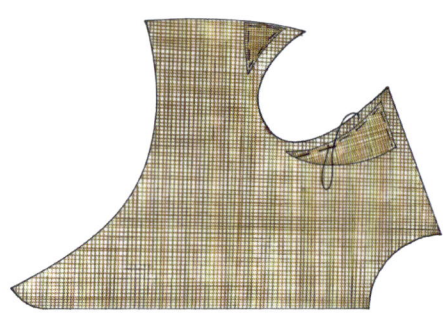

1 The front interlinings were CUT net at the CF. A seam allowance of ¼" was left on the shoulder seam and the same amount was probably originally left at the waist, neck and armhole to be TRIMMED at a later stage. Extra pieces of canvas, stiffened with glue, were CUT net and PLACED on the WS, along the front and back portion of the armhole. The pieces were then BASTED together with long RUNNING STITCHES worked in thick linen or hemp thread.

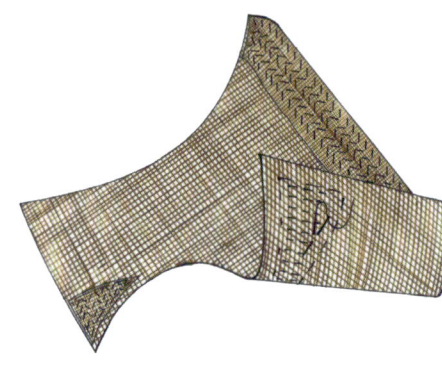

4 Using the basting line as a guide, each of the extra pieces of canvas was PAD STITCHED from the RS. The front was kept flat when the strip at CF was STITCHED. When sewing the pieces at the front and back of the armhole, the canvas was rolled to imitate the three-dimensional shape of the garment when worn.

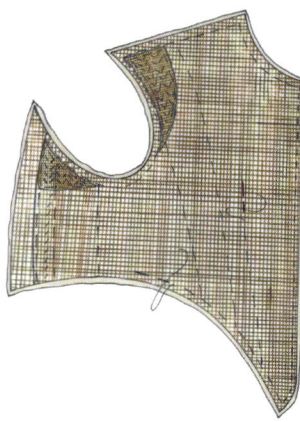

7 The RS of each front interlining was PLACED on the WS of the each satin front. They were BASTED in white linen thread around the outside edges and to mark the position of the decorated strips. The back panel was prepared in the same manner.

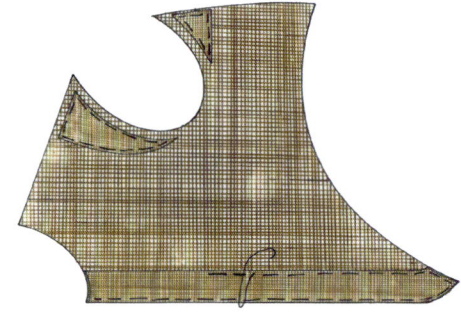

2 A strip of the same stiffened canvas was PLACED on the WS of the RHS front only and BASTED around all the edges with long RUNNING STITCHES.

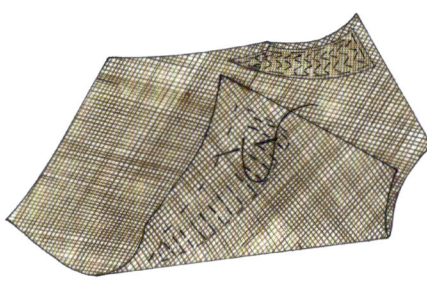

5 The extra pieces of canvas on the back piece were also PAD STITCHED from the RS in the same manner as the front.

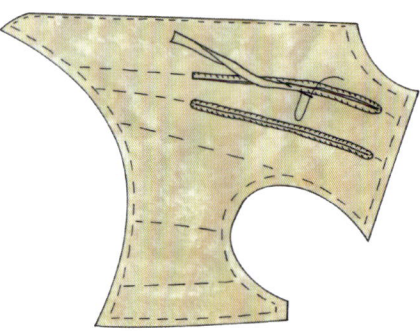

8 The vertical slashes were CUT on both fronts and the back. Starting at the bottom, the edge of each opening was bound with binding lace. This was FELLED with a single row of stitches, worked from the RS, going through all the layers of fabric and both sides of the lace with ivory silk thread. There are about six to seven stitches per inch.

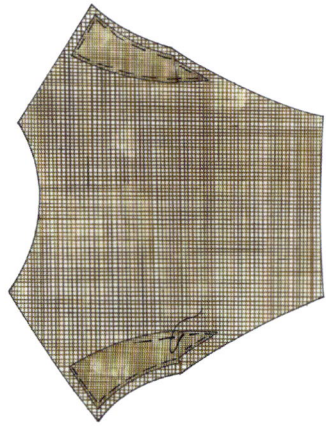

3 The back interlining was CUT with a ¼" seam allowance on the shoulder and the same amount was *probably* originally left on all the other edges. Two extra pieces of stiffened canvas, cut net, were PLACED on each side of the armhole's curve and BASTED with a long RUNNING STITCH along the edges.

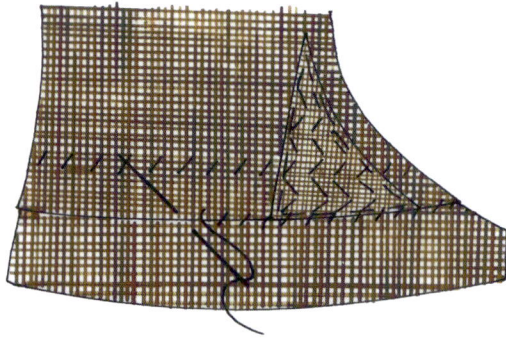

6 At one point, the side seams were altered by adding a piece of finer canvas on each side of the front. The piece was PLACED on the RS with an overlap of about ¾" and WHIPPED on both sides.

This alteration appears to have been done contemporaneously as it was done with the same thread as that used for the rest of the interlining. The doublet may have been let out after a fitting or altered, probably by the same tailor, after several years of wear.

9 The RHS front was STAMPED between the areas planned for the decoration. The stamped motifs are arranged in vertical lines, alternating flowers and branches of six different sizes, diminishing from large at the top to small at the waistline. The CF was stamped with a row of only the smaller motifs.

The raw edge at CF was then bound with binding lace. Using silk thread, the lace was FELLED with a single row of stitches worked from the RS and going through all the layers of the fabric.

5 | **Slashed doublet of stamped ivory silk satin**

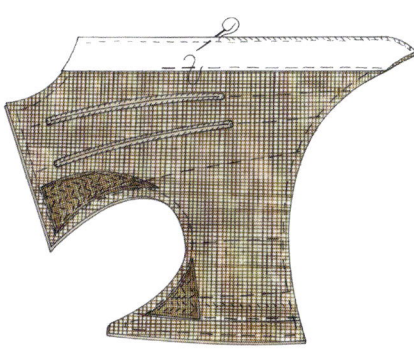
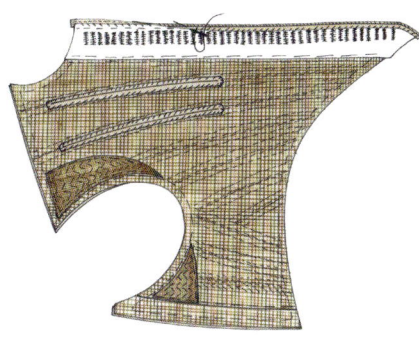

10 With WS together, a strip of white linen, CUT on the straight grain, was PLACED over the CF of the LHS front panel, WS facing. The strip was BASTED on both the CF and inner edge in white linen and then WHIPPED at the CF with silk thread.

13 The strip was then FOLDED over the CF edge and FELLED to the WS of the doublet, the number of stitches varies between six to seven per inch.

16 The side-seam allowances of the interlinings were TRIMMED to ⅛"–1/16". The seam allowance of the satin at the back is ¼" and was RUNNING STITCHED to the interlining. The seam allowances of the satin fronts are 1/16" at waist level and ⅛" to ¼" on the rest of the seam. The front-seam allowances were originally much wider to allow for alteration. The extra fabric at the front has been used, while the back was left untouched.

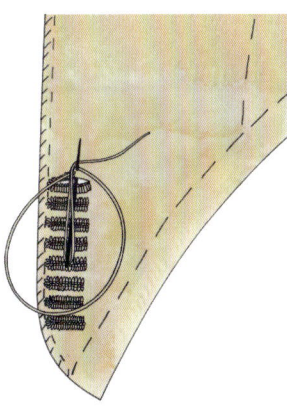
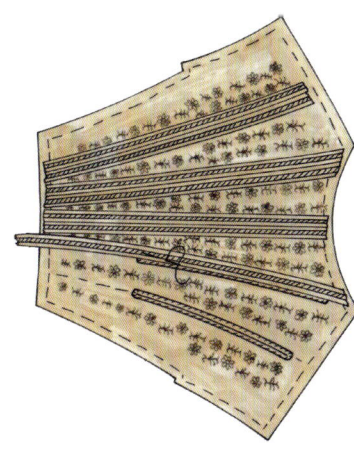

11 Forty-three buttonhole slits, ¾" wide and about ⅜" apart, were CUT along the CF of the LHS front, ¼" from the edge. Each slit was BUTTONHOLE STITCHED with ivory silk thread, starting from the lower right-hand corner, working towards and around the edge, and then continued on the other side.

14 The decoration was COUCHED on the back, a strip on each side of the bound slashes, with the same technique used for the fronts.

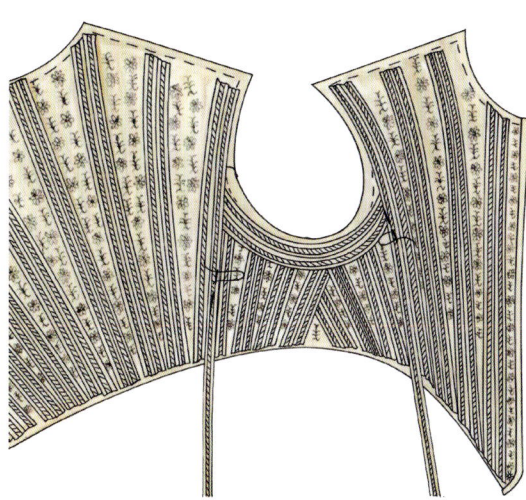

17 Two parallel decorated strips were COUCHED on the lower curve of the armhole. Starting from the outer corner of the shoulder line on both fronts and back, two more strips were sewn down to waist level. They cover the side seam at the back. On each side, they cover the raw edges of the strips under the armhole.

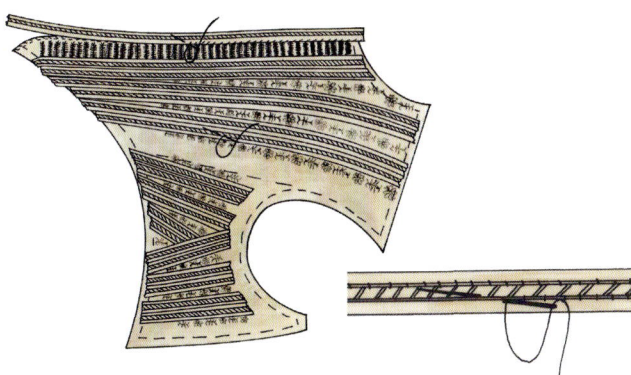
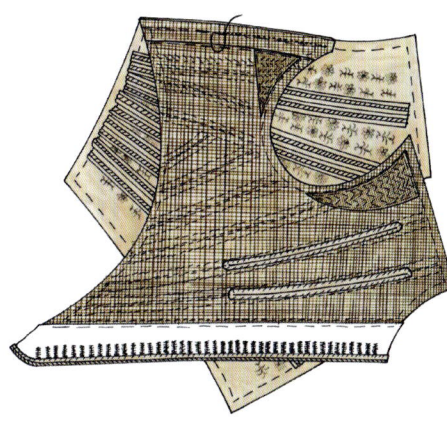
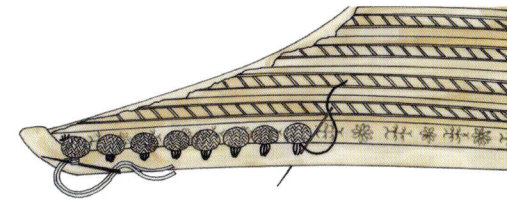

12 Decorated strips of bias-cut satin were STITCHED in parallel on both fronts. Each was attached with a COUCHING STITCH, worked over the thin silk threads already couched on each side of the central ribbon. The stitches were worked in silk thread, through the satin and interlining. A single strip was PLACED over the CF edge of the LHS front panel, covering the rounded end of the buttonholes and FELLED with silk thread.

15 With RS together, the side seams were *probably* BASTED together and BACK STITCHED with thick linen thread. These basting stitches were removed after sewing, while those marking the side seam on the back panel remain (fig. 5.15, page 115).

18 Forty-three buttons were STITCHED at CF on the RHS. Each was STAB STITCHED in the centre of the lace binding, with unbleached hemp or linen thread, leaving a shank of 3/16". Each shank was then WRAPPED and STAB STITCHED with doubled, white linen thread. Both threads were carried over from button to button and go through all the layers of the fabric.

Pattern by Luca Costigliolo

Construction of the body   CONTINUED

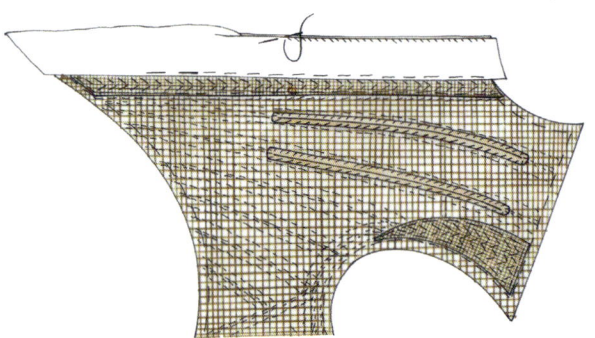

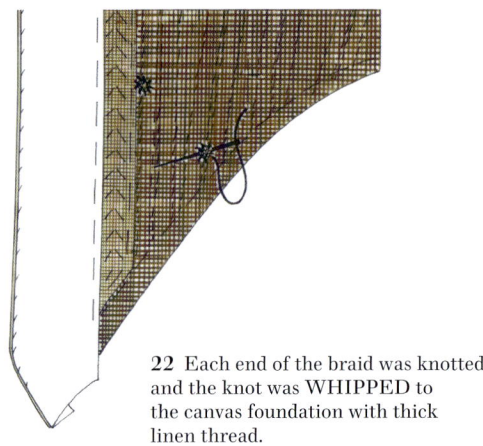

19 With WS together, a white linen facing was PLACED over the CF to cover the stitches holding the buttons. The inner edge was RUNNING STITCHED to the interlining, the other was TURNED and FELLED to the edge of the edging lace binding with thick white linen thread. There are about five stitches per inch.

22 Each end of the braid was knotted and the knot was WHIPPED to the canvas foundation with thick linen thread.

26 Each lap was STAMPED and the vertical decorated strips COUCHED in place. The sides and bottom edge were bound with lace. This was FELLED with a single row of stitches, worked from the RS and going through all the layers of fabric and lace with ivory silk thread.

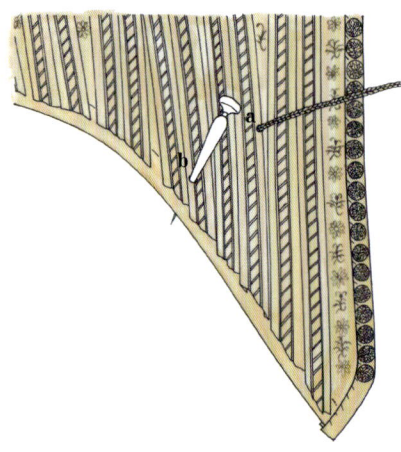

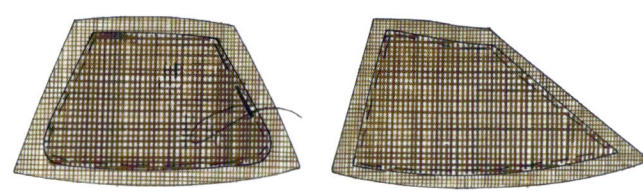

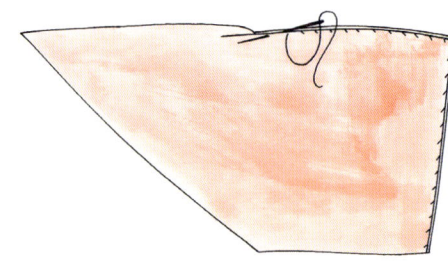

20 Two holes were PIERCED with a bodkin at a and b to create a girdle loop on each front. A length of plaited ivory silk was INSERTED through a from the WS.

23 The interlinings of the first and second laps of each front are one coarse layer and one slightly smaller canvas layer, stiffened with glue. These were RUNNING STITCHED together with thick linen thread. The interlining of the remaining laps is one coarse canvas layer only. All of the eight lap interlinings have a ⅛" seam allowance at the waist and are cut net on all other edges.

27 Two of the lap linings were PIECED and RUNNING STITCHED together with silk thread. With WS together, the pink satin lining was PLACED over each lap. It was FOLDED on the sides and bottom and FELLED to the edging lace with pink silk thread. There are about six stitches per inch.

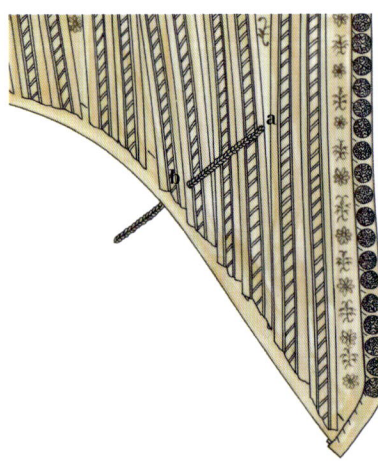

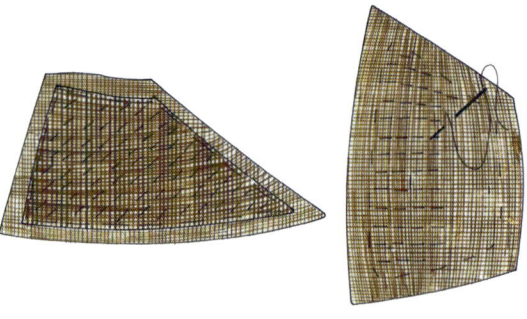

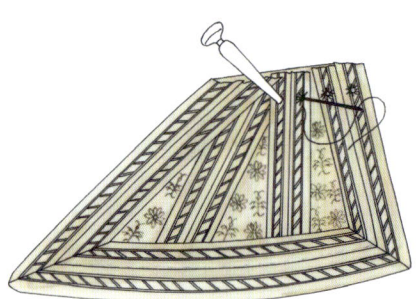

24 Each of the four front laps was PAD STITCHED from the RS through both layers of canvas while the piece was kept convex. The stitches were worked all in the same direction with thick linen thread.

28 Two decorated strips were COUCHED in parallel, starting at waist level, down one side, along the bottom edge and up the other side. Holes were PIERCED with a bodkin for eyelets. Each eyelet was WHIPPED with thick ivory silk thread.

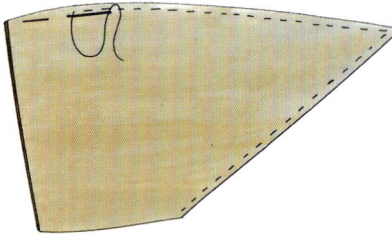

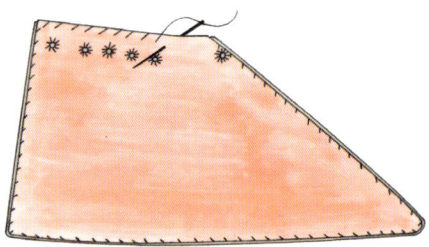

21 The plaited silk was INSERTED through point b from the RS.

25 A layer of satin, CUT net, was PLACED over the interlining of the back laps. On the four front laps, the WS of the satin is PLACED on the convex side of the interlining. Using silk thread, each lap was RUNNING STITCHED on the sides and bottom edge.

29 Each lap was WHIPPED at the top to neaten the raw edges of the fabrics. The stitches are worked through all the layers of the fabric in pink silk thread.

5 | Slashed doublet of stamped ivory silk satin

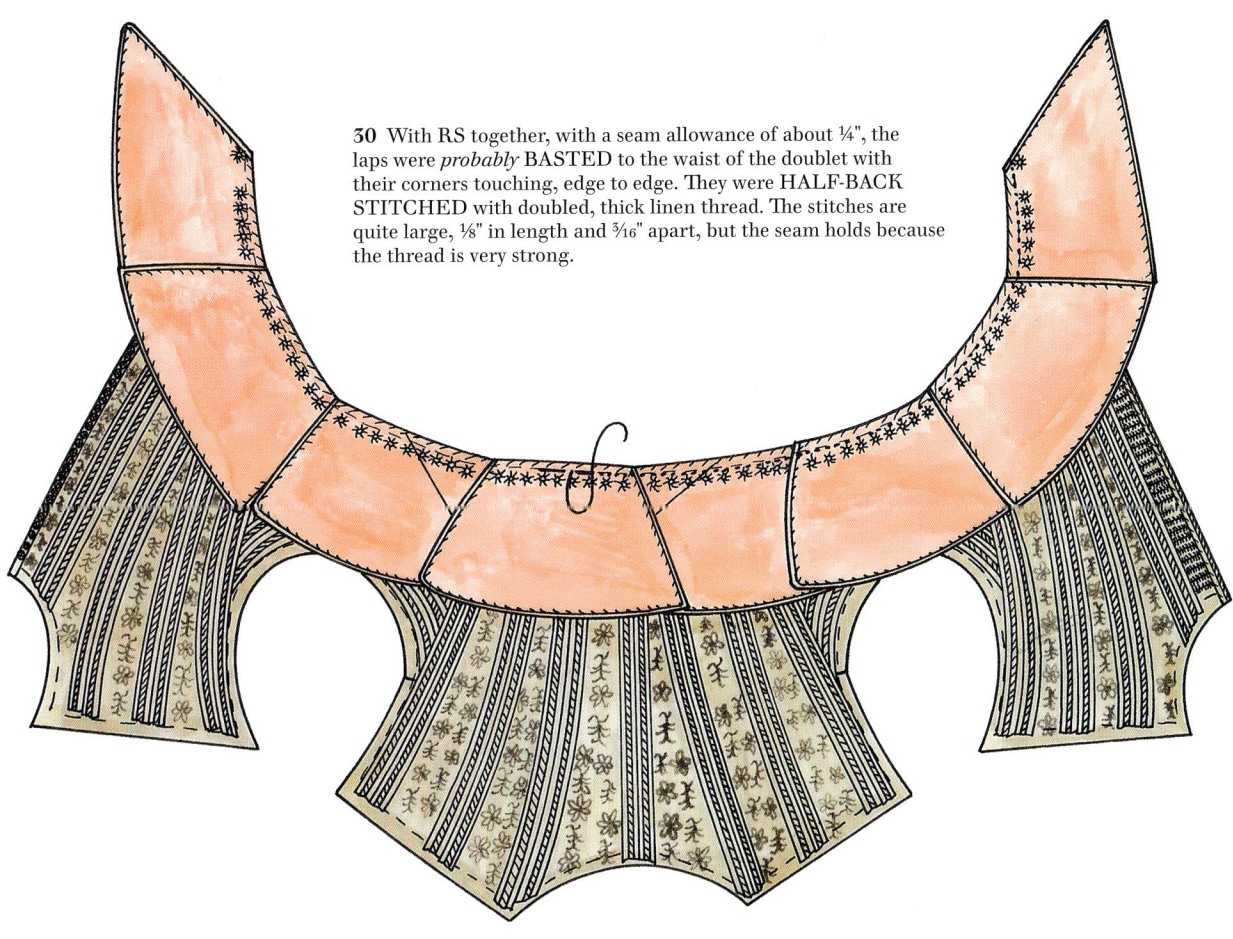

30 With RS together, with a seam allowance of about ¼", the laps were *probably* BASTED to the waist of the doublet with their corners touching, edge to edge. They were HALF-BACK STITCHED with doubled, thick linen thread. The stitches are quite large, ⅛" in length and ³⁄₁₆" apart, but the seam holds because the thread is very strong.

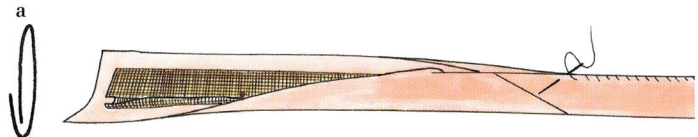

33 The waistband interlining was CUT on the straight grain, with a seam allowance of ¾" at the top and ⅛" at the bottom. These were FOLDED in to create a strong fold at the top to stitch to the doublet, and three layers of interlining below the eyelets (cross-section a). The waistband cover was PIECED from satin cut on the straight grain, RUNNING STITCHED together. The satin was FOLDED over the canvas and WHIPPED all around the edges with pink silk thread.

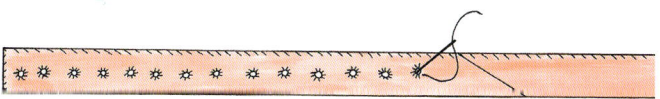

34 Forty-five eyelet holes, each about ¾" apart, were PIERCED with a bodkin in the centre of the waistband and WHIPPED with red silk thread.

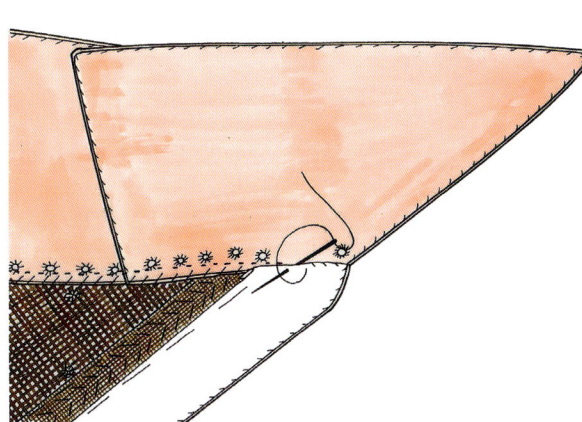

31 The lower ends of the strips of white linen, facing each CF, were FOLDED and FELLED to the front laps with thick linen thread.

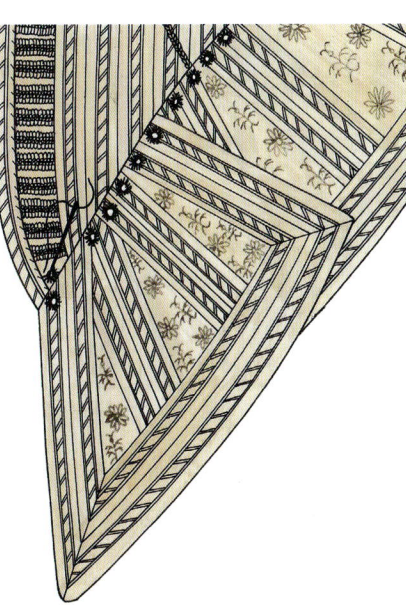

32 On both fronts, just above waist level, an eyelet was PIERCED with a bodkin, corresponding to the first eyelet of laps 5 and 11. It was WHIPPED with thick ivory silk thread. These pairs of eyelets are for the point fastening the doublet at the bottom and holding the girdle in position under the peak.

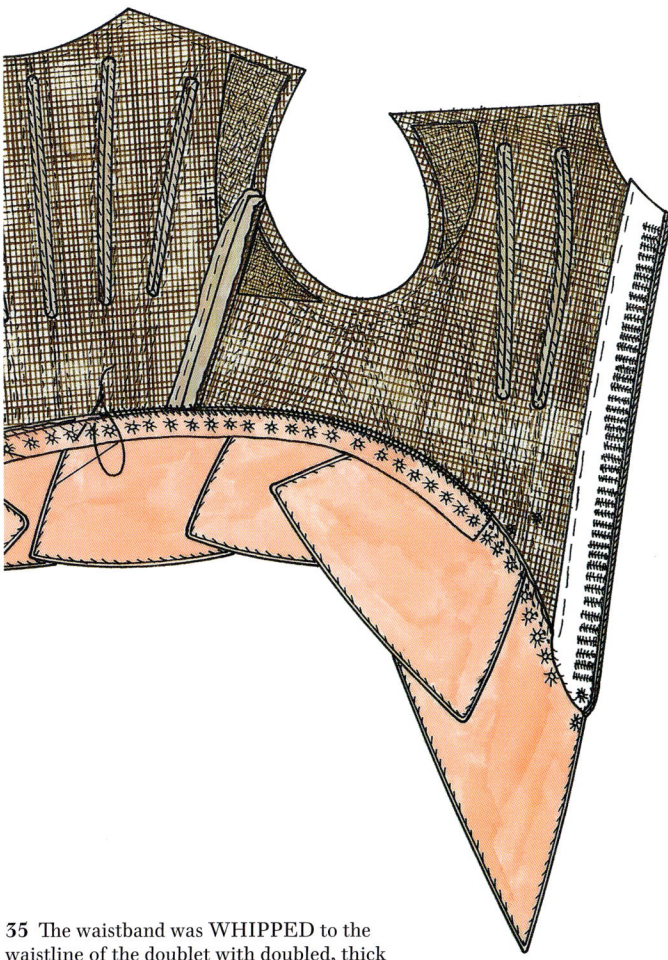

35 The waistband was WHIPPED to the waistline of the doublet with doubled, thick linen thread. There are about five stitches per inch and they are worked through the seam allowances of the waist and laps.

Pattern by Luca Costigliolo

Construction of the belly pieces and lining

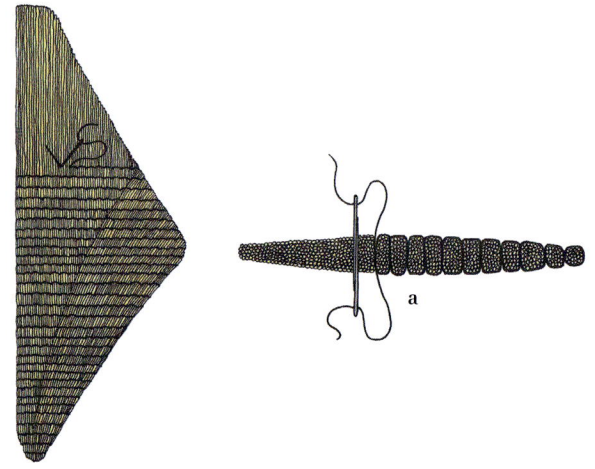

36 The belly pieces consist of a thick layer of bents PLACED vertically at CF and at an angle on the inner side, the thickness tapering at each end and on the sides. *Probably* starting from the lower edge, 51 rows of INTERLOCKING RUNNING STITCH in thick linen thread were STITCHED with two needles, worked simultaneously to keep the bents together (cross-section a).

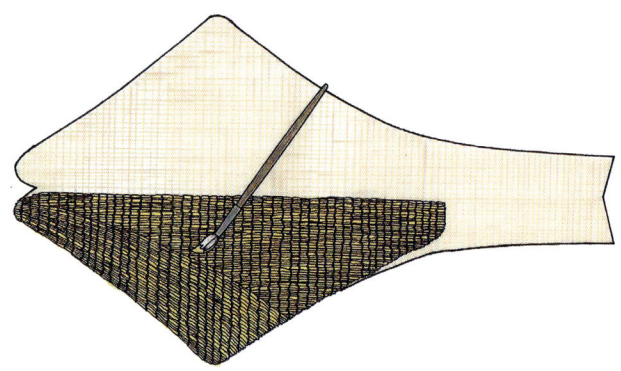

37 A layer of white wool, loosely woven, was CUT to FOLD at CF. Each belly piece was COATED with glue and the wool FOLDED over it.

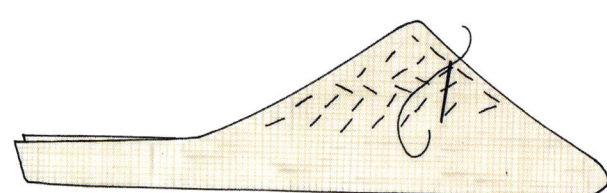

38 Once the glue was dry, each belly piece was PAD STITCHED with thick linen or hemp thread; the stitches were stabbed with the needle going through all layers. This further stiffens the belly pieces while retaining a certain degree of flexibility.

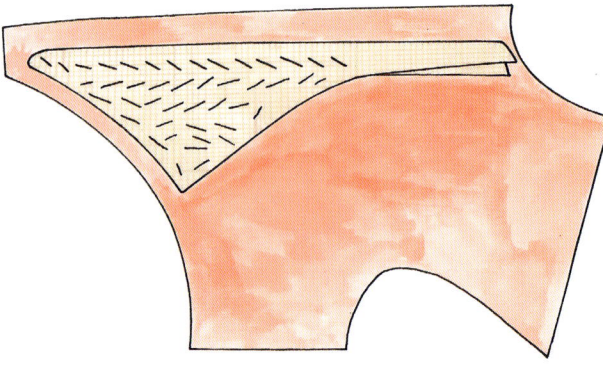

39 The pink satin lining for each front was CUT with a seam allowance of about 1" at CF. Each belly piece was PLACED on the WS of the corresponding front lining.

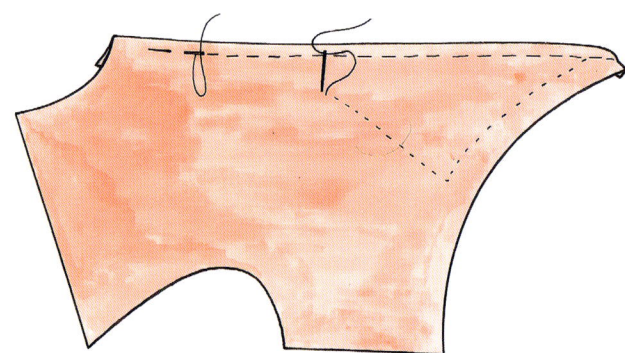

40 The seam allowance at CF was FOLDED over the edge of the wool-covered belly piece and BASTED from the peak to the neck, about ⅜" from the CF edge. Through the layers of bents only, the basting was worked as a STAB STITCH. A RUNNING STITCH in pink silk thread was STAB STITCHED around the lower and upper edge of the belly piece; there are about four stitches per inch.

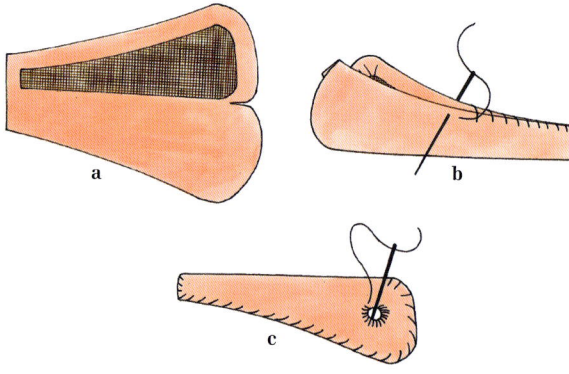

41 The interlining of the lacing tab was CUT net. The satin cover was CUT to FOLD with a seam allowance of ³⁄₁₆" (a). The satin was FOLDED over the canvas and WHIPPED all around the edge with red silk thread (b). On each tab, an eyelet was PIERCED with a bodkin and WHIPPED with red silk thread (c).

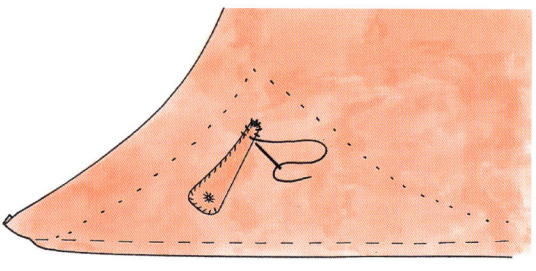

42 Each tab was WHIPPED at one end to the belly piece, with a STAB STITCH in red silk thread, through all the layers of silk, wool and bents.

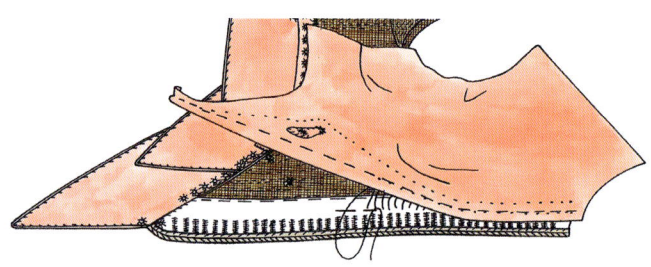

43 On the LHS, the lining was PLACED over the front of the doublet with WS facing. The CF of the lining is ⅜" from the CF of the doublet at the neck, tapering to ⅛" at the peak, with the ends of the buttonholes uncovered. With thick red silk thread, the two layers were sewn together with a firm RUNNING STITCH, partly worked as a STAB STITCH, along the line of basting at the CF of the lining.

44 On the RHS, the lining was PLACED on the doublet with the CF edge to edge and SEWN in the same manner as the LHS. On the RHS side only the folded edge of the lining is FELLED to the edging lace binding at CF, from the top of the belly piece to the neckline.

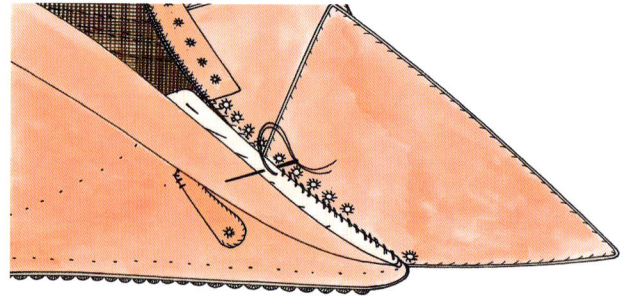

45 The lower edge of the belly piece was WHIPPED to the waist seam allowance of doublet and laps. The stitches are ⅜" apart and worked in white and occasionally in brown, doubled, thick linen thread.

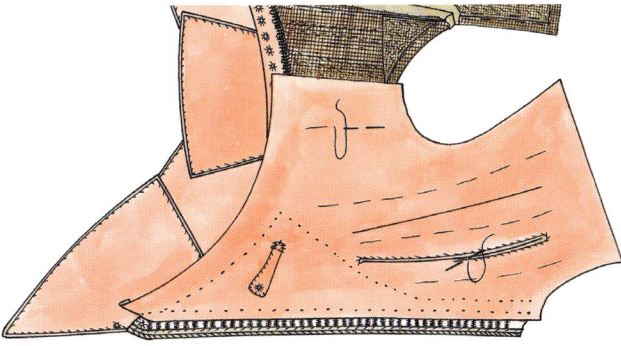

46 The rest of the front lining was *probably* BASTED to the interlining with long vertical stitches worked from the waist upwards. Slashes in the lining were CUT to match those of the doublet; the edges were FOLDED and FELLED to the edging lace with pink silk thread. There are about six or seven stitches per inch.

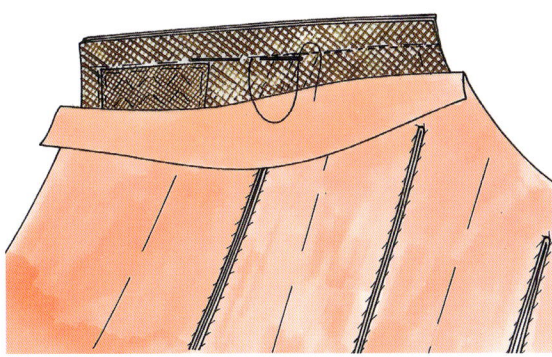

49 With the lining held back, the back shoulder of the doublet was eased to fit the front shoulder and *probably* BASTED together. The seam was HALF-BACK STITCHED with thick white linen thread.

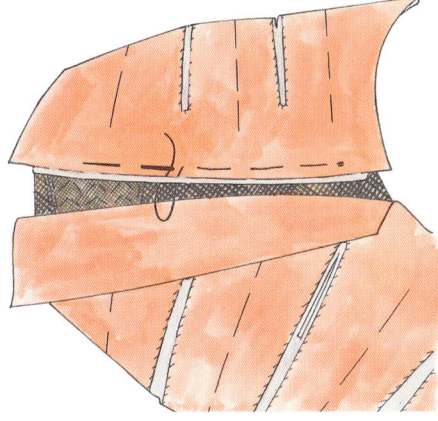

52 The shoulder seam allowance of the front lining was placed over the shoulder seam and permanently BASTED to the ivory satin seam allowance of the back shoulder.

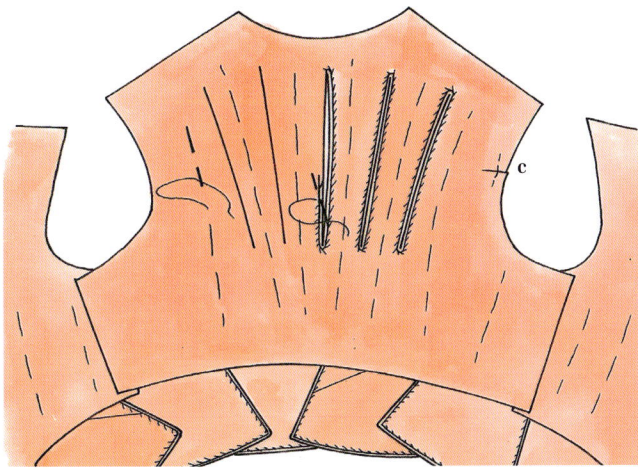

47 With WS together, the back lining was placed over the doublet and *probably* BASTED to the interlining with long vertical stitches. A pleat facing upwards (c) was BASTED on the LHS armhole only (see fig. 5.20, page 115). The five vertical slashes were CUT, FOLDED and FELLED with silk thread.

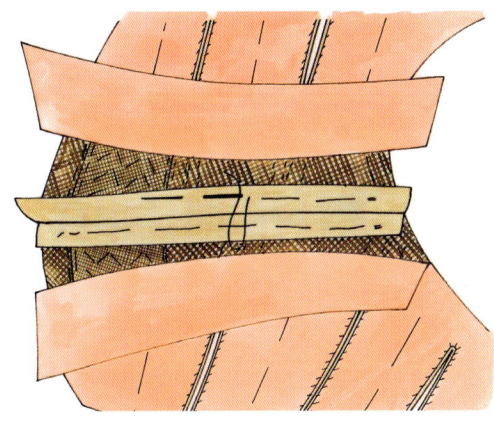

50 The seam allowances of the interlining only were TRIMMED to ⅛". The ¼" satin seam allowances were opened flat and RUNNING STITCHED to the canvas with linen thread.

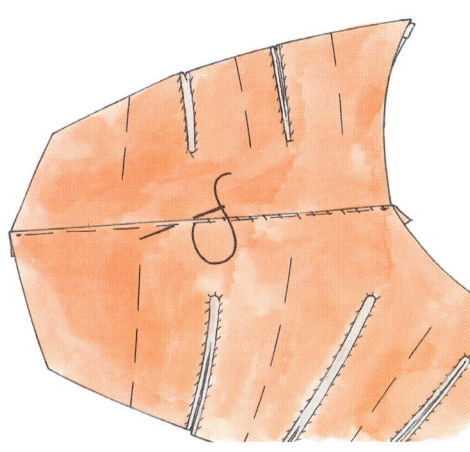

53 The shoulder seam allowance of the back lining was FOLDED over the centre of the seam, eased to fit the front and *probably* BASTED. The seam was FELLED with pink silk thread. There are about six stitches per inch.

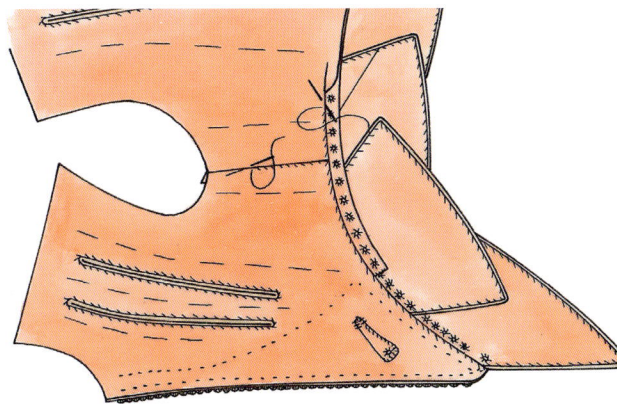

48 The side-seam allowance of the front lining was FOLDED over the back side seam and FELLED with silk thread. The seam allowance of the waist was FOLDED to cover the seams of the laps, waistband and belly piece and FELLED with pink silk thread. There are about eight stitches per inch.

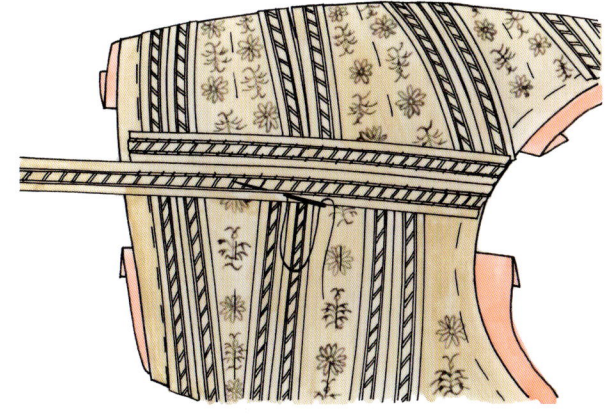

51 A decorated satin strip was COUCHED over the shoulder seams. On the back piece, a second strip was COUCHED immediately next to it.

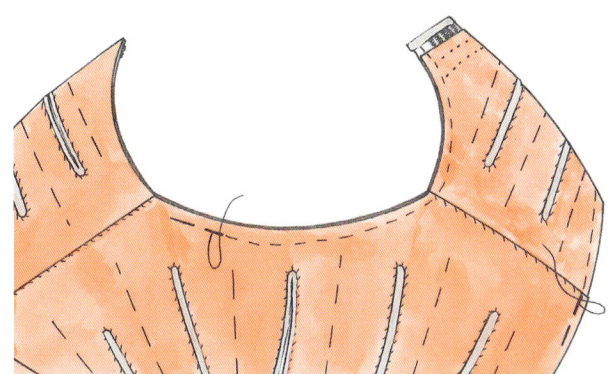

54 The neckline and armhole were *probably* BASTED to keep the layers together.

Pattern by Luca Costigliolo

Construction of the collar and wings

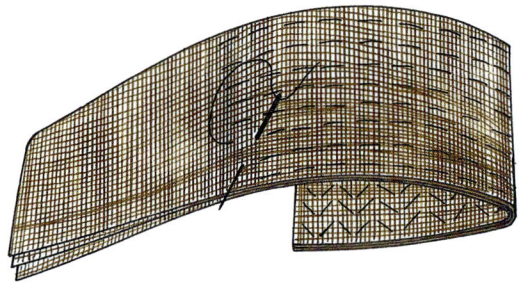

55 The collar was interlined with three layers of canvas; each was stiffened with glue individually. The three layers were PLACED together, kept in a convex shape and PAD STITCHED in vertical rows and worked on the RS in thick linen or hemp thread.

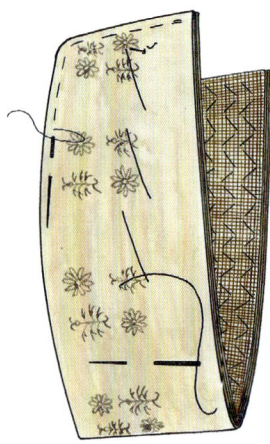

56 The satin layer of the collar was CUT net, STAMPED in the areas that would be left uncovered by the decoration and PLACED over the three layers of canvas. The satin was *probably* BASTED to the canvas with a central row of temporary PAD STITCHES. A permanent RUNNING STITCH was worked, in silk thread, around all the edges of the collar to keep the layers together.

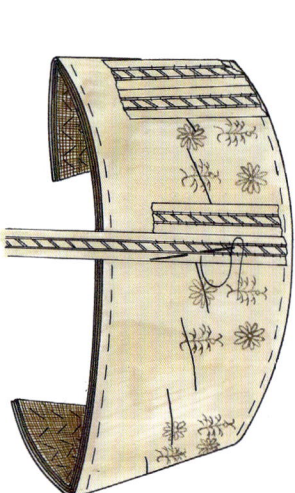

57 Decorated satin strips were PLACED on the collar vertically between the stamped motifs and COUCHED in pairs with silk thread.

58 The lower edge of the collar was WHIPPED to the neckline with doubled, thick linen thread and the stitches were worked through all the layers of the doublet.

59 A decorated strip was COUCHED over the neckline seam. A second strip was COUCHED above it.

60 On the RS, a length of ivory edging lace was FELLED, with ivory silk thread, along the top and CF edges of the collar.

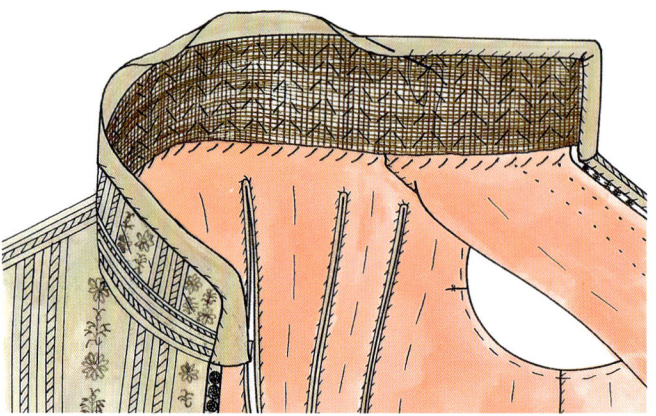

61 The binding lace was FOLDED over the edge of the collar and FELLED to the WS of the canvas.

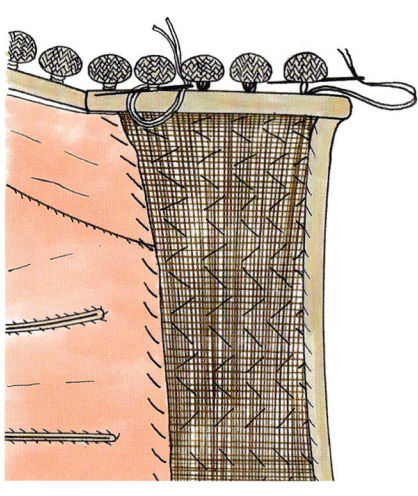

62 On the RHS of the collar, five buttons were STITCHED in the centre of the edging lace binding at CF. Each button was first STITCHED with thick unbleached hemp or linen thread, leaving a shank of ³⁄₁₆". Each shank was then WRAPPED and STAB STITCHED with doubled, white linen thread.

63 Five button loops were made by knotting together five lengths of plaited ivory silk. Five holes were PIERCED with a bodkin on the LHS of the collar and a loop was INSERTED in each hole from the WS.

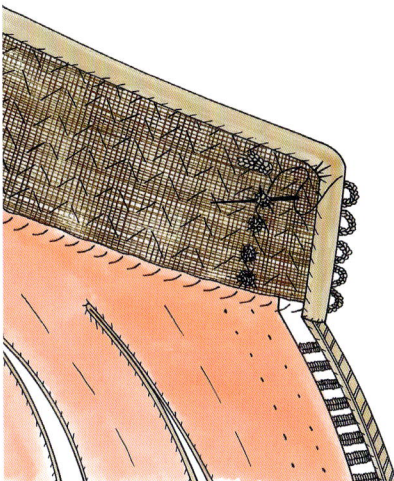

64 On the WS, the knotted end of each loop was WHIPPED to the canvas interlining with thick linen thread.

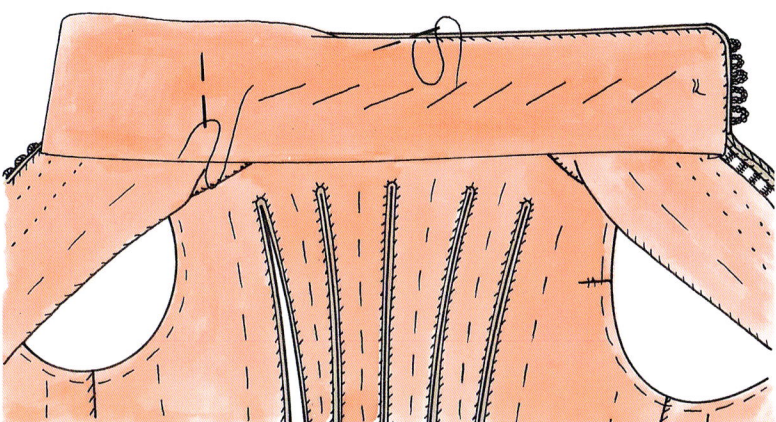

65 With WS together, the collar lining was *probably* BASTED to the collar, lengthwise along the centre, with a temporary PAD STITCH. Its seam allowances were FOLDED and FELLED, with pink silk thread, to the edge of the collar and to the neckline of the doublet.

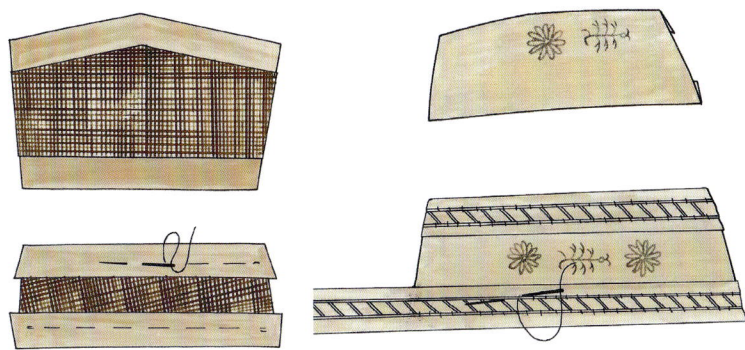

66 Each shoulder wing was made of 10 sections, each interlined with a layer of canvas CUT net. After the satin layer was STAMPED, the canvas was PLACED on it with WS facing. The seam allowances of the satin were FOLDED over its edges and RUNNING STITCHED with thick white linen thread. A decorated satin strip was COUCHED, with silk thread, to the outer edges of each section, but not at A–A, A1–A1, K–K or K1–K1 (see pages 118 and 120).

67 Each section was FOLDED on itself lengthwise. The sections were then joined together at the top with a continuous RUNNING STITCH worked with thick linen thread. On the RS, a worked bar in silk thread was made with silk thread between each section to hold them together.

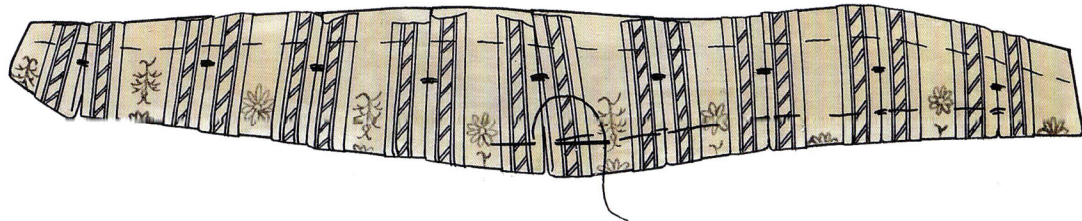

68 On the WS, the edges of each section were WHIPPED together with a single stitch, alternating with large RUNNING STITCHES, worked with thick linen thread, about ¼" away from the lower folded edge.

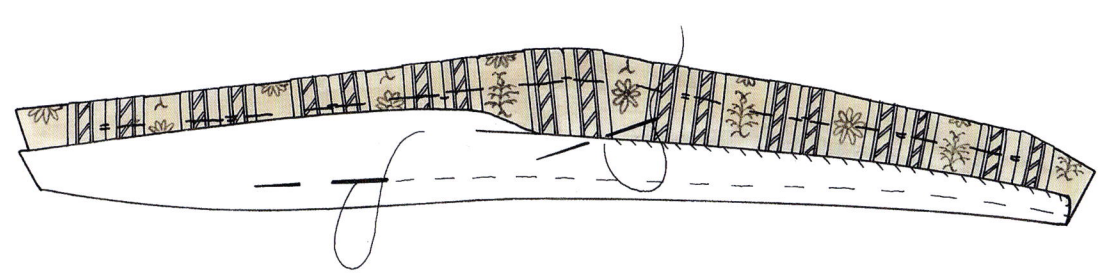

69 The bias-cut white linen lining was PLACED on the WS of the wing and BASTED with a RUNNING STITCH to its top edge with thick linen thread. The lower edge of the lining was then FOLDED and FELLED to the wing.

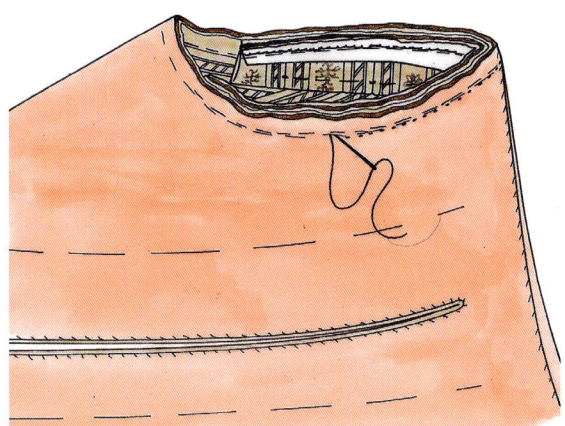

70 The wing was HALF-BACK STITCHED to the armhole with thick linen thread, between point A–A1 and point K–K1 (see pattern on pages 118 and 119).

Pattern by Luca Costigliolo

Construction of the sleeves

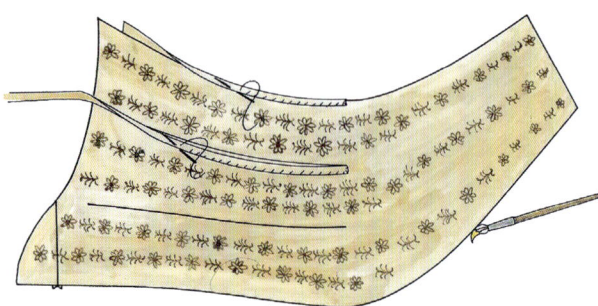

71 The ivory satin top and undersleeve were CUT net. The undersleeves piecings were BACK STITCHED with ivory silk thread. All the raw edges were BRUSHED with glue to keep them from ravelling and the sleeves were STAMPED. The vertical slashes were CUT and bound with a length of lace, FELLED from the RS with a single row of stitches worked through all the layers. A length of edging lace was also FELLED between points M/M1–N/N1 and Q/Q1–R/R1 (see pages 118 and 120).

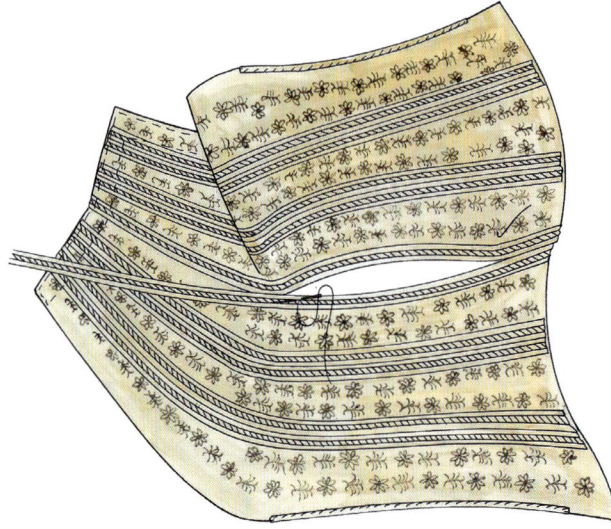

74 On the RS, a decorated strip was COUCHED on either side of the inner seam.

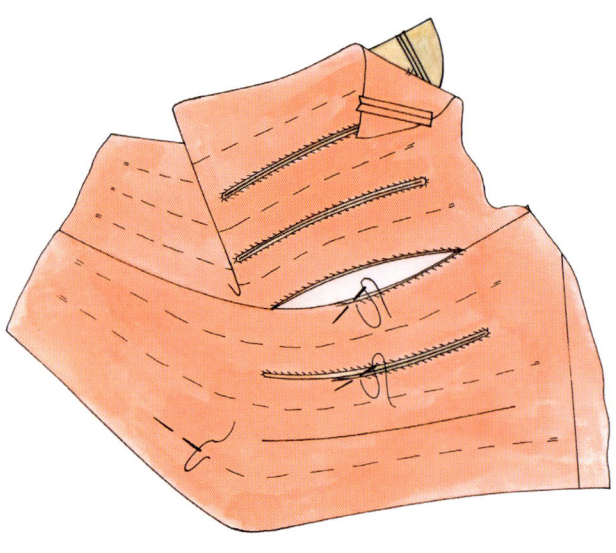

77 With WS together, the sleeves and linings were *probably* BASTED together with vertical rows of temporary RUNNING STITCHES. The slashes in the lining were CUT, the edges were FOLDED and FELLED, with pink silk thread, to the binding lace. On the inner seam, the raw edges of the lining were FOLDED and FELLED to the binding around the front opening.

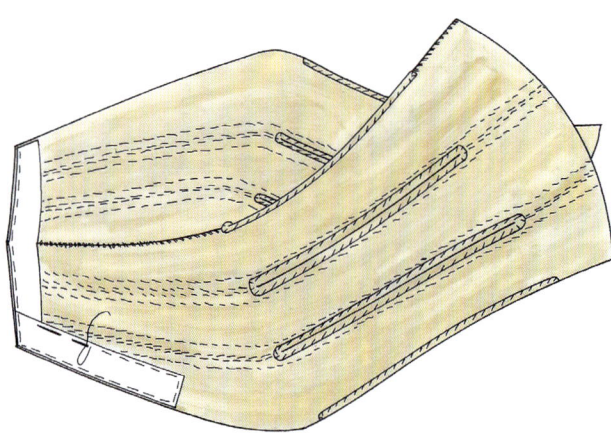

72 On the RS, decorated satin strips were COUCHED on either side of the slashes in the top and undersleeves.

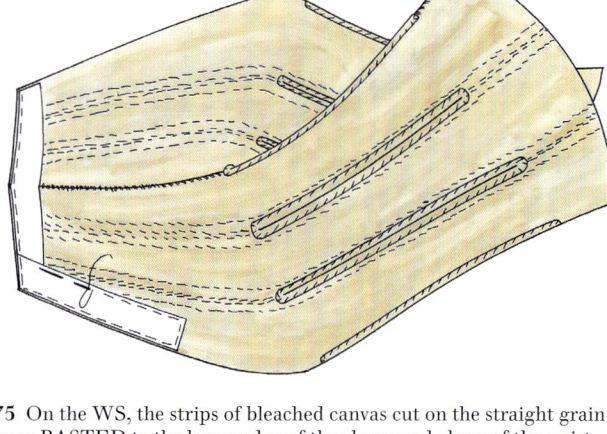

75 On the WS, the strips of bleached canvas cut on the straight grain were BASTED to the lower edge of the sleeve and along of the wrist opening of the top sleeve only. This was done to stabilize the satin which is cut on the bias in this area.

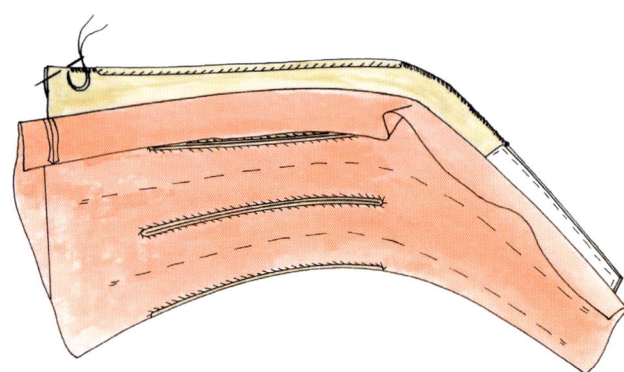

78 With the lining held back, the outer seam was WHIPPED with doubled, white linen thread between points S/S1–R/R1 and points Q/Q1–P/P1.

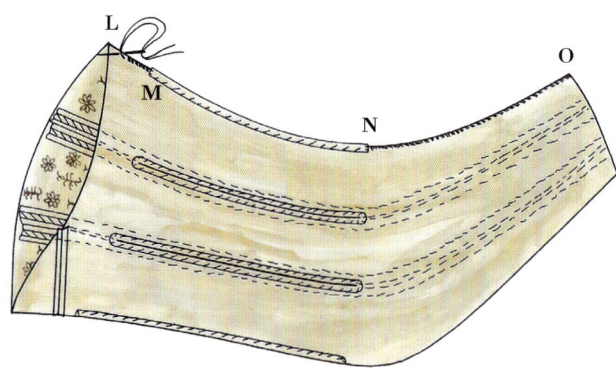

73 With RS together, the inner seam of the top and undersleeve was WHIPPED with thick doubled white linen thread, between points O/O1–N/N1 and points M/M1–L/L1.

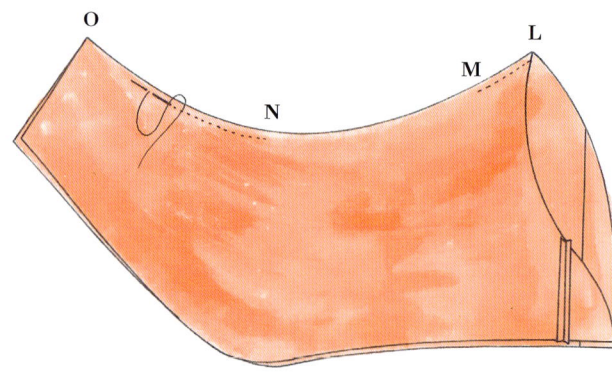

76 The lining of the top and undersleeves was CUT with a 1" seam allowance at the top and ¼" on all other edges. Piecings were RUNNING STITCHED with pink silk thread. With RS together, the inner seam of the top and undersleeve was HALF-BACK STITCHED with silk thread between points L/L1–M/M1 and points N/N1–O/O1.

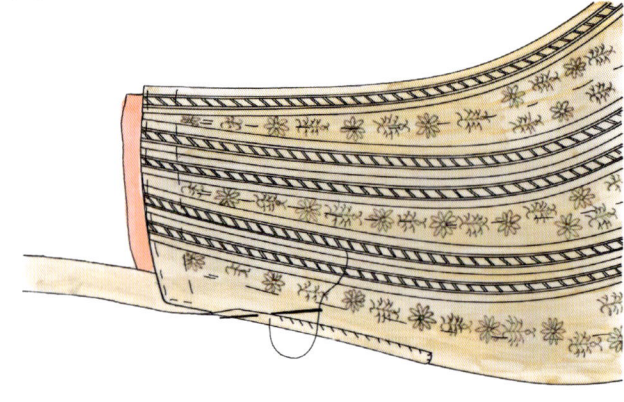

79 The sleeve was pulled to the RS. A long strip of binding lace was FELLED on the edge of the wrist opening of the undersleeve only, with a single row of stitches worked in ivory silk thread through all the layers. The rest of the length was left for step 81.

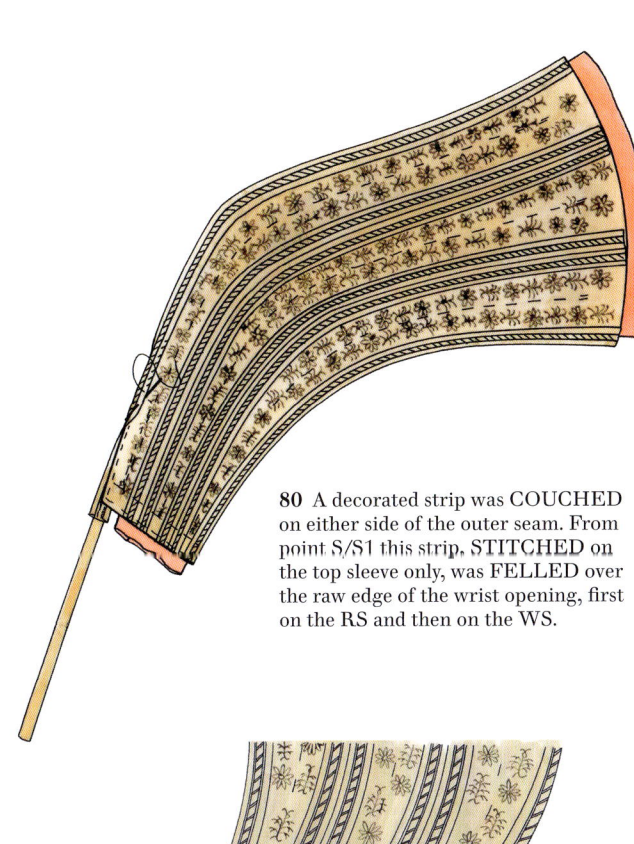

80 A decorated strip was COUCHED on either side of the outer seam. From point S/S1 this strip, STITCHED on the top sleeve only, was FELLED over the raw edge of the wrist opening, first on the RS and then on the WS.

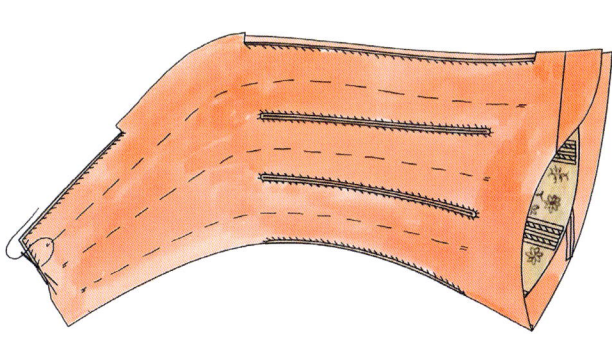

83 The seam allowance of the outer seam of the undersleeve lining was snipped on points Q/Q1, R/R1 and S/S1 and the raw edges were FOLDED and FELLED to the binding of the back opening, to one edge of the wrist opening and around the lower edge.

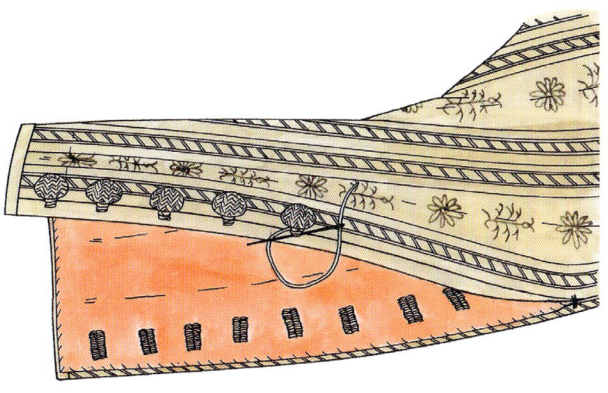

86 On the top sleeve, eight buttons were STITCHED, with thick white linen thread, in the centre of the binding lace of the wrist opening.

81 The length of binding lace remaining after step 79 was PLACED over the lower edge of the sleeve, RS facing, and BACK STITCHED.

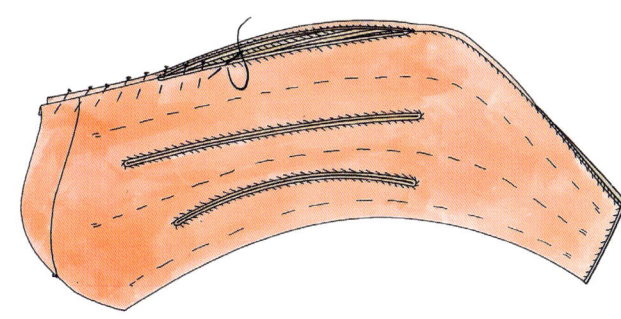

84 Starting at the wrist, the seam allowance of the outer seam of the top-sleeve lining was FOLDED and FELLED.

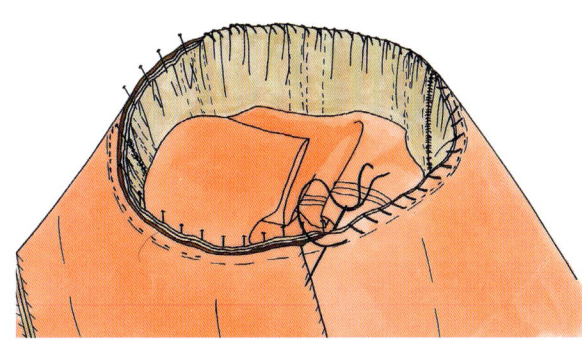

87 The sleeve was eased to fit the armhole, *probably* PINNED in place and WHIPPED with doubled, thick white linen thread. The stitches vary between five to nine per inch.

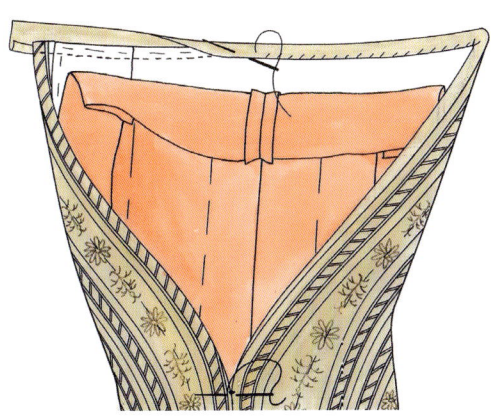

82 The binding lace was FOLDED over the lower edge of the sleeve and FELLED to the WS. The top of the wrist opening was reinforced with a few WHIP STITCHES in silk thread.

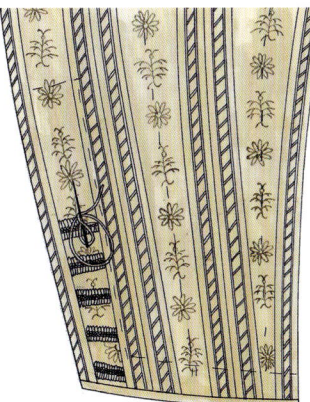

85 Eight slits were CUT for buttonholes on the edge of the wrist opening of the top sleeve. Each slit was BUTTONHOLE STITCHED with thick ivory silk thread.

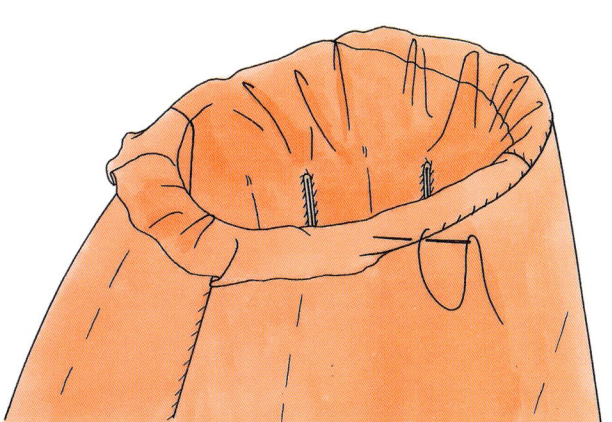

88 The seam allowance at the top of the sleeve lining was FOLDED and FELLED around the armhole with pink silk thread. There are about six stitches per inch.

Pattern by Luca Costigliolo

6 | Embroidered silk damask cloak

Spanish, *c.* 1560–1600 | V&A: T.202–1965

Pattern by Claire Thornton

This cloak was purchased in 1965 at a cost of £150, adding to the V&A's collection of Spanish cloaks, one of which is shown on the right. The cloak is of a rich red damask, with applied motifs and metal- and silk-thread embroidery. Damask is traditionally reversible with a pattern created by the contrast between the warp and weft faces of the same weave, usually satin.[1] This particular damask has a large-scale pattern repeat, showing stylized plants and crowns within ogees. The scale, foliate design and pattern repeat across the width are typical of damask designs of the mid-16th century. The condition of the cloak is good. The collar has been re-attached, probably when it arrived at the museum in 1965, and the wrong side of the motifs around the hem, centre fronts and collar have been covered for conservation purposes.

Cloaks appear regularly in contemporary portraits, worn over one or both shoulders, and were cut as full or half circles, or as a three-quarter circle, as this one is. In his book, *Tailor's Pattern Book*, the Spanish tailor Juan de Alcega offered patterns for cutting three-quarter circle cloaks, described as *Boemio* (Bohemian). He also suggested that for all garments made of damask, ½ ell more fabric must be cut than when other silks are used, to allow for aligning the pattern.[2]

This cloak is cut in three main sections with three small piecings, themselves made with even smaller piecings still, from a length of fabric 22½" wide, with ½" deep bright golden coloured selvedges. There appears to be a little ease around the hem. Embroidering normally pulls up the ground fabric, so the fullness here may have been to counteract this. However, when mounted as it would have been worn, the hem hangs beautifully.

It was probably once lined. The vibrant colour of the yellow thread on the wrong side of the cloak when compared to the same thread on the right side suggests that it was hidden. Surviving examples of red cloaks are lined with yellow or natural linen, including the one on the right.

Thirty-three stylized foliate motifs, couched in silver and silver-gilt filé, twist and red silk floss, decorate the hem and centre fronts, with a further six on the collar. Couching, or laid work, is a technique often used for expensive metal threads which are laid on the surface and then stitched down, often with a silk thread. Each motif was stitched separately onto a length of bleached linen stretched into an embroidery frame, first using linen thread, then couching down pairs of silver-gilt filé with a yellow silk thread. The motifs were then cut out and applied to the damask, one curving up, the next down, couching around the edge, first with red floss silk thread, then a silver-gilt three-ply twist. Each motif was joined to the next with a length of silver three-ply twist and edged with silver gilt.

Above: Red velvet cloak with applied yellow satin decoration, lined with saffron-yellow linen, *c.* 1580–90
Spanish
V&A: 832–1904

Two lengths of thick, two-ply linen twist were applied, one above and one below the motifs, framing them. Silver-gilt filé was then couched back and forth, completely covering the linen. A further length of silver-gilt twist was couched either side of the filé-covered linen thread. Five columns of scrolling 'S's (actually four 'S's because the left front column was reversed and appears as a 'Z') taper from the neck to the hem in a finer three-ply silver-gilt twist, invisibly couched. These were enhanced with a still finer, two-ply silver-gilt twist, worked through the damask ground. Two further lengths of silver-gilt twist were invisibly couched down either side of the 'S' scrolls.

1. Dorothy Burnham, *Warp and Weft: A Textile Terminology*, Toronto: Royal Ontario Museum, 1980, p. 32
2. Juan de Alcega, *Tailor's Pattern Book*, 1589, facsimile, Carlton: Ruth Bean, 1979, p. 19

Right: Philip IV of Spain, 1622
Rodrigo de Villandrando
From the private collection of David Leppan
He wears a heavily metal-thread embroidered doublet and hose, and a brocade-lined, watered-silk cloak with deep-embroidered guards. The cuffs and ruff are deep and narrow set.

Pattern by Claire Thornton

DETAILS
Right side (RS) details

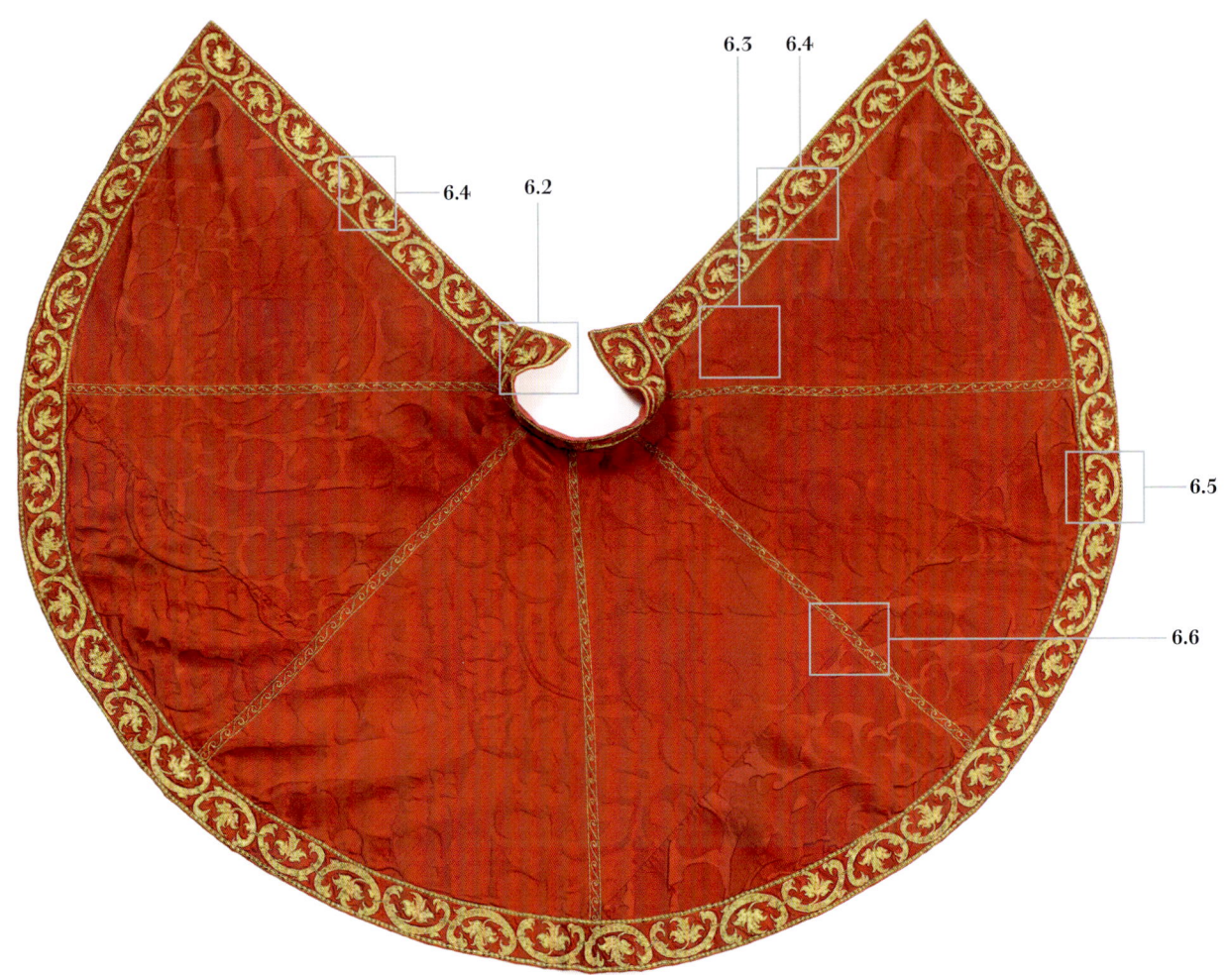

6.1 The cloak laid flat. The differences in grain are apparent in the way the damask reflects the light. The radiating columns of couching taper in size from neck to hem and perfectly segment the cloak.

6.4 Although the centre fronts appear mirror-imaged, the motifs are slightly staggered.

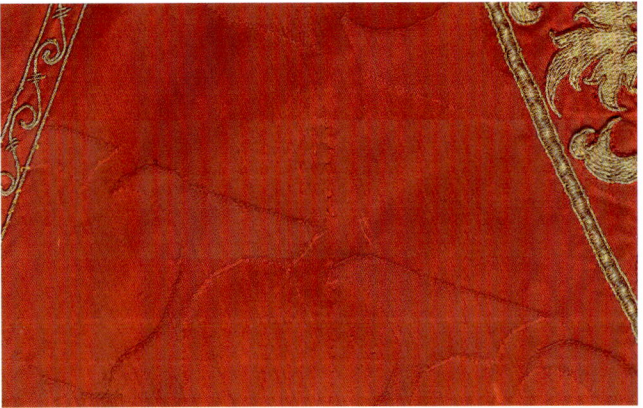

6.2 Silver-gilt filé was couched over a thick, plied linen cord, exposed here at the top of the collar front. The radiating column of couching seen here was worked as a scrolling 'Z'; the other four are 'S' scrolls.

6.3 A line of stitch holes in the damask could mean that the cloak was recycled from an earlier garment, or they were used to stabilize the fabric as the column of couching was worked on the bias. They appear to be running stitches.

6.5 The motifs were worked individually and then couched to the cloak first with a silver-gilt twist and then a red silk floss. The applied motifs have a three-dimensional appearance.

6 | Embroidered silk damask cloak

6.6 A vertical seam in the damask is completely hidden by the line of couched twist on the left. The seam allowance underneath made the surface onto which the twist was couched more stable.

Wrong side (WS) details

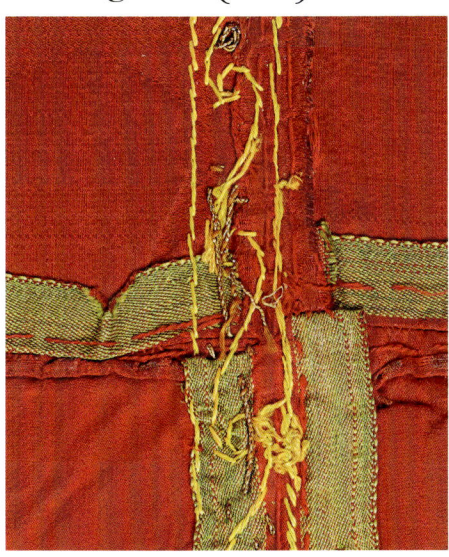

6.7 The reverse of the seam above. The bright gold-coloured selvedges were clipped so that the damask hung well. The raw seam allowances were wax coated to prevent fraying. Each seam allowance was running stitched open in red silk thread.

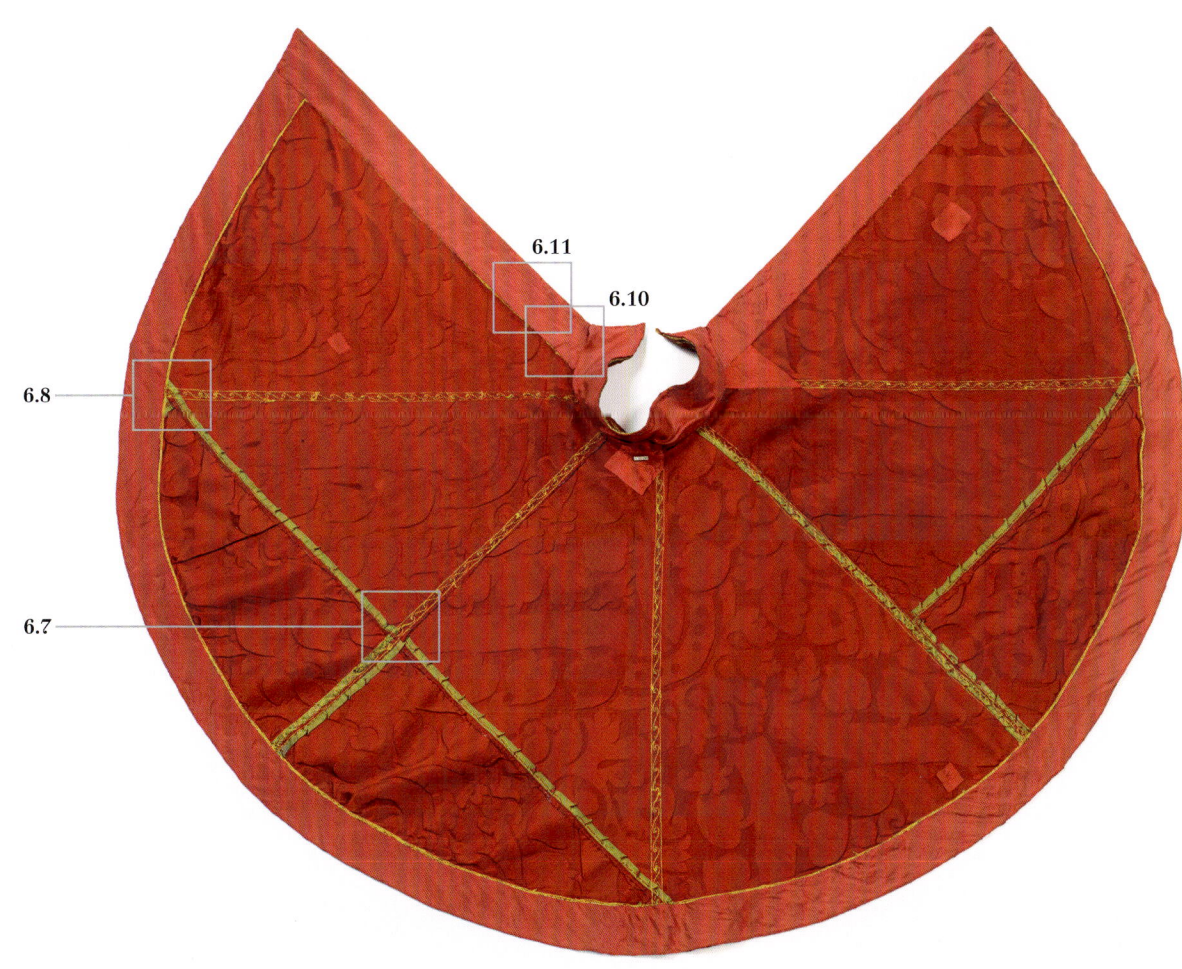

6.8 This column of couched 'S's was worked on the cross or bias grain of the damask. Unusually, the thin silver-gilt twist forming the little bars over the 'S' was worked through to the reverse. Expensive metal threads were worked almost entirely on the surface whenever possible.

6.9 The WS of the cloak laid flat. The embroidered hem, fronts and collar have been conserved and covered with fabric, but a small section of stitching is open, allowing a view of the reverse of the motifs (see 6.10 and 6.11).

6.10 Left: instead of applying a motif cut from the linen below the collar, a partial motif was couched directly onto the damask. Seen here are the gold silk threads holding the silver gilt to the right side of the damask. Also visible are the thick bleached linen threads providing the contours over which the silver gilt was couched.

6.11 Right: the reverse of the motif, worked on linen, cut and then sewn to the damask, appears as an outline only. The gold and red threads, couching down the edge of the motif, are seen here.

Pattern by Claire Thornton

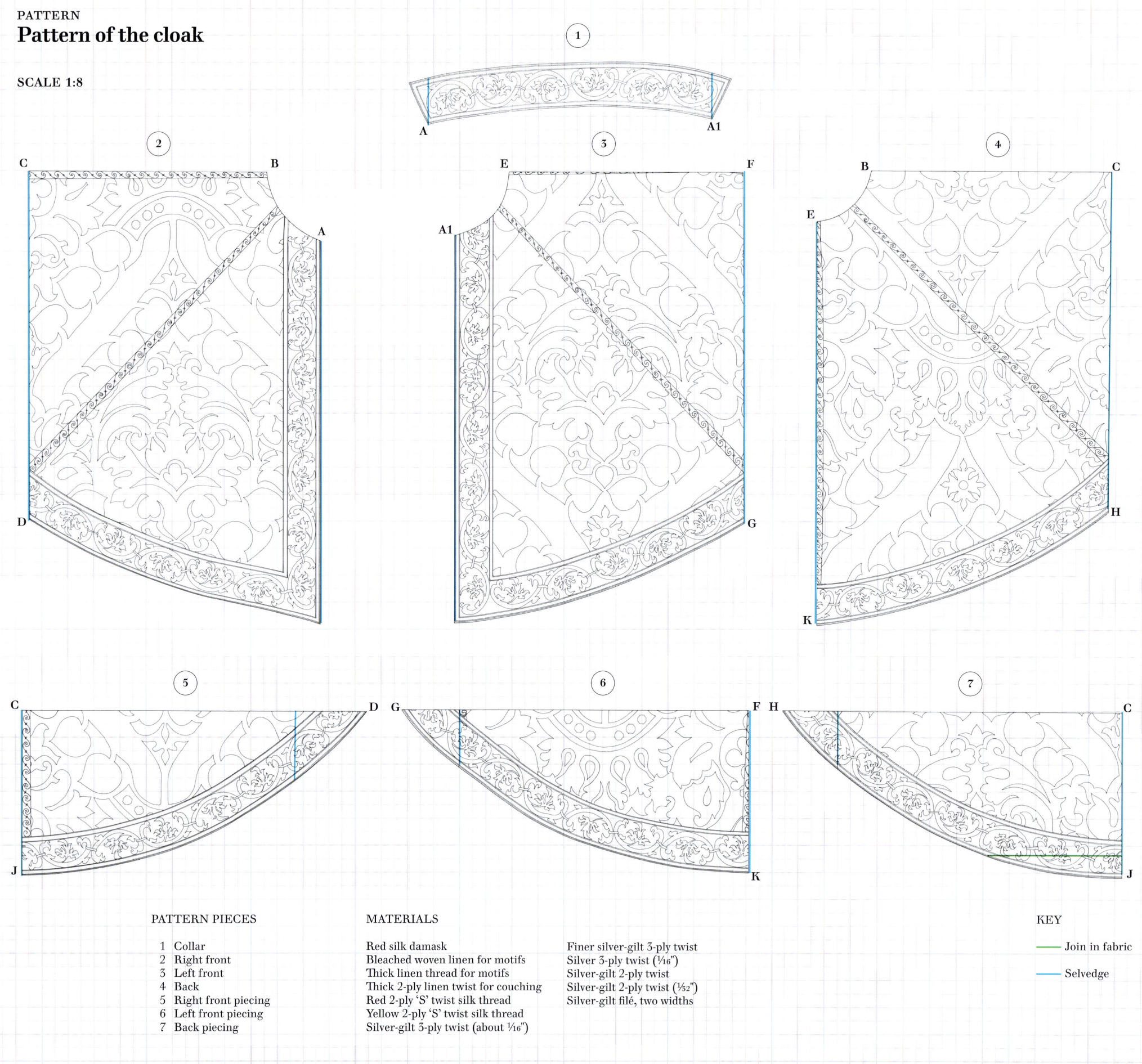

Actual size of embroidery motif
SCALE 1:1

Right: Crimson silk velvet couched guard, recto (above) and verso (below)
c. **1550–1600**
The School of Historical Dress, London
The guard is couched with silver and silver-gilt twist, and linen thread using the same technique as the cloak motifs.

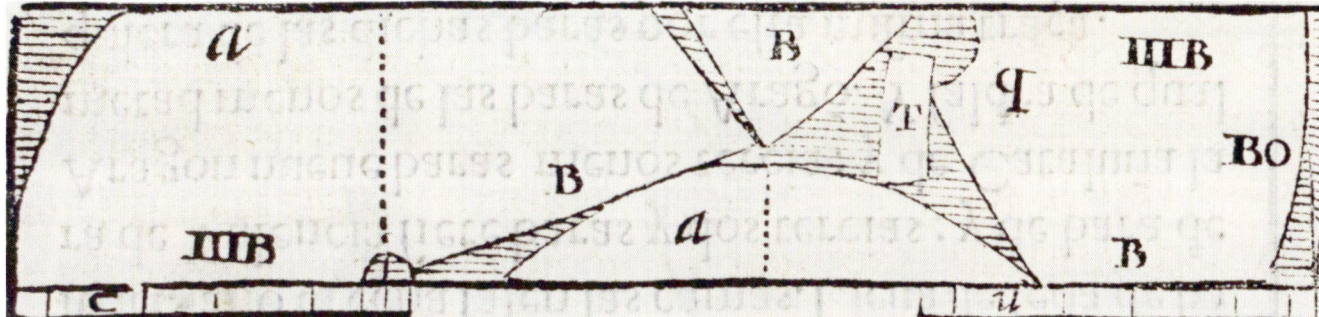

Pattern for a Bohemian cloak in damask. To the left is the back of the cloak; the front panel is to the right.
Francisco de La Rocha Burguen, *Geometria, y traca pertenenciente al officio de sastres*, Valencia, 1618, p. 142.

The pattern of the damask was designed to repeat horizontally when sewn together selvedge to selvedge, as well as vertically. Not to scale.

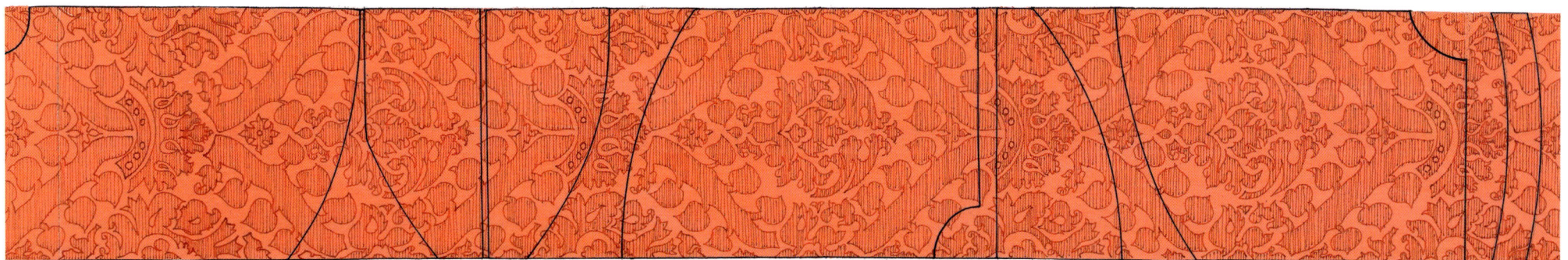

Conjectured cutting layout of the cloak using the woven pattern of the damask, not to scale. Based on the Castilian ell, or bara, measuring 33", the cloak would need four ells of 22½" wide damask. The 40" pattern repeat has not been matched.

Pattern by Claire Thornton

CONSTRUCTION
Construction of the cloak

The embroidered motifs were worked as in steps A–F.

Reconstruction of the embroidery motifs

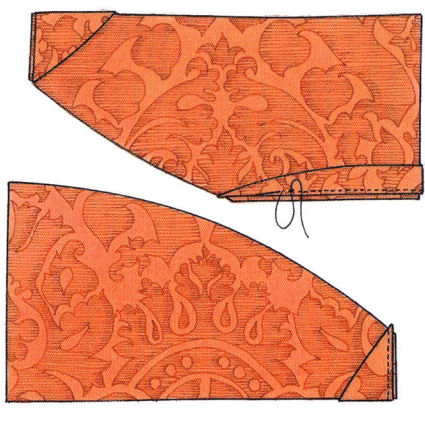

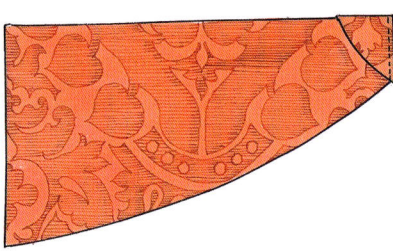

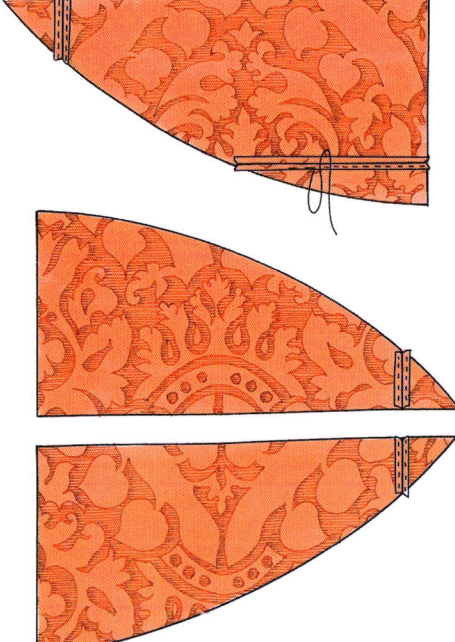

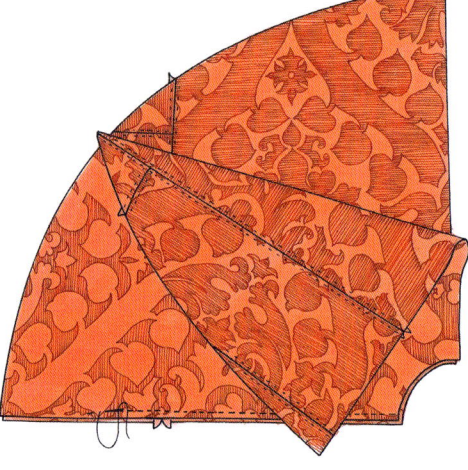

3 With RS together, the collar pieces were HALF-BACK STITCHED. All the seams were then HALF-BACK STITCHED open.

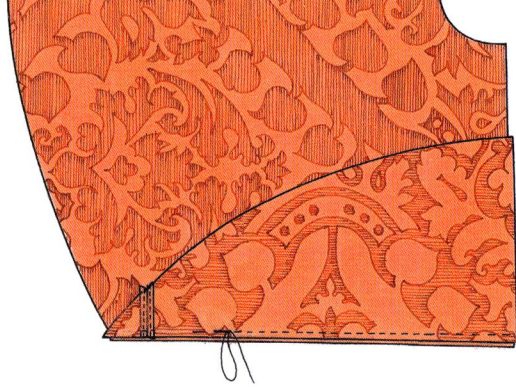

1 Four small piecings were made: two on pattern piece 7 and one each on pattern pieces 5 and 6. With RS together, each was HALF-BACK STITCHED with a seam allowance of ½" in red silk thread.

4 With RS together, piece 5 was HALF-BACK STITCHED to piece 2. Pieces 4 and 7, 6 and 3 were SEAMED in the same manner, using the same silk thread with a seam allowance of ½".

6 With RS together, piece 4 was HALF-BACK STITCHED to piece 3, with a seam allowance of ½". The seam allowances were HALF-BACK STITCHED open on the WS.

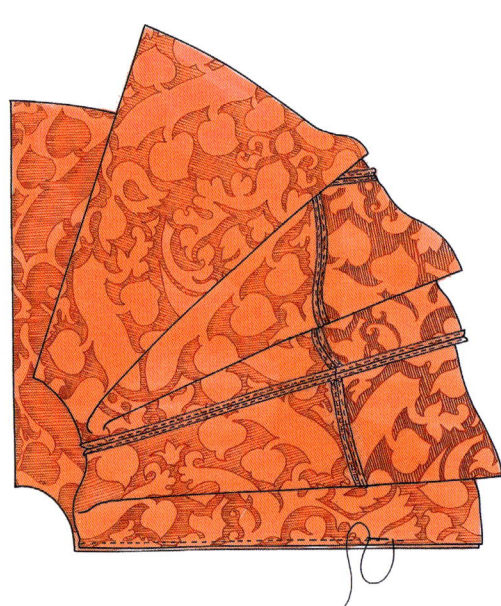

7 With RS together, piece 4 was HALF-BACK STITCHED to piece 2 with a ½" seam allowance. On the WS, the seam allowances were HALF-BACK STITCHED open.

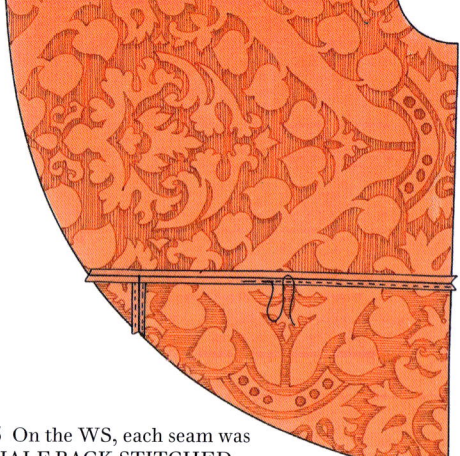

2 On the WS, each seam was then HALF-BACK STITCHED open along both edges in the red silk thread. The stitch length on the WS is about ½", showing as a little dot on the RS.

5 On the WS, each seam was HALF-BACK STITCHED open along both edges as in step 2.

The embroidery was probably worked in the following sequence:

The scrolling 'S' columns were couched.
The motifs were applied.
The thick linen twist was stitched on and the silver-gilt filé was couched over it.

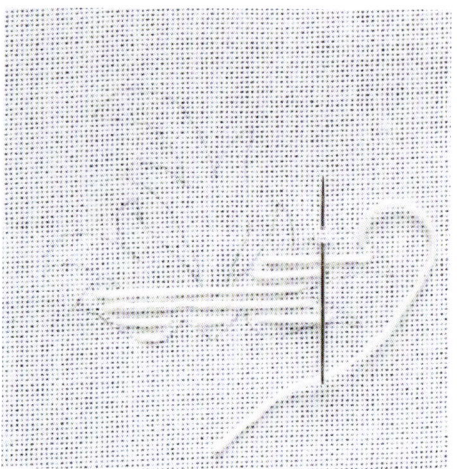

A Linen thread was STITCHED in parallel lines (perpendicular to the direction of the basket weave that will be worked over it).

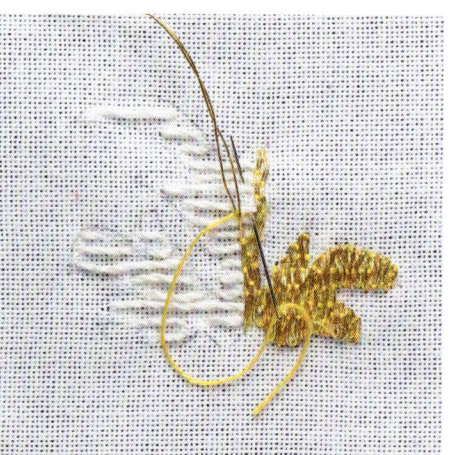

B Lengths of filé were COUCHED down in pairs, stitching between pairs of linen threads, to create the basket-weave texture.

C The motif was CUT OUT and, with multiple strands of red silk floss covering the edges of the linen, COUCHED to the damask with red silk.

6 | Embroidered silk damask cloak

Conjectured construction of the hem and lining

D Silver-gilt twist was INVISIBLY COUCHED around the motif edge.

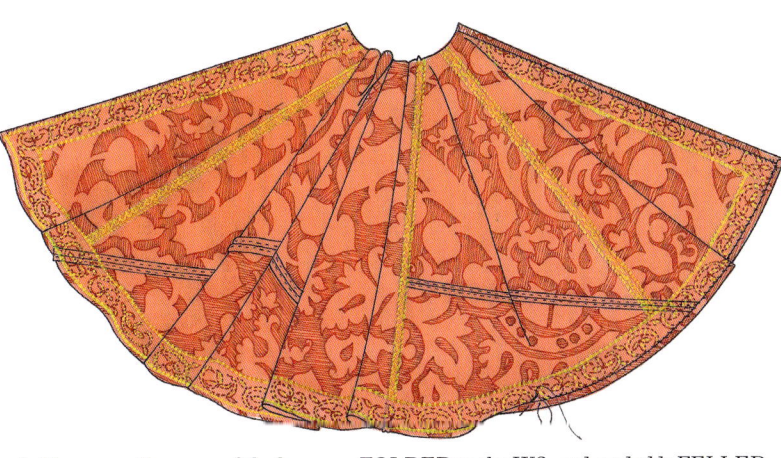

8 The seam allowance of the hem was FOLDED to the WS, and *probably* FELLED down the left front, around the hem and up the right front to the neck.

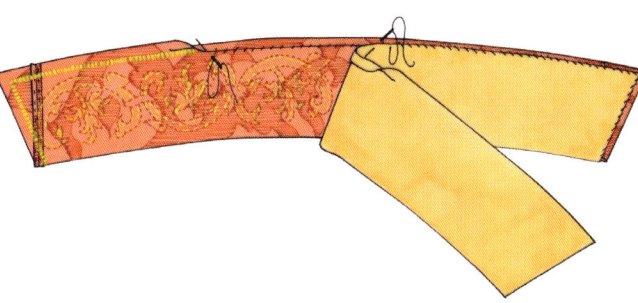

11 The seam allowance of the collar was FOLDED to the WS and FELLED around the three outside edges. The collar lining was PLACED on the collar, WS together, the seam allowances FOLDED to the WS and FELLED to the damask along the three outside edges.

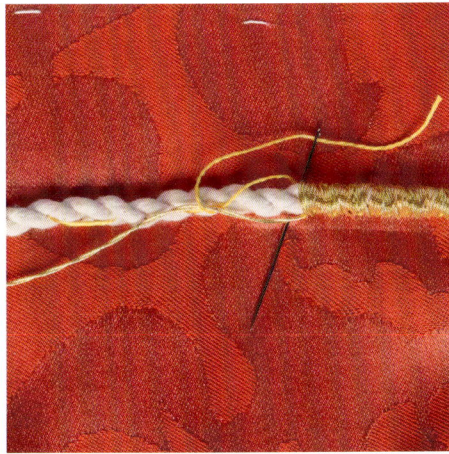

E The thick linen twist was STITCHED to the damask, and silver-gilt filé was COUCHED over it.

9 A yellow linen lining, CUT to the same shape as the cloak, was PLACED WS together, and FELLED to the vertical seam allowances of the damask.

12 With RS together, the collar was *probably* HALF-BACK STITCHED to the cloak neck.

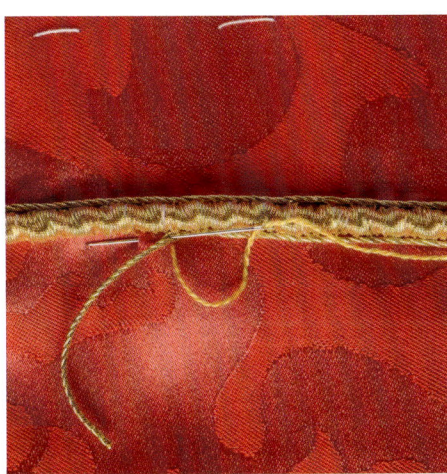

F Silver-gilt twist was invisibly COUCHED either side of the filé-covered linen twist.

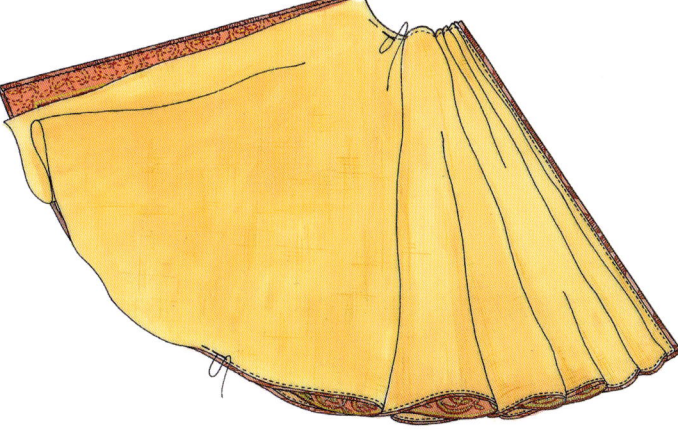

10 The edges of the lining were FOLDED to the WS and HALF-BACK STITCHED to the damask hem, down the left front, around the hem, and up the right front to the neck. The raw neck edges were *probably* BASTED together.

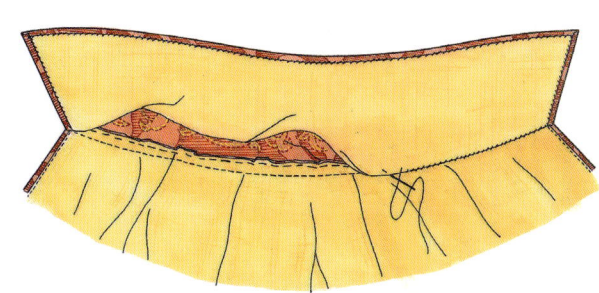

13 The lower edge of the collar lining was FOLDED to the WS and FELLED along the neck edge.

Pattern by Claire Thornton

7 | Felt hat

English, 1590–1620 | V&A: 752–1893
Pattern by Luca Costigliolo

This felt hat was donated in 1893 by John Seymour Lucas, a theatre costume designer and history painter who frequently advised the V&A on dress acquisitions. In the 16th and 17th centuries, hats were essential accessories, worn by men, women and children of all social classes, both indoors and out. With a crown 14¼" high, this is a rare example of the style described by Randle Holme as 'Sugar-Loaf-like' which was very fashionable in the 1590s.[1] By the 1620s such high hats were going out of style, but they were still worn by men and women of the middle and lower classes as late as the 1670s. Originally, the felt was probably dyed black; it is now discoloured with wear and damaged in some areas.

The brim has a diameter of 17" and does not lie completely flat; it appears to have been worn turned up at centre front. A series of stitch fragments in the lower part of the crown suggests that a 2½" wide hatband was worn around it. Such bands could be more precious than the hat itself. In the wardrobe accounts of Prince Henry from October 1608 there is payment for 'Embroidering an hatband with several sorts of pearle, having set among the pearle rubies, emrods, and opals, having also three scores of great pearls, £26' (this amount was only for the embroidery, not the jewels themselves).[2] A series of holes in the front of the crown suggests that a large hat jewel was also worn with it, probably pinned through the hatband and the felt, and secured by stitches of which some fragments remain. Hat jewels were precious possessions. In his will dated 1608, Francis Fitton, Esq. of Gawsworth, Cheshire, left to his nephew, 'my jewell of diamonds and gold like unto a starre, which I do usually weare in my hatte'.[3] A similar arrangement of a turned-up brim with hatband and jewel is seen in the portrait of James VI dated c. 1590, shown right. He wears clothes of the latest fashion and a richly decorated hatband and jewel. The portrait on the far right, dated c. 1630, features a man wearing an old hat, probably second-hand, battered and out of shape, but the crown is almost identical in proportion to this example. The hat was probably made between 1590 and 1610 as contemporary portraits show that large hat jewels were out of fashion by the 1620s.

1. Randle Holme, *The Academy of Armory*, 1688, Book III, chapter VI, p. 291
2. William Bray, '*Extract from the Wardrobe Account of Prince Henry, eldest Son of King James I*', Archaeologia, vol. 11, 1794, p. 94
3. John Parsons Earwaker, ed., *Lancashire and Cheshire Wills and Inventories 1571 to 1696*, Chetham Society, vol. 28, new series, 1893, p. 174

Right: King James I of England and VI of Scotland, c. 1590
Unknown artist
© National Portrait Gallery, London

Far right: Portrait of a man, c. 1630
Adriaen Brouwer
Museum Boijmans van Beuningen, Rotterdam, The Netherlands/Bridgeman Images

DETAILS
Right side (RS) details

Wrong side (WS) details

7.1 A front view of the hat.

7.2 A top view of the hat.

7.3 The pale line is the impression left by the pack thread, tied around the base of the crown when the felt was shaped over a wooden block. Below it, the back of the stitches, worked in silk thread, that held the crown's lining in place can be seen.

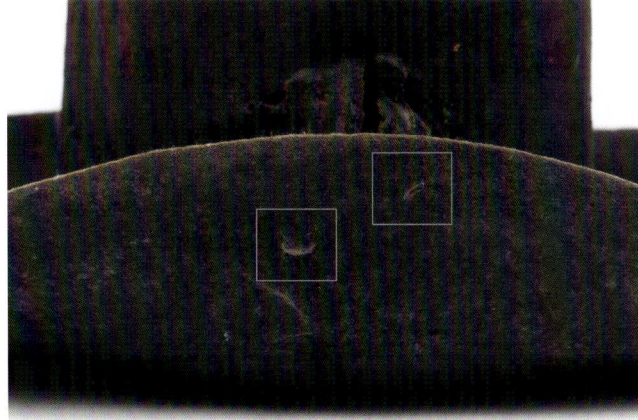

7.4 On the side of the brim that curves upwards there are two small holes near the edge (as shown in the white boxes). They correspond to others on the crown and were probably from stitches that originally held it in this position.

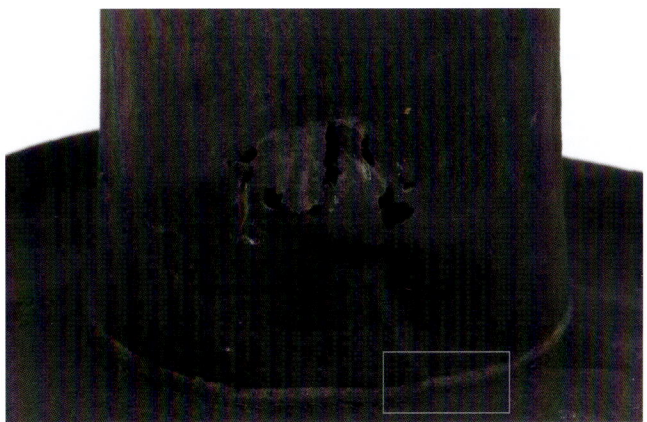

7.5 Various holes in the crown, together with remnants of linen thread, mark the area where a hat jewel was originally stitched or repeatedly pinned; they are on the same side where the brim was turned up.

7.6 Gold hat jewel, 1620–30, European, V&A: M.69–1975, H=3.2 cm, W=2.9 cm. Set with rubies and onyx, the jewel has a pin at the back so it can be quickly removed. A similar jewel might have been worn with this hat.

7.7 Inside the hat the stitch marks and remnants of linen thread that probably held a hatband in place are visible; they are around the base of the crown and about 2⅝" above it. The holes from the stitches that held the lining in place are also visible just above the hatband threads at the base.

7.8 There are remnants of silk fabric (possibly taffeta) caught in the stitches that originally held the hat jewel. It is not clear whether they were reinforcement pieces to support the weight of the jewel or part of the original lining.

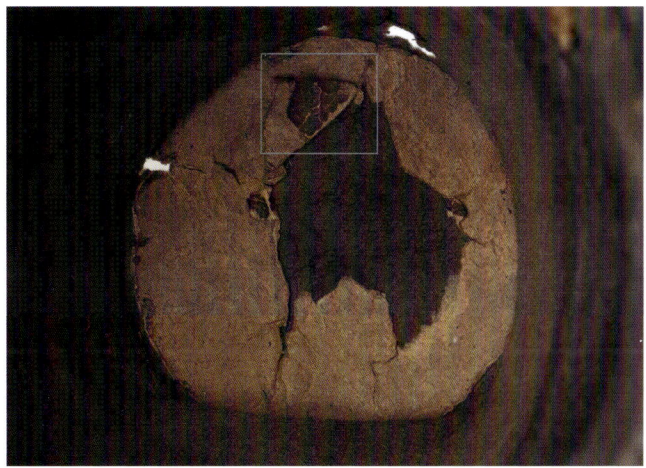

7.9 A layer of pasteboard, now partially disintegrated, was glued inside the top of the crown to hold it in shape. The glue, now dark brown, can be seen where the pasteboard was folded back on itself (shown in the white box).

Pattern by Luca Costigliolo

PATTERN
Pattern of the felt hat

SCALE 1:4

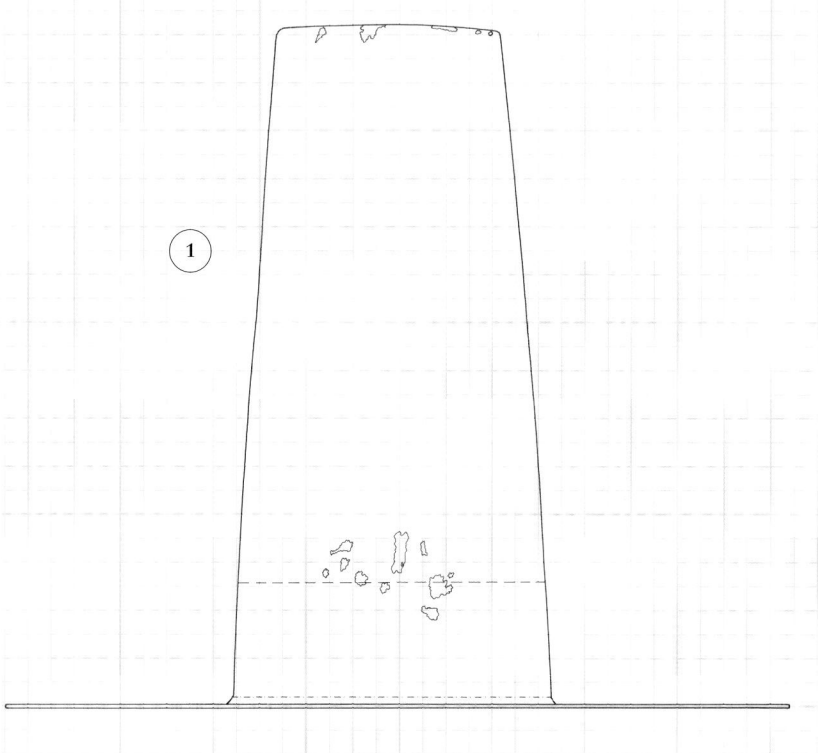

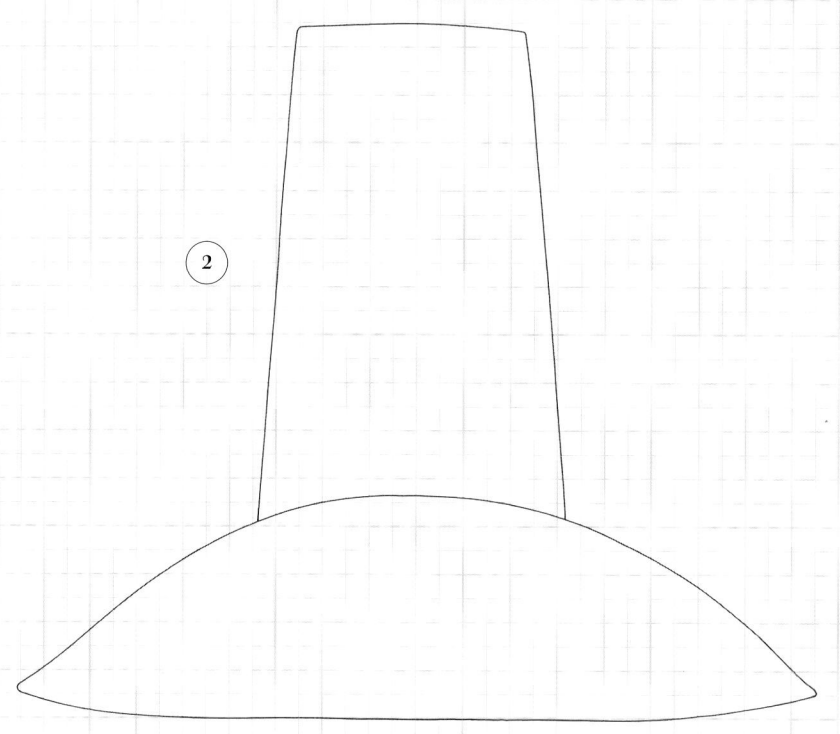

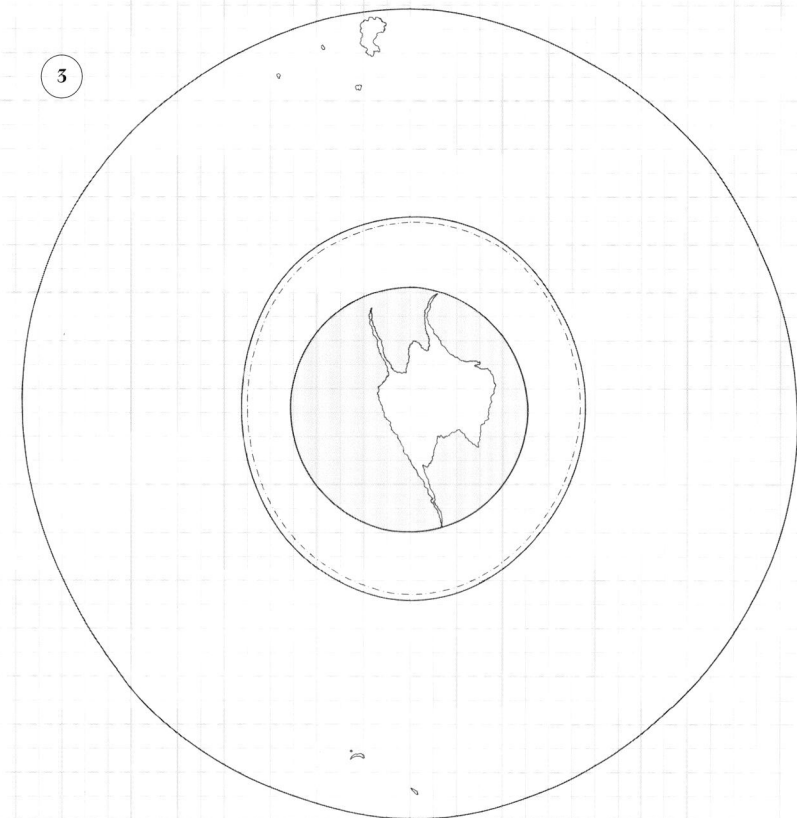

The felt is ¹⁄₁₆" thick and feels very light. Although damaged, it is still quite soft and supple. It was probably dyed black or dark brown originally but it is now badly faded in some areas: the colour changes from almost black to very light brown where the felt is worn or damaged. The fibres were examined under a microscope to determine the type of hair from which the felt was made. Its structure does not resemble that of hare or rabbit, but it was not possible to distinguish it as either beaver fur or sheep's wool.

The diameter of the brim measures 17", while the height of the crown is 14¼". When the hat was made the base of the crown was probably a perfect circle, but it has now turned into a slightly oval shape from years of wear. The direction of the oval shape, slightly narrower at one end, suggests that the hat jewel and the turned-up brim were worn at centre front.

Stitch marks around the edge of the crown show that the hat was originally lined. Fragments of silk found inside the crown suggest that the lining was probably cream taffeta.

TECHNICAL DRAWINGS

1. Side elevation with the brim lying flat
2. Side elevation with the brim turned up
3. Plan

KEY

— — — — Stitch line of the hatband

- - - - - Position of the pack thread

———— Damaged or missing areas

Pasteboard layer

7 | Felt hat

8 | Silk satin picadil

English, 1600–20 | V&A: T.32-1938

Pattern by Luca Costigliolo

In the early 17th century men wore linen neckwear in the form of bands and ruffs, either 'standing' or 'falling'. The latter draped over the doublet collar, but the former required some sort of support. This was usually in the form of a separate rebato (made of wire) or picadil (made of paper or pasteboard). Not many of either type survive; this rare example was acquired by the V&A in 1938 as part of the Spickernell collection, together with Sir Rowland Cotton's suit (see page 48). The picadil is made of two panels of pasteboard; the round outer edge of the upper panel is covered by 50 individual picadils made of a single layer of paper covered in ivory silk satin, which has now discoloured to a yellowish grey. On top of the upper panel a layer of carded wool covered in satin creates a soft and smooth surface around the face of the wearer. Underneath the upper panel is a smaller panel of pasteboard, also covered in satin, which provides extra support around the neck.

The picadil fastened at the centre front with a hook and eye, of which only the eye remains on the left-hand side; it is stitched to a fragment of pasteboard with thick linen thread. When the picadil is laid flat the two centre fronts sit almost an inch apart. The reconstruction of the picadil revealed that when the hook and eye are fastened and the centre fronts drawn together, the outer edge bends down in a gentle curve, enhanced by the wool padding around the neck. This three-dimensional shape allowed the starched linen band worn on top to fall gracefully from the neck of the wearer and gently over the bent edge of the picadil. The same curve can be seen in the portrait on the right, where a man wears a wide, darted and starched linen band over a picadil of a very similar shape. Although the band is much larger, the outer edge of the picadil does not create a ridge underneath it and the band falls in a smooth line.

A neckband of silk grosgrain lined in white linen was originally stitched around the inside edge of the picadil. The silk layer has now almost completely disintegrated: only the silk stitches that held it in place and the linen lining still survive. Examination of the grain of the remaining silk fragments of the neckband show that it was cut slightly on the bias, probably from a left-over piece, in order to use the fabric as economically as possible. The absence of eyelet holes at the centre back of the picadil neckband suggests that it would have been either stitched or basted to the inside of the doublet collar to keep it in place. Repeated stitching and unpicking of the picadil and the friction of wear would have hastened the disintegration of the satin of the neckband and it probably needed regular replacement. In the Shuttleworths' household accounts of July 1612 we find 'one past board, foure skeines of silke and threade to Harg: dublett' and on 15 January of the same year 'a pickadell to his dublett' suggesting that on some doublets the picadil was part of the construction of the collar.[1] This can be seen in two surviving examples, one at the Galleria Parmeggiani in Reggio Emilia, Italy, and one at the Metropolitan Museum of Art in New York.

1. John Harland, ed., *The House and Farm Accounts of Shuttleworths of Gawthorpe Hall*, The Chetham Society, vol. 35, part 1, 1856, pp. 201, 205

Detail of a Portrait of a Gentleman,
c. **1610–20**
Dutch School
Tomasso Brothers Fine Art, UK
He wears a cut velvet jerkin over a black slashed satin doublet. Around his neck a wide darted band made of fine white linen is supported by a picadil. This sits on the top edge of the doublet's collar which makes it stand at an angle, high at the back and lower at the front.

DETAILS
Right side (RS) details

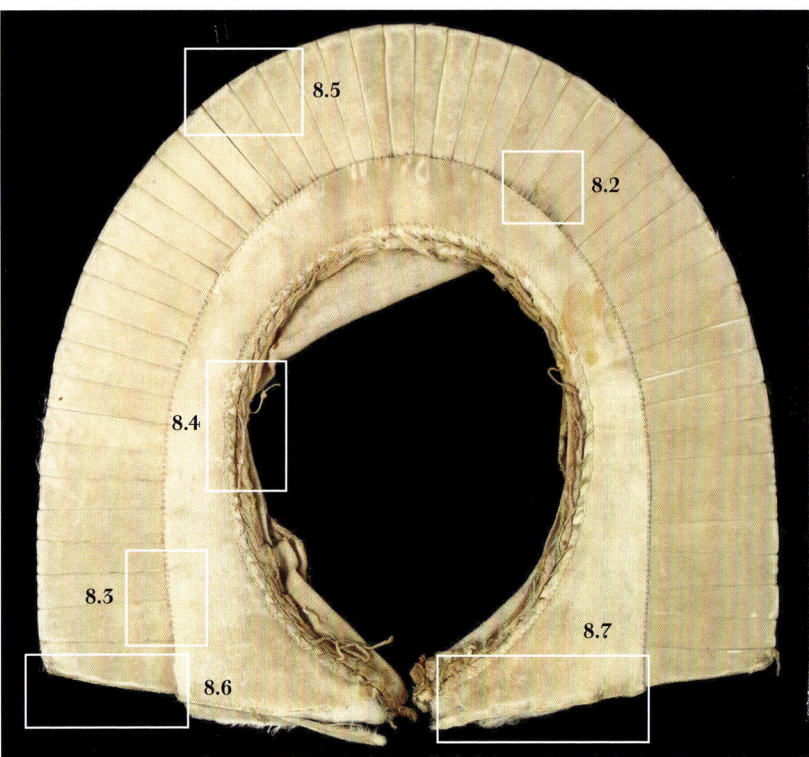

8.1 A front view of the satin picadil lying flat.

8.2 The ends of the individual picadils were whipped to the pasteboard and covered with a layer of carded wool and satin.

8.3 The satin layer that covers the wool padding was felled to the picadils with silk thread.

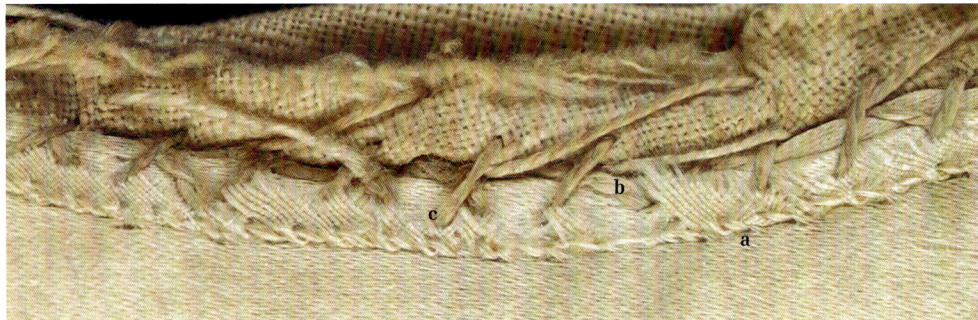

8.4 The remaining fragments of the silk grosgrain neckband can still be seen around the neckline; they were held by a row of felling stitches worked in silk thread (a). A row of thick linen stitches holds the picadil's layers together (b). There is another row attaching the linen lining of the neckband to the picadil (c).

8.5 The satin cover of the individual picadils has worn away around their folded edges, exposing the paper layer.

8.6 The whipped edges of the picadil on the RHS front have come undone, revealing the pasteboard upper panel, which was made of 15 layers of paper glued together.

8.7 The whipped edges of the wool and pasteboard lower panel have come undone on the LHS front. The pasteboard lower panel was made of six layers of paper glued together. Where the upper and lower panels overlap the thickness is about ¼".

Wrong side (WS) details

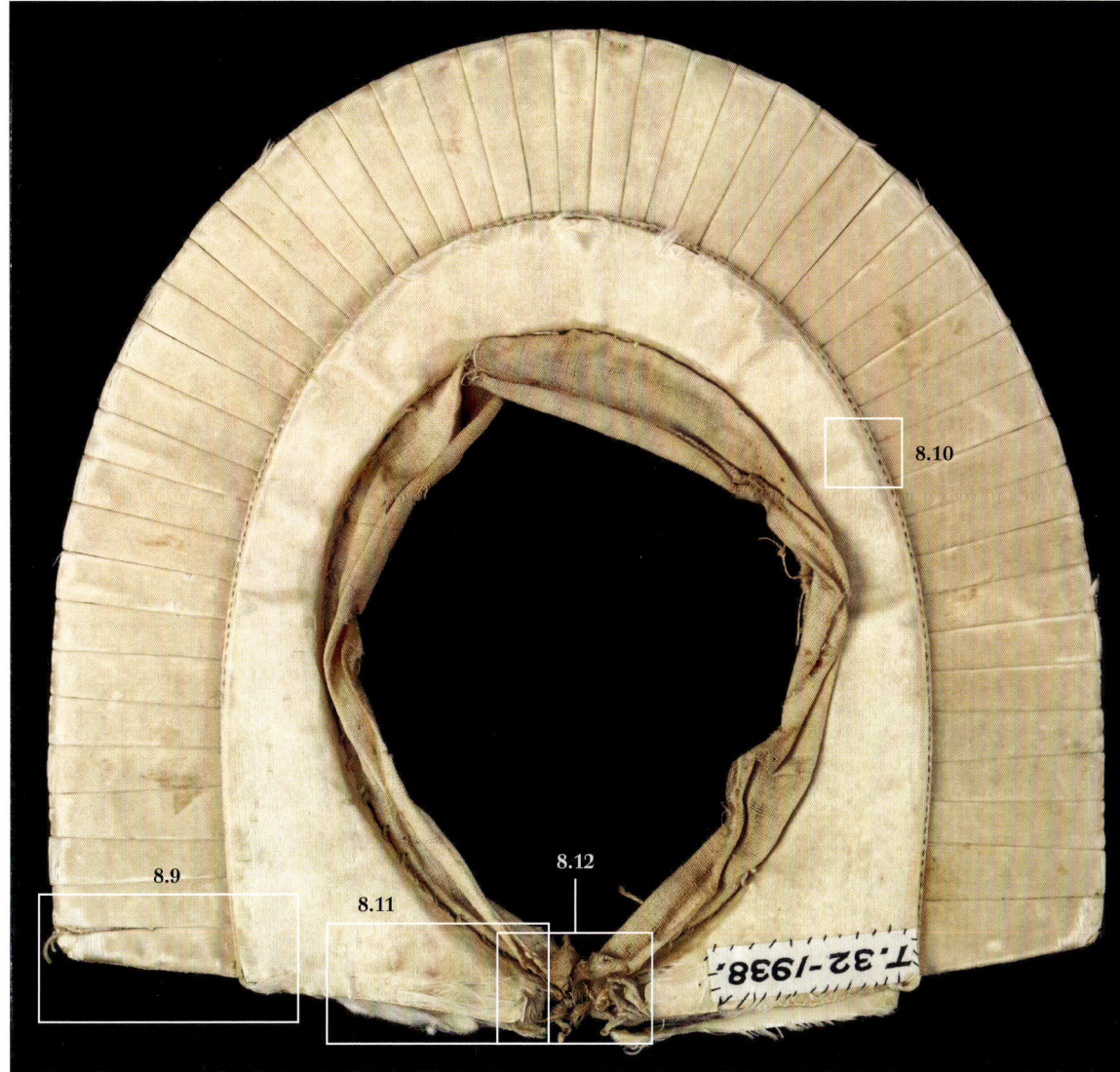

8.8 A back view of the satin picadil.

8.9 On the LHS, the individual picadil covering the front edge is joined to the edge of the next picadil by a single stitch, worked through all the layers and on both sides of the upper panel. The corner of the pasteboard lower panel can be seen on the right.

8.10 The satin cover of the pasteboard lower panel is back stitched closely with thick 2 'S' ply ivory silk thread.

8.11 Part of the satin cover has disintegrated on the LHS front edge, revealing a total of 21 layers of paper where the upper and lower panels overlap.

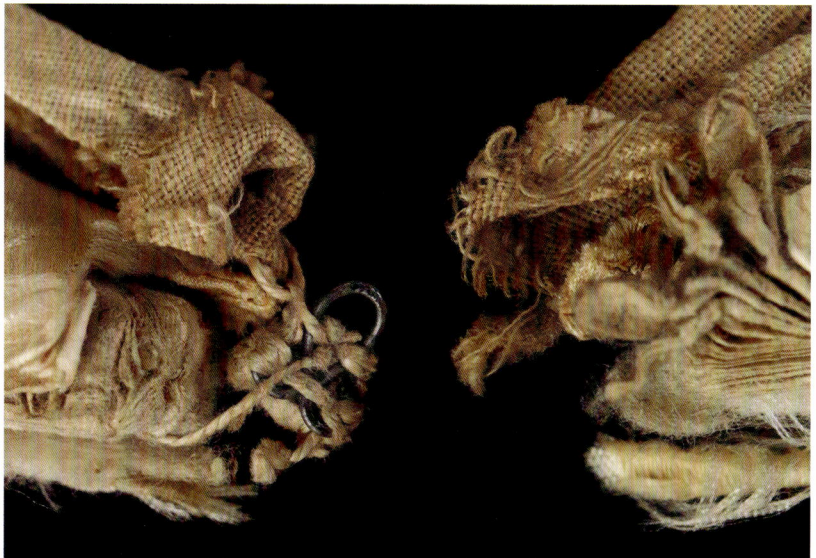

8.12 At CF on the LHS only the metal eye of the front closure survives. Although most of the pasteboard has disintegrated in this area, the strong linen stitches that held the metal eye in place still remain.

Pattern by Luca Costigliolo

X-ray images

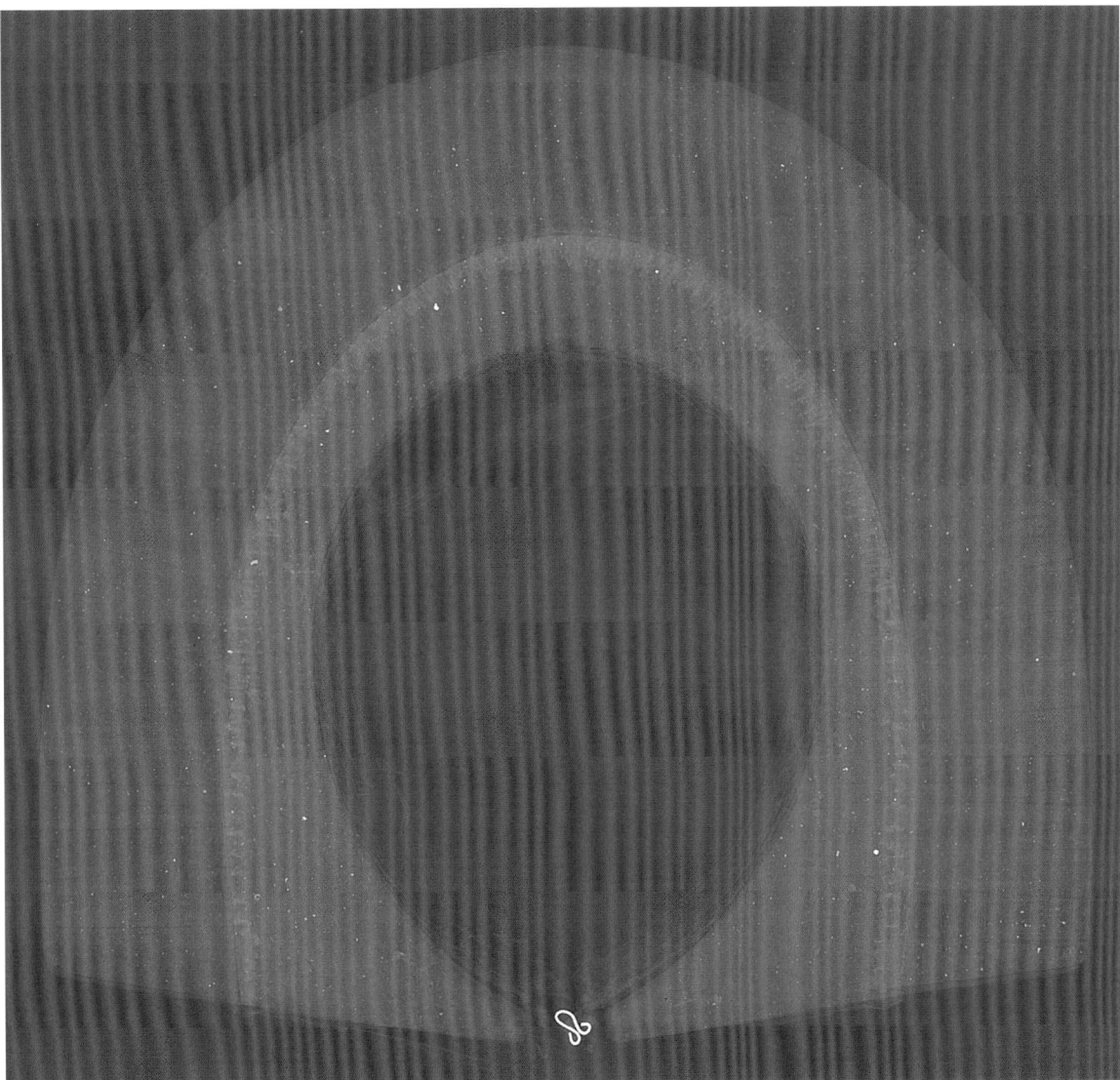

8.13 An x-ray image of the picadil from the RS. The cut shape of the pasteboard lower panel is clearly visible.

8.14 A detail of an x-ray image of the LHS front from the WS, showing the whip stitches worked around the edge of the neckline. The metal eye, still attached to a fragment of pasteboard, can be seen clearly, as well as the whip stitch holding the ends of each individual picadil to the pasteboard upper panel.

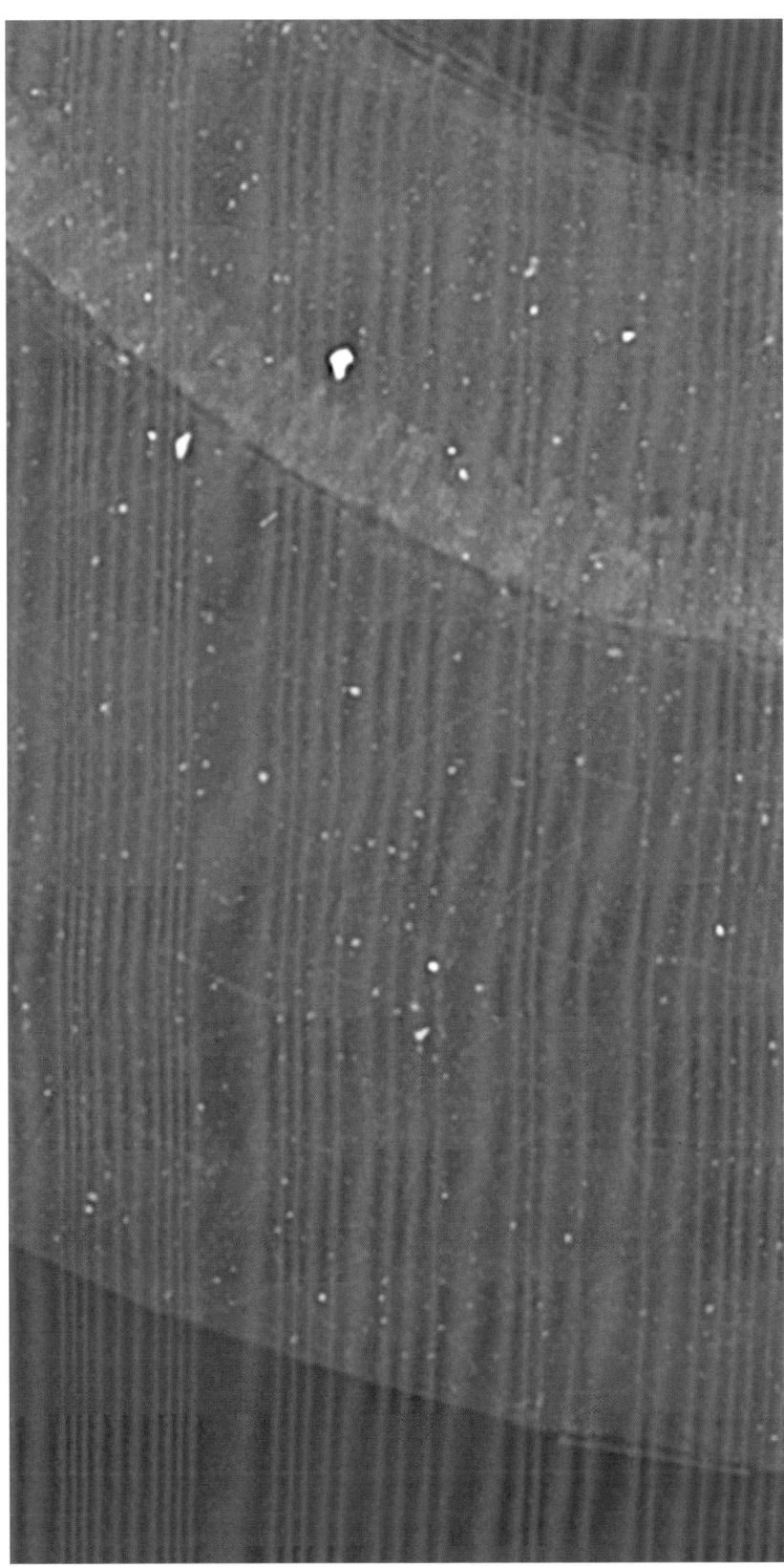

8.15 A detail of an x-ray image of the picadil. The whip stitches holding the satin cover of each paper picadil can be seen. Because each picadil is folded on itself widthwise, the single row of stitches overlaps itself in the image, giving the illusion of a cross stitch.

PATTERN
Pattern of the picadil

SCALE 1:4

All pasteboard pattern pieces are cut net.
All satin pattern pieces are cut with a seam allowance.

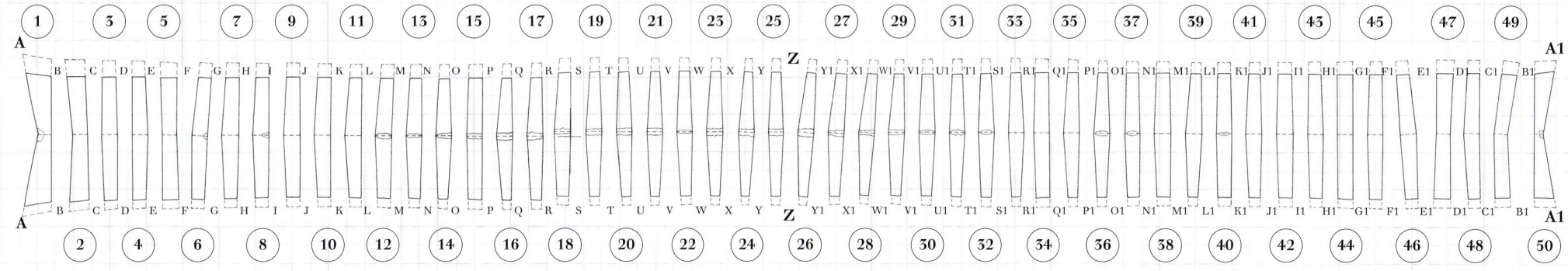

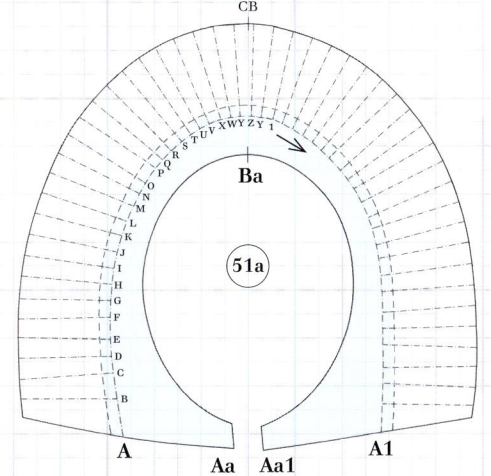
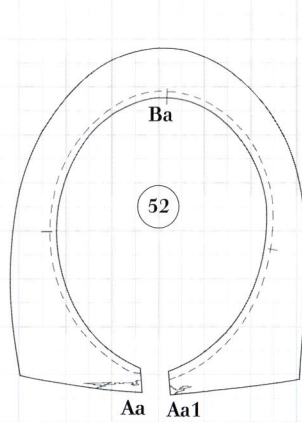
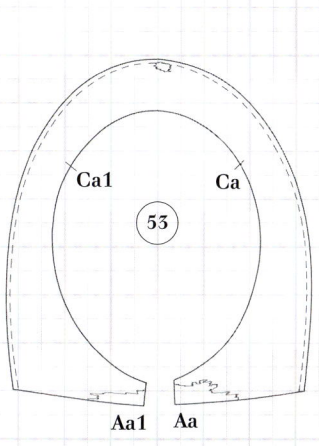
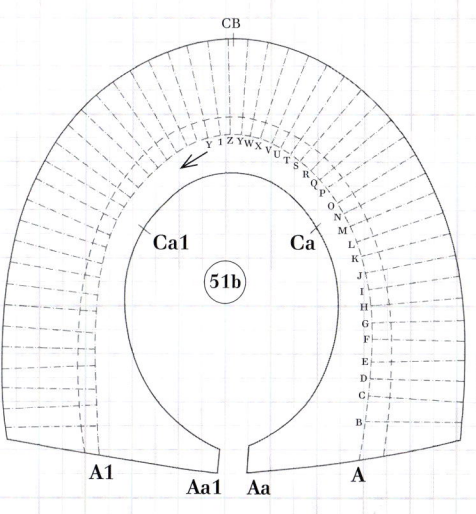

PATTERN PIECES

1–50 Picadils – satin and paper layers
51a Top view of pasteboard upper panel (15 layers of paper glued together)
51b Under view of pasteboard upper panel
52 Satin topside cover for the wool padding
53 Pasteboard lower panel (six layers of paper) and satin cover of the lower panel
54 Linen lining of the neckband

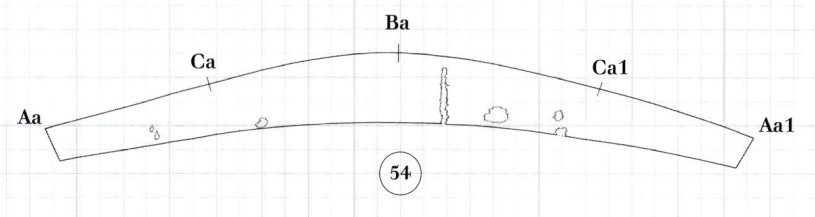

A cross-section of the different layers forming the picadil

Satin topside layer
Carded wool
Silk and paper picadil
Pasteboard upper panel
Silk and paper picadil
Pasteboard lower panel
Satin cover of the under panel

KEY

– – – – Position of picadils
- - - - Fold line of picadils
· · · · Concealed ends of the picadils
~~~~ Areas where the fabric has worn away
▬▬▬ Carded wool layer

MATERIALS

Ivory silk satin
Ivory silk grosgrain
Carded wool
Paper
Pasteboard
Partially bleached woven linen
Metal hook and eye
Thick linen thread, 2 'S' ply
Ivory silk thread, 2 'S' ply, two thicknesses

DETAILS

SCALE 1:1

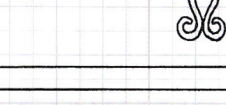 Actual size of the metal eye still attached at CF on the LHS

━━━━━ Thickness of the pasteboard upper panel
━━━━━ (15 layers of paper glued together)

━━━━━
━━━━━ Thickness of the pasteboard lower panel
(six layers of paper glued together)

Pattern by Luca Costigliolo   149

CONSTRUCTION
Construction of the picadil

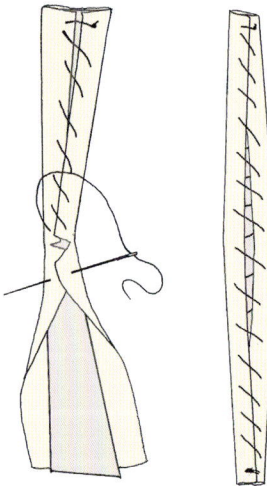

1 Each of the 50 individual picadils consists of a layer of paper cut net and a satin cover cut with a seam allowance of about ¼" on the long sides. The paper shape was PLACED on the WS of the satin, the seam allowance was FOLDED over its edges and secured with a WHIP STITCH worked in thick linen thread.

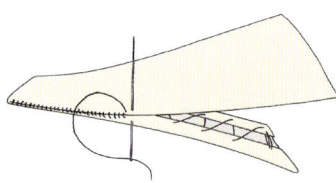

2 The two front picadils (pieces 1 and 50) were FOLDED widthwise with WS facing and the outer edges were closely WHIPPED together with the finer ivory silk thread.

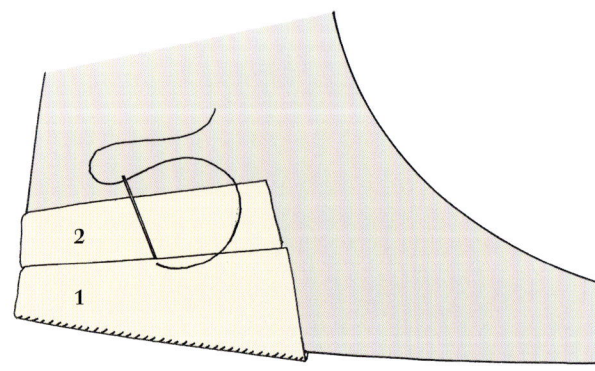

3 The upper panel consists of pasteboard made of 15 layers of paper GLUED together. Picadils 1 and 50 were PLACED respectively over the RHS and LHS outer corners of the panel with the whipped edges on the front edge of the pasteboard. Picadils 2 and 49 were FOLDED width-wise and PLACED next to them, covering either side of the pasteboard upper panel. The two picadils were STAB STITCHED together on both sides with a single WHIP STITCH, worked in silk thread and going through all the layers of silk, paper and pasteboard.

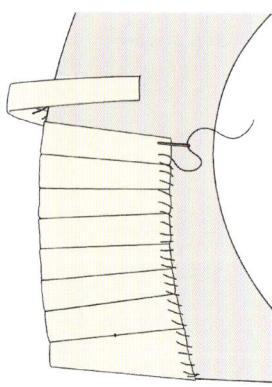

4 Starting on the RHS, the rest of the picadils were FOLDED widthwise and PLACED over the edge of the upper panel, covering both sides of the pasteboard. The ends of each picadil were STAB STITCHED on both sides with a single row of stitches worked through all of the layers with thick linen thread. There are about nine stitches per inch.

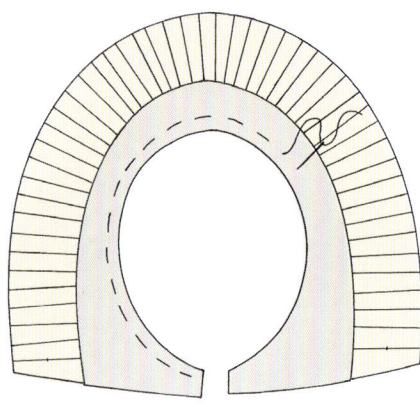

5 The pasteboard lower panel, made of six layers of paper GLUED together, was PLACED over the WS of the upper panel. The two pieces were RUNNING STITCHED around the neckline with large stitches worked in thick linen thread.

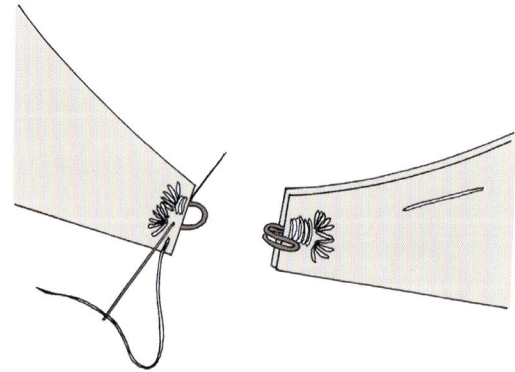

6 On the RHS, a metal hook was INSERTED at CF between the two layers of pasteboard and WHIPPED through all the layers, with a STAB STITCH worked in thick linen thread. On the LHS, a metal eye was INSERTED at CF and STITCHED to the pasteboard in the same manner.

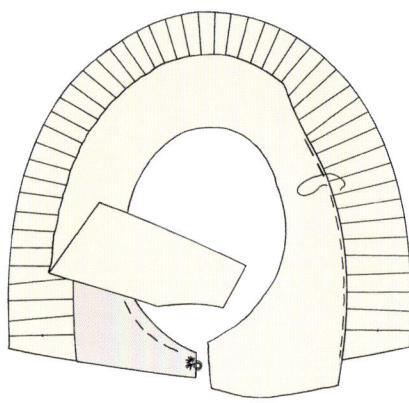

7 The satin cover was PLACED over the pasteboard lower panel. Its seam allowance on the outer edge was FOLDED and *probably* BASTED to the picadils.

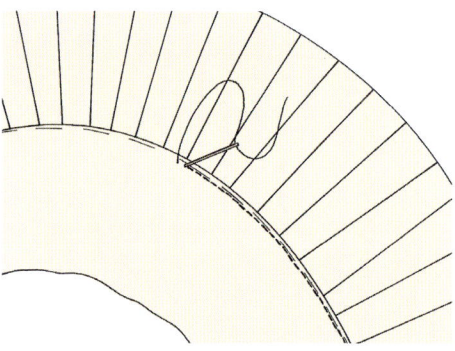

8 The satin cover of the pasteboard lower panel was closely BACK STITCHED all around the basted edge, with a STAB STITCH worked in thick silk thread. There were about 11 stitches per inch. The needle was pointed at an angle towards the neckline and although the stitches go through all the layers of pasteboard they do not catch the ends of the picadils to the other side.

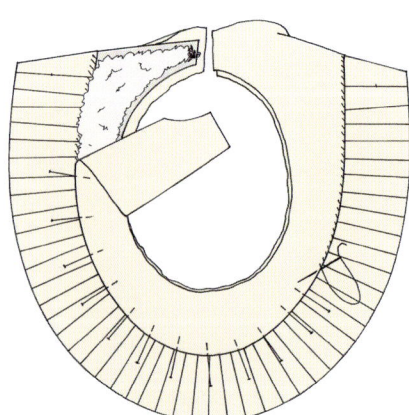

9 On the RS, a layer of soft carded wool was PLACED over the pasteboard and arranged around the neckline on the surface not covered by the ends of the picadils. A piece of satin was PLACED on top with the WS facing the wool. Its seam allowance at the outer edge was FOLDED and *probably* PINNED all around to cover the whipped ends of the picadils. The pinned edge was then FELLED with the finer silk thread. There are about 13 stitches per inch.

8 | Silk satin picadil

Construction of the neckband

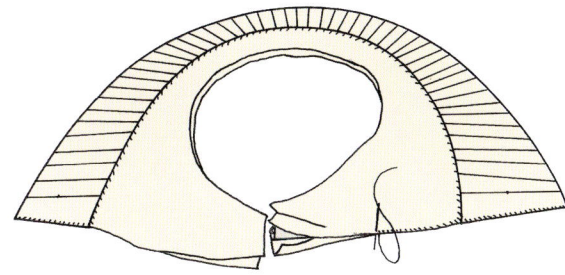

10 The seam allowances of the top and bottom satin covers were FOLDED along the two front edges and WHIPPED together with the finer ivory silk thread.

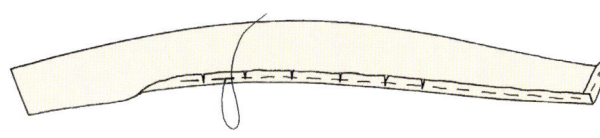

13 The seam allowance at the bottom of the silk grosgrain layer forming the neckband was *probably* SNIPPED. It was then FOLDED, as was the seam allowance of each CF. They were *probably* BASTED with a RUNNING STITCH.

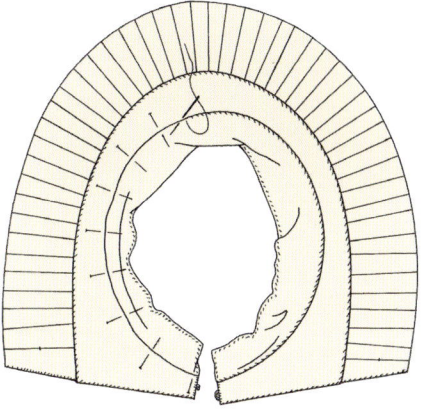

17 The seam allowance of the top edge of the satin layer of the neckband was FOLDED and *probably* PINNED around the neckline edge of the picadil. It was then FELLED into place with the finer silk thread. There are about 13 stitches per inch.

Reconstruction of the picadil

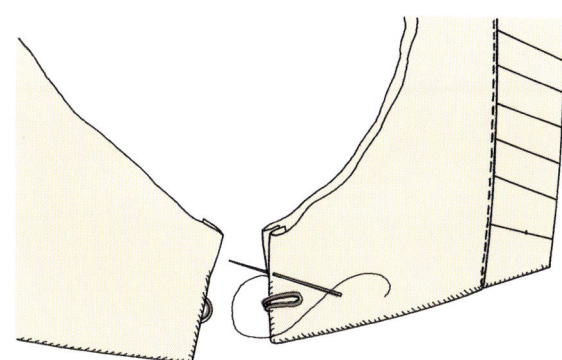

11 At CF, the seam allowances of the satin were FOLDED in on either side of the metal hook and eye and WHIPPED together with silk thread.

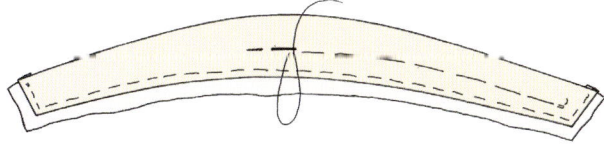

14 With WS together, the grosgrain layer was *probably* BASTED to the lining along the centre.

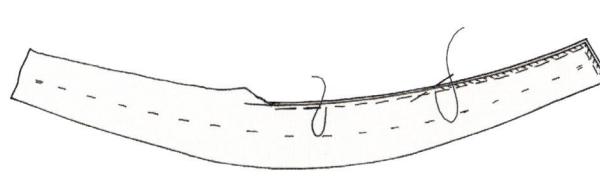

15 The seam allowances of the lining were FOLDED along each CF and at the bottom edge and *probably* BASTED. The three edges were then *probably* FELLED together with silk thread (this line of stitching is now missing).

Front view of a reconstructed picadil in full scale, showing how it would have appeared when worn. When the hook and eye at CF is fastened the picadil bends, creating a slightly curved surface.

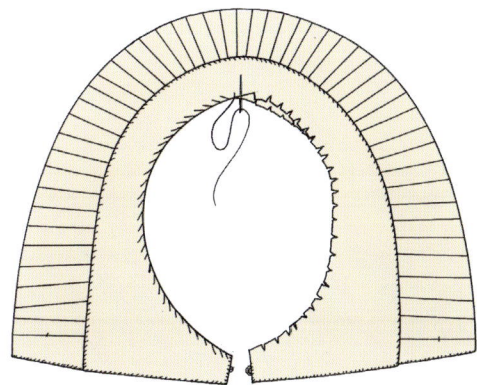

12 The seam allowance of the neckline was SNIPPED, FOLDED and WHIPPED with thick linen thread, with about four stitches per inch, working from left to right through all the layers of pasteboard and satin.

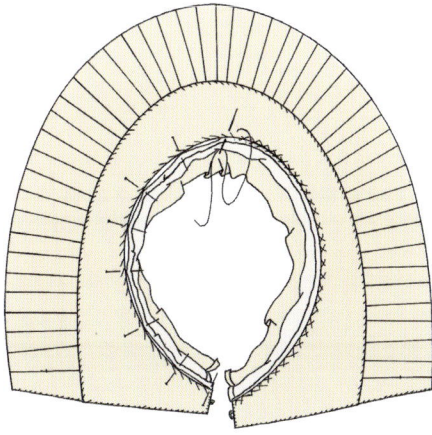

16 The seam allowance of the top edge of the lining was FOLDED and *probably* PINNED around the neckline edge of the picadil. It was then WHIPPED into place with thick linen thread, with about four stitches per inch, worked from right to left.

Side view of the reconstructed picadil.

Pattern by Luca Costigliolo

9 | Embroidered linen nightcap

English, 1600–25 | V&A: T.258-1926

Pattern by Claire Thornton

This nightcap was purchased in 1926 along with an embroidered waistcoat panel from Messrs Christie, Mason and Woods at a total cost of £68 5s. There are several extant nightcaps with similar embroidery in the V&A; they probably survived because they were too small to be re-modelled or recycled into another garment. Until the 19th century, a 'nightcap' was not worn in bed, but informally in the home as 'undress'. They appear occasionally in formal portraiture, as in the portrait opposite of the Earl of Nottingham.

The plain-weave linen was embroidered with polychrome silk floss and metal thread, and spangled bobbin lace. Although the silk threads are somewhat faded, the nightcap is in good condition and has been minimally conserved. This style of embroidery is typical of the early part of the 17th century. Scrolling stems with floral motifs were popular in the 16th century in the form of black-work; however, the metal-thread embroidered scrolls bearing colourful flora are characteristic of this later period and are found on nightcaps, coifs and waistcoats. It is possible that their increased popularity was due to the lapsing of the sumptuary laws, which meant that anybody could wear garments and accessories decorated with precious metals – if they could afford them.

Stem stitches worked in a dark green silk floss thread outline both the stems and motifs, and also the edges of the cap, allowing a simple whipped insertion seam to be worked in a light green silk floss. The scrolling stems on the nightcap carry vine leaves executed in different ways: a stylized striped leaf in a still-vivid blue-green and silver gilt, and a large, shapeless leaf, possibly a pansy. There are also borage, pansies, roses, acorns, rosehips and grapes, all worked in variations of detached stitches.

A detached stitch is not worked through the ground fabric, as is noticeable on the inside of the cap, where a minimal amount of the coloured silk thread can be seen, mainly as an outline. Silk thread was expensive, but not as costly as silver and silver-gilt filé, which was also worked mainly on the surface. The double-plait stitch used to work the stems is particularly thread-greedy, weaving through itself to give a faceted appearance, which would have twinkled when seen under candlelight. This stitch too appears only minimally on the wrong side of the linen ground.

Silver and silver-gilt filé bobbin edging lace, tipped with spangles, was stitched to the turned-up brim of the nightcap. A lace, similar in both design and execution, appears on a nightcap from the Middleton Collection in Nottingham (opposite). Pattern books that offered designs for embroidery and lace had been available for over a century to both amateurs and professionals. These gave very little in the way of instruction. Indeed, Richard Shorleyker in his *A Schole-House for the Needle* suggests that his designs are 'only but Patternes, which serue but to helpe and inlarge your inventions: but for the disposing of them into forme and order of workes, that I haue left to your owne skils and vnderstandings'.[1]

The nightcap is unlined, but was probably worn with a cap liner similar to that on page 158, as an embroidered garment such as this could not have been laundered.

1. Richard Shorleyker, *A Schole-House for the Needle*, 1632, facsimile edited by John and Elizabeth Mason, Much Wenlock: RJL Smith & Associates, 1998, fol. A2

Nightcap, *c.* 1615
Middleton collection,
Nottingham City Museums and Galleries:
Lord Middleton Collection
Museum no. CTLOAN 3/28
Embroidered with floral motifs in scrolling stems, the style of this cap is very similar to the V&A one. The lace is also very similar, but is worked here in silver-gilt filé only.

Two designs from the Trevelyon Miscellany of 1608
Folger MS V.b.32, fol. 268r and fol. 219r (facsimile)
By permission of the Folger Shakespeare Library
At the top is a design for a nightcap of similar shape and style to the V&A cap, showing floral and fruit motifs within scrolling stems. The design below shows a borage motif, present on both the cap in the portrait on the right and the V&A example, which features bunches of grapes, also on the Trevelyon design.

Right: **Charles Howard, 1st Earl of Nottingham,** *c.* 1620
Daniel Mytens the Elder
© National Maritime Museum, Greenwich, London, Greenwich Hospital Collection
He wears an embroidered linen nightcap with Garter robes, including the garter of the Order of the Garter worn around his left knee. This is an unusual combination for a formal portrait. The doublet and hose are cloth-of-silver and he wears a multi-layered ruff.

Pattern by Claire Thornton

DETAILS
Embroidery details

9.1 Two grape leaf motifs, both with stem-stitched outlines, and radiating lines of stem stitches as filling. Although they sit side by side, brought together by the seam, they would have been worked at opposite ends of the embroidery frame, maybe accounting for the differences in execution.

9.2 A bunch of grapes, again worked at opposite ends of the frame. One half has silver-gilt filé grapes worked in a two-stage weaving stitch, the other has eyelet holes worked in pink silk floss.

9.3 Borage flower, with detached-buttonhole stitched petals in blue silk floss and silver-gilt filé. The blue petals were embellished with a doubled, silver filé chain stitch. Pairs of silver-gilt filé filling the vine leaves were couched down with blanket stitch in green silk thread.

9.4 Rose motif, worked in chain, stem and detached stitches. The hem at the top of the image was decorated with a two-stage edging stitch.

9.5 Pansy motif (above) and reverse (right). The pansy was worked in chain, stem and detached stitches. The double-plait stitch is silver-gilt filé. On the reverse only the stem and chain stitches are visible as an outline. Scant amounts of metal thread can be glimpsed, indicating that all the work was carried out above the surface of the fabric, with only minimal amounts of thread anchoring it through to the reverse.

9.6 A stylized, striped leaf in green silk floss and silver-gilt filé, in a detached buttonhole stitch, was enhanced with chain-stitched silver filé. The rosehips were also worked in a detached buttonhole stitch.

Cap details

9.7 An unusual view of the nightcap, from above the crown, showing the four pansies each in its own quarter. The pattern by Thomas Trevelyon on page 153 would have formed a single motif at the crown. The light green silk floss insertion seam is clearly visible against the dark green stem stitches.

9.8 The brim is turned down, showing both right and wrong sides of the embroidery, and the unworked gap between them. The acorns, barely visible when the brim is turned up, were worked in chain and detached stitches. The full pattern repeat can be seen here.

9.9 The inside of the nightcap. The seam allowances are unfinished, but have not frayed. Small lengths of selvedge are just visible at the crown where all the points meet. Although the nightcap is in good condition, the embroidery has faded. The colours of the silk threads here give an indication of how vibrant the cap would have been originally.

Pattern by Claire Thornton

PATTERN
Pattern of the nightcap

SCALE 1:2

The nightcap was cut from a single length of linen, with the selvedge at the top.

KEY

—— Selvedge

—·—·— Edge of turned hem

∴∴∴ Reversed embroidery

– – – Seam allowance

MATERIALS

Partially bleached linen,
  thread count 88 warp × 88 weft
Linen thread
Polychrome silk floss
Silver and silver-gilt filé
Silver-gilt spangles

156   9 | Embroidered linen nightcap

CONSTRUCTION
Construction of the nightcap

A length of linen was stretched in an embroidery frame and the pattern marked, or 'pounced', onto it.

The coloured silk threads were worked first, followed by the silver and silver-gilt filé. This is designated the RS.

The frame was then turned over, in order to work the turned-up brim. This is designated the WS.

1 At the bottom of the cap a 5⁄16" seam allowance was TURNED to the RS and HEMMED with a fine linen thread, from A–F–F–A; the finished hem is just over 1⁄8" deep.

2 A two-stage edging stitch was worked on the WS in a light green silk floss thread, again from A–F–F–A, completely covering the hem.

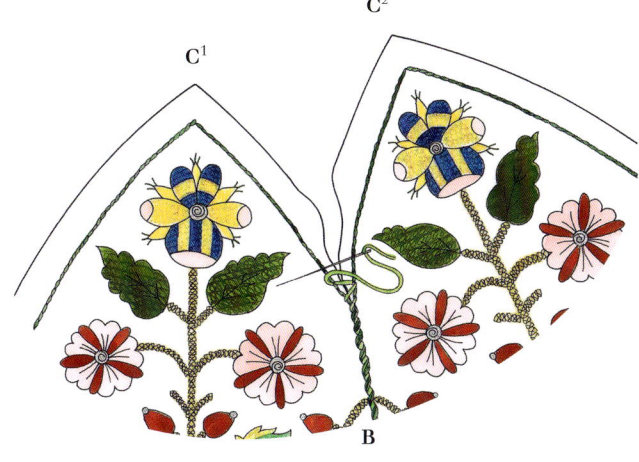

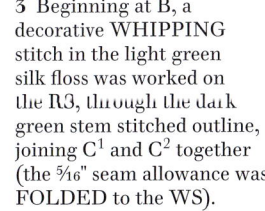

3 Beginning at B, a decorative WHIPPING stitch in the light green silk floss was worked on the RS, through the dark green stem stitched outline, joining C¹ and C² together (the 5⁄16" seam allowance was FOLDED to the WS).

4 The seam allowances at C³ and C⁴ were FOLDED to the WS, then the WHIPPING was continued through them, drawing all the Cs together, and finishing at E. F and F were brought together and WHIPPED in the green silk floss, joining A and A, through C¹, C², C³ and C⁴, finishing at D.

5 Working from the CB, a length of silver and silver-gilt filé bobbin lace was WHIPPED to the RS of the hem with the light green silk floss, stitching only through the green silk edging.

Bobbin lace pattern

Spangled edging lace of a pointed design worked in silver and silver-gilt filé.

6 pairs of bobbins:
4 wound with silver gilt and spangles
2 wound with silver and spangles

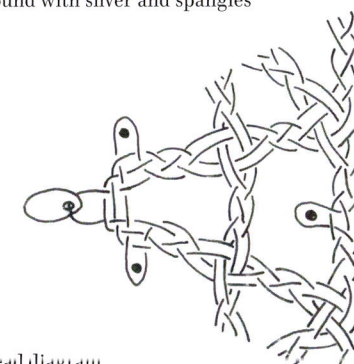

Thread diagram
SCALE 4:1

SCALE 2:1

The pattern is shown here in the style of the early lace-pattern books. Only the pin positions are shown, allowing the lacemaker to interpret the pattern as she wished. Pins could possibly be PLACED at the pink asterisk along the straight right edge of the pattern, but it is likely that an 'experienced seventeenth-century lacemaker, working with relatively stiff metal threads, would not have needed these pins'.[1]

1. E-mail communication with Gilian Dye, 25 October 2015.

Pattern
SCALE 1:1

Pattern by Claire Thornton

10 | Linen nightcap liner

English, 1600–80 | V&A: T.68–2004

Pattern by Susan North

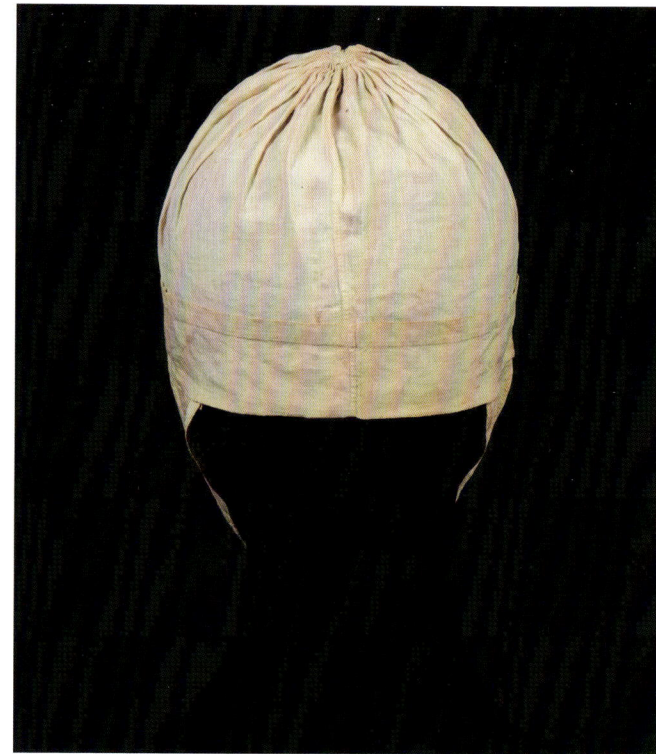

This rare, but very plain accessory answers the question living historians frequently ask: were nightcaps lined? Most are thinking in terms of a sewn-in lining, for which there is very little evidence, but objects like this one correspond with written accounts referring to 'cap liners', which could be removed and laundered. For example, the laundry list of Sir Henry Slingsby senior in 1612 included five shirts, nine bands and four 'Cap Lyninges'.[1]

Far more of the decorative caps worn over these are found in museum collections (like the one on page 152), although a matching cap and liner of Christian IV of Denmark survives in Rosenborg Castle.[2] The Museum of London has a fine example of a cap liner with a needle-lace edging, said to have been worn by Charles I at the wedding of one of his servants in 1646. The elderly gentleman on the right wears a nightcap liner with ear flaps to tie under the chin, a style very rarely seen in portraiture.

The construction of this liner is distinct from that of the decorative nightcap worn over it. The liner is made of a rectangle of linen and gathered at the top, illustrating the traditional techniques of the seamstress: a sew and fell seam, hemming and counted-thread gathers. A monogrammed 'C' is embroidered under the brim at the back. The liner was purchased from Kerry Taylor Auctions in 2004 for £3800. Like the other garments with which it was sold, it is associated with ancestors of the Chaffyn Grove family in Wiltshire.

1. Daniel Parson, ed., *The Diary of Sir Henry Slingsby*, London: Longman, 1836, p. 270
2. Janet Arnold, Santina Levey and Jenny Tiramani, *Patterns of Fashion 4*, Basingstoke: Macmillan, 2008, p. 42, plate 40C

Nightcap liner edged with needle-lace, c. 1630–40
© **Museum of London**
The edging of bobbin lace would have been turned back over the decorative nightcap worn on top of the liner.

Detail of an unknown man, formerly known as Charles Howard, 1st Earl of Nottingham
Unknown artist
© **National Portrait Gallery, London**
The liner inside his embroidered nightcap has ear flaps like this one and a brim edged with bobbin lace.

DETAILS
Right side (RS) details

Wrong side (WS) details

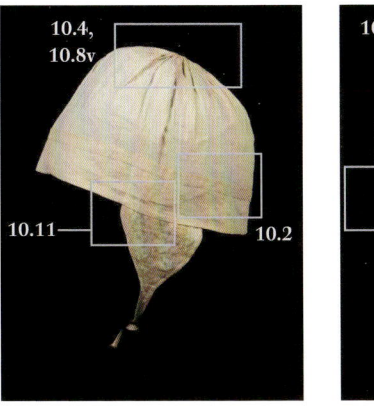
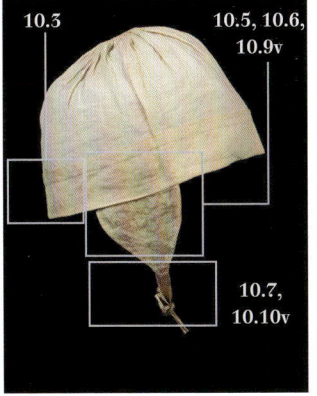

10.1 The LHS of the liner (left) and the RHS of the liner (right).

10.4 The circular piece of linen at the crown of the liner, to which the counted-thread pleats are individually stitched.

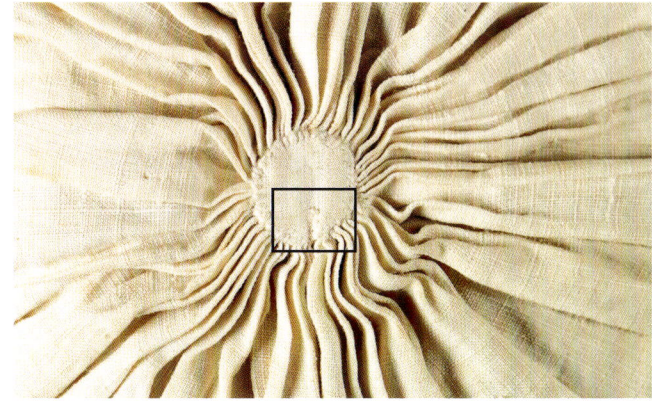

10.8 Another circle of linen is stitched to the counted-thread pleats on the WS of the crown, exactly as on the RS, covering the raw edges of the gathers. The stitch below the centre of the crown piece (shown in the box) probably anchored the first gather.

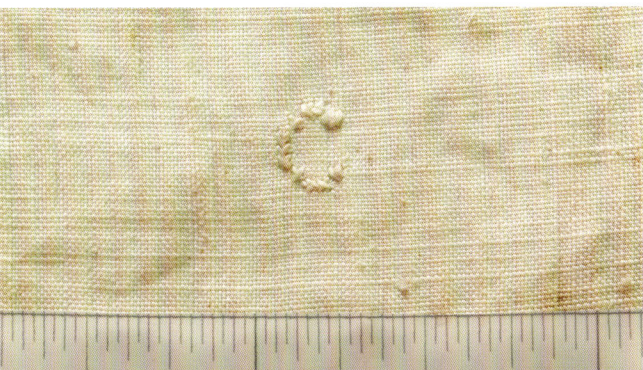

10.2 The monogram 'C', cross stitched in white linen thread under the brim, between the left ear flap and the CB seam. The ruler indicates the fine weave of the linen fabric.

10.5 The RS of the whipped seam joining the right ear flap to the nightcap liner.

10.9 The WS of the right ear flap, showing how its top edge is whipped to the fold of the cap brim. The ear flaps were hemmed ⅛" on all three sides.

10.6 Inside the fold of the brim, showing the back of the whip stitches attaching the right ear flap.

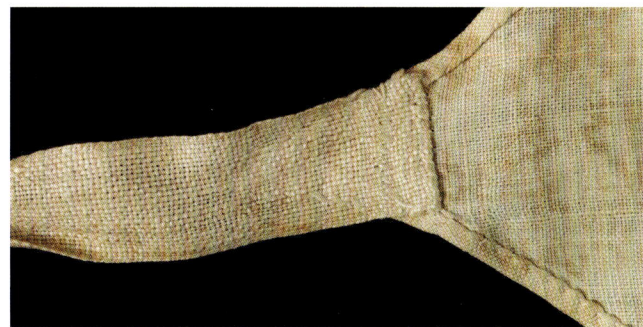

10.10 The WS of the right ear flap, showing the felling of the linen-tape tie to the bottom of the flap.

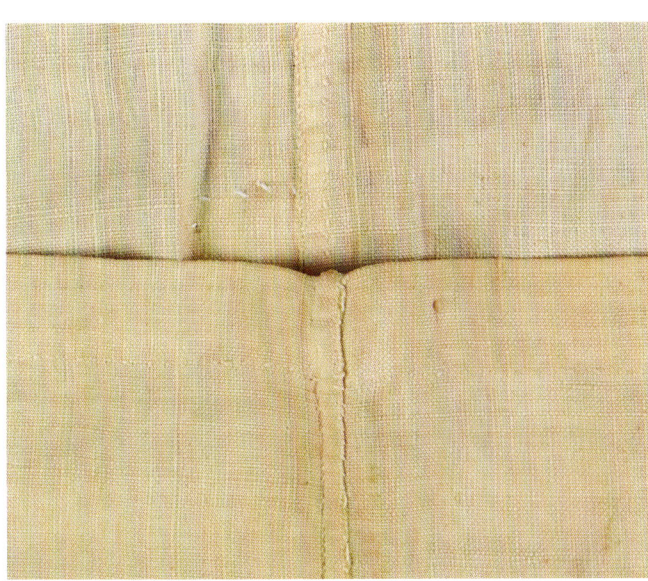

10.3 The bottom of the nightcap liner was hemmed first, then a sew and fell hem seam was made at CB. The crude stitching of the museum number is seen to the left of the seam.

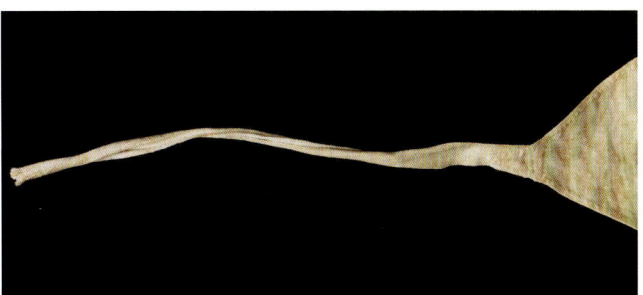

10.7 A length of linen tape, (7½") at the bottom of the right ear flap. The ends of the tapes are raw; they may have been hemmed originally and come unstitched, although there is now no evidence of this.

10.11 The hem binding the top edge of the left ear flap has come unstitched.

Pattern by Susan North

PATTERN
Pattern of the nightcap liner

SCALE 1:2

PATTERN PIECES

1. Left ear flap
2. Right ear flap
3. Linen tape, × 2
4. Crown piece, × 2
5. Liner

KEY

- - -   Fold of the liner hem
- · - · -   Fold of the brim
· · · · ·   Placement of linen tape
C   Position of the monogram
———   Selvedge

MATERIALS

Bleached linen with an average thread count of 88 × 88 per inch (no visible selvedges)

Bleached linen tape, ½" wide

Fine white linen thread, 2 'S'-plied

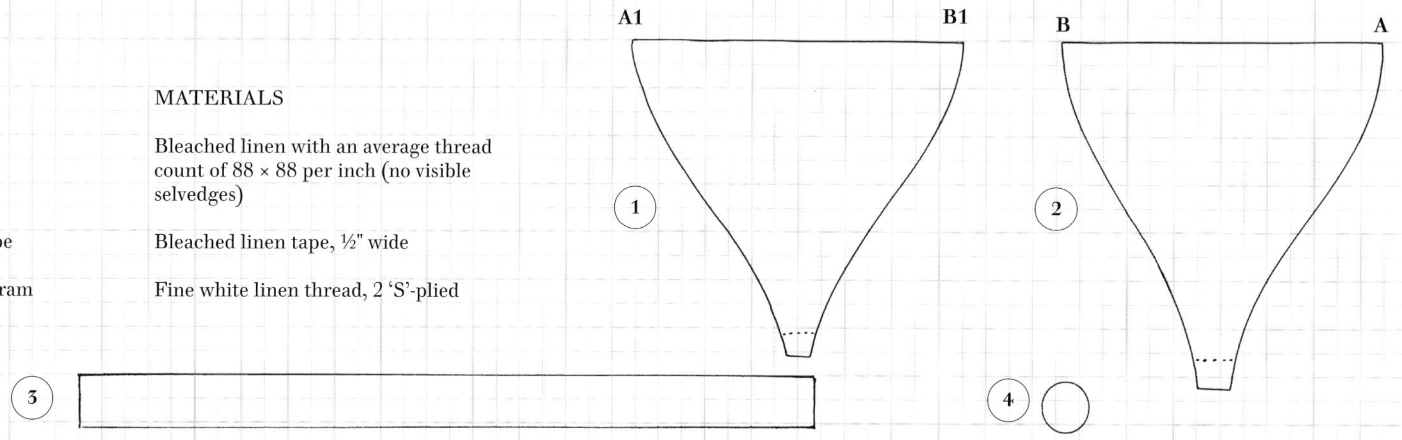

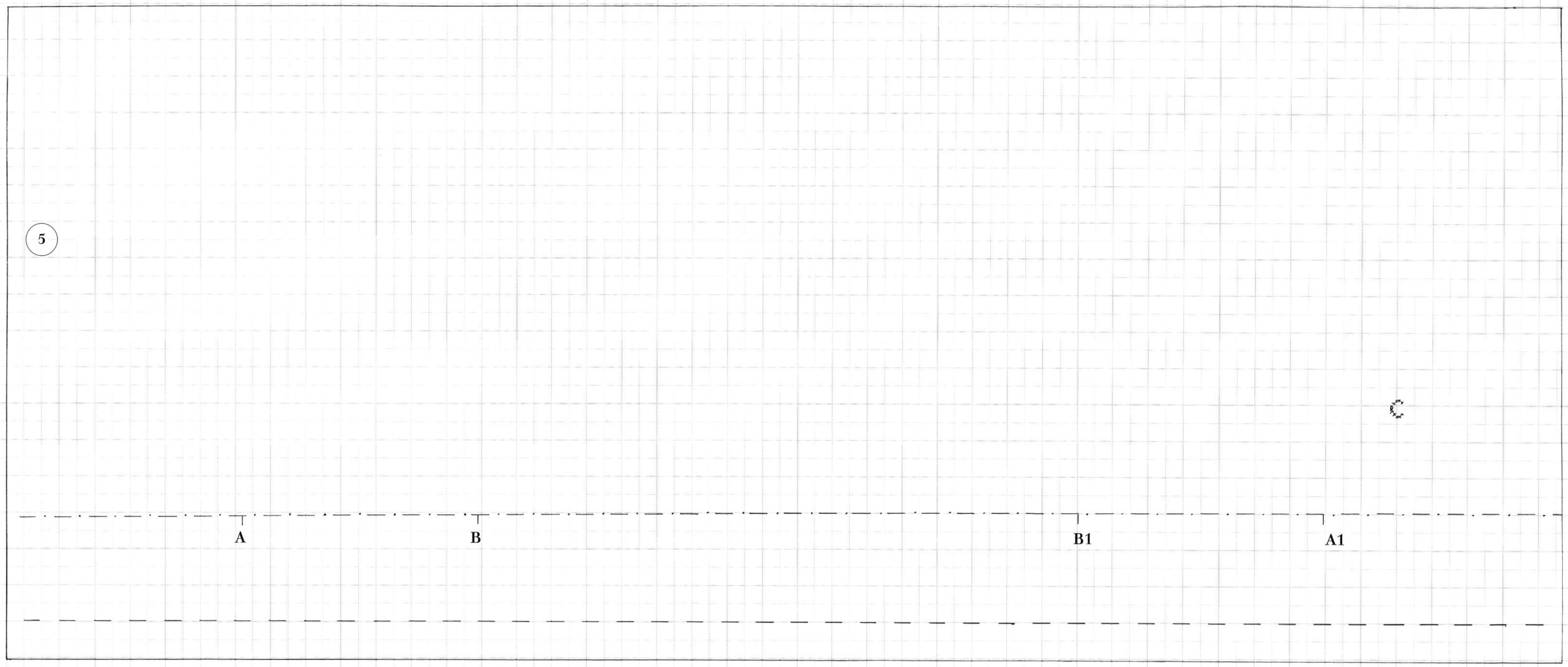

MONOGRAM

SCALE 2:1

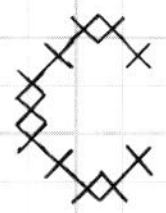

CONJECTURED LAYOUT

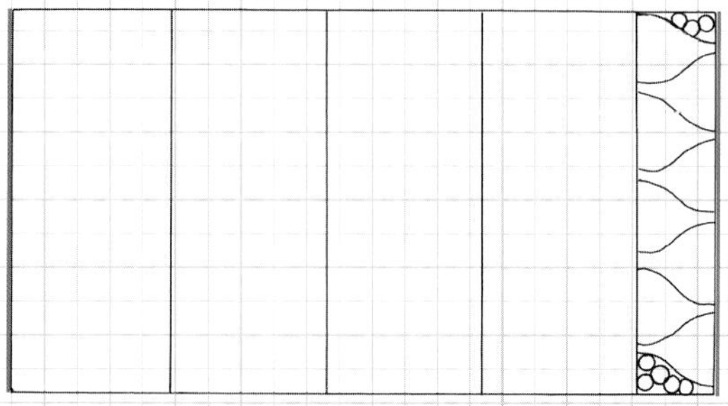

SCALE 1:16

There are no visible selvedges on the cap, suggesting a layout of four liners using ¾ of a yard of ell wide (45") linen.

GATHERING THREAD DIAGRAM

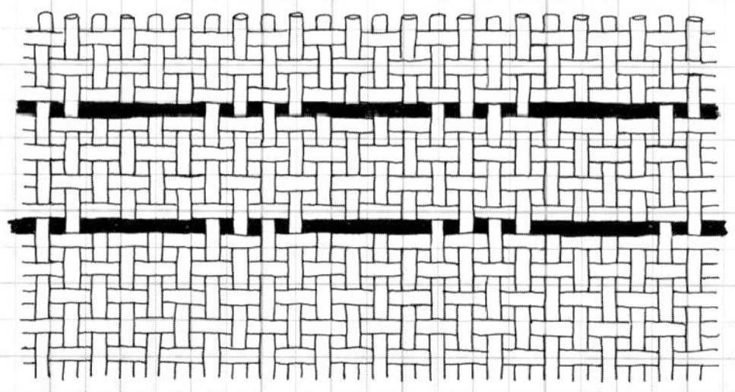

NOT TO SCALE

Diagram of the counted-thread running stitch used to make the gathers at the crown of the liner.

160   10 | Linen nightcap liner

CONSTRUCTION
Construction of the nightcap liner

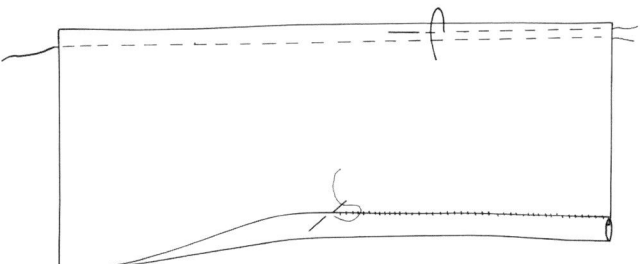

1 The bottom of the cap was FOLDED 1/16" and then 5/16" and HEMMED on the RS. Two lines of counted-thread running stitches for 1/4" pleats were worked, one 1/8" and another 3/16" from the top edge of the liner.

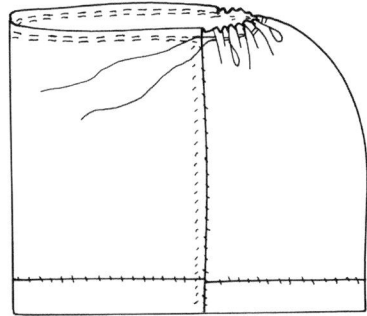

3 The two rows of running stitches at the top of the liner were PULLED UP evenly and gathered into a tight circle.

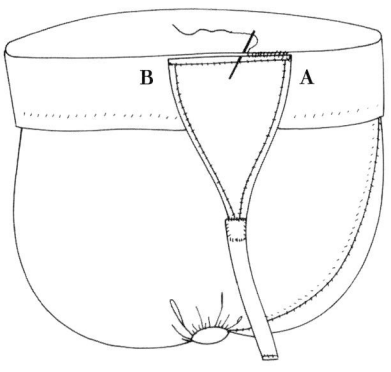

6 The bottom of the liner was FOLDED up 1¾" on the RS. With RS together, the ear flaps were WHIPPED to the fold at the bottom of the liner, 3⅜" from the back seam, between points A/A1 and B/B1.

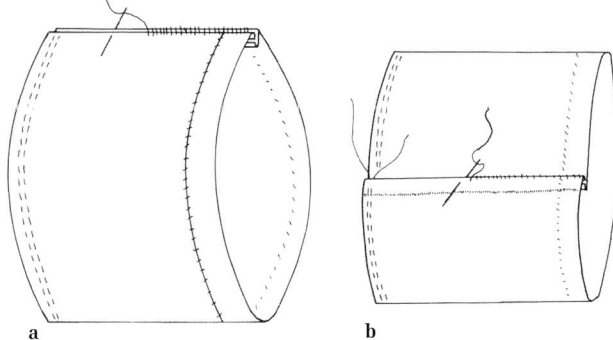

2a The back seam of the liner was WHIPPED on the RS.
b The back seam of the liner was FELLED on the WS.

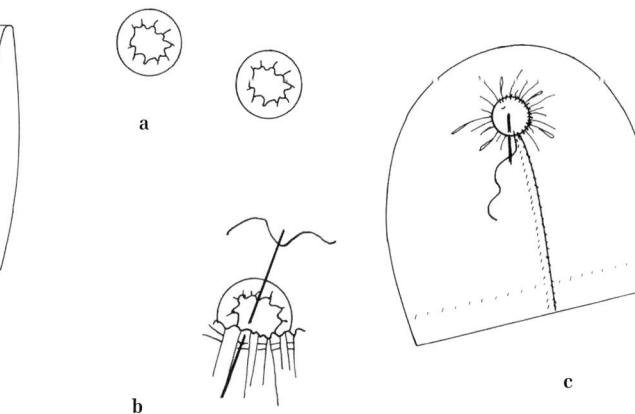

4a The seam allowances of the crown pieces were FOLDED to the WS **b** One crown piece was sewn to the WS of the liner. A pleat was *probably* first CAUGHT to the WS of the centre of the crown piece with a single stitch to hold it in place. Then the RS of the crown piece was WHIPPED to the WS of the liner, stitching through each pleat.
c The other crown piece was WHIPPED to the RS of the liner, stitching through each pleat.

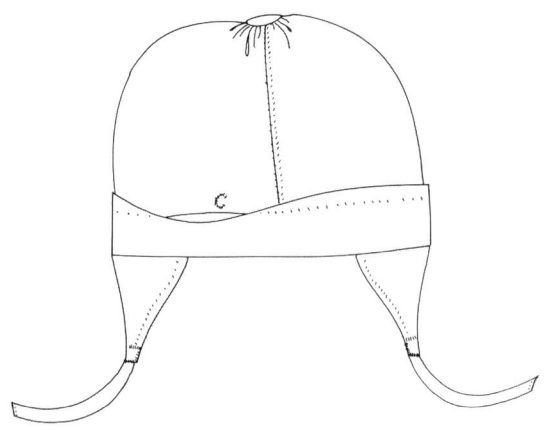

7 A 'C' was CROSS STITCHED in white linen thread, under the brim, between the left ear flap and the CB seam.

Reconstruction

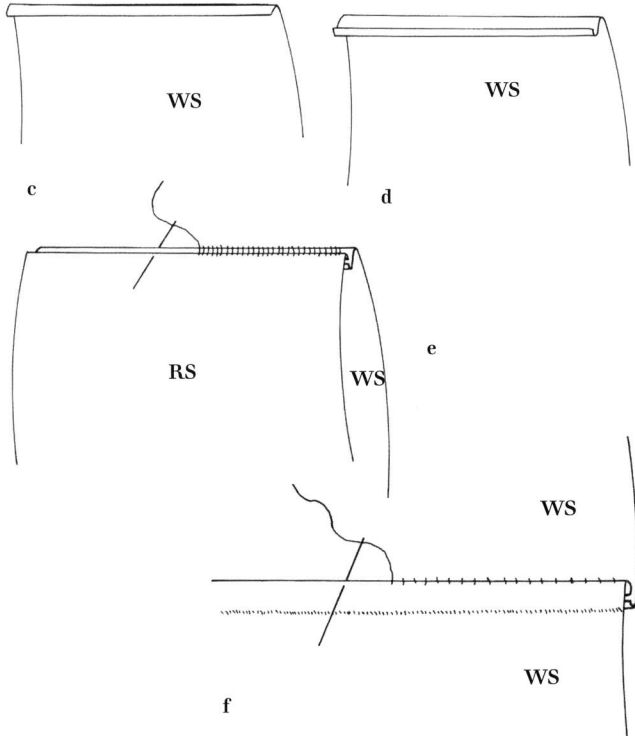

c and d Detail of the folding of the seam allowances for a sew-and-fell seam.
e The 'sewing' or WHIPPING of the seam on the RS
f The FELLING of the seam on the WS

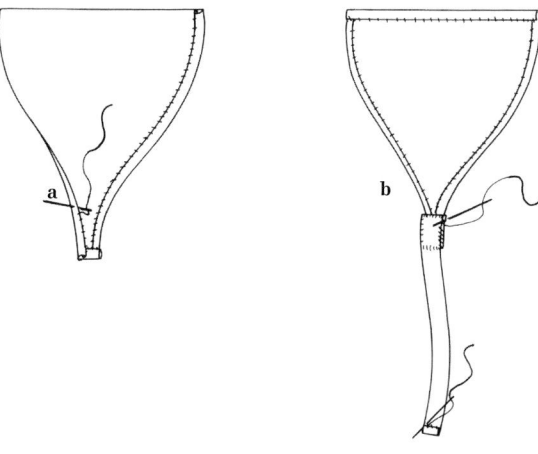

5a The sides of each ear flap were TURNED 1/8" and FELLED.
b One end of the linen tape was FOLDED under 1/4", and WS together, FELLED to the lower point of each ear flap. The other end of the tape was *probably* TURNED and HEMMED (see fig. 10.7, page 159).

Pattern by Susan North

11 | Crimson silk velvet mittens with embroidered tops

English, *c.* 1600 | V&A: 1507&A–1882 Given by Sir Edward Denny

Pattern by Jenny Tiramani

These splendidly worked mittens are said to have been a gift from Elizabeth I to her maid of honour, Margaret Edgcumbe (1560–1648), wife of Sir Edward Denny (1547–99), in about 1600. At some point, they were given or acquired by the Earl of Arran, and were purchased from his estate by a member of the Denny family in 1759: 'the mittens given by Queen Elizth. to Sir Edwd. Denny's lady for £25 4s 0d'.[1] Together with a pair of gloves and a military scarf, they were donated to the South Kensington Museum by Sir Edward Denny in 1882. Although they were described as a pair of women's mittens, they could equally have be worn by a man. Numerous other examples survive and they vary in their quality and materials, demonstrating their use by all classes of society. Durable mittens of leather have survived from the 1627 shipwreck of the *Vasa*, a warship of Gustavus Adolphus of Sweden, as have woollen ones in the Historisches Museum, Hannover, as well as other examples in British collections.

The term 'mitten' for a glove without fingers may have originally referred to a practical item connected with difficult manual labour. Randle Holme describes the mitten as follows, 'He beareth Argent, a **Mitten** Gules. This is of some termed, an **hedged Mitten**, or **Glove to hedg with : a Tethering Glove**'. Holme also describes 'The **Gauntlet**, all that reacheth behind the Hand to the Wrist', although this term can now mean the whole of a glove, not only the 'cuff'.[2] Another term used in the early 17th century for the cuff was the 'top'. Of the seven pairs of gloves listed in the 1619 inventory of Richard Sackville, 3rd Earl of Dorset, five pairs are described as having 'topps', such as 'Item one paire of gloves with topps of greene sattin embroidered and edged wth gold lace' and six pairs were part of matching ensembles of doublet, hose, cloak, hatband, sword girdle and hangers.[3]

The mittens have silk velvet hands and silk satin tops, embroidered in polychrome silks and metal threads. All the seams and edges are bound in silver and silver-gilt woven lace, some of which is now missing. They are interlined with two types of stiffened linen and lined in pink silk velvet. The red velvet of the hands was probably coloured with an insect dye, given the lack of fading over decades of display. Like many Renaissance silk velvets, the warp and weft threads of the ground weave are much paler than the rich crimson velvet pile warp threads. In this case, the ground threads are pale yellow, adding more depth and texture to the fabric than if all the threads in the weave were the same crimson colour. The mitten tops have a design that is mirror-imaged on the fold line. The overall pattern of obelisks, swags and scrolls was probably compiled from design elements found in a variety of sources including emblem books. The embroidery pattern on page 167 works more coherently as a flat design. When folded the symmetry of the design is lost.

Henry Cary, 1st Viscount Falkland and detail of his mitten top, 1603 (below) Marcus Gheeraerts II Sarah Campbell Blaffer Foundation, the Museum of Fine Arts, Houston

The mittens worn by Henry Cary appear to have matching gloves inside them, the fingers of which are visible as they protrude from the slits across the palms of the mittens. Alternatively, these fingers could be part of the mittens themselves, and be stitched just inside the slits. Cary married Elizabeth Tanford in 1601 and this portrait may have been painted to celebrate their marriage. The mittens are striking in the depth of their colours against the soft ivory and silver tones of his other clothing. The embroidered gilt motifs, including a rainbow, are framed by clouds. These would have been significant to Cary.

1. *The Annual Register, or a View of the History, Politicks, and Literature, of the Year 1759*, London: R. and J. Dodsley, 1760, p. 84
2. Randle Holme, *The Academy of Armory*, 1688, Book III, chapter II, p. 18, XIX and fols. 16, 18
3. Peter and Ann Mactaggart, 'The Wearing Apparel of Richard, 3rd Earl of Dorset', *Costume*, 14, 1980, pp. 41–55

Early 17th-century mittens and patterns

Pair of silk mittens, 1600–30, private collection.
Photograph: Mark Asher Photography

Woollen mittens, belonging to Moritz, Duke of Sachsen-Lauenburg, *c.* 1600–12, Historisches Museum, Hannover.
Photograph: Jenny Tiramani

 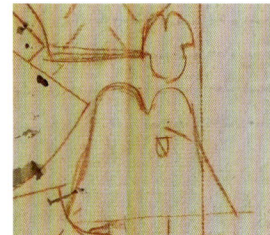

Above left: simple mitten pattern with one pattern piece from *The Book of Patterns by the Guild of Tailors from Český Krumlov*.

Above right: mitten pattern, 1604 (with separate thumb piece), from *The Book of Patterns by the Guild of Tailors from Chomutov*.

Both published in Martin Šimša, *Tailor's Pattern Books in the Czech Lands in the 16th–18th Centuries* (NULK, 2013). Photographs © Martin Šimša, 2013

DETAILS
Right side (RS) details

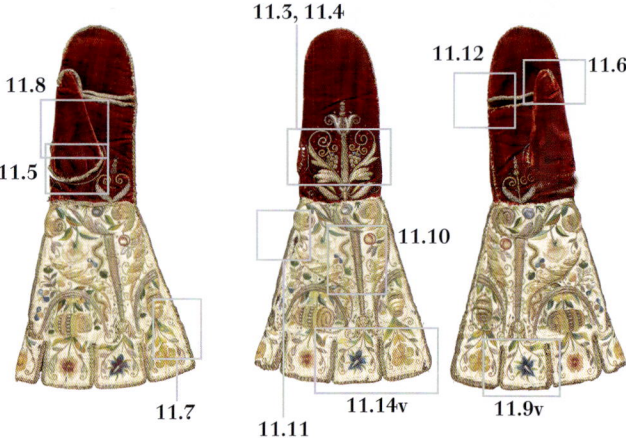 

11.1 Left mitten. **11.2** Right mitten.

11.5 The velvet at the base of the thumb on the left mitten was eased in. An impression of the missing filé remains in the velvet. Scale 2:1

11.3 Detail of the embroidery on the back of the right mitten hand that depicts a vine with bunches of grapes hanging from it. The pale spots on the velvet indicate the original positions of missing metal spangles and purl. One spangle is visible below the grapes on the right.

11.6 The tip of the thumb on the right mitten. Where the whip stitches have worn away, the linen interlining, stiffened with a black substance, is visible. Scale 2:1

11.4 The grape motifs were worked over a base of linen threads, in mingled silk threads of blues, greens, yellow and mauve. The laid threads of the leaf motifs were couched in green silk thread.

11.7 The seam down the outside of the left mitten top, stitched up to the opening between two tabs. The seam was covered in the silver-gilt woven lace.

11 | Crimson silk velvet mittens with embroidered tops

Wrong side (WS) details

11.8 The seam between the hand and thumb of the left mitten with the whip stitches in heavy linen thread, visible where the silver-gilt woven lace covering the seam is missing. Scale 2:1

11.10 Detail of the right mitten top, showing the padding of linen threads under the silver filé, worked to create a raised area down the obelisk. Pairs of stitch holes on the satin indicate the original positions of short lengths of purl and spangles, which are now missing.

11.12 A view through the finger slit in the right mitten. The pink velvet lining is detached, showing the back of the hand embroidery. The pale yellow ground threads of the red velvet can be seen here.

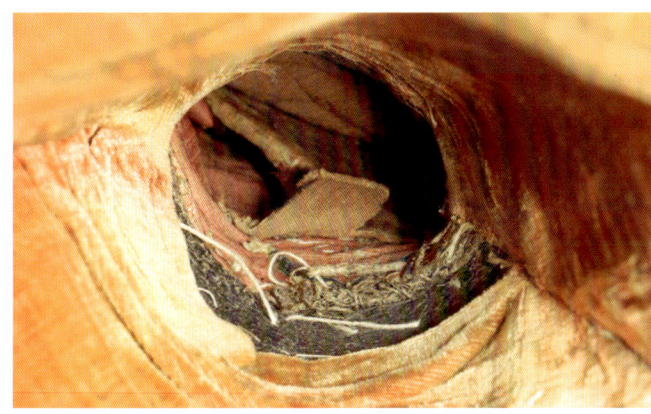

11.13 Inside the left mitten the velvet lining has come loose and the black linen interlining of the mitten top is visible. Long basting stitches were worked through the satin and interlining layers of the top.

11.9 A split tab on the right mitten top, showing the ink outline where the silver-filé thread outline is now missing. The blue borage motif was worked in overlapping satin stitch. Scale 1:1

11.11 Coarsely woven black linen interlining can be seen where the satin on the right mitten top has worn through.

11.14 The inside of the right mitten top lined in pink velvet piecings. The edges of the top were neatly bound in the silver-gilt woven lace.

Pattern by Jenny Tiramani

X-ray image

Above: X-ray of the right mitten. The partially detached pink velvet lining in the hand is now scrunched up towards the finger-tip end. The patterns of the embroidery and lace in metal threads are very clear here as white shapes. Scale 1:2

PATTERN
Pattern of the right mitten
SCALE 1:2

PIECES
1. Hand
2. Thumb
3. Top lining
4. Top

All the pattern pieces were cut with a seam allowance of ⅛" or less – just enough to WHIP the raw edges together.

KEY
— Selvedge
– – Fold line
– – – Edge of silver lace
↑→ Direction of velvet pile
–·–·– Edge of second interlining layer

MATERIALS

Hand
Crimson silk velvet

Top
Ivory silk satin

Lining
The thumb, the hand and the top are lined in pink silk velvet, possibly recycled from an older item of dress or furnishing.

Interlinings
The thumb piece is interlined in a fine linen, stiffened with a black substance.

The top is interlined with a coarsely woven, thick linen, stiffened with a black substance.

EMBROIDERY
Silk threads of many single colours were used for the flower, insect and fruit motifs on the top and for two leaves on the hand. Mingled coloured silk threads were used for the grapes on the hand.

Silver and silver-gilt filé were used for both outlines and fillings, worked singly, in pairs or two-plied together into a twist to be couched as single threads. The diameter of these threads varies from ¹⁄₆₄" to ¹⁄₁₆".

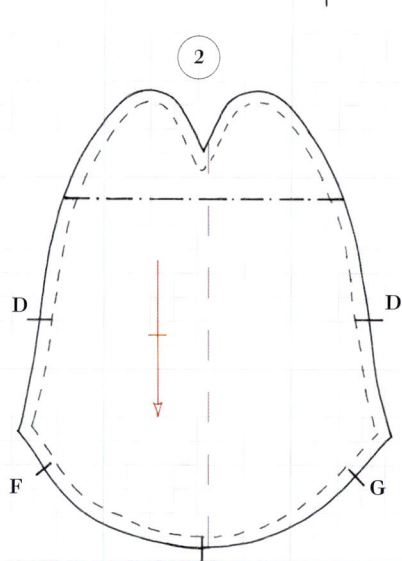

The thumb piece was cut in the red silk velvet, a fine black linen interlining and the pink silk velvet lining. The upper portion of the thumb has a second layer of interlining.

Lengths of silver and silver-gilt purl, both wire and flat strip, were used as fillings on the mitten top and hand, and short lengths were scattered on the satin ground around the motifs on the tops.

Split-ring spangles, both silver and silver-gilt, were stitched to the crimson velvet hand and to the satin ground of the top, secured by short lengths of purl. The diameter of the spangles varies from ¹⁄₁₆" to ⅛".

11 | Crimson silk velvet mittens with embroidered tops

The black linen interlining was cut to the same shape and grain as the silk satin layer.

The embroidery was worked through the satin layer only.

honeysuckle
borage
carnation
sunflower
carnation
borage
honeysuckle
rose
rose

Embroidery and lace details

GRAPE MOTIFS
SCALE 1:1
The grape motifs on the hand of the mitten have a colour scheme that suggests the depiction of ripening fruit as the grape colours worked in silk threads graduate from purple at the top to green and white at the bottom of each bunch.

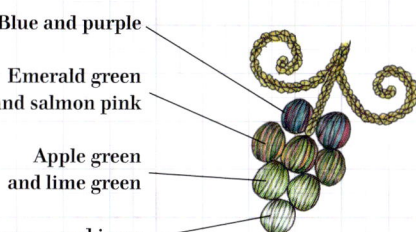

Blue and purple
Emerald green and salmon pink
Apple green and lime green
Pale green and ivory

The vine and tendrils holding the bunch of grapes consist of two silver-gilt filé threads couched together, following the path shown below.

LEAF MOTIFS
SCALE 2:1
The large leaf motifs on the hand of the mitten are worked in pairs of silver filé couched down with green silk threads.

The main stem on the large leaf motifs is made of a bunch of white silk threads [a] wrapped in a length of white silk threads [b] and then wrapped in silver filé [c].

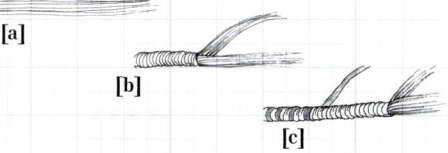

[a]
[b]
[c]

BINDING LACE
SCALE 2:1
The binding lace has 28 warp filé threads. They alternate between silver (now tarnished) and silver gilt. The weft filé is also silver gilt.

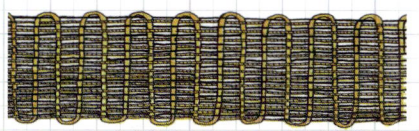

Pattern by Jenny Tiramani

CONSTRUCTION
Construction of the right mitten

The embroidery for all pieces was worked first. All the WHIPPING was in natural linen thread. The FELLING of the metal lace was worked in white silk thread.

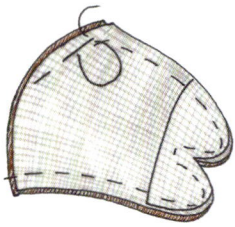

1 The whole thumb piece was interlined in fine, black stiffened linen. The upper portion of the thumb had a second layer of black linen, *probably* all BASTED together.

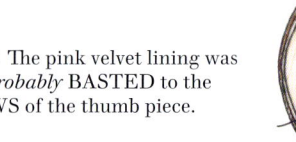

2 The pink velvet lining was *probably* BASTED to the WS of the thumb piece.

3 The thumb seam was WHIPPED with linen thread, through all the layers of crimson velvet, black linen interlining and pink velvet lining, treating them as one layer.

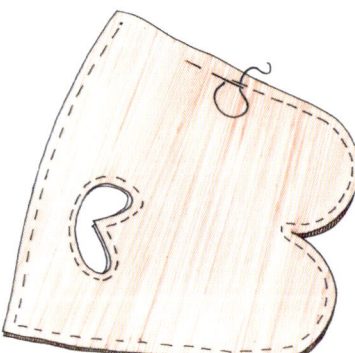

4 The pink velvet lining was *probably* BASTED to the crimson velvet hand.

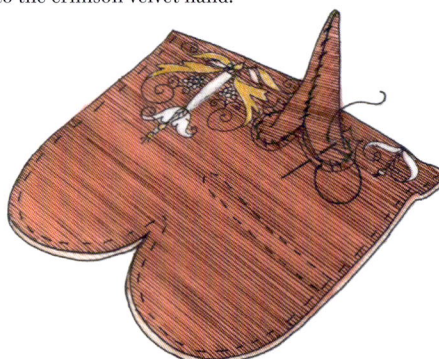

5 The thumb piece was PLACED on the hand and WHIPPED onto it. From point G to point F it was eased onto the hand.

6 The seam joining the base of the thumb to the hand and the seam up the thumb were covered in a length of woven silver and silver-gilt lace, FELLED down on both sides of the lace.

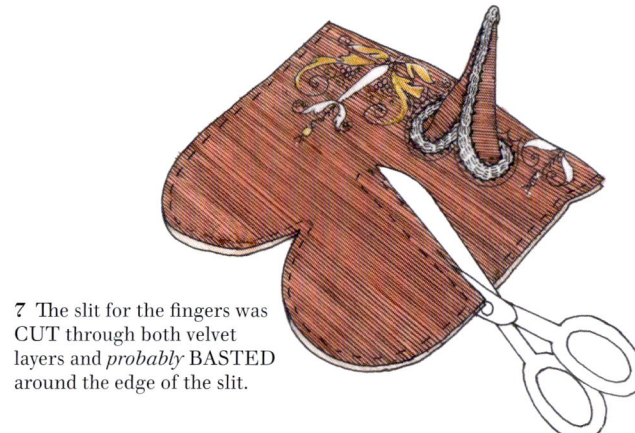

7 The slit for the fingers was CUT through both velvet layers and *probably* BASTED around the edge of the slit.

8 The metal lace was FELLED, ¹⁄₁₆" from the edge, on the RS, down both sides of the split for the fingers.

9 The lace was FOLDED over the edge to the WS and FELLED to the pink velvet lining, binding the slit.

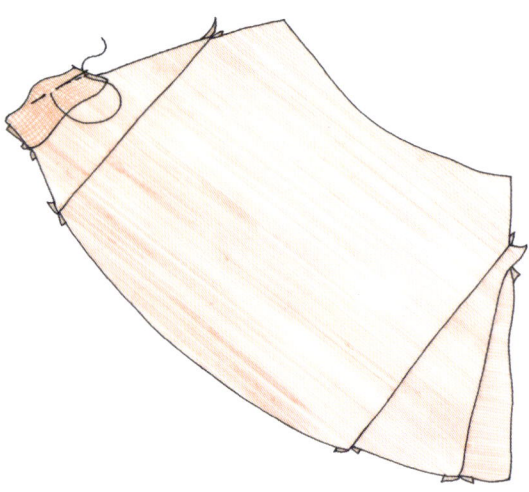

10 The pink velvet for the lining of the mitten top was PIECED together from scraps with HALF-BACK STITCH. Several of the piecings look as though they were recycled from a previous item.

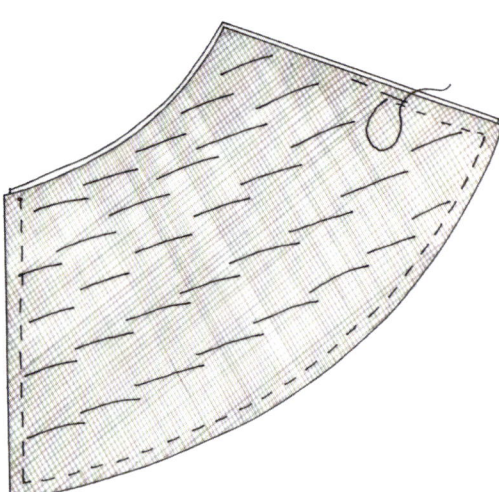

11 A layer of coarsely woven black stiffened linen was PAD STITCHED and BASTED to the embroidered silk satin top.

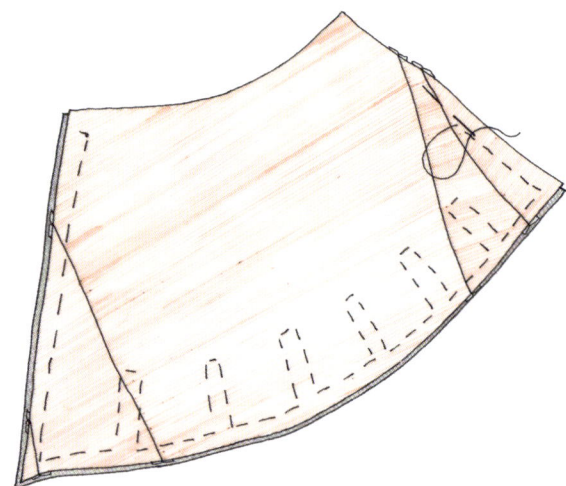

12 The embroidered satin, interlining and the pink velvet lining of the mitten top were *probably* BASTED together, along the lines for the split tabs.

13 The raw edge of the top was WHIPPED to the hand around the wrist seam from the RS. Some of the stitches are in pink silk and some are in white.

16 The seam between the hand and top was covered in metal lace, and CATCH STITCHED.

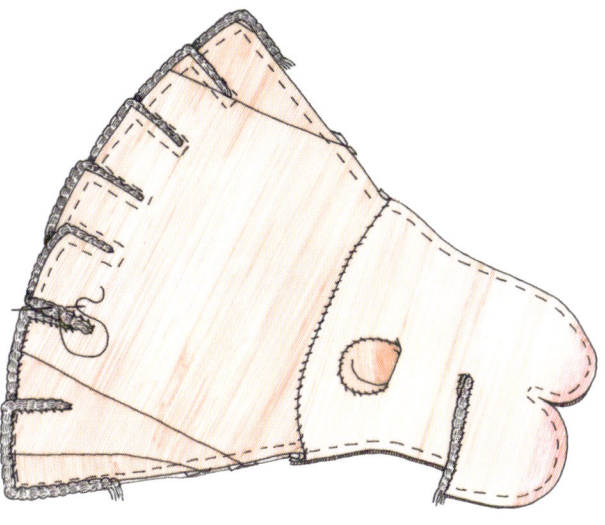

19 The lace was FOLDED to the WS and FELLED to the lining, binding the slits.

17 The slits between the tabs were CUT.

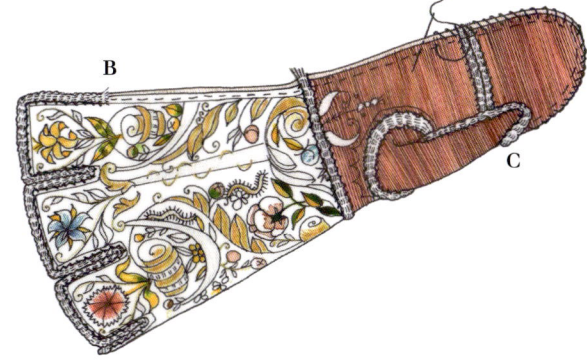

20 The seam from point C down to point B was WHIPPED together.

14 The raw edge of the hand lining was FELLED to the linen interlining of the mitten top.

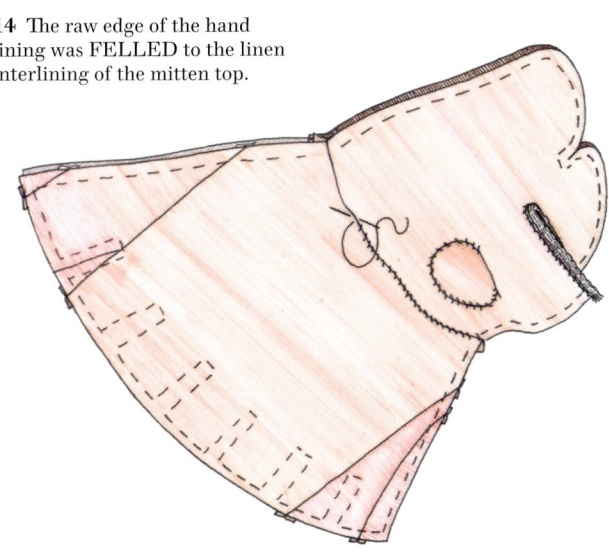

15 The seam allowance of the mitten top lining was FOLDED and FELLED to the lining of the hand.

18 A length of metal lace was CATCH STITCHED ⅛" from the outer edge of the split tabs of the top, on the RS.

21 A length of metal lace was FELLED to cover the seam from point B to point C.

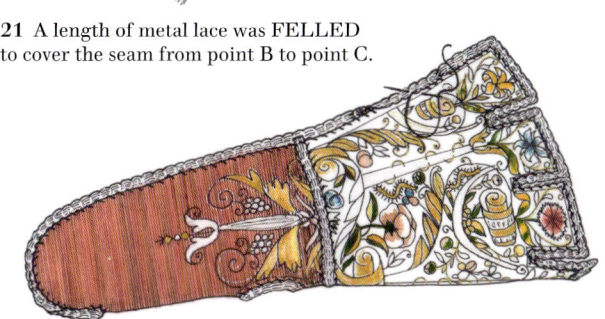

22 The length of metal lace was FOLDED over the edge and FELLED to cover the seam from point B to point C.

Pattern by Jenny Tiramani

12 | Embroidered linen stocking

English, 1590–1630 | V&A: T.126:A–1958

Pattern by Susan North

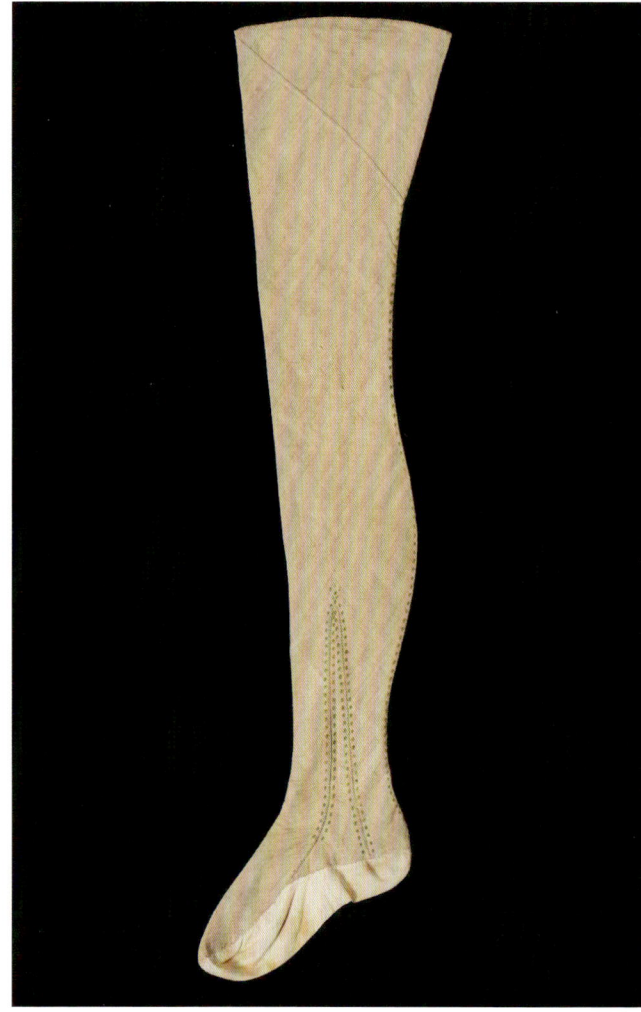

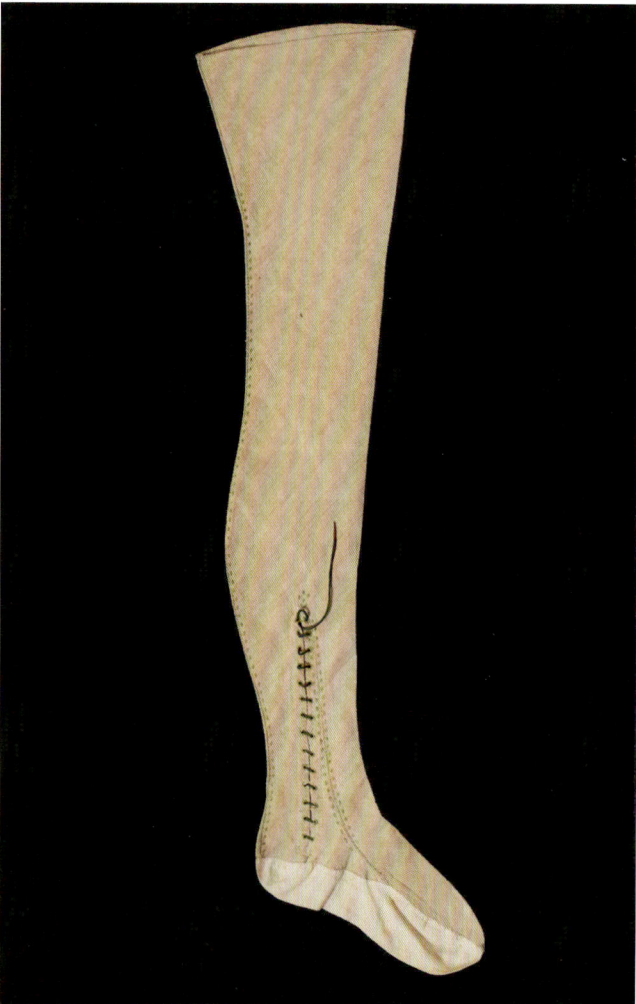

Above: Thomas Meautys, 1620–25
Daniel Mytens
Photograph by the Photographic Survey of Private Collections
The Courtauld Institute of Art, London
Meautys wears white stockings inside his boots.

In 1931, Miss Phyllis Brockman offered a pair of linen stockings, along with a 1630s crewel-work woman's waistcoat and a 1720s embroidered man's waistcoat, to the V&A on loan. In 1938, the objects were purchased for £30. The stockings are made of a medium-weight half-bleached linen, embroidered with half-back stitch and spaced chain stitch in green silk floss. They represent an element of the masculine wardrobe for which there are very few documentary references or visual images showing them in use.

Linen stockings may be equivalent to a man's linen shirt, in terms of underwear for the legs. However, the embroidery at the ankles of this pair suggests that they were meant to be seen. They also relate to the cut hose of the 16th century, which were made of woollen broadcloth and cut on the bias. These were gradually replaced by knitted versions, which had greater stretch and therefore kept their shape better when worn. The stocking examined here is one of a pair of 'cut hose' of linen. It is often difficult to distinguish cut hose from the knitted variety in inventories. The '8 pere of linyinge hosses', in the 1573 probate inventory of Richard Goddard of Southampton, might have been cut linen hose or stockings similar to this pair.[1] At present, the earliest documentary evidence found for knitted linen – or thread stockings, as they were called – appears in the household accounts of James Master, dated 12 May 1659, 'For ½ a po[und] of thred to knit me a pair of stockings, 2s, For knitting of them, 4s 6d'.[2] It is likely that both cut and knitted linen hose were made and worn between these dates.

Only one of the pair was available for study and it is probably the left stocking. The lacing is assumed to be on the inside leg, based on surviving boots, similarly laced, and a 16th-century pair of conjoined linen hose, in the Bayerisches Armeemuseum in Ingolstadt, Germany. How this pair was fastened to the breeches remains a mystery. Those in the portrait of Thomas Meautys (above right) must have had eyelets for the points seen at the bottom of the hose. Gartering the stockings or basting them to the breeches were other ways to secure them. The white stockings in the portrait are probably boot hose, protecting the fine silk ones underneath; they could be either cut or knitted. This stocking and its mate may well have been worn as boot hose.

It was probably made by a tailor, as the seams and shapes used to make it are different from those employed by a seamstress (see the nightcap liner on page 158). The stocking has a curved shape cut on the bias, a run-and-fell seam, and the cut edges of the seam allowances are left raw, relying on the embroidery to keep them from fraying. Leaving the seams unfinished would also minimize bulk and reduce chafing when worn inside a boot. There is an opening at the ankle with worked eyelets and a laced point for fastening. This dark green silk lace has a weft of finer blue silk and could have been tablet-woven or made with finger loops. The foot of the stocking is a different weight and shade of linen, and is probably a replacement during the lifetime of its wear. Payments for re-footing stockings appear regularly in household accounts throughout the 17th century.

1. Edward Roberts and Karen Parker, eds, *Southampton Probate Inventories, 1447–1575 I*, Southampton Record Society, vol. 34, 1992, p. 356
2. Canon Scott Robertson, ed., 'The Expense-Book of James Master, Esq., A.D. 1646 to 1676', *Archaeologia Cantiana: Being Transactions of the Kent Archaeological Society*, vol. 17, 1887, p. 330

DETAILS
Right side (RS) details

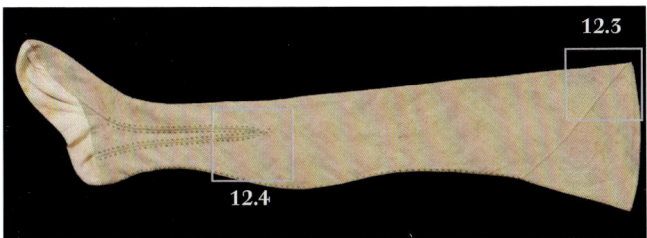

12.1a The outside of the left stocking.

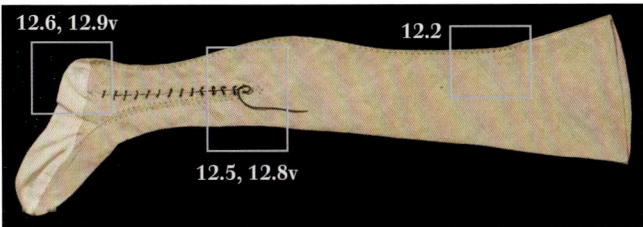

12.1b The inside of the left stocking.

12.2 The half-back stitch and spaced chain stitch along the back seam of the stocking.

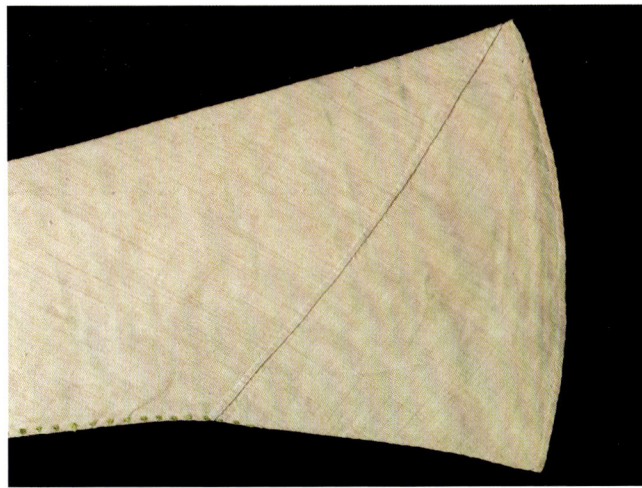

12.3 The piecing in the upper part of the outside of the stocking. The spaced chain stitch on both sides ends just above the seam.

12.4 The half-back stitch and spaced chain stitch outlining the top of the gusset on the outside of the stocking. There is a simple clock in spaced chain stitch above the gusset.

12.5 The dark green silk lace and metal aiglet, with a mended tear at the top of the clock. The aiglet was rolled and crimped.

12.6 The seam of the sole to the stocking leg, and the stitch joining them. There is a short line of half-back stitch in green silk, joining the gusset to the heel of the stocking, below the bottom eyelets.

Wrong side (WS) details

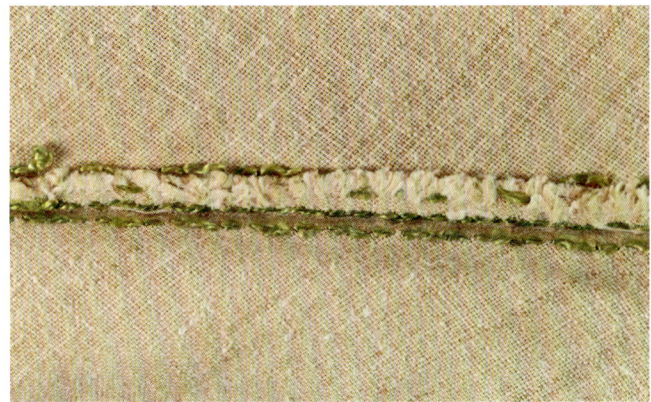

12.7 The WS of the back seam, showing the raw edges held in place by the half-back stitch, with a line of spaced chain stitch on either side.

12.8 The WS of the lacing gusset showing the raw edges held by the half-back stitch with spaced chain stitch on either side. Below it are the facings and eyelets on either side of the opening.

12.9 The WS of the bottom of the lacing gusset showing the end of the lace, tied in a half bow. The seam allowances of the stocking leg/sole seam are caught down.

Pattern by Susan North

PATTERN
Pattern of the left stocking

SCALE 1:4

PATTERN PIECES

1. Leg
2. Outside gusset
3. Lacing gusset facing, × 2
4. Inside lacing gusset
5. Sole

KEY

× × × Position of the eyelets

——— Join in fabric

MATERIALS

The stocking leg, gussets and gusset facings are made of a partially bleached linen with a thread count of 55 × 58 (no visible selvedges).

The linen of the replacement sole is lighter in colour and finer with a thread count of 60 × 58 (no visible selvedges).

The stocking is sewn with 2 'S' ply linen thread and the embroidery worked with green silk.

The finger-looped lace is worked with dark green silk, and a mid-blue silk weft of half the diameter.

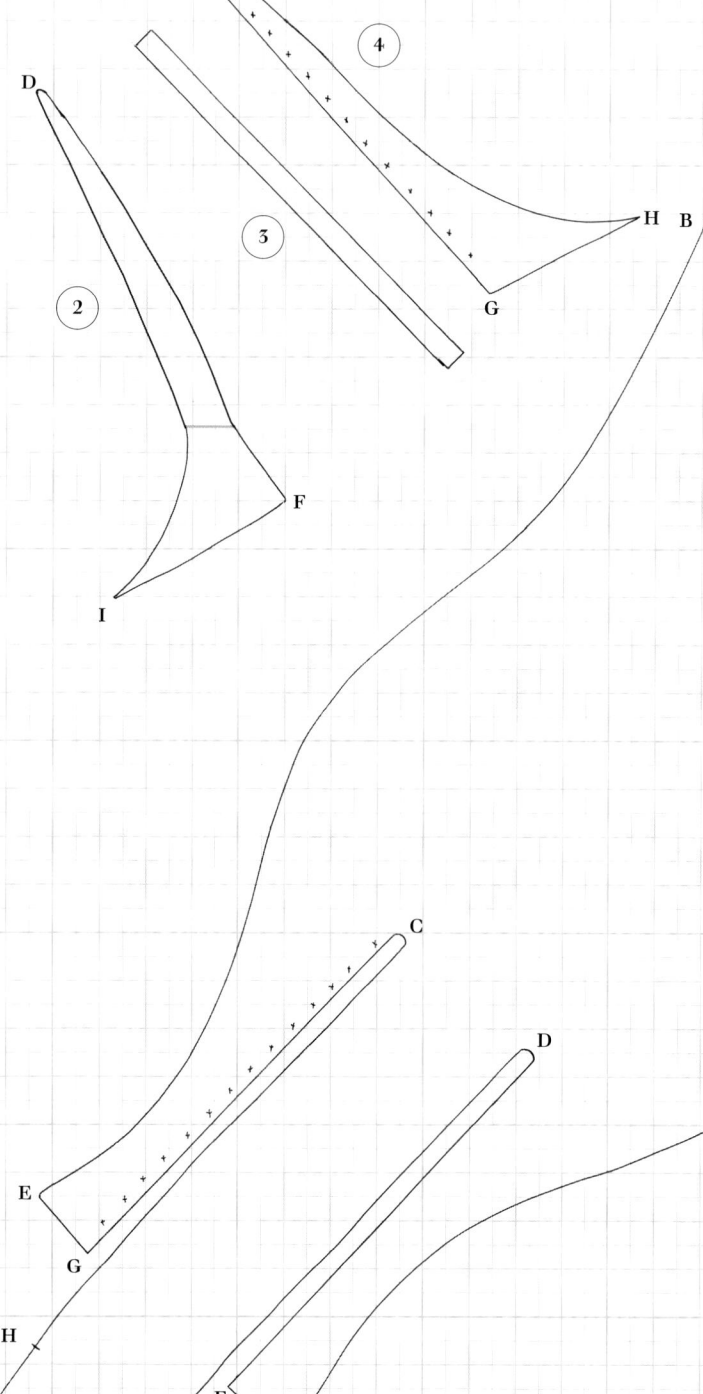
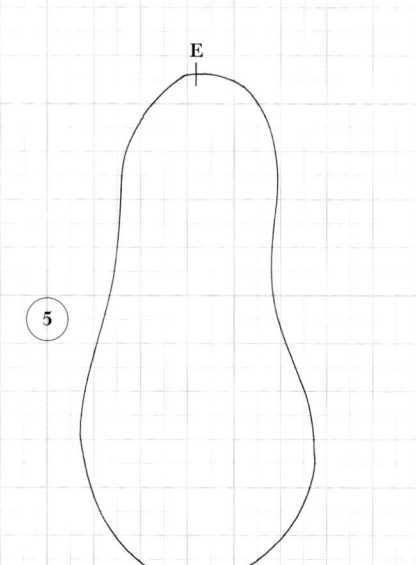

CONSTRUCTION
Construction of the left stocking

For the purpose of distinguishing WS and RS, the eyelet holes markings on the inside leg are shown

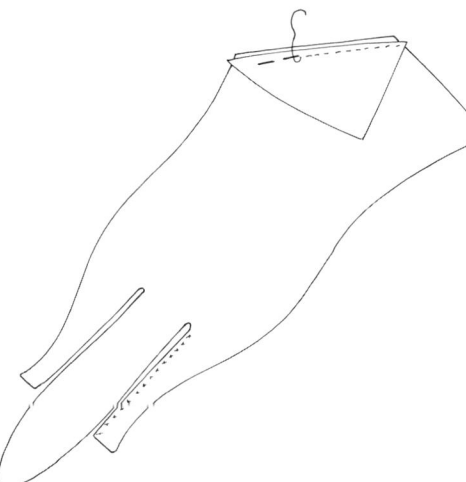

1 With WS together, the upper leg piecing was RUNNING STITCHED to the leg, with a ³⁄₁₆" seam allowance, and about six stitches per inch, with linen thread.

2 On the RS, the seam allowance was FOLDED ⅛" and FELLED to the leg piecing, sewn with about nine stitches per inch.

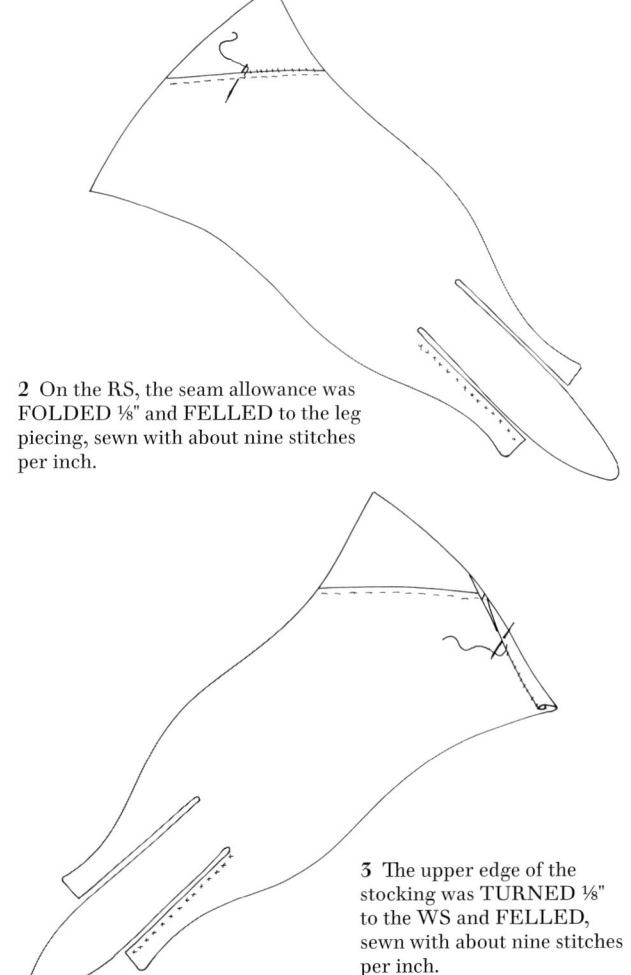

3 The upper edge of the stocking was TURNED ⅛" to the WS and FELLED, sewn with about nine stitches per inch.

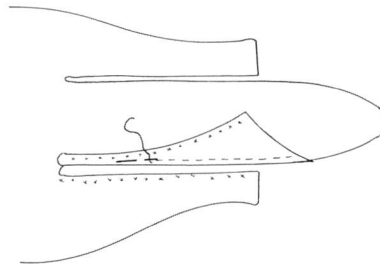

4 With RS together, the long, curved edge of the lacing gusset was *probably* RUNNING STITCHED to the edge of the foot; the seam allowances were FOLDED towards the foot. The subsequent embroidery obscures the stitches.

5 With RS together, the gusset piecings were *probably* RUNNING STITCHED, about 15 stitches per inch; the seam allowances were opened.

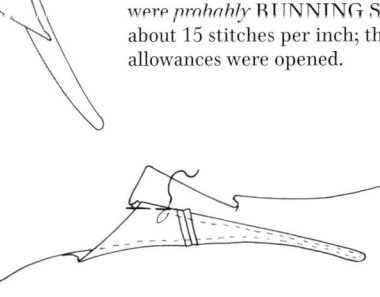

6 With RS together, the pieced gusset was *probably* RUNNING STITCHED to the clock opening of the stocking on both sides. The seam allowances were FOLDED towards the foot on the long side and the heel on the short side.

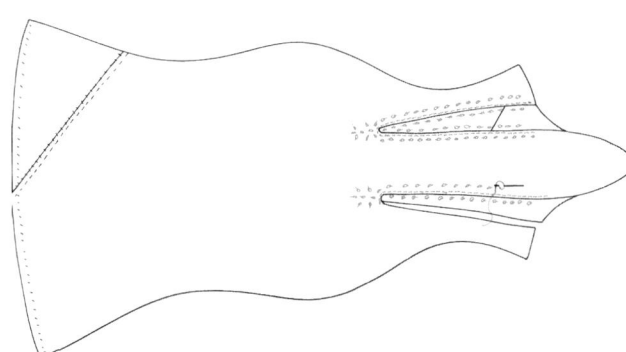

7 The gussets were EMBROIDERED on the RS with green silk thread, with half-back stitch, on the outside of the seams (holding the seam allowances in place), and two lines of spaced chain stitch, one outside the half-back stitch and one line inside the gusset seam, with a simple clock in spaced chain stitch at the top of the gusset (see 12.4 and 12.5, page 171).

8 The ³⁄₁₆" seam allowance around each piece of the lacing gusset facing was FOLDED to the WS, and the seam allowance on either side of the lacing gusset was FOLDED to the WS.

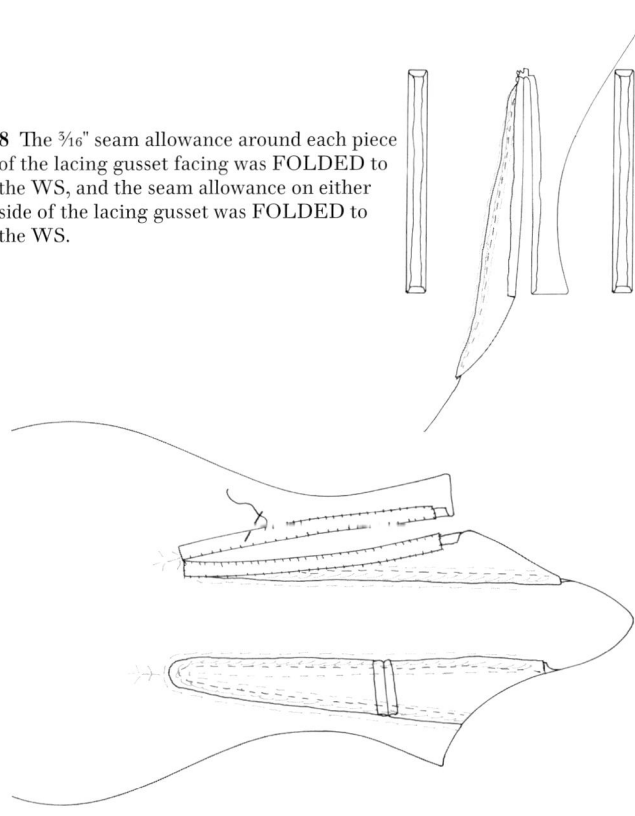

9 A lacing gusset facing was PLACED on the WS of each side of the lacing opening, and FELLED around all edges, with linen thread.

10 The edges of each lacing gusset facing were WHIPPED together where they overlap at the top.

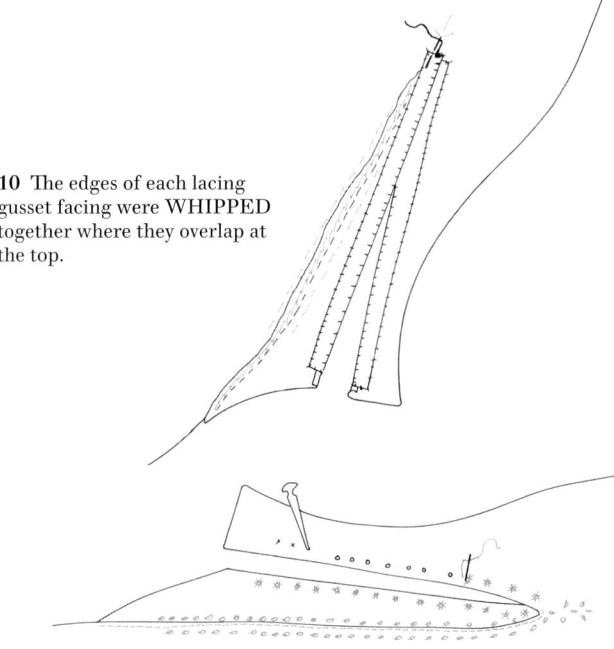

11 Fourteen lacing holes were PIERCED with a bodkin, along the side of the lacing gusset and the heel of the stocking, and WHIPPED with green silk thread.

Pattern by Susan North

Construction of the left stocking CONTINUED

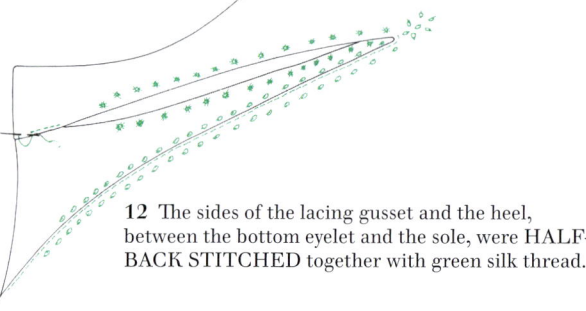

12 The sides of the lacing gusset and the heel, between the bottom eyelet and the sole, were HALF-BACK STITCHED together with green silk thread.

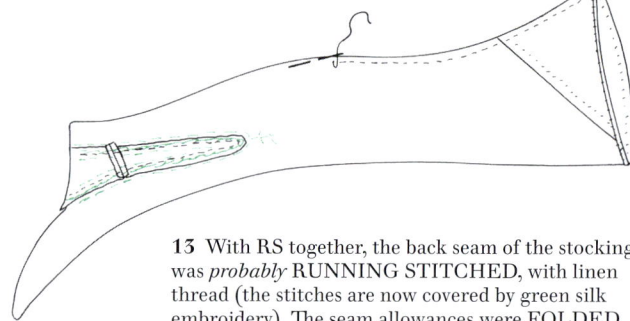

13 With RS together, the back seam of the stocking was *probably* RUNNING STITCHED, with linen thread (the stitches are now covered by green silk embroidery). The seam allowances were FOLDED to the inside leg.

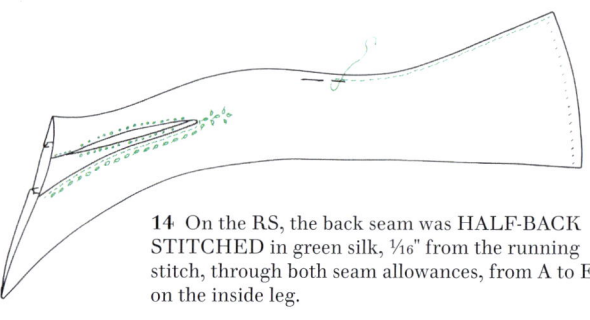

14 On the RS, the back seam was HALF-BACK STITCHED in green silk, 1/16" from the running stitch, through both seam allowances, from A to E, on the inside leg.

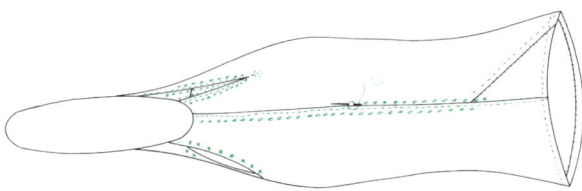

15 A line of spaced chain stitch was EMBROIDERED from B to E, on either side of the back stitched seam (see detail 12.3, page 171).

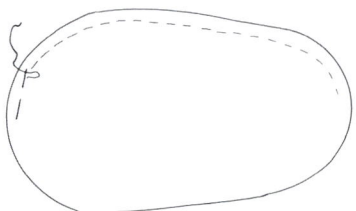

16 The sole was *probably* BASTED around the outside edge, with linen thread 3/16" from the edge, and the thread DRAWN UP slightly to ease the sole into the stocking. This makes a three-dimensional shape for the foot.

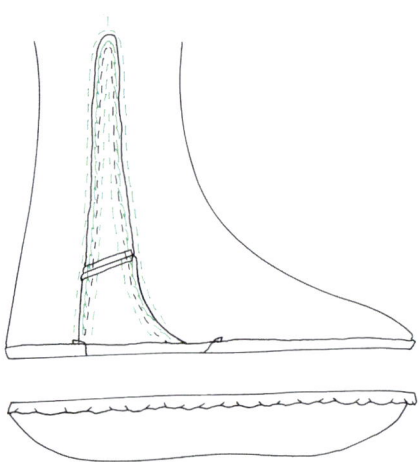

17 The seam allowances of the stocking and the sole were FOLDED 3/16" to the WS.

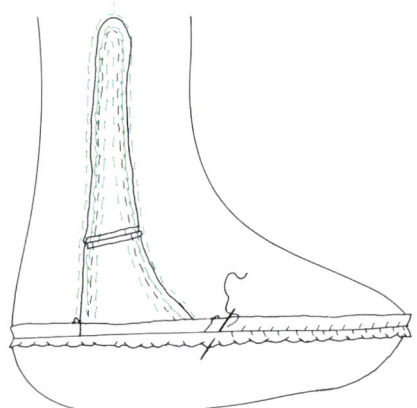

18 The sole and stocking leg were STITCHED together with a joining seam (see page 20), easing the outside curves of the sole.

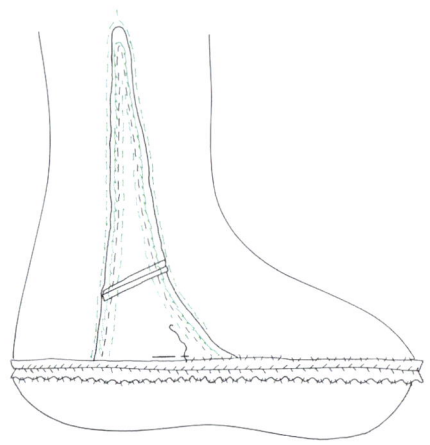

19 The seam allowances of the sole/stocking leg seam were SEWN down on either side with RUNNING STITCHES in a zig-zag path.

Reconstruction

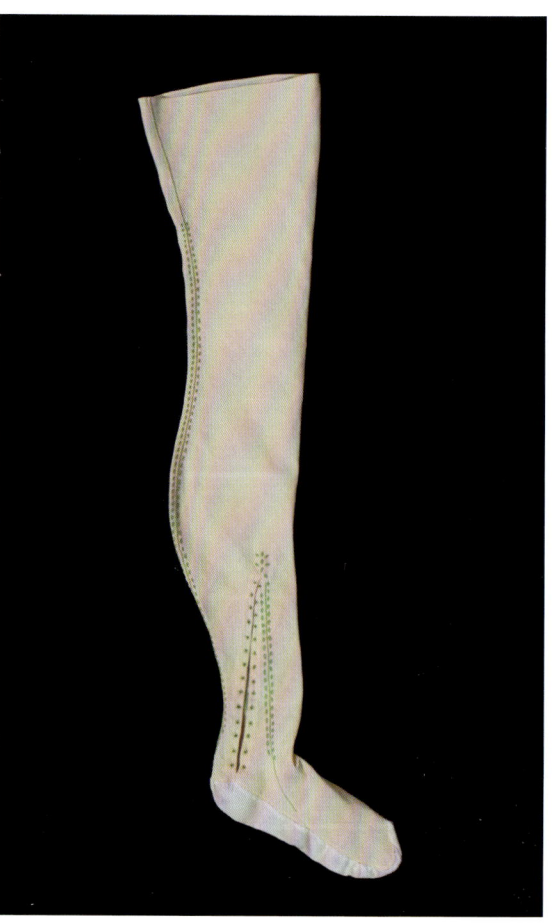

174   12 | Embroidered linen stocking

Construction of the lacing

12.10 Detail of the finger-looped lace on the stocking.

The lacing resembles one described by Noemi Speiser in *The Manual of Braiding* (1983, page 120), and the pattern here is adapted from hers. It requires two people: one to work and tighten the loops with both forefingers and another to work and tighten the weft. There are six positions that the four loops take during braiding:

Lb = left back loop Rb = right back loop
Lm = left middle loop Rm = right middle loop
Lf = left front loop Rf = right front loop

Tighten loops between each move by pulling hands apart.

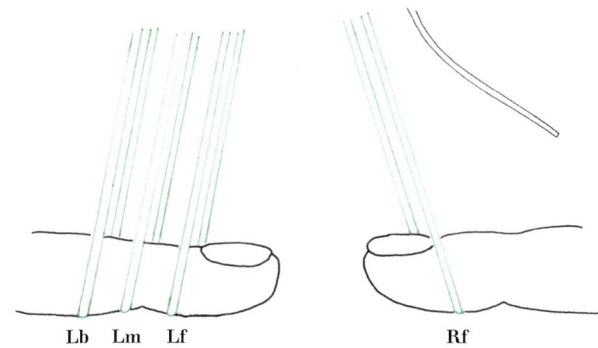

1 Start with three loops on the left finger and one loop on the right finger.

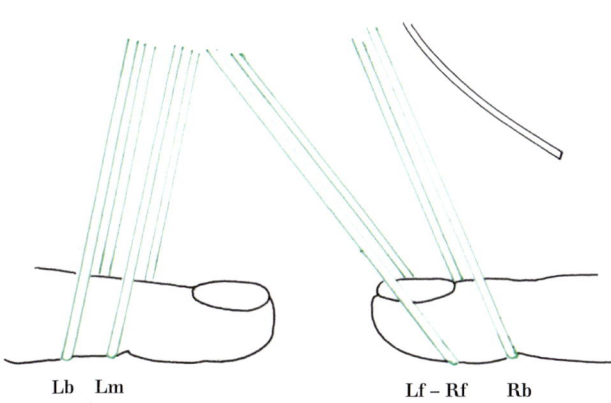

2 The Lf loop moves to the right finger.

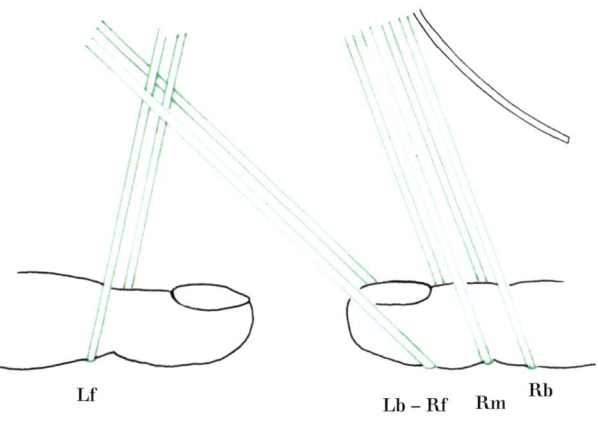

3 The right finger pulls the Lb loop over the Lf loop, onto the right finger.

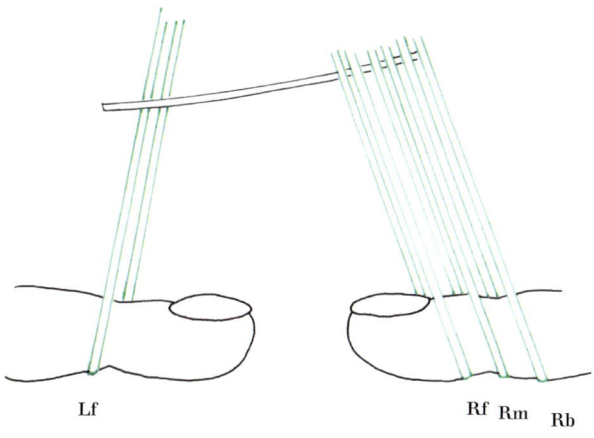

4 The weft goes from right to left, between the fingers. Pull up to tighten.

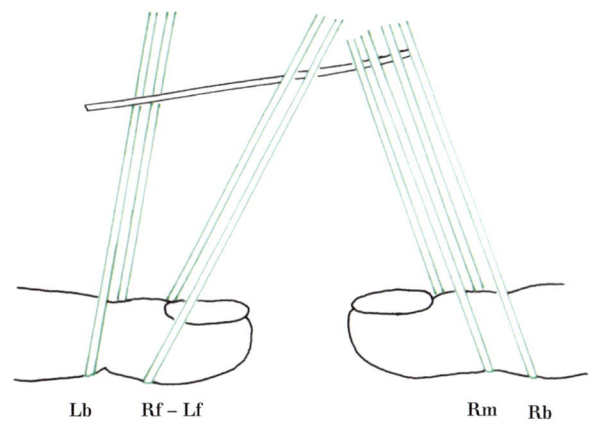

5 The Rf loop moves to the left finger.

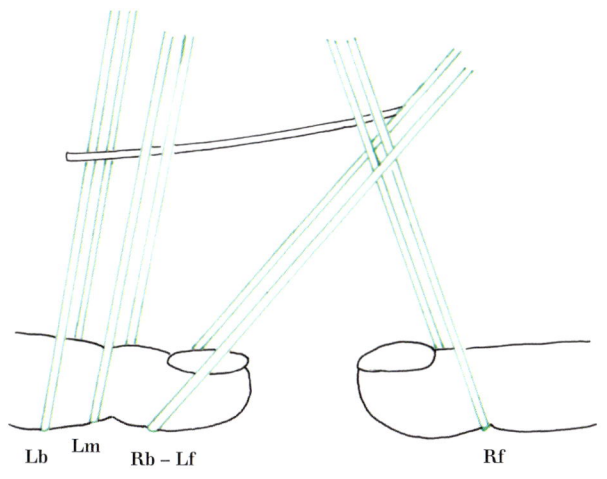

6 The left finger pulls the Rb loop over the Rf loop onto the left finger.

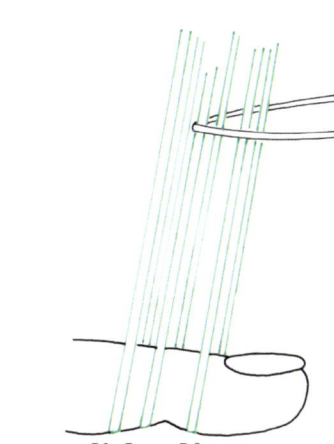

7 The weft goes from left to right, between the fingers. Pull up to tighten.

8 Repeat steps 2 to 7 to make the lacing.

Reconstruction

Pattern by Susan North

Select Bibliography

Anonymous, *The Annual Register, or a View of the History, Politicks, and Literature, of the Year 1759* (London, 1760)

Arnold, Janet, 'Sir Richard Cotton's Suit', *Burlington Magazine*, vol. 115, 1973, pp. 326–29

———, *Patterns of Fashion 3: the Cut and Construction of Clothes for Men and Women 1560–1620* (London, 1985)

Arnold, Janet, Santina Levey and Jenny Tiramani, *Patterns of Fashion 4: the Cut and Construction of Linen Shirts, Smocks, Neckwear, Headwear, and Accessories for Men and Women c. 1540–1660* (London, 2008)

Atkinson, J. A., et al, eds, *Darlington Wills and Inventories 1600–1625*, Surtees Society, vol. 201, 1993

Bagley, J. J., 'Matthew Markland, A Wigan Mercer: The Manufacture and Sale of Lancashire Textiles in the Reigns of Elizabeth I and James I', *Transactions of the Lancashire and Cheshire Antiquarian Society*, vol. 68, 1958, pp. 45–68

Batho, G. R., *Household Papers of Henry Percy*, Camden, 3rd series, vol. 93, 1962

Bestall, J. M., and D. V. Fowkes, eds, *Chesterfield Wills and Inventories 1604–1650*, Derbyshire Record Society, vol. 28, 2001

Bray, William, 'Extract from the Wardrobe Account of Prince Henry, Eldest Son of King James I', *Archaeologia*, vol. 11, 1794, pp. 88–96

Brinkworth, E. R. C., and J. S. W. Gibson, eds, *Banbury Wills and Inventories: Part Two 1621–1650*, The Banbury Historical Society, 14, 1976

Burnham, Dorothy, *Warp and Weft: A Textile Terminology* (Toronto, 1980)

Cotgrave, Randle, *A Dictionarie of the French and English Tongues* (London, 1611)

Cunnington, Willet and Phyllis, *A Handbook of English Costume in the Seventeenth Century* (London, 1955)

Davies, Godfrey, *Autobiography of Thomas Raymond and Memoirs of the Family of Guise of Elmore, Gloucestershire* (London, 1917)

de Alcega, Juan, *Tailor's Pattern Book 1589*, facsimile (Carlton, 1979)

de Anduxar, Martin, *Geometria y trazas pertenecientes al oficio de sastres* (Madrid, 1640)

Dye, Gilian, *Gold & Silver Edgings* (Glasgow, 2012)

Earwalker, J. P., ed., *Lancashire and Cheshire Wills and Inventories 1571 to 1696*, Chetham Society, vol. 28, new series, 1898

Foakes, R. A., *Henslowe's Diary, 2nd edition* (Cambridge, 2002)

George, Edwin and Stella, eds, *Bristol Probate Inventories, Part 1: 1542–1650*, Bristol Record Society, vol. 49, 2002

Gibson, J. S. W., ed., *Banbury Wills and Inventories: Part One 1591–1620*, Banbury Historical Society, vol. 13, 1985

Harland, John, ed., *The House and Farm Accounts of Shuttleworths of Gawthorpe Hall*, The Chetham Society, vol. 35, part 1, 1856

Herridge, D. Marion, ed., *Surrey Probate Inventories 1558–1603*, Surrey Record Society, vol. 39, 2005

Hodgson, J. C., ed., *Wills and Inventories from the Registry at Durham, Part III*, Surtees Society, vol. 112, 1906

Holme, Randle, *The Academy of Armory* (London, 1688)

Jones, Jeanne, ed., *Stratford-upon-Avon Inventories 1538–1699: I 1538–1625*, The Dugdale Society, vol. 39, 2002

King, Donald, Three Spanish Cloaks, *Victoria and Albert Museum Bulletin*, vol. IV, 1968, pp. 26–30

Larminie, Vivienne, ed., *The Undergraduate Account Book of John and Richard Newdigate, 1618–1621*, Camden Miscellany XXX, 4th series, vol. 39, Royal Historical Society, London, 1990

MacTaggart, Peter and Ann, 'The Rich Wearing Apparel of Richard, 3rd Earl of Dorset', *Costume*, vol. 14, 1980, pp. 41–55

McGrath, Patrick, ed., *Merchants and Merchandise in Seventeenth-Century Bristol*, Bristol Record Society, vol. 19, 1955

Moore, John S., ed., *The Goods and Chattels of our Forefathers: Frampton Cotterell and District Probate Inventories 1539–1804* (London, 1976)

———, ed., *Clifton and Westbury Probate Inventories 1609–1761* (Bristol, 1981)

Nevinson, J. L., 'A New Suit', *Connoisseur*, vol. CXXIII, 1949, pp. 99–101

O'Connor, Sonia, and Mary Brooks, *X-Radiography of Textiles, Dress and Related Objects* (London and Amsterdam, 2007)

Ornsby, George, ed., *Selections from the Household Books of the Lord William Howard of Naworth Castle*, Publications of the Surtees Society, vol. 68, 1877

Parker, Meryl, ed., *All my Worldly Goods II Wills and Probate Inventories of St Stephen's Parish, St Albans 1418–1700* (St Albans, 2004)

Parson, Daniel, ed., *The Diary of Sir Henry Slingsby* (London, 1836)

Patterson, A., *Fashion and Armour in Renaissance Europe* (London, 2009)

Phillips, C. B., and J. H. Smith, eds, *Stockport Probate Records 1578–1619*, Record Society of Lancashire and Cheshire, vol. 124, 1985

Pietsch, Johannes, and Karen Stolleis, *Kölner Patrizier- und Bürgerkleidung des 17. Jahrhunderts*, Riggisberger Berichte 15 (Riggisberg, 2008)

Pixton, Paul B., ed., *Wrenbury Wills and Inventories 1542–1661*, Record Society of Lancashire and Cheshire, vol. 144, 2009

Rangstrom, Lena, *Modelejon Manligt Mode; Lions of Fashion: Male Fashion of the 16th, 17th, 18th Centuries* (Stockholm, 2002)

Reed, Michael, ed., *The Ipswich Probate Inventories 1583–1631*, Suffolk Record Society, vol. 22, 1981

Robertson, Canon Scott, ed., 'The Expense-Book of James Master, Esq., A.D. 1646 to 1676', *Archaeologia Cantiana*, vol. 17, 1887

Rothstein, Natalie, ed., *Four Hundred Years of Fashion* (London, 1982)

Shirley, E. P., 'An Inventory of the Effects of Henry Howard', *Archaeologia*, vol. XLII, part 2, 1869, pp. 347–78

Shorleyker, Richard, *A Schole-House for the Needle 1632*, facsimile edited by John and Elizabeth Mason (Much Wenlock, 1998)

Šimša, Martin, *Kniy krejčovských střihů v českých zemích v 16.až 18. Století / Tailors' Pattern Books in the Czech Lands in the 16th–18th Centuries* (Strážnice, 2013)

Speiser, N., *The Manual of Braiding* (Basel, 1983), vol. 93, 1962, p. 108

Sykas, Philip A., 'Re-threading Notes towards a History of Sewing Thread in Britain', *Textiles Revealed: Object Lessons in Historic Textile and Costume Research*. Ed. Mary M. Brooks (London, 2000), pp. 123–36

Vaisey, D. G., A Charlbury Mercer's Shop, 1632, *Oxoniensia*, vol. XXXI, 1966, pp. 107–16

Victoria and Albert Museum, *A Picture Book of English Costume: Part I. 17th Century* (London, 1937)

Waugh, Norah, *The Cut of Men's Clothes: 1600–1914* (London, 1964)

Webster, John, *The White Devil* (London, c. 1610)

Williams, Iris Lorelei, and Sally Thomson, eds, *Marlborough Probate Inventories, 1591–1775*, Wiltshire Record Society, vol. 59, 2007

Wood, Herbert Maxwell, ed., *Wills and Inventories from the Registry at Durham, Part IV*, Surtees Society, vol. 142, 1929

Acknowledgments

Thanks are due to many members of staff at the V&A. We are very grateful to our former editors, Anjali Bulley and Mark Eastment, for initiating this series. Many thanks to Tom Windross and Kathryn Johnson in V&A Publishing and the team at Thames & Hudson for taking over the 'shepherding' of this volume. Henrietta Clare and Pip Barnard did the beautiful and precise photography, while Paul Robins captured the splendid x-ray images. Jo Hackett and Tina Cogram in Textile Conservation helped with access and identification of materials.

Colleagues outside the V&A provided essential assistance: many thanks to Sonya O'Connor for identifying the cork in the belly piece of the crimson silk grosgrain doublet. We are very grateful to Gesa Werner for making Sir Rowland Cotton's suit camera-ready and to Emma Treleaven for sewing underpinnings for the other garments. Friends, family and colleagues provided professional expertise, technical assistance, pairs of hands, tea and sympathy, moral and financial support, hospitality, patience and brutal honesty in the preparation of this volume. We are indebted to William Kentish Barnes, Stefano Cioncoloni, Gilian Dye, Evienna Goodman, Gosia Hryskiewicz, Tiziano Musetti, Frits Nieuwland, Scottie North, Simone Olivieri, Johannes Pietsch, Davide Ragazzi, Jessica Rae Drader, Karl Robinson, Jane Ruddell, Elizabeth Trapnell, Peter Trapnell, Nikola Velkov and Anna Watkins.

The reappearance of the portrait of Sir Rowland Cotton, not seen since 1961, was most serendipitous. Costume students at the Centro Sperimentale di Cinematografia in Rome alerted us to its presence online when it had come up for sale at auction. It was purchased by the Weiss Gallery in London and we are very grateful to Mark and Catherine Weiss for the opportunity to study the painting and for a colour image. Many thanks to other institutions and individuals who also let us use their images free of charge: the Rijksmuseum in Amsterdam, the Art Institute of Chicago, the Sarah Campbell Blaffer Foundation at the Museum of Fine Arts in Houston, Tomasso Brothers Fine Art in London, the Regional Museum in Mikulov, the Ufficio Diocesano Beni Culturali Ecclesiastici e Arte Sacra in Naples, as well as a private collection, Judith Hodgkinson, Roberta Orsi Landini, David Leppan, Martin Šimša and Lt. Col. Rhodri Traherne.

V&A pattern books:
Seventeenth-Century Women's Dress Patterns, Book One, 2011
Seventeenth-Century Women's Dress Patterns, Book Two, 2012